ISBN 978-1-333-67712-1
PIBN 10534480

For support please visit www.forgottenbooks.com

English
Français
Deutsche
Italiano
Español
Português

www.forgottenbooks.com

Mythology Photography **Fiction**
Fishing Christianity **Art** Cooking
Essays Buddhism Freemasonry
Medicine **Biology** Music **Ancient
Egypt** Evolution Carpentry Physics
Dance Geology **Mathematics** Fitness
Shakespeare **Folklore** Yoga Marketing
Confidence Immortality Biographies
Poetry **Psychology** Witchcraft
Electronics Chemistry History **Law**
Accounting **Philosophy** Anthropology
Alchemy Drama Quantum Mechanics
Atheism Sexual Health **Ancient History**
Entrepreneurship Languages Sport
Paleontology Needlework Islam
Metaphysics Investment Archaeology
Parenting Statistics Criminology
Motivational

LIFE

OF

CHARLES BLACKER VIGNOLES

F.R.S., F.R.A.S., M.R.I.A., &c.

SOLDIER AND CIVIL ENGINEER

FORMERLY LIEUTENANT IN H.M. 1st ROYALS

PAST-PRESIDENT OF INSTITUTION OF CIVIL ENGINEERS

.

A REMINISCENCE OF EARLY RAILWAY HISTORY

BY HIS SON

OLINTHUS J. VIGNOLES, M.A.

ASSISTANT MINISTER OF S. PETER'S CHURCH, VERE STREET, LONDON

LONDON

LONGMANS, GREEN, AND CO.

AND NEW YORK: 15 EAST 16th STREET

1889

.

TO

HER MOST GRACIOUS MAJESTY THE QUEEN
AND EMPRESS

THIS MEMOIR OF ONE WHO IN THE EARLY PART OF THE
CENTURY RECEIVED MUCH KINDNESS FROM HER MAJESTY'S
ROYAL FATHER, AND WHO WAS PERSONALLY KNOWN TO
HER MAJESTY, TO H.R.H. THE DUCHESS OF KENT, AND TO
H.R.H. THE LAMENTED PRINCE CONSORT, IS, WITH THE
QUEEN'S GRACIOUS PERMISSION, HUMBLY DEDICATED BY
HER MAJESTY'S MOST DUTIFUL AND GRATEFUL SERVANT
AND SUBJECT,

THE AUTHOR.

PREFACE.

THE subject of this memoir having passed away more than thirteen years ago, this work may very naturally be charged with appearing 'late in the field.' A reasonable excuse, however, is found in the necessity that existed for great labour and care in examining and selecting papers, letters, journals, reports, and documents of every kind placed at the writer's disposal—all of them requiring close inspection, as well as the exercise of anxious judgment; necessitating many visits to distant places, and involving, moreover, much laborious condensation when the story came to be written, for this was indispensable to a work in one volume that professes to give everything essential in a life of active and constant labour extending over half a century.

An undertaking of such a kind is, when possible, rightly entrusted to a near relative; although the value of the result, in the present case, is no doubt to some extent diminished by the writer's previous training and occupation lying in a sphere remote from engineering.

I may here quote, not inaptly, a passage from the preface to Southey's Life and Letters [edition of 1849, published by Longmans, in six volumes], by his son, Rev. Charles Southey, in which he says: 'Although a son may not be a fit person to pass judgment upon a father's character, he may yet faithfully chronicle his life, and is, undoubtedly, the most proper person to have all private and family letters intrusted to his judgment.'

But, again, I would suggest that the present memoir gains

something from the efforts of a writer outside his father's profession to confine technical details to the very narrowest limits consistent with a just description of all special engineering work fairly entitled to the credit of originality or novelty, or which, by its general environment, is invested with an interest likely to be shared by the public at large.

The delay that has taken place may also serve to put the story of C. B. Vignoles's life in a truer perspective. Old controversies have passed away; personal friction and prejudice have disappeared; so that, what this record of the pioneering days of modern engineering loses in respect of some delay in its production, it may gain in time having been thus allowed to grasp the full importance of work carried out in that early era, and to form a truer and fairer estimate of Mr. Vignoles's position amongst the English engineers of this century.

But the author further hopes that this biography will be found to possess intrinsic interest from the diversity of events it has to deal with, the historic importance of much of the work it endeavours to describe, the changes of fortune and circumstance experienced by him whose life is here sketched, and the varied scenes, both of war and peace, in which Mr. Vignoles was an actor during a life of more than eighty years.

The writer is indebted to many relatives and friends for kind help and counsel. Amongst these, he is proud to mention his brothers, Hutton and Henry Vignoles; to the latter more especially for valuable aid in many engineering and personal details, and to the former for unrestricted use of all family letters and papers, as well as for much judicious criticism.

To these must be added a few names of kind helpers out of the many who, though not mentioned, are gratefully remembered by the writer.[1] In England, he is greatly indebted to Sir James Allport, a director of the Midland Railway, and to Messrs.

---

[1] Mr. S. Reay, the lately-deceased Secretary of the London and North-Western Railway Company, rendered much kind service to the author.

James Williams and John Noble, A. A. Langley and W. Needham, the principal officers of that Company. The writer wishes also to express his best thanks to Mr. Edward Lawrence, the Auditor, and to Mr. Henry A. Dibbin, formerly one of the Engineers of the London and North-Western Railway Company; also to Messrs. J. Morgan and J. Hadfield, the Secretaries respectively of the London, Chatham, and Dover, and of the Great Eastern Railway Companies; also to Mr. Edward Ross, the Secretary of the Manchester, Sheffield, and Lincolnshire Railway. He also gladly owns his obligations to Sir George Grove, D.C.L., Sir Charles H. Gregory, K.C.M.G., Professor Pole, F.R.S., and to Mr. Philip Sewell, of Norwich, for friendly and helpful criticisms. His acknowledgments are also justly due to the President and Council, and to Mr. Forrest, the Secretary of the Institution of Civil Engineers, for the free use of their valuable Library; and he wishes to express his best thanks also to the Committee of Management and to the Librarian of the 'Brown's Free Library' of Liverpool; also to Mr. J. P. Griffith, President of the Institution of Civil Engineers of Ireland, and more particularly to Mr. Grierson, one of its leading members, for the aid derived from a perusal of his very valuable and lucid account of the Dublin and Kingstown Railway, contributed to the 'Transactions' of that Institution, of which Mr. Vignoles was one of the founders in 1835.

Lastly, the writer's cordial thanks are tendered to his relative, Mr. de Barri Crawshay, for the kind and very serviceable help rendered in the shape of constant and careful criticism of the memoir, and for the map of Vignoles's early surveys in Wales, and much local information concerning the Principality.

O. J. VIGNOLES.

ATHENÆUM CLUB, LONDON: *April* 1889.

CONTENTS.

PART I.

LIFE AS A SOLDIER; AND EARLY SURVEYS IN THE UNITED STATES.

CHAPTER I.

1793–1813.

PAGE

Brief genealogy—Connection with family of Sir Isaac Newton—Vignoles's parentage—Death of father and mother in Guadaloupe—Vignoles a child-officer in the British army—Placed by his grandfather, Dr. Charles Hutton, at Royal Military Academy, Woolwich—Early education—Estrangement from grandfather—Probable visit to Spain—Reconciliation with grandmother and aunt—Goes to Sandhurst—Meets Miss Griffiths and becomes engaged to her—Correspondence with her—Interview with Duke of Kent   1–15

CHAPTER II.

1813–14.

Vignoles gazetted to York Chasseurs—Stationed in Isle of Wight—Severe winter of 1813–14—Vignoles promoted to 1st Royals (foot regiment)—Sails for Holland—The siege of Bergen-op-Zoom—Descriptive letter 16–28

CHAPTER III.

1814–15.

Vignoles ordered to Canada—Shipwrecked on the isle of Anticosti—Residence in Quebec—War with the United States—Sir George Prevost, &c. 29–42

CHAPTER IV.

1815-16.

PAGE

Vignoles in Scotland—Visits to Professor Dugald Stewart . . . 43-51

CHAPTER V.

1816-17.

Vignoles stationed at Valenciennes as extra aide-de-camp to Sir Thomas Brisbane—Life at Valenciennes—Prepares series of computations for H.R.H. the Duke of Kent—The Duke of Wellington—Correspondence with his aunt and Miss Griffiths—Difficulties and disappointments—Leaves Valenciennes 52-61

CHAPTER VI.

1817.

Vignoles returns to Sandhurst—His marriage—Sails for America—Obtains employment as assistant State surveyor for South Carolina . . 62-72

CHAPTER VII.

1817-22.

Life at Charleston, U.S.A.—Birth of his daughter and eldest son—Correspondence with his wife—Letters from Professor Leybourne—Vignoles's claims on property in Florida — Description of Southern States—Changes in the military and scientific world—Visit of himself and wife to England—Vignoles returns to Charleston—Moves to Florida—Various surveys—Dangers incurred—Difficulties in his civil employments—He visits New York 73-90

CHAPTER VIII.

1822-25.

Unsettled state of things in Florida—Vignoles at New York—Publishes his Map of Florida — Returns to England — Practises as a civil engineer 91-104

PART II.

EARLY RAILWAY ENGINEERING IN THE UNITED KINGDOM.

CHAPTER IX.

1825-27.

PAGE

Introduction of railways into England—Vignoles on the Liverpool and
Manchester Railway 107-120

CHAPTER X.

1827-29.

The Institution of Civil Engineers—Government survey of the Isle of
Man—Improvements of the Oxford Canal—Proposals for completing
the Thames Tunnel—Controversy with the elder Brunel—The locomotive question—Ericsson's 'Novelty'—The competition at Rainhill—
Vignoles's notes made at the time—Success of the 'Rocket,' &c. 121-135

CHAPTER XI.

1829-30.

Letters from America—Vignoles's engagement on the St. Helens, Newton,
Wigan, and 'North Union' Railways—General condition and working
of early lines—Opening of the Liverpool and Manchester Railway 136-154

CHAPTER XII.

1831-34.

Vignoles elected member of Athenæum Club—His habits—First introduction of 'atmospheric' system of traction—Letter on early railway work
in the United States—Vignoles's activity and readiness as consulting
engineer—Value of his opinion—Proposed 'London and Paris' Railway—Visit to France—Letters from Paris — Interviews with King
Louis-Philippe and M. Thiers—Accompanies latter on English tour—
The project of line to Windsor—Vignoles's surveys in Gloucestershire 155-176

CHAPTER XIII

1832–34.

PAGE

Dublin and Kingstown Railway—Interview with H.R.H the Duchess of Kent and Princess Victoria 177–192

CHAPTER XIV.

1835–37.

Visits Hamburg, Hanover, and Brunswick—Proposed railways—References to Mr. Walker, Mr. Brunel, Mr. C. H. Gregory—Letters from Dr. Gregory, Sir John Burgoyne, M. Poussin—Gives evidence on various railway schemes—The ' Vignoles Rail '—Appointed consulting engineer of Eastern Counties Railway—Reminiscences of this line—Rival projects of London and Brighton Railway—Early surveys in Wales and Ireland for the first Irish Railway Commission—Various letters—Professional visit to Scotland 193–212

CHAPTER XV

1835–39.

The Midland Counties Railway 213–229

CHAPTER XVI.

1835–40.

The Sheffield, Ashton-under-Lyne, and Manchester Railway . . 230–244

CHAPTER XVII.

1888–43.

Miscellaneous letters—The second Irish Railway Commission—Vignoles's article on Ireland—Welsh surveys—Professor of Engineering at University College, London 245–264

CHAPTER XVIII.

1845.

Sir Robert Peel and railways—Great development of railway enterprise—Vignoles's railways in England and Ireland—The 'atmospheric' system—Vignoles invited to become engineer for Indian railways 265–288

PART III.

FOREIGN ENGINEERING ENGAGEMENTS. SUMMARY OF VIGNOLES'S WORK AND CHARACTER. CONCLUSION.

CHAPTER XIX.

1843-44.

PAGE

Vignoles's visit to Stuttgart—The Würtemberg Railways .   .   . 291–316

CHAPTER XX.

1846-47.

The Suspension Bridge at Kieff—Vignoles visits St. Petersburg in winter – Returns to England—Visits St. Petersburg in summer –Important interview with Emperor Nicholas—Meets the Emperor at Kieff—Chooses site of bridge—Brief account of dimensions of bridge .   .   . 317–332

CHAPTER XXI.

1848-50.

Further visits to Kieff—Floods in Dnieper—Fascine work for coffer-dams —Inspection of the bridge by Emperor Nicholas 333–348

CHAPTER XXII.

1851-53.

Model of Kieff Bridge—Visit to St. Petersburg– The total eclipse of the sun—Visit of Emperor Nicholas to Kieff—Completion and opening of the bridge—The Crimean War—Death of the Emperor Nicholas— Conclusion of Vignoles's Russian engagements 349–368

CHAPTER XXIII.

1853_60.

PAGE

Summary of Vignoles's works in later years—The Cheshire lines—Central
Station at Liverpool - Railways on the Rhine, in Switzerland, and in
the Brazils-- Railway through the Cantabrian Pyrenees—"Himalaya"
Eclipse Expedition--Astronomers in Spain . . . . . . 369_384

CHAPTER XXIV.

1865-75.

Vignoles becomes President of Institution of Civil Engineers--His position as a man of science--Estimate of his general work as an engineer
Peculiarities of his character—Concluding remarks—His death
in November 1875 . . . . 385_398

INDEX 399-407

LIST OF ILLUSTRATIONS.

PAGE

PORTRAIT OF C. B. VIGNOLES IN EARLY LIFE . . *Frontispiece*

PLAN OF STEPHENSON'S FIRST ROUTE FOR LIVERPOOL AND MAN-
    CHESTER RAILWAY 109

OPENING OUT OF THE EDGE HILL TUNNEL 112

'ROCKET' LOCOMOTIVE 129

VIEW OF 'NOVELTY' ENGINE AND TRAIN OF 'COACHES' IN 1830 . 130

RUNCORN AND ENVIRONS 138

BRIDGE ON THE ST. HELENS RAILWAY 141

BRIDGE OVER THE ST. HELENS RAILWAY 145

A WAYSIDE RAILWAY STATION IN 1832 147

OPENING OF LIVERPOOL AND MANCHESTER RAILWAY. . . . 150

CAST-IRON RAILWAY BRIDGE OVER THE TRENT, ERECTED BY C. B.
    VIGNOLES, 1838–39 216

REDHILL TUNNEL, NEAR KEGWORTH 218

SKETCH MAP OF MIDLAND COUNTIES RAILWAY 219

THE EARLY FORM OF THE 'VIGNOLES RAIL' 224

MAP OF VIGNOLES'S WELSH SURVEYS 260

SKETCH MAP OF THE WÜRTEMBERG SURVEYS 296

VIEW OF FASCINE MATTRESS 339

SECTION OF COFFER-DAM OF KIEFF BRIDGE 341

SUSPENSION BRIDGE AT KIEFF. 361

SECTION OF MAP OF BISCAY PROVINCE IN SPAIN, SHOWING SHADOW-
    PATH OF TOTAL ECLIPSE OF THE SUN, JULY 18, 1860, AND VIG-
    NOLES'S RAILWAY THROUGH THE CANTABRIAN PYRENEES *To face* 378

STATUETTE OF C. B. VIGNOLES AT SEVENTY-SIX YEARS OF AGE   „   386

LIST OF ILLUSTRATIONS.

PAGE

PORTRAIT OF C. B. VIGNOLES IN EARLY LIFE . . *Frontispiece*

PLAN OF STEPHENSON'S FIRST ROUTE FOR LIVERPOOL AND MAN-
CHESTER RAILWAY 109

OPENING OUT OF THE EDGE HILL TUNNEL 112

'ROCKET' LOCOMOTIVE 129

VIEW OF 'NOVELTY' ENGINE AND TRAIN OF 'COACHES' IN 1830 . 130

RUNCORN AND ENVIRONS 138

BRIDGE ON THE ST. HELENS RAILWAY 141

BRIDGE OVER THE ST. HELENS RAILWAY 145

A WAYSIDE RAILWAY STATION IN 1832 147

OPENING OF LIVERPOOL AND MANCHESTER RAILWAY. . . . 150

CAST-IRON RAILWAY BRIDGE OVER THE TRENT, ERECTED BY C. B.
VIGNOLES, 1838–39 216

REDHILL TUNNEL, NEAR KEGWORTH 218

SKETCH MAP OF MIDLAND COUNTIES RAILWAY 219

THE EARLY FORM OF THE 'VIGNOLES RAIL' 224

MAP OF VIGNOLES'S WELSH SURVEYS 260

SKETCH MAP OF THE WÜRTEMBERG SURVEYS 296

VIEW OF FASCINE MATTRESS 339

SECTION OF COFFER-DAM OF KIEFF BRIDGE 341

SUSPENSION BRIDGE AT KIEFF. 361

SECTION OF MAP OF BISCAY PROVINCE IN SPAIN, SHOWING SHADOW-
PATH OF TOTAL ECLIPSE OF THE SUN, JULY 18, 1860, AND VIG-
NOLES'S RAILWAY THROUGH THE CANTABRIAN PYRENEES *To face* 378

STATUETTE OF C. B. VIGNOLES AT SEVENTY-SIX YEARS OF AGE „ 386

the whole biography the subject of it has been allowed, whenever possible, to tell his own story.   But it is a source of deep regret that so many of Vignoles's letters, reports, and original drawings have perished, or for some reason or another are not forth-coming.[1]   This, however, has at least resulted in the memoir thus acquiring a more condensed form, and appearing in a single volume.

The author wishes to apologise for wholesale compression in the concluding chapters, which must be viewed rather as a summary than an adequate account of the engineer's later labours; the writer considering that enough had been related in the previous portions of the book to do justice both to the character and the work of C. B. Vignoles in that epoch of engineering history in which his lot was cast.

[1] The writer learne1 only last year that the engineer's offices in the original Midland Counties railway station at Derby were burnt down several years ago, and thus many of Vignoles's papers and drawings were destroyed.

PART I.

EARLY LIFE AND EDUCATION.

OFFICER IN THE BRITISH ARMY; SERVES IN HOLLAND, CANADA,
SCOTLAND, AND WITH ARMY OF OCCUPATION IN FRANCE;
LEAVES EUROPE; WORK AS AN ENGINEER ETC. IN
UNITED STATES OF AMERICA; ALSO IN ENGLAND
PREVIOUS TO THE RAILWAY EPOCH.

———

1793–1825.

CHAPTER I.

Brief genealogy—Connection with family of Sir Isaac Newton—Vignoles's
parentage—Death of father and mother in island of Guadaloupe—Vignoles
a child-officer in British army—Placed by his grandfather, Dr. Charles
Hutton, at Royal Military Academy, Woolwich—Probable visit to Spain—
Reconciliation with grandmother and aunt—Goes to Sandhurst—Meets
Miss Griffiths—Becomes engaged to her—Letters from and to this lady—
Interview with the Duke of Kent.

1793-1813.

THE late Mr. C. B. Vignoles was descended from a Huguenot
family which settled in Ireland at the end of the seventeenth
century, after the revocation of the Edict of Nantes. Two
hundred years earlier, the De Vignolles' (the double ' ll ' being
the then mode of spelling the name) were a noble family,
possessed of considerable property in Languedoc; but a still
earlier ancestor, De Vignolles, is mentioned in the French
accounts of the life of the celebrated Xantrailles (or Saintrailles,
as it is often spelt), who fought under Joan of Arc in 1430, and
was afterwards made a Marshal of France by Charles VII.
in 1454.

Etienne de Vignolles won distinction in arms in the suite
of this celebrated warrior ; and it seems as if he had also shared
something of that intimate friendship which his chief enjoyed
with La Hire, his inseparable companion in military exploits,
for the appellative ' La Hire ' is often found as a Christian name
in the Vignoles' genealogical tree, and now belongs to C. B.
Vignoles's youngest grandson. From the marriage of Jean de
Vignolles in 1559 sprang the heads of four branches, of which
one of the descendants, Jacques, seems to have been the first
who became Protestant, and is marked in the genealogies as
' Sieur de Prades,' a place of some importance in the Cevennes.
He was married in 1637, and, like most of his line, was blessed

with a numerous offspring. Amongst his descendants was a Charles de Vignolles who died in Dublin in 1721, aged seventy-seven, after being thrice married, and having become the father of thirteen sons and daughters. Of the former, the youngest was James Louis, who was the progenitor of the two branches of the family that still survive—viz. that of the late Rev. Charles Vignoles, D.D., for many years Dean of the Chapel Royal in Dublin, afterwards Dean of Ossory, and that of the subject of this memoir.

At least four or five of Vignoles's ancestors (the name having lost the superfluous 'l') were officers in the British army in the eighteenth century; but of these it is sufficient here to mention the grandfather and the father of C. B. Vignoles, the subject of this memoir. The former was a major in H.M.'s 31st Regiment of Foot, and his fourth child was Charles Henry, who afterwards became a captain in the 43rd Regiment. In the year 1790 this young officer was quartered at Woolwich, and there became enamoured of Camilla, the youngest of the three daughters of Dr. Charles Hutton, F.R.S., the eminent Professor of Mathematics in the Royal Military Academy. The letter in which Captain Vignoles proposes for the hand of the 'lovely Camilla' is still in existence, bearing date October 31, 1790, and is written in a manly and straightforward style. He describes himself as 'belonging to a sphere of life in which he had been accustomed to competence, but he did not aspire to affluence.' He further pleads :

'I long for happiness, and Camilla alone is capable of bestowing it. My choice is fixed, and, if disappointed now, I shall drop all thoughts of marriage.'

The young captain's suit was successful, and he married Camilla Hutton early in the year 1792. A very graphic and interesting letter from the bride, dated March 1792, gives a glowing account of their early married life. It is written from Arklow, just after their visit to an old friend of her husband's family of the name of Blacker,[1] from whom was derived the

---

[1] Mr. Blacker was a brother of Lady Duncan. His seat was Woodbrook, near Enniscorthy.

second name of their only son, Charles Blacker, whose life we are about to narrate, and who was born (probably at Woodbrook) on May 31, 1793.

It is interesting to observe that through his mother, the daughter of Dr Hutton, Vignoles could claim affinity with Sir Isaac Newton.

Dr. Charles Hutton was first cousin to the eminent geologist James Hutton, their respective mothers being sisters. The grandmother of James Hutton and the mother of Sir Isaac Newton were also sisters.

On account of this connection Lord Stanhope [1] bequeathed the admirable portrait of Sir Isaac Newton by Vanderbank, which had come into his possession, to his friend Dr. Charles Hutton. He in turn left it to his maiden daughter, Isabella Hutton, who bequeathed it to her nephew, the subject of this memoir. Vignoles presented the picture (an admirable and most valuable portrait) to the Royal Society in 1841. This painting now hangs over the President's chair in the rooms of the Society at Burlington House.

The scene of this narrative is now changed to the West Indies, to which region Captain C. H. Vignoles had been ordered with part of his regiment when hostilities between the British and French forces had broken out in Guadaloupe. This island had remained in British possession from 1759 till 1763, when the French (who had originally colonised it) again became its masters ; and they retained their hold, notwithstanding the defeat of their cruisers by Rodney in 1782, until 1794. In the spring of that year our forces, under Sir John Grey and Admiral Jervis, once more obtained a footing in the island ; but it was only for a few weeks, for, on June 2, Pointe-à-Pitre was successfully assaulted, with the enthusiastic aid of its inhabitants, and the tricolour was again hoisted on the ramparts of the little fortress. On this occasion the father of the infant Vignoles was severely wounded, and, with his wife and child, was left a prisoner in the hands of the enemy. Whilst thus

---

[1] This Lord Stanhope (Charles) was the third earl, noted for his love of practical science. He died in 1816.

deprived of liberty he was attacked by yellow fever, and for a few days carefully nursed by his wife, as well as tended with great humanity by a M. Courtois, a French merchant resident in the island. But all was of no avail, for both husband and wife succumbed to the terrible disease, and were buried in the same grave. An extract is here given from the letter in which many years subsequently this good Samaritan, M. Courtois, tells the sad tale of the early death of Vignoles's parents, and of 'their decent sepulture,' which must have been in those stormy days of war, according to the Roman poet's suggestion,

> . . . sepulchri
> Mitte supervacuos honores.

From M. Courtois to Mr. Charles Vignolles, à Londres.

'Paris : le 18 Janvier, 1805.

' Dans le désordre du siège, lors de la reprise par les Français de la ville de Pointe-à-Pitre, Guadeloupe, vers 1794, je donnai l'asile à M. Vignolles, officier au 43e Régiment, et à son épouse, qui tenoit un enfant dans ses bras : c'étoit vous, Charles, vous n'aviez pas un an.

' La fièvre jaune exerçoit ses ravages ; votre père et votre mère en furent victimes, mes soins n'ayant pu les sauver : je leur fis donner une décente sépulture.

' Vous fûtes également atteint de cette maladie. Le lait altéré de votre mère en avoit porté le germe dans votre sang ; une nouvelle nourrice vous conserva à votre famille.

' Dix mois s'étoient écoulées quand le Capitaine d'artillerie Hutton, votre oncle, veut en parlementaire vous reclamer.

' Quelle joie il eut de vous trouver au milieu des horreurs où nous étions livrés ! Je lui ai remis avec votre personne, le prétieux écrit que sa sœur, votre mère, traçoit dans ses derniers moments, lorsque s'entretenant du chagrin que la nouvelle de sa mort causeroit à son père, qui s'étoit opposé à son départ, et voulant lui faire ses adieux, la plume tomba de ses mains.'

The touching record alluded to by M. Courtois is still in the possession of the Vignoles family. On it the dying mother had feebly scrawled the name and address of Dr. Hutton, of Woolwich, the grandfather of her infant son; but ten months elapsed before Captain Hutton, R.A. (the boy's uncle), could reach Gaudaloupe to seek for the orphan child. His task was by no means an easy one, as is shown by a memorandum of Brigadier-General Colin Graham, dated July 20, 1796, which stated that 'Captain Hutton had reached the camp in the island by permission of Sir Charles Grey, but that, finding it destitute of any artillery officer able to do duty, and an attack being every moment expected, Captain Hutton in the handsomest manner had offered his services, and unfortunately had lost his right eye by a musket ball.'

Another interesting document that has been preserved shows that Captain Hutton must have been some months in the island, and virtually himself a prisoner of war, for he was only released on parole by a special order signed by Victor Hugues, the Commissary-General, who writes in the name of 'La Convention Nationale aux Iles du Vent,' the document bearing date 'le 7 Frimaire[1] de la République Française une et indivisible.' It specially covenants that Captain Hutton was to be permitted to withdraw to Grenada with his nephew, and his expenses to be defrayed to St. Bartholomew, only on the condition that he should not bear arms against the Republic until exchanged, according to the code of war, with a French officer of equal rank. It is another feature of the romantic story of this orphan child that he was already an officer in his Majesty's army. This curious fact (which in those days was by no means unprecedented) is best stated in the laconic terms of the official appointment :—

'Martinice: Nov. 10, 1794.

'Dear Sir,—The Commander-in-Chief, General Sir C. Grey, has appointed your nephew Vignoles an ensign in the 43rd Regiment, *vice* Cameron, deceased; and his commission bears date October 25, 1794.

'The terms are what you proposed, that he shall exchange to

[1] Our month of November.

half-pay immediately, as he is too young to serve; and I write
to the agents of the regiment to that effect for the colonel's
information by this opportunity.—I am, dear Sir,

'Your obedient and humble servant,

'G. FISHER,

'Lieut.-Col. 9th Regt., and Secretary.

'To Captain Hutton, Royal Artillery.'

In the 'Army List' of 1795 the date of the child's appointment[1] is given as November 10, 1794; and his name is found in
the subsequent lists of officers on half-pay up to the end of 1813,
in which year C. B. Vignoles, then just twenty years old, was
gazetted to the York Chasseurs by H.R.H. the Duke of Kent,
the father of her Majesty the Queen.

The youthful officer, who was thus early launched on the
troubled sea of life, remained for nearly forty years in the service
of his sovereign. In after life he was sometimes heard humor-
ously to boast of the far-off date of his commission, which in
1865 was, we believe, the oldest in the British army, with the
exception of that of Viscount Combermere, who died in February
of that year, his commission being dated 1791.

The youthful ensign was about the age of two years when
he was placed under the care of his grandfather; and he re-
sided at Woolwich, with a short interval at school, till the old
Professor resigned his appointment at the Royal Military
Academy in 1809, the boy being also for a year or two an inmate of his house afterwards at Bedford Row, where Dr. Hutton
passed the remainder of his days. Family documents (at least
the few referring to these early years which remain in the
possession of the Vignoles family) throw very little light on this

---

[1] Many amusing stories have been told of this mode of recompensing a
deceased officer's family by bestowing a commission on some youthful member
of it. Even female children (so the writer has been assured) were sometimes
the recipients of such favours! Vignoles used to relate a very humorous
illustration of the custom itself from his own experience in Scotland. He was
staying with some friends, when early one day in the morning-room he heard
the distant sounds of infantile wailing. The lady rang the bell, and demanded
of the domestic who answered the summons 'what was the matter now?'
'Oh, Mam,' was the reply, 'it's naethin' but the Colonel greetin' for his pap!'

part of the grandchild's[1] career. A few incidental remarks in Vignoles's letters to Miss Griffiths, the lady to whom he was engaged in his twenty-first year, and who afterwards became his wife, form almost our only sources of information; but we can see that there are two facts which stand out plainly in his early history—first, that he was very much indulged by his (step)-grandmother and his maiden aunt Isabella, his mother's sister; and secondly, that he was a very clever but not very industrious boy.

These habits and influences unquestionably affected Vignoles's youthful career; and of this he was himself fully conscious, for he often in after years lamented that his studies had not been more wisely directed, and that he had too often given to a desultory worship of the Muses and the Graces time which had been much better devoted to the systematic cultivation of his mind and character.[2] For years together the only ray of light which is thrown directly on the obscure story of his boyish days is found in a brief letter to Dr. Hutton from Mrs. Gilbert Austen (a distant relative), of Leixlip, near Dublin, dated August 13, 1806.

'. . . I hope my dear little cousin Vignoles is well, and proceeding in his studies so as to merit your approbation.'

There is no trace of the reply.

With regard to his residence at the Royal Military Academy, Vignoles has often in converse with his family referred to the mathematical tables compiled by his grandfather, and has spoken with some little pride of his own share in their computation. The writer of these pages has often heard him say that the whole of the logarithmic and other tables in Dr. Hutton's published works had been gone through by himself. No doubt this explains the secret of the grandson's attainments in that line, of which he gave early proof when preparing the tables[3] for Sir Thomas Brisbane, at Valenciennes, in 1816-17.

[1] A brief note in Vignoles's diary for 1853 refers to a visit he paid to Hayes in Kent, which place, he says, he had not seen since he was there at school for a short time, nearly fifty years before.

[2] Cf. some remarks on Vignoles's scientific attainments in Chap. XXIV.

[3] See Chap. V.

Another, and equally obscure circumstance, at least as to its cause, comes out clearly enough as a matter of fact from extant family letters—viz. that an estrangement took place between Dr. Hutton and his grandson when the latter was approaching early manhood; and it proved to be a breach which was never afterwards entirely healed. It was probably the growth of years, for their dispositions were almost diametrically opposed; but it culminated (so far as can now be ascertained) when C. B. Vignoles was about eighteen years old. At any rate, he then left his grandfather's house, to which he never returned; nor would the doctor permit him to resume his old footing of affectionate and personal intercourse, although he visited his aunt and grandmother when they were alone, and always dutifully corresponded with them. As the narrative will show, Vignoles once more found shelter in the old home at Bedford Row in 1823 (after his grandfather's death), when the house had become the solitary residence of his aunt, Isabella Hutton, who remained (as she had always been) his firm and faithful friend to the last hour of her life. In fairness to her nephew it must be said that he tried often and very earnestly to become reconciled to his grandfather, but without success. The old man seems to have been of a severe and somewhat implacable disposition; at any rate, he took sorely to heart the offence (whatever it was) committed by his grandson, who was a young fellow of a generous but proud spirit, and who, more than once, in the letters which we shall give, expresses himself very defiantly, and avows his determination to carve out an independence for himself, in which resolve, but not without many stern struggles with Fate, he succeeded in the long run. Still, one cause of the separation we speak of is not altogether conjectural. The writer has before him a long legal indenture, showing that Dr. Hutton had paid a large sum of money to place his grandson with a leading firm in Doctors' Commons. Vignoles on many occasions, in the hearing of his sons, has referred to his acquaintance with the forms and terms of law; indeed, in his humorous way he at times made something of a boast of his legal acquirements; and it is very probable that he owed to this short apprenticeship something of that precision which was a marked feature of his professional reports. But it is clear that this legal apprenticeship did not last long—a year or two at the outside, perhaps only a few months. It was broken, no doubt, by Vignoles himself; but *when* it is impossible to say.

The writer abstains from inflicting on his readers a tithe of the trouble he has himself taken to obtain any light on the two years 1811–13, immediately preceding Vignoles's residence at Sandhurst, which dates from the late summer of 1813.

That portion of the history is an absolute blank ; but there is this possible explanation, which, in the judgment of most of his family and all his friends, may be the true one—that Vignoles ran away from London in 1811 or 1812, and joined the army in Spain.

This solution is not only probable in itself—Vignoles being already an officer, and of an ardent temperament—but it also serves as the best (to the writer's mind the only) elucidation of the difficulty inseparable from such a visit by Vignoles to the Peninsula some time in his early career.

The writer ventures to call it a difficulty, because of the extremely troubled state of the continent of Europe in those days, and the immense obstacles in the way of a young volunteer officer reaching such a destination without a proper permit from the military authorities, for, as we shall soon see, Vignoles did not become a commissioned officer till November 1813. However, it was no doubt as true then as it is now that 'where there's a will there's a way ; ' and it is beyond all question that Vignoles often spoke about his early visit to Spain, and went into some details on the subject, and that in the presence of old campaigners like Sir John Burgoyne, his life-long friend. So that his historian is compelled to admit the fact, and only regrets that more light cannot be thrown on such a record of boyish enterprise and peril as the visit to Spain must have been.

The earliest letters from Vignoles himself in the possession of the family were written from London to his future wife, Miss Mary Griffiths, in October 1813. She was at the time on a visit (which had lasted several months) to Professor and Mrs. Leybourne at Sandhurst. This college for cadets had only been opened on its new site in the previous June, having been transplanted from Great Marlow, in Bucks, by order of the Duke of York. It originally consisted of two departments : the senior, established first at High Wycombe, and the junior at Great Marlow; but in the year 1813 the former was removed to Farnham, and the latter to Sandhurst. There is nothing to show that Vignoles was one of the resident cadets; he seems rather to have gone to the college in the capacity of a private pupil, or something between that and a visitor in the family of the Leybournes, with whom Dr. Hutton had made some kind of arrangement for his grandson to prepare for the army under the tuition of the Professor. This was, of course, after young Vignoles had broken his engagement with the law, and we can easily conjecture that he had expressed a determination to take up active service as an officer in the army, to which his commission would eventually entitle him.

From the following extract of a letter to Miss Griffiths, we find that the estrangement between young Vignoles and his grandmother and aunt had ceased, and that any opposition to his preparing for the army, which had previously existed, had been overcome.

‘ London : October 7, 1813.

‘ . . . . I have seen Mrs. and Miss Hutton, and have had a most affecting reconciliatory interview with them. My equipment will be ready by Saturday morning.’

To make the story clearer it should here be told that Vignoles had quite recently become engaged to Miss Griffiths, whom he had met during a previous visit to the Leybournes' about a month before. He at once formed a strong attachment to this young lady, and was faithful to her through all subsequent changes and trials. Their engagement, however, was to be kept as a strict secret, and this gave rise to many complications, and brought with it in its course many serious troubles.

In the interval between this and the next letter the lovers had contrived a meeting at Hounslow, the last stage between Sandhurst and London; for Miss Griffiths was returning to town on the conclusion of her visit. We give a pretty full quotation from the latter epistle, which is of more general interest. It must be observed that Captain C. H. Vignoles, the father of the young ensign, had been one of the secretaries to H.R.H. the Duke of Kent; and this Prince always evinced a warm and kindly interest in the son's career, as will appear in later parts of our narrative.

Extract from a letter to Miss Griffiths, dated Sandhurst October 12, 1813 :—

' . . . . On Sunday morning about eight o'clock Mr. Leybourne and myself set out from Hatton Garden, and no sooner had we entered the street than the rain fell in torrents, till we came to the top of the Haymarket. In a few minutes the Oxford coach stopped at the " White Bear," and at once we mounted. At ten we got to Brentford, and had breakfast ; and here we found the chaise which was to convey us to the Duke of Kent. At one o'clock precisely I was presented by Mr. L. to his Royal Highness,[1] who received me with very great politeness, and asked me many questions, which I answered as well as I could. After an audience of twenty minutes we were dismissed, the Duke promising to give me a letter to Lord Wellington and the commander of my regiment.[2]

' We then returned to Brentford, and at six o'clock set off for this place, where we arrived at eleven o'clock on Sunday night. When we came to Staines the storm of wind and rain was dreadful, and continued with increasing violence all the rest of the way. It was one of the coldest nights I ever was out in. When I got off the coach I could scarcely move my limbs, and was, besides, completely wet through. It was the first time I

---

[1] It is not easy to say where this interview took place. Possibly at his Royal Highness's residence near Ealing. The very handsome iron gates which formed the entrance to that domain are still to be seen in the neighbourhood.

[2] This probably means the 43rd Foot, his father's regiment, in which he had received his commission as before explained.

wore my regimentals, and I took it as a preliminary seasoning or specimen of my future winter campaign!

'I fear that we shall not meet again before my departure for the Peninsula. By-the-by, Mrs. Leybourne tells me in plain terms that I am in love with you, for I have somehow or other dropped out your name when addressing her! Both Mr. and Mrs. L. are extremely kind to me, and I am in high favour.'

The portion of the correspondence next given is taken from the first of many letters which his *fiancée* wrote to Vignoles, extending over an interval of nearly four years, up to the time of their marriage in 1817.

From Miss Mary Griffiths to C. B. Vignoles.

'London : October 14, 1813.

'I can hardly calm my feelings sufficiently to render it a pleasure, as I once promised myself it would be, to write to you in answer to your dear letter of this morning. What a day of misery was yesterday in not hearing from you as I fondly expected! Had I for a moment supposed that our last adieu would so shortly arrive, nothing would have induced me to leave Sandhurst while you were there. When the merciless storm beat about the windows on Sunday night, I pictured you exposed to its inclemency, and I felt miserable lest you had not the means of withstanding its effects. My full heart could write you volumes, but time denies me the pleasure. . . . . When do you think you shall leave Sandhurst? Let me know when you write next.'

This letter was answered immediately and at great length, but we give only a brief extract.

From C. B. Vignoles to Miss Mary Griffiths.

'Sandhurst : October 14, 1813.

'Judge with what delight I sit down to address you with news that I have just received from Captain Erskine, a communication by which I learn that *I am not to go to Spain*,' and

---

¹ Only words underlined in the original are printed in italics.

that the Duke of York has noted my name for an ensigncy in the Royals, which I shall receive as soon as if I had gone to Lord Wellington's army. But do not be too sanguine in your hopes that I shall remain in England. I fear that it will be expected that I shall offer my services to join the fourth battalion, which is now doing garrison duty at Stralsund, in Germany, under the Duke of Cumberland. It is the battalion which I must, at all events, join in obtaining my commission; and Mr. L. thinks the sooner I am off the better. It is, however, possible that I may continue here till I get my commission. By the advice of Captain Erskine I have written to the Duke of York's secretary, requesting to be called immediately into active service; and the captain is very sanguine about a favourable answer, which I may expect before Sunday. It is more than probable that I shall be stationed at the depôt in the Isle of Wight for some months, or at some other place within a hundred miles of London.'

The young and ardent lover seems to have dealt very honestly with his *fiancée*, so far as his own personal failings were concerned; but although the following extract is only a sample of many similar passages in the correspondence, we never get any clear evidence to show what his grievous faults had been.

Miss Griffiths writes :—

'I know the extent of your faults, and confess your great culpability; yet it was more than likely your maturer years would teach reformation and wisdom. I, however, know how to appreciate the qualities of your heart, on the intrinsic worth of which I build my fondest hopes.'

Miss Griffiths's letters (which always mingle good sense with assurances of affection) were much rarer in the winter and spring which followed her engagement; but many of those written to her by Vignoles have been preserved, and they certainly show that he was possessed of high spirit, versatility, and fortitude, all which qualities he retained midst scenes of danger and difficulty, soon to be experienced, and through many strange vicissitudes of fortune.

CHAPTER II.

Severe winter of 1813_14—Stationed in Isle of Wight—Discipline of army—
Shooting of deserters—Gazetted to York Chasseurs, &c.—Siege of Bergen-
op-Zoom—Descriptive letter.

1813–14.

YOUNG VIGNOLES was still at Sandhurst at the end of October
1813, and evinced no little impatience at the delay on the part
of the War Office with respect to his appointment.

He spent a good portion of his time in correspondence with
Miss Griffiths, and many of his letters sparkle with irrepressible
vivacity. He sometimes touches on his youthful follies, of which
he makes a full acknowledgment; but he consoles himself and
her by his conviction that ' nothing is so likely to guard a young
man from evil as an attachment to a beautiful and deserving
object.' In one of these letters he makes amusing reference
to his acquaintance with the law as gleaned from his short
apprenticeship in Doctors' Commons; and he recommends her
to study the Marriage Acts that of the year 1754—and particularly the new Act on Marriages which passed last year.
(1812).

Soon after this he got into disfavour with his tutor, who had
seen the outside of one of Miss Griffiths's letters; but this had no
worse consequence than a severe lecture. His characteristic
comment is, ' I will not repine if Mary will continue to love me.
" All for love, or the world well lost," is my motto.'

Meanwhile the college on November 4 was *en fête* on account
' of the glorious news ' of the battle of Leipzig, which had raged
for four days, October 16–19, and ended in that decisive victory
for the Allies which has long been famous. On hearing of this
great event, Vignoles wrote and begged Miss Griffiths to procure

a copy of the next ' Gazette ; ' and in her reply she says : ' After trying in vain at several shops I was at length told that they were published in Westminster. I, therefore, went down myself to the office, where a ruffian-like fellow told me I could not have one for some hours. I went into three different rooms in the hope of getting one, but they all assured me there would not be any out of the press before eight o'clock, which I knew would be too late for the post. What with the impudence of the people and the distressing disappointment for you, I returned home in the worst possible humour.'

On November 9 he writes :—

' You will observe that I am noted for an ensigncy in the Royals ; ' and a day or two afterwards he says : ' You will rejoice when you hear that I have at last got my commission, the Prince Regent having appointed me to the York Chasseurs. That regiment is with Lord Wellington in Spain, but I shall first proceed to the depôt in the Isle of Wight. The appointment will be in next Saturday's " Gazette." My pay will be only about 100*l.* a year, so that I must begin for the first time in my life to be economical.' He left Sandhurst on November 29, 1813, and in a letter of wild delight from Southampton he sings ' Io Triumphe ! ' at what he calls restoration to liberty. There is extant a very sensible answer to this production full of good counsel from Miss G. She speaks highly of the Leybourne family to begin with : ' I really consider him one of my best friends, as he is one of the earliest. It would occasion me much unhappiness to be ever thought unworthy of their friendship.' Then, with reference to his remark that in all probability he would shortly be sent abroad, she says : ' I know I shall have little else but fear and anxieties ; a thousand more from your being a soldier. How happy it would make me if you were reconciled to Dr. Hutton before you went ! I shall myself be miserable without one more interview, and would readily venture fifty miles to see you before you go.'

Ensign Vignoles writes from Newport on December 7 : ' I have been busied all day in looking for lodgings and paying my respects to the staff officers. Will it please you to hear that my regimentals are very dashing? Green hussar jacket with scarlet facings, gold buttons and ornaments, white pantaloons, Hessian boots, and a large sabre, &c. I have just secured comfortable apartments at 7s. 6d. a week.'

This last item belongs to those good things of olden days which we do not expect, however we may wish, to enjoy again.

In another place he says : ' Our regiment is raised on pur-pose to serve at the Cape of Good Hope, and is not expected to sail before late in the spring.'

In the same letter he assures her that he has ' made an attempt to be reconciled to Dr. Hutton, but that must be the event of time.' He tells her that at the depôt he had the satisfaction of knowing he could not get into debt, for the officers have so bad a character that he was ' obliged to pay for everything or go without.'

The colonel of the regiment had come down, and all were kept fully employed; or, as he describes it : ' Very dull here— no parties, nothing new ; in the morning, parade, all day at drill, and at night busy with the regimental books.'

On December 27 it was his fate to see something of the dread discipline of war as enforced in those merciless times ; and the painful feelings he experienced are best described in his own words :—

' The awful ceremony of shooting no less than fifteen deserters has occupied almost the whole of the forenoon. There was no time to write to you, and, had there been, the agitation and horror I was thrown into at beholding so many fine men sent out of the world in a very great degree affected me, and rendered it impossible to write. You will most probably see some account of this dreadful scene in the papers.'

He managed to spend Christmas in London, and on his return he came in for the beginning of the terrible frost which set in early in the year 1814. The account of his journey back from London is worth quoting : ' When I got to the " Gloucester "[1] on Sunday night, after quitting my terrestrial paradise, I found the

---

[1] The well-known coffee-house in Spring Gardens. Old Mr. Telford had rooms in one of these old-fashioned taverns all the latter years of his life.

mail had been waiting a quarter of an hour for me, so that the moment I mounted the box we drove off. It was one of the sharpest frosts I ever felt, and, though my feet and legs were buried in dry straw and my box coat wrapped close, I was almost frozen. It was near eight in the morning before we got to Southampton, for, as the mail carried no letters, they delayed a good deal on the road; and at one place where we changed horses they started off before they were harnessed, and it was upwards of half an hour before they could be retaken. My hat and coat were completely covered with a white frost, and the instant I got off the coach I was obliged to go on board the packet boat; and as Æolus had, to spite us, locked up every breath of wind, we were obliged to be rowed the whole way to Cowes, which occupied three hours and a half, and the fog on the water felt still more cold than the frost.' His correspondent, writing a week later, also refers to 'the dreadful fog which has now for six days without intermission enveloped the whole metropolis. Not an object, however near, can be distinguished, and the suffocating feeling which it occasions has made me quite unwell.'

On January 14 the York Chasseurs were removed to Sandown Barracks. The weather was still very severe, and, Vignoles says, ' so great was the fall of snow on this island all last week, that the roads to Newport this morning are completely impassable for man or beast. I am reluctantly obliged to break off, for I have got to trudge the ten miles through the snow, and be home before dark.'

In the letter from which this extract is taken young Vignoles mentions that he had made another application to the Duke of Kent, and evidently a successful one, for before the end of January he had been transferred to the 4th battalion Royal Scots, and had joined the depôt at Hilsea Barracks, Portsmouth.

He was almost immediately ordered on active service in Holland; and in an amusing letter from Harwich, dated February 2, 1814, he writes: 'I have been all this morning undergoing the pains of Purgatory in the Custom House, where among about fifty rascally Dutchmen I have at length despatched

my business after being fleeced by the officers, porters, land-
and tide-waiters, &c., besides paying for my passage, bill at
the inn, and various other impositions. I shall, I hope, have
enough cash to carry me to Williamstadt, where the head-quarters
are, and which I may reach by Friday evening. Harwich is
everything that is nasty and villainous; Little Dublin at the
end of Oxford Road is a fair specimen of its streets and alleys.
A Dutch merchant who came down with me in the coach is
sitting near me, and, happening this moment to raise my eyes,
the spirit of Democritus for a moment overpowered me, and I
burst into a loud laugh. Imagine an animalcule dressed *à
la Hollandaise*, with an immense wrapper and a military cloth
forage cap, his legs on the fender and his arms on his knees
supporting his face, from which I cannot decide whether his
nose or the pipe in his mouth projects furthest! This noble
specimen was holding forth in the above attitude to the fire in
Dutch! The *tout ensemble* was worthy of the pencil of Holbein
or Hogarth.'

His next is a hurried line from the island of Goree, off the
coast of Holland, in which he describes himself as 'landed on a
desolate island, blocked up with ice;' but this is followed three
days later by a longer despatch from Williamstadt: 'You will,
I doubt not, be happy to hear I have at last arrived at a place a
little more civilized than the desolate island of Goree. It was
not till Thursday afternoon that we left Harwich, having been
detained on account of a King's messenger with despatches. I
will not attempt to describe the misery I endured on the voyage,
which lasted forty-eight hours. I was not able to get a berth,
and I was wrapped up in my boat cloak on the cabin floor
surrounded by a crowd of beastly Dutchmen all as sick as
myself. However, I will not add to the misery I endured by
relating all I have gone through, but conduct you at once to
the island of Goree, where I was landed with the rest of the
passengers late on Saturday afternoon.

'The channel up to Helvoetsluys was so filled with masses
of floating ice that the packet could not get through, and,
though we might have done so with the ice boats, the captain

obliged us to go on shore at once, for which, though only half a mile from the vessel, we were obliged to pay a guinea a head. We slept at Goree, and endured every possible imposition from the Dutch.   On Sunday we attempted to get into Helvoetsluys, but could not, and landed on another Dutch island called Vlackyll, where we again made a vain attempt to get through the floating ice.   At length we succeeded in reaching Helvoet-sluys, having been driven about since Sunday and expended nearly ten pounds apiece.

'The very thoughts of the imposition I endured make me sick ! I will turn to the brighter side of the picture.

. 'From my knowledge of French and Dutch I hope to get a staff situation as soon as I reach head-quarters, which will about double my pay and give me a horse to ride on.   My thoughts are for ever recurring to England and your fireside.   How faded appear now all those bright scenes of happiness my warm imagination once pictured !   Surrounded here by the bustle of troops and stores in constant motion, I seem a solitary being ; and your image alone throws light on my dull sensations. There has been a terrible skirmish between the English and French at Antwerp, in which we have been defeated with great loss.   There are several officers killed and many wounded. Government has offered 25,000*l.* for the destruction of each ship of war at Antwerp (there are twenty there), and 500,000*l.* for taking that town ; in all a million of prize money !

'We have heard a very strong report that Buonaparte has been defeated at Châlons, with the loss of forty thousand men ; but there is nothing official.'

Amongst C. B. Vignoles's papers we fnd a draft of his application to Major Evatt. commandant at Williamstadt, for employment as assistant-engineer, a general order having been issued inviting qualified officers to send in their names.   He says : 'I received my education originally as an engineer, and I am conversant with the French and German languages, and have studied Dutch grammatically.'

Meantime his friends in London were not forgetful of his interests.   Mr. Leybourne writes to him from Sandhurst on

February 15 : ' You will perceive by Captain Parker's letter to me what the Duke of Kent's opinion was with respect to a staff appointment.   However, I had written to Colonel Mudge and to Dr. Gregory, who informs me that the Colonel is acquainted with two or three officers in Holland and will write to them at once.

' Let me again, my dear fellow, caution you in your conduct. Do not push yourself too much ; be modest.   You will in the end be better looked after.   Do not give the Duke any reason to be displeased with you.   I have no doubt you will excel most of the officers in regimental duties, as I know you do in many other things.'

We subjoin a letter from Captain Parker, the Duke of Kent's secretary :—

' Kensington Palace : February 22, 1814.

' With regard to your letter of yesterday in favour of Ensign Vignoles, H.R.H. desires me to inform you that at some future period he will be very happy to forward your views in that young officer's behalf as a candidate for staff employment.

' But at present H.R.H. thinks it will be more desirable for him to learn the duties of a regimental officer as the best foundation for service hereafter.

' Mr. Vignoles is a young man whom H.R.H. is disposed to think very favourably of, and you may, therefore, rest assured that his interests will not be forgotten when they can be promoted agreeably to a due regard to those of his regiment and the service.'

As we read these encouraging statements we can readily understand the feelings of disappointment with which young Vignoles regarded the peace that was so quickly to ensue.

The following interesting and very graphic letter was written immediately after the failure of the British assault upon the citadel of Bergen-op-Zoom.   A full description of this disaster is given by Alison in his ' History of Europe,' and an account of the circumstances of the siege may also be read in the ' Memoir of the Life of the late Field-Marshal Gomm.'

The story of this well-conceived but badly managed attempt to take the fortress was one of Napoleon's favourite reminiscences both at Elba and St. Helena :—

'March 15, 1814.

'I am afraid the few lines I hastily scratched you from Bergen-op-Zoom frightened you a little. We marched out the next day on our " paroles," and I have delayed writing that I might inform you whether there was a certainty of our returning to England till exchanged. During my stay in Willemstadt Sir Thomas Graham announced that officers who were capable of undertaking the situation of assistant-engineer should give in their names. Accordingly I sent in my name to the commandant, who desired me, as a proof of my capability, to make a plan of the fortress and town. Here was a task for me, unfurnished with a single instrument ! But that did not deter me, and with a pencil and paper in my hands, and my feet as measures, in three days I took the dimensions of the ramparts, and in two more of the town. This, by the help of a pair of old compasses, I laid down upon paper, and I finished my sketch with pen and ink, and on comparing my work with a perfect plan I found I had come within ten yards of length and three of breadth of the true dimensions. On the 1st of March I set out, having a detachment of 100 men under my command to conduct to head-quarters. Our party arrived at a town called Oudenbosch in the evening, where I found the Royals had just come in, and I was soon met by poor Captain Wetherall, at whose quarters I spent the evening, and it was the happiest I had had since I left you. We talked of old times, and your name was mentioned. He rallied me on my acquaintance with you, and asserted—it was indeed true—that you had stolen my heart before I left England. Poor Ned ! he confided to me an attachment which he had formed. But more of this presently. I marched in the morning, and arrived at head-quarters at Grool Tondert about four o'clock in the evening. I waited upon Colonel Macdonald, the Adjutant-General, to whom I presented my plan, and was desired to call in half an hour. I did so, and had the pleasing information given me that I was

appointed assistant-engineer, and was to go immediately to
Colonel Carmichael Smyth, the commanding officer of Engineers,
and report myself. He first asked me where I learnt engineering,
and I told him with my grandfather, Dr. Hutton. He then said
that my appointment should be in general orders the next day.
I slept that night at Grool Tondert, and pursued my way in the
morning in a little Dutch cart, attended by a lad of the country,
whom I have hired as my servant, to this town, where the Royals
had preceded me from Oudenbosch. My journey, though through
a heavy fall of snow, was delightful. It was in the afternoon of
the 3rd inst. that I attended the first parade of the Royal Scots.
Colonel Müller is our commanding officer. I was introduced to
my brother-officers, and soon found myself at home. Captain
Wetherall had, in his journey to Stralsund, found a handsome
little Cossack boy of twelve years of age, whose story you shall
hear another time. He is armed in his own style with a pike,
a sword, and pistol, and is mounted on a small Cossack pony.

'On the evening of the 7th of this month I received orders
to proceed as engineer to Spaltern, which is only two miles from
Bergen-op-Zoom. This order I instantly took to Colonel Müller,
but he refused his permission to my quitting the regiment.
Though excessively incensed with him at the moment, yet I
believe to his refusal I owe my life.

'I must now proceed to give you a history of the dreadful
night at Bergen-op-Zoom, in the course of which I was completely broken in to stand fire. At about seven o'clock on the
morning of the 8th a sudden command came to march in light
order. In a quarter of an hour we were under arms and set off.
To reach our place of attack it was necessary to take a circuitous
route; and all day we marched, and then had a few hours' rest
at the very village of Spaltern to which I was to have gone.
In about two hours more we came to the foot of the glacis, and
marched along the grand dyke of the river Zoom. The night
was dark, and no light was afforded but the reflection of the
snow. All was dead silence, and orders were given to halt.
The clock from the church tolled ten, and at that moment the
firing began. The pickets exchanged shots, but before they

could retreat to the garrison the flank companies of our regiment
took them prisoners, and in five minutes a joyful shout pro-
claimed us masters of one of the bastions. The shout drew the
fire of another bastion upon us, as we were still halted upon
the dyke, and the grape and round shot whistled incessantly
over our heads. Orders were now given to proceed, and we
immediately scrambled over the opposite side of the dyke and
plunged at once into a morass. We advanced by companies,
each filing separately. We thought the morass bad ; but worse
was to come, for we had to ford the river Zoom. The water was
only a few inches deep, and when I, with my captain, plunged
in, we were instantly up to our breast in mud. It was in vain
we attempted to wade along, we only stuck the faster. From
the " curtain " before us a heavy fire of grape played upon our
men, who were unable to return a shot. My face was covered
with spots of mud struck up into it by the grape as it fell all
around. An unlucky ball killed one of the sergeants. I
immediately seized his halbert, and, laying it along, crawled
through the shallow water and over the mud till I reached a
piece of ice, on which I stood and collected the men as well as
I was able. At this moment poor Wetherall called out to me
to help him, being up to his neck in mud. With much labour
I pulled him out with my sword and pike. After some minutes
we reached the opposite dyke ; but it was near two hours before
we collected the men together, and many were smothered in the
mud. Though across the river, an obstacle apparently formidable presented itself—immense palisades of wood. Not a single
pioneer was attached to us ; but by main strength a part of the
barrier was torn away, and the men passed through. We were
now on the bank of the ditch, which was frozen over, but the
ice had been cut away for some feet all round. We were so
close under the walls that the shot passed over our heads,
whistling sweetly through the air ! The drawbridge of the
gate was up, and Captain Wetherall was sent by the Colonel
with two men to cut it down. By the assistance of the palisades
they got upon the firm ice, and reaching the foot of the rampart
scaled it, and ran along the parapet. One of the men was

killed by a musket ball from the flanking bastion, but not a
Frenchman was on the wall. Wetherall descended to the gate
and found it deserted by the enemy. He opened it, and, proceeding to the drawbridge, cut it down, and the regiment
marched upon the wall and remained waiting for orders. As
the Grenadiers and Light Infantry (the flank) had been detached,
there were only eight companies on the bridge ; so we now had
time to look about. We mustered the men, and the officers,
collecting together, began to discuss the mode of attack. From
twelve o'clock at night till seven in the morning did the Royals
remain on the bridge, without receiving a single order except to
retreat ; although we could at any time have gone to a different
part of the town, and have supported the other troops in their
attack, for, instead of being seriously opposed (as the despatches
say), not a single Frenchman came within 200 yards the whole
night. By way of keeping the enemy in play, three companies
were sent into the town alternately, and the one I belonged to was
one of them ; and over a small footbridge we passed to attack a
fortified guard-house. The lieutenant of the company had been
wounded in crossing the river, and the captain and myself were
the only officers. We drew the men up and commenced a brisk
fire with good effect ; but their numbers tripled ours, and the
men fell fast around. At this moment the captain received a
wound through the lungs and was carried off, and I was left to
command the company. The blaze of the fire, the incessant
report of the firelocks, the whistling of the balls, the darkness
of the night, the cries of the wounded, the shouts of the
soldiers—all produced such a confusion in my brain that I was
senseless of danger. I at length brought the men to charge
with the bayonet, and we got to the door of the guard-house, but
it was impossible to enter. Before I could resolve what to do, the
Colonel ordered the men to be brought off, and I returned with
only thirty unkilled or wounded out of sixty-four. It was during
this brush that a musket ball passed so close to my cheek as to
make it black for a fortnight ; and in retiring across the small
footbridge three poor fellows fell before me, and I stumbled over
them and fell off the bridge. Somehow I caught hold of one
of the iron rails and recovered myself ; but I received a sprain,

of which I still feel the effects. But the worst was yet to come. It was about three o'clock in the morning when I returned to the bridge; and I found that poor Wetherall had attempted to recross the river Zoom, then full of ice, the tide being up, but had failed, and returned completely frost-bitten, and cramped in every limb. He was taken to the French guard-house close by the gate, where a fire had been lighted. The place was crowded with the wounded, of whom many had died, and the others moaning most dreadfully. No light, but the sickly blaze of the fire that just rendered " darkness visible," which shone feebly on the ghastly countenances of the men nearest to it, their cheeks streaked with blood, the eyes convulsed, and every feature distorted with pain and agony. In the background the figures were scarcely discernible through the smoke, and the whole formed a scene that made my heart sicken within me. No pen could describe it; no pencil do it justice. I tied Wetherall's head up with his sash ; but this was all I could do, as my duty forced me away. Hitherto, the exertions I had gone through prevented my being sensible of pain ; but when I left the crowded guard-house and met the keen blast of the night frost the agony I endured was almost intolerable. Not a rag about me but was soaked through and had been frozen to my skin, and my feet were benumbed. One cheek was as cold as ice, and the other, where the swelling was, pained me much ; nor was any comfort added to me by the sprain I had got, which at this time renders me scarce able to walk.

'At seven o'clock we received orders to retire, which we did under a heavy shower of grape and musketry, but it was impossible to recross the river. The redoubt now began to open on us, and the men fell around us thick, for we were completely in a cross fire without the possibility of escaping. In this dilemma Colonel Müller called for a sergeant's halbert, and I being next him gave him my white pocket-handkerchief, which was tied to the top of the pole, and I mounted the crest of the dyke and waved the flag of truce ; but in vain. The firing continued incessant, and a shot struck the staff a few inches above me and carried the top off.

'I then asked Colonel Müller's leave to go into the town with

There are many eyes upon you, and, go where you will, you will always find someone acquainted with your grandfather, who, for his sake, will be kind to you.'

The above is a good example of the letters which Mrs. Hutton wrote to her grandson from time to time, showing that her attachment to him was deep and unchangeable. The closing sentence of her letter has an additional pathos from the fact that Mrs. Hutton never did see young Vignoles again, though she lived two years longer, and that the reconciliation so earnestly desired never took place.

If from these sad reminiscences we turn again to his correspondence with his *fiancée*, we find her (as she says) 'bewildered with the wonderful succession of events, and half distracted at the idea of not seeing him before he again left England.' He evidently chafed at not being able to get to London, and seems to have confessed to her that 'he was tired of a soldier's life.' To this she replies : 'You remember, from the first of our attachment, it was painful and objectionable to me that you should be compelled to join the army. You have abilities that, I should think, would point out a variety of ways to support yourself, and in due time a wife ; but without a competence, where'er we might go, we should be pursued by poverty's evil eye, and all its attendant miseries.'

He in turn remarks as to his prospects : 'Peace is likely to be long, but as my only dependence is on the army, I must remain in it ; for it is only by my rise in that profession I can expect a reconciliation with my friends and the Doctor. There is no more to be said upon it, and I must leave my fate with the Duke.' [1]

The battalion being under positive orders for embarkation early in May, Miss Griffiths determined on a visit to Portsmouth with her maid. This she safely accomplished, and after remaining two days Vignoles accompanied them back to town, returning, however, at once to Portsmouth ; and on May 4 writes that they 'would march out to Southsea Common the next day, and embark immediately for Canada.'

[1] H.R.H. the Duke of Kent.

On May 8 he writes from H.M. ship "Leopard," off Spithead, and it is a letter of some interest, for it is perhaps the only one out of a large collection which gives any insight into his earlier years, or which attempts any analysis of his own character. He says:—

'I am extremely sensible of my own carelessness of disposition and habitual want of thought. When I first was blessed with a sight of you, I informed you of my temper and disposition. At an early age I loved reading, and before I was eight years old I loved it enthusiastically. But two sorts of books filled my grandfather's library—scientific and classical. The Doctor, pleased to observe me reading, forgot to regulate my taste, and I imbibed all I read; but instead of drawing from my books the useful, I only remembered the ornamental.'

In a subsequent paragraph he speaks of two young ladies whose fascinations had once exerted their rival charms upon him.

' 'Tis now five years[1] since I first met them, and for four years their attractions made me by turns the adorer of each. I continued nearly equally divided in my choice, when the *thunderbolt* burst on my head, and I left home!

'My extravagance and imprudence have been unbounded, unpardonable; but the boyish inclinations I may have felt for my fair enslavers is banished by the solid and rational attachment of my riper years. You are, I believe, acquainted with almost every action of my life; but, notwithstanding, I shall employ myself in writing for your amusement some account of myself.'

Most unfortunately for his biographer our hero stops short in the very crisis of his narrative. The rest of his letter is filled with comments on his fellow-voyagers, some of which are very caustic and amusing; and becoming thus diverted from what he had promised to enlarge upon, he completed his letter without returning to the topic which would have been the most interesting of all. If he took it up again, it must have been

---

[1] From this it appears that Vignoles must have been nearly nineteen years of age when he left his grandfather's home.

in some of those letters, written from Canada, that never came to hand. On May 10, 1814, the " Leopard " was under way, with the breeze blowing fresh and fair, he himself very unhappy, though, as he adds philosophically, ' repining is vain, and I endeavour to persuade myself that our stay in America will not be long. I raise my spirits by conceiving the most extravagant ideas, but as suddenly the thermometer of my gaiety falls to zero.'

On May 13 he sends a letter from the Cove of Cork. ' If we had not been obliged to keep company with a rascally convoy, we should have been at the Cove of Cork ere now.' Then, giving reins to his fancy, he adds :—

' Hope, the nurse of young Desires, has been paying me a long visit, and I see myself already a quartermaster-general, or colonel, and fifty other great people. But I will tell you also the scheme of my more rational hours—to lay myself out on my arrival in America to make my superior officers my friends.'

Still, he is evidently afraid of the possible results of ' hours of idleness,' for he adds: ' If we shall only have garrison duty, I expect I shall employ my faculties to write epigrams on the officers, sonnets on the ladies, and to laugh at and ridicule the Yankees. In the drawing-room, I shall be as strict as a parson, and whisper soft nonsense to the wife and daughter of some general who wants an aide-de-camp, and then I shall make a fresh start by talking scientifically on military discipline and tactics!' He brings this rhapsody, however, to an end by the very proper observation: ' But I find I am dreaming again.'

Farther on, he gives a brief reference to his early efforts in literary composition, for which he possessed undoubted talent :—

' I must acquaint you that my poetic mania, which has lain dormant upwards of a year, has revived ; and although I was so careless as to leave the MS. of my tragedy, and also the plot, at Sandhurst, I recollect it enough to put it in black and white again. I have also a comedy on the stocks, and lots of verses of all kinds. In Quebec, all the world runs mad on theatricals, so I shall exert my wits that way.'

Speaking of his brother-officers on shipboard, he says :—

' I cannot find one except Captain G. who has any ideas beyond smoking, drinking, and swearing. I was at first prejudiced against this gentleman, but I have learned to esteem him, and find him very well informed on every subject. This shows we should not judge by first impressions.'

As to their fare on board, he writes with more satisfaction :—

' We have got a most excellent stock of provisions, and dinners that would not disgrace an East Indiaman or our own mess on shore.'

The " Leopard " did not get away from the Irish coast till May 18, and at the very end of the month he writes :—

' I am pleased with the delightful voyage we have ; the wind ever since we left Cork has been favourable, and, had we sailed direct from Portsmouth to Quebec, we should have been there by this time.'

On June 1, however, things were not so comfortable. He says :—

' Yesterday was my birthday (he was twenty-one years of age), but I did not enjoy it, as the wind has changed, and for forty-eight hours has blown a violent gale. We are still 1,200 miles from Quebec, but part of our convoy is bound for Halifax when we reach the Banks of Newfoundland. We indulge in the reasonable hope of being at Quebec by the 24th. The " Diomede," in which is the other wing of the battalion, quitted the convoy a day or two ago, to run by herself to Quebec, on account of the prevalence of ophthalmia and scurvy among the soldiers. We are very lucky in being free from any disorder on board the " Leopard." '

The next letter he wrote was two months later, and in the meanwhile the ship he was sailing in had been wrecked on the island of Anticosti, at the mouth of the river St. Lawrence. The circumstances cannot be better related than in his own words :—

D

' I am anxious to relieve the anxiety you must all have felt on the report of the loss of the " Leopard," which no doubt reached England in an exaggerated form.

' A severe illness, occasioned by long exposure to cold and wet, has confined me to my bed for nearly a month. It was on the morning of June 28 last, with a very light wind and thick fog, that the " Leopard " struck upon a reef of rocks at the eastern point of the island of Anticosti, in the mouth of the river St. Lawrence. It was Tuesday, and until Thursday evening everything appeared a confused dream. All on board were safely landed; but it was on a low flat shore, with some ice yet remaining from the long severe winter. A small Halifax fishing schooner came in sight at last, and was brought to, and I was the officer pitched on to carry the news to Quebec. The sailing master of the " Leopard " came with me, but owing to the contrary winds and adverse currents we were seventeen days before we could work up the 500 miles to Quebec.

' The last ten days of the time I lay in my berth very ill; and when we landed on July 17 I was carried to lodgings and put to bed, from which I have only risen these last two days. At first I was quite unable to write, and then was unwilling, until I could acquaint you with my recovery, which is now rapidly proceeding, but I am still very weak, and am reduced to a skeleton. Our regiment is so thinned by sickness that we shall not take the field this campaign, but shall remain snug in Quebec.

' Besides, there is great talk of peace. Still we have in Canada 20,000 troops, and lots of artillery; and the most formidable preparations are now making to drive the Americans from the lakes.

' I seem to be a great favourite with Colonel Müller, who has written to the Duke of Kent very kindly about me.'

There is an interesting letter which was written to him about the same date by Mrs. Hutton, in which she gives some account of the rejoicings which were taking place in honour of the peace just formally concluded, and to which the Prince Regent had made prominent reference in his speech at the prorogation of Parliament on July 30, when he said that 'all the objects for which the war had been entered on were now accomplished, and the final deliverance of Europe had been effected.' This gratulation, as events proved, was twelve months too soon. In the same document, the Prince Regent lamented the troubles in Canada, which were due to the unprovoked aggression of the United States:—

'I find that since you wrote you have been in some danger, as we see by a letter in the newspapers that the "Leopard" has been wrecked on an island at the entrance of the river St. Lawrence, but that the crew and passengers were saved.

'Our little world of England since June 7 has been in a constant uproar, and the people almost mad. The great folks, emperors, kings and princes, &c., whirling about, have turned the brains of most people; and the "Fairs," as they call them, in the Parks, completed the business. Mr. Hansom seldom comes to London, and the marriage of his daughter, Lady Portsmouth, seems to have hurt his business much.[1] I am much afraid you will have hard warfare in America. May the Almighty God, my dear youth, protect you! Let it not be said that a grandson of Dr. Hutton lived in vain. The letter you wrote to your aunt Isabella has been much admired.'[2]

Ensign Vignoles's next letter to Miss Griffiths is also of some interest:—

'Quebec: August 18, 1814.

'I have long waited for this opportunity of addressing you. In spite of the croaking of the doctor, I have been for some time on my legs, and am as well as ever. Colonel Müller being about to make up a large packet of letters to the Duke of Kent, I enclose this in one, and I expect it will reach you in less than six weeks. I have been much disappointed at not finding Quebec such as I had hoped and expected. There are only

---

[1] A brief account of the divorce suit which was the unhappy result of this union may be found in the *Annual Register* for 1814.

[2] This letter has not been preserved.

French settlers near it, and they will not be at the pains of cultivating the fruitful soil, but content themselves with gathering the wild fruits and bringing them to the market. The meat is far from good, and everything almost as expensive as in England. Wine is much dearer, and a couple of garrets unfurnished cost ten shillings a week. This is the consequence of the war. Montreal is 180 miles farther up the river St. Lawrence; Kingston about as much more, and it is near there that the Americans are in great force. We have plenty of troops and military materials, but we want a good head!

'Sir George Prevost is rather sleepy. They talk of his being recalled. Quebec is at present very dull, but I am told it is gay enough in the winter. I am in hopes of getting introduced to some of the principal families in the town, without which the military must not expect much amusement. The Canadians are not over-fond of the English, and besides, they have two of their own militia regiments here. The scenery is very fine, and from the highest part of the town the surrounding plains appear like a large map. There are some grand falls of rivers, and mountains, covered with impenetrable forests, are visible from the heights of the town. The woods here abound with fruit trees in a wild state, and the underwood is mixed with currant bushes, cranberries, blueberries, &c. A little English industry would make the farms of the settlers into little Edens.

'Our first battalion has been so much cut up in the last campaign that it is supposed the fourth will be incorporated with it, all the old men and boys discharged, and the extra officers sent home. I shall stay, at all events, as the late promotions have brought me high up in the regiment. Our officers talk of getting up some plays this winter, to be performed for the benefit of the poor. You may guess I am not a little pleased with this idea.'

Sir George had reached Quebec nearly a year previous to the date of this letter—viz. on September 25, 1813—the war having begun in January. The check of the United States

forces in the thick forests[1] which young Vignoles refers to was
due to the skilful manœuvres of Colonel de Salsberry, and by
November the commander of the United States troops (General
Wilkinson) had given up all idea of attacking Lower Canada.
Sir James Yeo was subsequently the chief promoter of the
charges against Sir George Prevost, who resigned his command
and returned to England. Strange to say, both these officers,
accuser and accused, died before the court-martial could assemble.[2]
About this time Vignoles received a letter from his cousin
Charles (son of General Hutton), who was a pupil in the Royal
Military Academy. We give here a short extract from the
letter because of its frank schoolboy-like criticisms on the com-
missariat of that establishment :—

'I like the Academy very well, for we have everything we
want except good victuals, which appear to be scarce. We
have for breakfast dry bread and cold milk—plenty of chalk
and water; for dinner we have sometimes boiled beef and sometimes roast mutton; for our supper we have bread and stinking
cheese, and some sour beer. So much for the eating part. Our
studies are from eight in the morning till twelve, after which we
have leisure time till a quarter-past two, when we go to dinner,
and generally sit about a quarter of an hour; then we go to study
again at three, and there remain till six. After that we have
leisure till ten o'clock, when we go to bed and the barracks are
locked up. I was very sorry to hear of the shipwreck of the
"Leopard," but hope you have escaped unhurt. I am staying
with my grandfather for the vacation.'[3]

Vignoles writes from Quebec on September 17 :—

'Another packet has arrived about eight days since, bringing
letters and London newspapers to July 16, but not a line from

---

[1] It was, however, in this same district that General Robinson was en-
tangled, when marching on Plattsburg, by a *ruse* of the American commander,
and the British lost severely.

[2] Cf. Cust's *Wars of XIX. Century*, vol. iv. p. 308.

[3] This very promising youth died at an early age of consumption. Afterwards another son was born to the General, who grew to man's estate, gradu-
ated at Oxford, and was subsequently Rector of Woburn, Beds, and then of
St. Paul's, Covent Garden.

anyone to console me. We learn, however, that two of the
bags containing the June packet were burnt accidentally in the
immense forest tract lying between this town and Halifax,
through which the mail is carried on foot. One of the July
bags also was destroyed by violent rains, which reduced the
contents to hasty pudding. I devoured the papers which our
mess received, and I see by the " Star " evening paper of June 19
that a detachment of our regiment was under orders for immediate embarkation to join us here.

'Your last letter is dated May 6, so that four months and a
half have elapsed without a line or a word for me. By this
time the London papers have told you of the events that have
happened in Canada, which are none of the most glorious to
Great Britain—indeed, quite the contrary. A recent affair will
most probably cause the recall of the Governor, Sir G. Prevost.
We attacked the fort of Champlain, upon the lake of that name,
by water and land. The ships unfortunately grounded, and
were all destroyed or taken ; and a British army, seeing this, ran
away from a quarter their own number ! It is said that Major-
General Brisbane is under arrest for refusing to retreat when
ordered. The walls here are covered with reflections upon the
affair, so highly inimical to the Governor that I am really afraid
to copy them in my letter. It is whispered that we lost several
hundred men on our retreat, but everything is hushed up. An
attack upon Sackett's Harbour—the naval arsenal and depôt
of the Americans upon Lake Ontario—is now talked of. We
have plenty of troops and material for an army here; we only
want a Lord Wellington to send the Yankees to the d—l ! In
the United States, Lord Hill and his army have burnt Washington and Baltimore, and they are now proceeding to Philadelphia.

'The Yankees are in a terrible fright, but they fight well.
Indeed, we have taught them. Out first battalion is enduring
all the hard knocks and deprivations of this campaign. I do not
as yet know how I shall send this letter. When the river St.
Lawrence is blocked by ice, which is for half the year, the
packets only come to Halifax, and the mail is brought overland.'

An interval of two months occurs without letters to or from Vignoles and his family. It appears from what Mrs. Hutton writes that letters had been sent by her and Miss Hutton in the beginning of July, August, and October, but these seem all to have been lost. The same fate befell some of Miss Griffith's communications, for on November 20 she writes from London :—

' It is truly unfortunate that I should have written by those very packets. Daily, hourly, do I sigh for your return. It is the only source, save Heaven, from which I can draw any pleasure. I have only a few days since returned from Wales, where you will be surprised to find I spent full eleven weeks. Most happily did they pass away, at least as much as in your absence I could expect. My friends are universally kind and hospitable, and I returned looking quite well.

' With what pain and sorrow do I read over your letter which informs me of the melancholy event of the shipwreck ! Do not laugh when I tell you that a most singular dream that night made me sure that something had happened to you, and I could not shake off the gloom which it left upon me. When I think of the perils you have encountered the anguish I endure is not to be described, and Heaven only knows what still may be your fate.'

About the same time that the foregoing letter was penned, young Vignoles wrote again from Quebec on November 17 :—

'. . . A few days ago I sent you a Quebec newspaper, which contained an account of a ball given by our battalion in honour of the birthday of his Royal Highness the Duke of Kent. I had the honour of painting the portrait of the Duke there mentioned, which was a transparency ; and by the aid of a gay dress and high colouring (like many ladies both at the ball and elsewhere !), it passed off tolerably well. The wreath surrounding the name " Edward," also mentioned, was done by young Clarke from designs of mine. We kept treading the rounds of the mazy dance till five o'clock in the morning, at which time, the ladies having retired, and the claret operating rather strongly, I, with a few others, prevailing on the drowsy musicians to strike up once more, finished the night's amusements with a few reels, the last of which was a *reel* to bed!'

A little later he writes:—

'The Colonel has issued an order permitting the soldiers of the Royals to wear *whiskers*. I intend to avail myself of this privilege to appear with an extraordinarily large pair.[1] There is no army news except that the Americans have blown up the celebrated Fort Erie and returned to their own side of the frontier line.[2] In Congress they are speculating about raising 100,000 men by conscription. This prospect Jonathan won't much like. Should the war continue, the campaign will open with renewed vigour. Perhaps some friendly ball will lay me low, and then all will be well.'

This is Vignoles's last letter (during his stay in Canada) which came to hand. The few extracts that follow complete the story up to the end of 1814. Mrs. Hutton writes on November 21 :— ·

'Colonel Wright, at my request, wrote to his brother, Major George Wright, of the Engineers, strongly recommending you. Also, if you ever meet Colonel Gordon Drummond, mention to him that he was an inmate of our house at the time you were born.

'Now I must tell you all the news. Lord Byron has married Miss Millbank,[3] who is heir to her father, Sir Ralph, and to her brother, Lord Wentworth. I believe you have seen the Millbank family at our house. Miss M. is a very charming and highly educated young lady—I am afraid much too amiable for his lordship!

'The " Attic chest "[4] has not been opened since you left us; a little poetic effusion from you would be very welcome!'

---

[1] It is more than likely that he did not carry out this notion. Mr. Vignoles, as all his portraits show, to the end of his life always kept his face, neck, and chin clean shaven.

[2] It was an American fort. Its destruction took place on Nov. 5, 1814. Cf. Cust, iv. pp. 297, 309.

[3] The marriage did not actually take place till the beginning of January 1815.

[4] The 'Attic chest' was a name given by Vignoles in his youthful days to

At the very end of the year Miss Griffiths writes :—

'I read in to-day's paper that Sir George Prevost is to be tried by a court-martial on charges preferred by the subordinate generals and Sir James Yeo.[1] Sir G. Murray is expected to leave immediately for America. All this most likely you know, as you get all the news by every packet. I forget whether or not you saw Kean, the actor, at Drury Lane. He has been quite the star, and a new actress[2] has lately made her appearance at Covent Garden, of whom report speaks in the highest rapture. I have not seen her, but will give my opinion in another letter.'

We conclude the correspondence of this year by a very gratifying incidental testimony to our young hero's good conduct in Canada. It is reasonable to infer, from the extract given below, that he had not sought to commend himself to his colonel by reason of his relationship to Dr. Hutton. It is a Mr. John Vignoles, a distant connection, who writes from Tewkesbury on January 3, 1815, to Dr. Hutton :—

'I must express my satisfaction that an act of kindness intended for my son should have turned so much to the advantage of your grandson ; and more particularly as he appears from undoubted testimony to be deserving of it. A friend of mine who is well acquainted with Colonel Müller has lately had a letter from that officer, out of which he transcribes the following passage :—

'"Should you meet Mrs. Vignoles, tell her that her son has, in this unfortunate shipwreck, given me fresh proof of zeal and devotedness to the service and his own particular duty, for which I have not failed to recommend him for a staff appointment to the Commander-in-Chief."

'This son, whom my friend supposed to be in America, was gazetted for a commission in the 41st in Canada, but the

---

a collection of original papers, read from time to time at the meetings of a literary society which assembled at the Huttons' residence in Bedford Row. Vignoles seems to have contributed tales, dramas, and sundry poetical effusions to this academic store.

[1] Sir J. Yeo commanded the naval force on the Lakes.

[2] This was Miss O'Neill.

Governors at Woolwich would not allow him to accept it *yet*, and there he still is.'

To this letter we may add a few extracts from the only one that remains of those that were probably written in the earlier months of the year 1815. It is from his aunt Isabella, and is dated March 24 :—

'I find that the 4th Royal Scots is to remain in America. I hope it will be to your advantage. With your talents, my dear Charles, you will always meet with friends if you are but your own friend.

'King Louis is on his way again to England, and Buonaparte is once more in Paris! So many wonderful changes have happened lately that we shall be surprised at nothing.

'The "Attic readings" have been going on this winter, but since you left us I may say our chief interest has been taken away; I still fondly hope and trust we shall yet meet again to be happy.

'Your grandfather has had his health much better this winter than he has had for several years past. I had almost forgotten to tell you that Miss Porden is going to publish a poem of "The Veils" in six books, to which you will recollect having contributed. Buonaparte has got safe to Paris without any fighting at all. You see what wonderful events have come to pass within these twelve months !'

CHAPTER IV.

Vignoles in Scotland—Various letters to and from him —Visits to Professor
Dugald Stewart.

1815-16.

A BLANK of four months intervenes before we get further tidings
of C. B. Vignoles, and then he is again off the shores of old
England.   He writes to a friend:—

'On board the transport "Hector," Spithead: July 15, 1815.

'Our battalion, which is part of a force of 10,000 men,
arrived this day about two o'clock.   We have had a most delightful short passage of five weeks from Quebec, and are only
now arrived time enough to hear of the dreadful battle,[1] which
has apparently decided the fate of Europe.   Our third battalion
has suffered much—eight killed and twenty-four wounded among
the officers.

'I will tell you how we passed away the long Canadian
winter in acting plays, in which amusement your devoted
servant was a principal performer.   There were no ladies to be
procured for love or money, and I was pitched on to perform
those parts, and as the newspapers say, "brought down the
plaudits of a brilliant and overflowing audience."   Our friend
Macartney was a lady as well as myself, and we were pronounced
by the whole *male* part of the spectators to be much better
figures and faces than any real lady in Quebec, all of whom
indeed are rather stunted in their growth.[2]

'Imagine me dressed as Floranthe in the *Mountaineer*,

---

[1] Waterloo.   It is evident that but for his rapid promotion Vignoles would
have been in this action.

[2] Vignoles was of rather short stature for a man.

Emily Worthington in the *Poor Gentleman*, Julia in the *Rivals*, and Cora in *Pizarro*! Add to this the part of Miss Penelope Snap in *Yes or No*.'

Vignoles was bitterly disappointed at being refused leave of absence to visit his London friends on his arrival at Hilsea Barracks; but Miss Griffiths had the courage to go once more to Portsmouth, this time to welcome him home, and at least set eyes on him before he sailed with his company for Edinburgh.

Writing later he says :—

' The policy of the Duke of Kent contrived to have the 4th battalion sent to France instead of the 1st, as originally ordered; but whether that arrangement will continue I cannot say. Rumour has it that H.R.H. is going to the Continent to retrench. Query—Will the Ministry in that case suffer him to retain a regiment of four battalions when almost all the others are reduced to one?'

Vignoles sailed for Scotland on the last day of July 1815, and what he thought of the voyage may be seen in one or two extracts from his letters :—

' It is the intention of the master of the transport to call or rather touch at several of the towns on the sea coast, particularly at Sunderland, where his own wife resides, and he will certainly stop there to take her on board. I hear the seamen at this moment raising the anchor; a few more hours, therefore, will bring us to the Downs.'

He writes again off Sunderland on August 8 :—

' Our voyage has been uncommonly long and dull; but I have been plagued by the people on board much more than by the weather. There are no less than nine officers, four of whom are married and accompanied by their wives and children. Among the rest is the Quartermaster, who has risen from the ranks, and is possessed of a wife who is an Irishwoman, and she is possessed of the d——, for such a gift of the gab never was bestowed on any female. I would certainly pit her against any fishwoman for volubility and vulgarity of tongue. The other three are much better, but two out of those are the wives of

private soldiers since become officers. You may, therefore, conclude, when any quarrel ensues between the aforesaid *ladies*, that
their previous habits of life rush in and pour themselves forth
in the most vulgar innuendoes and insinuations. There are nearly
a dozen children of all ages from five months to ten years; and
of course every variety of pipe, from the highest squall of a baby
to the hobbledehoy of a schoolboy. I am fortunately secluded
from much of this, as I have engaged the master to board me
during the voyage, and I am accommodated with the use of the
cabin by day and the mate's berth by night.'

The " Albion " reached Leith on August 12, and the military
portion of the passengers was quartered in Edinburgh Castle
the next day. The accommodation being limited, Vignoles and
two brother-officers hired a lodging in the city and found themselves very comfortable. Some breach of discipline had occurred
on board the transport, and his first duty in his new quarters
was to appear as witness on the court-martial. He goes on to
say :—

' I have another piece of news to tell you. The Royal Scots,
in consequence of the very gallant manner they have behaved
in the present war, are to be in future called " The First, or
King's Own Royal Highlanders ; " the men are to be dressed in
the high tartan bonnet and plumes, and are to wear the kilt
and philibeg—in short, everything *à l'Ecossais* ; and the officers
will also wear the feathers, the kilt, &c., and a silk tartan plaid.
The three words " Egypt, Niagara, Waterloo," will shine con-
spicuously on our breast-plates.'

He goes on to tell of the amusements of the place, and
especially of Miss O'Neill's triumphant success in Edinburgh :—

' I saw her last night in the character of Isabella in the
Fatal Marriage. She is, in my opinion, infinitely beyond any
actress I have ever seen.'

A few days later he writes :—

' I must now inform you that I have introduced myself to
several people here who were acquainted with my grandfather ;
among the rest is Mr. Jeffrey, the editor of the " Edinburgh
Review," and Professor Dugald Stewart. From the latter I

the orders of the evening. The place is rainy, and my mornings,
when I cannot stir out, are fully employed in my accounts,
writing and drawing, &c. I have four large rooms, two men
servants, and a maid ; and were I to remain every day at home
the expenses of my establishment would not exceed two shillings
a day, but I am so much out that it never amounts to more
than half-a-guinea a week. Mutton and beef are only fourpence
per lb., fourpence a dozen for new-laid eggs, sixpence for a fine
fowl, &c.; best fresh butter one shilling a pound ; and I have
also a garden belonging to me as the commanding officer.
Bread is the only dear article, and I am not yet Scotchman
enough to be reconciled to eat cakes. I am well supplied with
books. By-the-by, in my walks, I have often been taken for
a young laird, which you will allow is justified by my dress,
consisting of a scarlet jacket, with gold bullion, straps on each
shoulder, tartan trousers, an elegant Highland bonnet with
heron's tail and feathers, and a large plaid.'

On November 2 he writes :—

' You doubtless have seen in the papers that I have at length
got my lieutenancy. This, however, will not remove me hence,
until the veterans relieve us, which will be about Christmas ;
after which I have my own option to go to India or to Paris.
You need not doubt but the latter place will be my choice. I
am writing to the Duke of Kent by this post. Since I sent my
last I have been to the top of Ben Nevis, which is considered
the highest mountain in Great Britain, being nearly a mile in
altitude above the level of the sea. I was much gratified by the
trip.

' Mrs. Stewart of Kinniel is first cousin to General Brisbane,
who commands a brigade under the Duke of Wellington, and
he is at this time without an aide-de-camp. I am to have
letters of introduction and recommendation to this said general,
and it is not impossible that he may please to take me on his
staff.'

In a postscript he adds :—

' I have been much amused at purchasing a shoulder of
mutton for sixpence. It is, however, small, like the Welsh

mutton, only weighing a pound and a half, but better than any in London, and at all events very cheap.'

A few days previously, Vignoles had received a letter written by Mr. R. Wetherall, brother of the officer who was killed at Bergen-op-Zoom. He tells the fate of the Cossack boy mentioned in Chapter II., who had recently died of decline at Bath. It seems he had just attained a fair knowledge of the English language and writing, and, had he survived, he was to have gone under the protection of the Duke of Kent, who had written to Mr. Wetherall to that effect.

Vignoles writes again on December 5, 1815 :—

' I have been full of gaiety since I wrote last ; first, with the ball, and then on a little tour I made among some old veterans who served with my father in the American War nearly thirty years ago. I was received by them with every kindness and true Scotch hospitality. I went from this on last Monday, and returned only for the ball on the 29th. Such handsome women, and such delightful dancers! At seven o'clock in the morning our gaieties concluded with the favourite dance of " The Haymakers." '

The following letter is given verbatim :—

'Kensington Palace: December 6, 1815.

' Captain Harvey is instructed by the Duke of Kent to acknowledge Lieutenant Vignoles's letter of the 28th ult., and to state to him in reply thereto that, most natural and proper as his Royal Highness considers it in him to wish, for the reasons he has assigned, to pay a visit to Monsieur Courtois[1] near Tours, the Duke cannot sanction it at present. But, if the 4th battalion should remain in France, his Royal Highness hopes it may not be difficult to obtain for Lieutenant Vignoles, during the winter, the leave of absence necessary to enable him to perform the duty towards the individual who behaved with such kindness to his departed parents, at the time when the heavy

---

[1] The gentleman mentioned in Chapter I. who had taken care of Vignoles after the death of his parents.

B

hand of sickness cut them both off untimely in the West Indies.'

It was not till nearly the end of January 1816 that the order arrived from the Adjutant-General's Office in Edinburgh for Lieutenant Vignoles to make over the command of the party of the Royal Scots of which he had been in charge. Thus the event he so much dreaded had come about, and he was placed on half-pay; but it was not till a month later that he actually left Fort William.

Vignoles writes on March 2, 1816 :—

' I have received orders to quit this place, but no officer has yet come to relieve me. I have a strong inclination to be in London, now that I am again on half-pay. I may consider myself quite sure of a staff appointment with the army in France.

' Professor Stewart still continues his friendly correspondence His only (surviving) son has just returned from India; he is a lieutenant-colonel in the army and senior major of the York Rangers. I am earnestly requested to spend a few weeks at Kinniel on my way south. Such a friend must not be neglected.'

The closing paragraph shows how undecided he still feels as to the main business of life :—

' Let me hear all your arguments as to the future—whether the life of a soldier is still to be pursued, and I continue to seek the " bubble reputation at the cannon's mouth," or whether I should sit contentedly down as a farmer and hide myself for ever from the world. To die a soldier or live in obscurity, that is the question ! '

We conclude this chapter by a few passages from an interesting and spirited letter dated March 13, 1816 :—

' I am with a brother-officer at his father's house about fifteen miles from Fort William. Before me are the highest mountains in Great Britain, covered with snow many feet in depth. Half way down commences the region of clouds and mists which hang like a thick veil waved about by the blast of the storm. At their feet is a rapid roaring river, broken by rocks, shallows, and cata-

racts. Its banks are covered with trees and shrubs, still divested
of their foliage, through which the storm shrilly whistles, while
the deep sound of the waters forms a solemn bass to the music
of the tempest.   This is the very heart of the land and country
of Ossian.   Every hill bears the name of one of his heroes;
every path that is trod by the wild Highlander preserves some
characteristic of his poems. The very names of the neighbouring
farms translated into English sound romantic : " The Land of
Brambles," " The Great Battle-field," " The King's Glen," "The
Stag's Burn," &c.   In this part of the world, were it not for the
papers, we might imagine ourselves in America.   Yesterday
morning while at breakfast we were agreeably entertained by the
London journals brought from Fort William by my orderly, who
had started at daybreak and travelled in a heavy storm, cursing
me, no doubt, for his walk on such a morning.   Our mode of
living, too, is somewhat different from yours in London. Venison
daily covers the table, and moor fowl, black cock, ptarmigan,
&c., are as plentiful as barn-door poultry in the south.   Adieu!
At present " my honour calls me from thee," but expect soon
to behold your ever-sincere and affectionate

' CHARLES.'

CHAPTER V.

Valenciennes—Extra Aide-de-Camp to General Brisbane—H.R.H. the Duke of Kent—Letters—The Duke of Wellington—Correspondence with his Aunt and Miss Griffiths—His prospects — Difficulties and disappointments—Leaves Valenciennes.

1816-17.

No record remains of Lieutenant Vignoles's visit to London on his way to France. His removal took place some time in April 1816, and from the tenor of his first letter after his arrival at Valenciennes it is evident that he had taken his farewell of Miss Griffiths a few days before.

Valenciennes was one of the four places first occupied by the allied forces in 1793–4, the others being Le Quenoi, Landrecies, and Condé. Valenciennes was taken by the Duke of York in March 1793 after a six weeks' siege. Its fortifications were planned by Vauban, much of whose work still remains.

Young Brisbane, then an ensign in the 38th Regiment, took part in the warlike operations which brought about the surrender of the citadel and of the town in which, twenty-two years later, he was to occupy so conspicuous a position. At the time Vignoles was quartered at Valenciennes, as related in this chapter, Major-General Sir Thomas Brisbane, K.C.B., had shared in the honours and promotion which rewarded the chief actors in the terrible drama of war now completed, and he was still in command of the second division of Wellington's army.

Vignoles writes :—

'Valenciennes: May 1, 1816.

' I arrived here in safety last Friday evening. I wrote a few hurried lines from Calais, whence the Duke of Wellington's dispatches were forwarded through me to Cambrai ; but now let me narrate my farther adventures.

'I waited on General Brisbane and delivered my letters, and have received his commands to remain with him for the present. I have got a good billet, though neither pay nor allowances ; but I must submit to some temporary deprivations to attain a situation which presents a prospect of independence. This town is very dull, and but for the army would be intolerable. . . .

'Theatricals are the order of the day ; to-morrow is to be acted the *Honeymoon* and the *Irishman in London.*

'I find here most of the officers [1] I knew before. Colonel Müller has paid me great attention, and all the lads were rejoiced to see me again. I can but envy those officers who have their wives and families with them ; they are all so well lodged, and living is so cheap, and all their cares and wants are amply provided for. The Duke of Wellington is at the Hague, and has no idea of coming to England for the wedding,[2] as the English papers say.'

Vignoles writes from Valenciennes on May 16 :—

'Now I will reply to your question, and tell you how I like the General. I shall first answer categorically very much, and then proceed to inform you that he combines the manners of the accomplished gentleman and officer with the knowledge and learning of the scholar. He treats me with the greatest kindness, but says nothing. At first the ceremonious title of " Mr." preceded my name ; but within these few days that has been dropped, and the simple sound of " Vignoles " generally intimates he is speaking to me. He keeps me very well employed all day, and, I perceive, is sounding my depth and making his own observations ; consequently, I am on the *qui vive*, but apparently as easy as possible. A French mathematician lives with him, and I am learning from him several astronomical calculations, which the General [3] particularly has occasion to make use of. I am

---

[1] General Brisbane had held a command in the army in Canada. He led the troops in the battle of Plattsburg.

[2] Of the Princess Charlotte.

[3] The General himself was an accomplished astronomer, and in 1882 built

as silent and indifferent as the General, who comes quietly every morning about ten or eleven and remains till five or six; which time, with the exception of riding out now and then, is passed with him and M. Dobisson (the French mathematician) in calculations of different kinds. Sometimes, when anything is wanted particularly neatly copied or drawn, I am employed; and about a week since I drew out some tables comparing the French and English measures, with scales, &c., for the Duke of Wellington.

'On the whole I am very well contented, and argue with myself thus : Sir Thomas Brisbane would not keep me employed about him, encouraging hopes which he never means to fulfil, unless he had some determinate object in view.

'I have been introduced to several French families, and find myself daily improving in the language, my knowledge of which, by-the-by, seemed to please my new governor, as neither of his present aides-de-camp knows a word of it.'

He writes again on June 13 :—

'The General continues to behave most kindly to me, and I am more than ever with him. Every day that he does not dine abroad I take my knife and fork at his table, and am now often included in his invitations to public dinners, &c.

'My time is wholly devoted to him, and I assure you that I have scarcely a moment to myself.

'I will give you a sketch of one day, which will answer for every other. Out of bed by eight (by-the-by, you will call this laziness); breakfast by half-past nine (you will remember I was always a considerable time at my toilette); walk to the "Grande Place," pick up a few mouthsful of news, and arrive at Sir Thomas's by ten. From that hour to two, hard work of all descriptions, chiefly with my pen and noddle together. At two, if the weather is fine, one of the General's horses is ready for me, and I accompany him in a ride till four; if bad, the staff amuse themselves at shuttlecock, &c., or we continue our calculations. From four to five, walk in the garden making observations, &c.,

the first Australian observatory at Paramatta, near Sydney. Sir John Herschell long afterwards spoke of General Brisbane as the 'father of Australian science.'

and return home to dress for dinner at six. Whatever place I dine at I cannot rise from table till nine or ten; and there is always a rout, a ball, a play, or billiards, to fill up the time till midnight, when I retire, to begin the same course again. To all this add the important office of property man and dress manager of our elegant theatre, which absolutely snatches from myself every moment I should steal from the General. Valenciennes is filled with a most elegant English society at present. I will put down the names of some of the principal ladies: the wife of General Sir John Kean; Lady Cameron, the wife of Sir John Cameron, colonel of the 9th Regiment; the wives of the following officers: Colonel Spring, 57th Regiment; Colonel McGregor, 88th Regiment; Major Cully, 5th Regiment; Major Wolcroft, Royal Artillery, all of whom I know. Adieu! A thousand tender regards and every good attend you.'

Miss Griffiths writes on July 25 :—

' Your friend M. informed me yesterday that he had been to Bedford Row, and was grieved to find you had not written to your relatives there. He says that if you had not neglected them you would long ago have been put on full-pay through their means.'

Considering what had gone before, we think this assumption quite improbable; for it is evident that the grandson of Dr. Hutton had become very tired of repeated efforts towards reconciliation, which had hitherto produced not the least effect.

Vignoles replies on August 2 :—

' I wrote to Mrs. Hutton about a week since explaining my silence, and will write again by Colonel Müller's son, who is returning to Sandhurst College. I have been to Paris since you last heard from me, on business for the General. More particulars in my next.'

On August 3 Vignoles's grandmother once more writes to him, and the letter affords a good illustration of her sterling character :—

' You were indeed long in writing, and I had begun to fancy you had left France without thinking of your relations. I am sorry for your situation, but not at all surprised. Had you remained in Doctors' Commons you would now have been your own master; but as you thought otherwise you must struggle on. I cannot think that a gentleman of Sir Thomas Brisbane's character will let you fag for nothing. However that may be, your neglect of real tried friends has hurt only yourself. All your best advisers think that you should keep to the Royals and not change your situation, but you ought to know best. I have no doubt but that you will soon be restored to full-pay, and it will then be a proper time for you to come to an explanation with Sir Thomas. In the meantime I think your dining at his table no advantage to you, as it must expose you to the company of men you cannot cope with in dress and other respects. We must be first in some measure just to ourselves and our own friends, which no one can be who gets into debt.

' I find that Colonel Müller is on the spot with you, and I am assured that he is well-disposed towards you.

' I am still in hopes, my dear Charles, that you will make compensation to us all for the sorrow and care we have suffered for you.

' I have to add my prayers for your happiness, and to beg your steady perseverance in doing right; depend on your reward some time.'

In a postscript she adds :—

' What a dreadful wet season we have had! We are sitting over the fire this moment, August 3, shivering with cold.'

All this time poor Vignoles was carrying on a gallant struggle against surrounding difficulties. It was easy for his relatives to lecture him about debts, but these were simply inevitable under existing conditions.

We cannot blame him for trying to retain the honourable post he had been placed in by Sir Thomas Brisbane, who would probably have dealt more liberally with his young *attaché* could he have dispensed with some of the aides-de-camp already on his staff. It was hard lines indeed for our lieutenant, on half-pay, and with no private income, to perform gratuitously the services he evidently rendered to the General, and at the same time to keep up the appearance his position demanded.

Had his grandfather abated something of the bitterness of his wrath for offences committed four or five years previously, and which his young relative's privations and perils, not to mention his high character as an officer, might be considered as in some measure atoning for, Vignoles would have been partly relieved from his embarrassment, and enabled to hold on until better times should come.

His grandmother sent him a little, very little, pecuniary aid from time to time ; but he seems to have been chiefly indebted to his own friends and those of his future wife for supplying his more urgent requirements.

From another long letter written by Vignoles we give only a brief extract here :—

'Valenciennes: September 5, 1816.

' I have just been attending the brilliant races, which on this lovely day are graced by the presence of Wellington and the chief Russian, Prussian, and English Generals, and their staff. The races began yesterday, and perhaps out of England a more noble assemblage of men and lovely beings of your sex were never met together. For the last fortnight, and for a week to come, balls, routs, concerts, French and English plays have been, and will be, our nightly recreation.'

In one of Miss Griffiths's letters she had informed him of a possible visit to France in the company of some friends. To this he says :—

' The best way that you can come is in the packet that leaves Billingsgate for Calais direct ; from that to Valenciennes is two days' easy journey, and even only one by starting early. You must form a party large enough to fill a coach, for you will find it much cheaper and in every way more agreeable to hire a travelling barouche in London, as the expense will be much less than carriages in this country. The smallest conveyance you can hire in France will not cost you less than sixpence per · English mile, and is liable to break down. The posting in France is regulated by law, and every expense on the road can be calculated to a penny.

'I have every reason to believe that at least two years must elapse before Sir Thomas Brisbane will go to New South Wales;[1] and also, till he goes, my remaining with him will probably depend upon myself. I feel that something decisive will soon take place—at least so I hope.'

There is nothing to show what were Vignoles's experiences during the next three months. Mrs. Hutton writes to him towards the end of the year, and tells him of his uncle's (General Hutton's) retirement from the army with an allowance of eleven hundred a year, 'more than he could ever have expected.'

She says further :—

'I always show your grandfather your letters. It is one step gained in your favour that he will read them to me, and I hope it is a very comfortable thought for you also.'

It appears from a subsequent allusion that her grandson (Vignoles) had been ill. In condoling with him she begs of him not to think of coming to England just then, and adds :—

'Great is the general distress in this country; it would sadden you to see and hear the complaints amongst all classes of people, and God knows what may be the consequences to the poor this winter.'

The letter we now give from Vignoles to H.R.H. the Duke of Kent at Brussels shows that he had occupied his time to some purpose under General Brisbane :—

'Valenciennes: December 29, 1816.

'Sir,—At the desire of Sir Thomas Brisbane I have the honour of enclosing to your Royal Highness a collection of tables comparative of the English and ancient French measures, with those established upon the metrical system. These tables have been considerably enlarged and various alterations made in them, under the direction of General Brisbane, since they were first brought to the notice of your Royal Highness. It is a fortnight since I received the final approval of the General to their present arrangement, and I have endeavoured to make

---

[1] Sir T. Brisbane did not go out as Governor of New South Wales till 1821, and he remained there ten years.

the copy as correct as possible, to render it more worthy the acceptance of your Royal Highness. On the return of Sir Thomas from Paris, he intends to have circulated similar comparative tables of the new measures of capacity and weights, also founded on the metrical system and the decimal division, which when completed will be forwarded to your Royal Highness.

'I have the honour to be, with the greatest respect, your Royal Highness's most obliged and very obedient servant,

'CHARLES VIGNOLES,
'Lieutenant 4th batt. Royal Scots.'

The acknowledgment of this communication is also given here :—

'Brussels : January 3, 1817.

'Captain Harvey is directed by the Duke of Kent to acknowledge Lieutenant Vignoles's letter, which arrived yesterday, together with the interesting collection of tables forwarded to him at the desire of Major-General Sir Thomas Brisbane, to whom it is his Royal Highness's wish that he should convey his best thanks for this further mark of the General's obliging recollection of him.

'To this Captain Harvey is commanded to add the Duke's best acknowledgments to Lieutenant Vignoles for his great attention to their execution, which certainly does him much credit.

'The comparative tables of the new measures of capacity and weight, intended to be calculated by Sir Thomas on his return from Paris, will be particularly acceptable when completed, and Lieutenant Vignoles is requested to express this to the Major-General when he arrives.

'Captain Harvey has the pleasure of stating, by desire of the Duke, that, Lieutenant John Campbell having been recently recommended from half-pay to succeed Lieutenant Thomas Stewart, there is only one on the half-pay list of the 4th battalion—viz. Lieutenant John Miller—who stands before Lieutenant Vignoles, who may, therefore, in all probability expect ere long to be brought on full-pay into the 3rd battalion.'

We shall close this chapter by a brief extract from Vignoles's last letter from Valenciennes.   It is clear that the hopes of his being placed on full-pay, held out in the letter of the Duke of Kent's secretary, were not fulfilled.   No family papers throw any light on the subject, but we may conjecture that this severe disappointment proved too much for the young lieutenant's endurance.   Indeed, his position must have been rendered almost intolerable by pecuniary embarrassment; and, moreover, the Convention of Paris being now near at hand, it is probable that the General's presence was required in the city, and that he had no immediate need of the services of his extra aide-de-camp.   All this, however, is purely conjectural.

What we are now sure of is that our hero saw plainly there was nothing to be gained by his remaining in France, and, as he was kindly received by his old tried friend and adviser at Sandhurst on his return to England in the spring of 1817, we may fairly conclude that he did not take this important step without that gentleman's concurrence.

'Valenciennes : February 6, 1817.

'You will be surprised to learn that my situation with regard to Sir Thomas Brisbane remains precisely as it did, except his increasing kindness and even intimacy.

'He has only lately returned from Paris, where he was nearly three months, during the whole of which period he kept me as busily employed as ever—indeed, so constant has been my occupation, that since the Grand Review by the Duke of Wellington in October I have not been outside the gates of Valenciennes.   His present extra aide-de-camp was formerly with him in Spain ; he is a captain in the 74th, which is now in Dublin, and so long as that regiment remains in Great Britain he will continue with the General.   All idea, therefore, of recompense from Sir Thomas Brisbane for any service I am or may have been to him will be his interest in my promotion.

'You are aware of the dreadful reduction that took place

in the army on the 24th of last month. Nearly a thousand lieutenants have been placed upon half-pay; of these, twenty in the Royals are reduced, and I, who was the very first to come in from the half-pay of the 4th battalion, have now not the smallest chance of being brought in for years, without the greatest interest exerted by all my friends. Whether it will be successful I cannot tell.

' Mr. Leybourne's I can rely on; Sir Thomas Brisbane will, I have reason to think, use his; with regard to my grandfather, I am uncertain.

' I keep up a constant intercourse with Mrs. Hutton and all the family, and the doctor even is amused with hearing the rattle of my letters.

' I would willingly fill this sheet entirely, but I am too much occupied, and have already given you every moment I can spare.

' Once more, Farewell ! '

CHAPTER VI.

Vignoles returns to Sandhurst—His marriage—Sails for America—Obtains
employment as Assistant State-Surveyor for South Carolina.

1817.

FROM the last letter written by Miss Griffiths to Lieutenant
Vignoles during his stay in Valenciennes we get tidings of his
grandmother's death; but of the exact date of that event there
is no record, nor is there any allusion to it in his own extant
letters.

That he felt it acutely may be inferred from one sentence in
his correspondent's letter, which is dated March 30, 1817 :—

' No consolation that I could offer can have power to cheer
you in the irreparable loss you have sustained.'

It was probably towards the end of April that Vignoles left
Valenciennes, for we find that early in May he is once more a
visitor at Sandhurst. He writes :—

' I arrived here safe on Monday morning, and was received
in the most friendly manner by Professor and Mrs. Leybourne.

' We had an immediate explanation : but he would not consent to the Mexican expedition until he had used his utmost
endeavour to get me upon full-pay in the British service.

' *En attendant*, he insists on my remaining with him.'

On May 29 he writes :—

' Within these few days the adventure to Spanish South
America has been revived as a topic of great interest between
Mr. Leybourne and myself; and if I could persuade him to consent to my going, there would be a certain prospect of promotion
and independence.

' The revolt of the colonies both of Spain and Portugal is

daily increasing, and the whole continent of South America from the Isthmus of Panama to the Gulph (*sic*) of California is rising to regain its pristine liberty.'

A few days later he writes again with enthusiasm on the same subject:—

'The Spanish colonies in South America have already peaceably secured their liberties by land, but they are now threatened by attacks from sea, and are in consequence exerting themselves to the utmost to put their towns in a proper state of defence. To do this they require European officers to assist them in the Artillery and Engineering department; and as I fancy myself qualified to act in that capacity I am anxious to do so.'

The extracts which follow are from a very animated and interesting letter which he wrote in the early hours of the morning of June 20 :—

'Being half distracted at the state of affairs, I suddenly thought of asking Mr. Leybourne to try what could be done through General Gordon. He agreed, and on the spur of the moment I wrote the sketch of a letter, which Mr. Leybourne copied out, and presented to General Gordon through the hands of Sir Howard Douglas, at the Board meeting last Wednesday. On Friday the Farnham examinations took place, when I accompanied Mr. Leybourne there; and he then received the Duke of York's answer to a strong application made by General Gordon, the substance of which was that "his Royal Highness regretted that the case of Lieut. Vignoles was that of 2,000 other young men similarly situated; consequently, Mr. Leybourne must be aware how impossible it was to expect any early appointment for his *protégé* to full-pay. Nevertheless, what General Gordon had stated so strongly would have its due effect and consideration." But meanwhile Mr. Leybourne has come round to my way of thinking, since a long interview he had this morning with Colonel Butler, which has induced him to go up to town and see the agents of the Independents in London.'

A passage towards the end of this letter shows that he foresaw what in fact came to pass :—

'I have not merely in view a warlike expedition; I should prefer, and even may accept, a civil situation of equal if not superior advantages.'

In this and numerous other letters to Miss Griffiths the main purpose of his argument was always the same—that she should consent to be married to him, and accompany him on his intended expedition. Writing on June 24, he speaks of his probable embarkation from Portsmouth, and adds:—

'It is more than likely that the ship will not sail immediately, and in such case I have only this alternative.

'I see it is impossible you can come with me, so will you consent to marry me before I go away? For God's sake, write and say if you could contrive to meet me half way; or come down to Portsmouth by the coach of Saturday.'

On July 3 he writes from London; but on the 11th he was again in Gosport, and had settled all the preliminaries of the marriage. He then writes:—

'I waited till this day's post before I procured the sacred authority which is to unite us. Finding there was no letter from you, I concluded you really will come down to-morrow as you so faithfully promised, and so I waited on the clergyman of the parish, and obtained the long-wished-for licence, and Sunday morning at eight o'clock precisely has been appointed for the completion of the ceremony.'

He gives a few other details, which after seventy years may yet be read with some interest:—

'The parish church of Gosport is about a mile in the country from my lodgings, No. 3 Upper South Street. I have secured your place in the mail, the price of which was 1*l.* 14*s.*, and you need not start from New Bond Street till half-past seven o'clock P.M. [on July 12].

'Portsmouth is seventy-two miles from London; and half way, at a village called Molesey, the mail stops for supper. You will leave again at about half-past one; and at half-past six in the morning you will arrive at the Crown Inn, Portsmouth, where I shall be in readiness to receive you.

'At seven precisely we must start from Portsmouth, that we

may arrive at the church quietly; and after the ceremony which will bless me with the hand of my beloved we shall come at once back to Gosport and find our breakfast ready. The only objectionable point in all these arrangements is having been obliged to pay four guineas for the licence, an enormous sum out of our little stock. Till Sunday morning, then, adieu!'

Notwithstanding the evident imprudence of the step she was about to take, Miss Griffiths—though with some reluctance and many misgivings—set off according to the ardent wishes of her *fiancé*, and they were married in Gosport Church on July 13, 1817, without the knowledge of any near relative or friend.

The honeymoon of the newly-married pair was cut very short, for on July 26 they were separated.

He writes to his bride on the 27th :—

' It was long after we parted before I could muster resolutions to return home, and how can I describe the deep sinking of heart on entering that desolate abode! I dared not look at the tearful eyes of my adored, as I wrung her hand when we parted; and on leaving Hilsea I strolled on the ramparts, having resolved to go on board with Ryan at two o'clock.

' When we came to the point of embarkation the wind had increased to a gale ; but notwithstanding, we ventured off, and after half an hour's buffeting with wind and tide we found ourselves drifted opposite the bathing machines on Southsea Common. We were obliged to run the boat among the breakers, and being now completely wet through I was compelled to return.'

In a day or two he writes again :—

' I had yesterday a long conversation with Mr. ——, who, on the strength of his presence at our wedding, wished for more particulars concerning ourselves. I informed him of the truth : how you were an orphan, how the portion your father had left you and your sisters had been placed in the hands of a friend, and how you had completed your education in London. 1 also said that we had no reason for concealing our marriage except the fear of displeasing Dr. Hutton ; that my object in marrying before I left England was to secure to you my pension, and

F

anything my family might leave me, in the event of my death abroad. He appeared fully satisfied, and complimented me highly on my bride and my own good taste.

'Last night I had a delicious but melancholy walk on the ramparts and listened to the distant drums beating the *Taptos* at nine o'clock. The moon was just rising in all the glory of her full. Every golden-tinted cloud, every sigh of the rising wind, every object of Nature reminded me of my Mary.'

In another letter he writes:—

' One thing fills me with ardent expectation—there are few or no French officers going to the Caraccas, and not a single officer of Artillery or Engineers has yet left England ; I shall therefore be almost the first.

' Read well the papers, and endeavour to see the "Times ; " you will there find an accurate account of the progress of the Independent army. Endeavour also to get a sight of the " Star " of yesterday ; it contains a long official account of the successes of the Independents up to a very recent date.'

Lieutenant Vignoles embarked on board the ship "Two Friends" on the night of August 3, 1817. Some of his experiences will be described in his own words ; but a good notion of what the major part of the intending adventurers were like may be formed from a hurried line despatched at the moment of sailing :—

' About a dozen unlucky fellow-passengers of mine have been arrested here ; some of them have got off, the rest remain in limbo.'

Whatever may have been the imprudence of Vignoles's conduct as to his marriage, which certainly for many years to come involved both husband and wife in sore difficulties and privations, it is evident that he needed these strong ties of duty and affection to keep him from a career of aimless adventure. His temperament was so elastic, his spirits so mercurial, the love of excitement and change so deeply ingrained in his nature, that, in all probability, but for the new and sacred claims of wife and children, he must recklessly have thrown away his life in some of those perilous undertakings which presented the only apparent opening for the disbanded half-pay officers of the English army at the close of the great war.

Vignoles writes to his wife on August 18 a letter which he continued in the form of a diary till the arrival of his ship at the Madeiras :—

' 'Tis three weeks since we parted, and already I have had many adventures. Almost drowned the day you left me, I have since suffered the miseries of a persistent contrary gale of wind— a circumstance that has brought forward the real character of all, and in some measure enabled me to choose my acquaintance.

' The whole conduct of this voyage has been one system of deception, and even swindling. We have scarcely a single comfort, and, had I not in some measure provided for myself, I should be ill off indeed.

' We proceed to Madeira to get a fresh supply of provisions and water ; and, as I am one of the committee that has been appointed, I shall have the privilege of going on shore, and seeing my present dispatches safely sent off.

' With the exception of half a dozen, the whole of our party is one compound of selfishness, presumption, and ignorance. Among the few who keep together is a young naval officer, whose name is H., and another young man who is going into the army, of the name of Rattenbury, who has been married some years, and whose wife is about to join him ; and we have proposed that our dear better halves should all come out together.

' Mr. R. has been married about seven years to a Miss Ball, daughter of Admiral Ball. She is cousin to Lady Wilson, who lives in that beautiful park at Charlton, near Woolwich, the village where poor Mrs. Hutton is buried.[1]

' . . . . We are rapidly approaching Madeira, and the old seamen assure us we may now expect fair winds, as we are very near the *trades.*

' I begin to be ashamed of the appearance of my paper, but I cannot attempt to copy it out, although it has been so often

---

[1] Dr. Hutton is also buried in the graveyard of Charlton Church.

opened and reopened;[1] so you must even take the scrawl as it appears.

'Since I began this, land has appeared, and I have now the supreme satisfaction of finding that my reckoning of the ship's course is right within five miles.

'This morning at eight o'clock I told the captain the land was distant eighty miles due west; it is now four o'clock, and in those eight hours we have run sixty-four miles. Consequently, by me it should be distant sixteen miles; and it now appears in sight, distant twenty-one miles.

'This is a great triumph for me over the old sailors, who laughed at the idea of a soldier knowing how to keep a ship's reckoning.

'It will be about midnight before we come to an anchor in Madeira Roads, making exactly three weeks since leaving Spithead—rather a long passage for this time of year.

'Probably we shall stay here a day or two. The rest of the voyage will be delightful when we have well provided ourselves at the island.'

In a brief postscript he adds :—

'This is a most heavenly climate, and we are well feasted on grapes, oranges, pomegranates, and *turtle*; while the finest wines flow abundantly round us. As a vessel sails to-night, I must close my dispatch and bid my Mary adieu.'

The bright visions of the remainder of the voyage, which our hero and his friends no doubt pictured over their grapes and turtle at the Madeiras, were far from being realised. In his next letter, ' Off the Virgin Isles,' he writes on September 20, 1817 :—

'A tedious passage of seven weeks is at length approaching its close, and we shall be relieved from an experience of all the horrors that have been almost as bad as any which ever accompanied the captive negroes off the Gold Coast.

'But I will not complain of the past, as we are sailing smoothly along now with a rapid current and a fair breeze.

'This morning at daylight we found the little island of Bar-

---

[1] It has been no easy task to decipher the original—aged seventy years. The paper is thin, the writing small, and all four pages closely crossed.

badoes on our larboard quarter ; and we have since been gradually making the islands of St. Bartholomew, St. Kitts, Antigua, &c., and expect by sunset to-morrow to be landed at St. Thomas. . . . .

'Of all my confederates, the one I esteem the most is young H. He has all the open-hearted qualities of the British tar, sings a jovial song, and loves his wife almost as well as I do you.'

Vignoles's thoughts of shipboard are now diverted—not very agreeably—by their arrival at St. Thomas, from which place he continues his letter :—

'September 27, 1817.

'We have been here since Monday, but are rather disappointed in our ardent expectations from a variety of discouraging circumstances.

'Do not let my preamble alarm you, for my maxim through life has been that of Mentor in his address to Telemachus, when they had thrown themselves into the sea from Calypso's island : "Avant de s'y jeter dans les périls, on doit les regarder et les craigner ; mais, quand on y est, il faut les mépriser ! "

'My account is collected from individuals of high respectability in the island, partisans of both the Royalist and the Independent causes, and this is the essence of it.

'The army of the patriots is ever successful, but the conduct of their chief and general (Bolivar) has caused great disgust, not only to the English officers already in the service, but to his own generals, who have divided interests, each contending against the other ; and the Danish commandant, who is hostile to the Independents, wishes to get rid of us as soon as possible.

'Nine-tenths of the passengers are panic-stricken, but the rest have seized on perhaps the only means of success, which I will relate.

'We heard that Sir G. McGregor had quitted the Caraccas, and gone to America to raise money and men.

'Learning that the Americans were favourable to the cause, I immediately waited on the American Consul here, and he has given myself and some twenty-five more of our crew the offer of a schooner. He also assures us that, his Government being

anxious to obtain possession of the Floridas, the New Orleans
merchants have subscribed a hundred thousand dollars, and sent
them to Sir G. McGregor at Amelia Island, which lies about 3°
to the south of Charleston ; and he says that adventurers from
all parts of the United States are flocking to his standard.

'Disbelieve all you read in the papers about the dreadful
state of affairs.   The cause is ever successful, but the conduct
of the chief is repulsive.

'Bolivar is in reality the despotic head, but his manners are
tyrannical and disgusting.'

He adds in a postscript :—

'I shall write a duplicate of this by a gentleman who is
going direct to Portsmouth.'

This duplicate is still extant, and is a striking and admirable
example of Vignoles's powers of composition.   It summarises
with terseness and vivacity all the particulars fully detailed in
the preceding letter, and bears the same date (September 30,
1817).   He still gives (from hearsay only) a very unattractive
account of the General-in-Chief—Bolivar—whom he describes
as 'actual and sole despotic ruler of the States, and a man of
turbulent, violent, and irritable disposition.'

There was also a sanguinary general who was bent on the
extermination of the whites, named 'Piar, a Spanish Creole ;'
and he had 'openly avowed his intentions of establishing the
St. Domingo Constitution as now upheld by Christopher in
Hispaniola.'

In very vigorous language he again entreats his wife 'not
to pay any regard to the reports and alarms raised in England
by the pusillanimous scoundrels who are returning home at the
first check, and who will doubtless have a powerful effect upon
the nerves of the croaking frequenters of the London coffee-
houses.'

There is actually a triplicate of this letter ; affording another
proof of the writer's versatility, for it differs from the duplicate
in being even more condensed, though written fluently, and
having some vivid and characteristic remarks of its own.

The struggle of the Independents was only beginning; and it was not till fully seven years later that Bolivia actually acquired a separate government, and renamed herself after her able and patriotic liberator, whose worst qualities alone seem to have been impressed on Lieutenant Vignoles.

His next letter is dated Charleston, October 17, 1817, but not finished until November 24. He begins by a brief *résumé* of his previous communications, and then proceeds :—

'Before we left old England, Mr. Mendez had represented the Government of Venezuela (in whose service we had entered) as being in great measure permanently established.

'To fill the various gradations that existed in the naval and military as well as the civil departments, a rush of adventurers had come from all quarters. Some had formerly held commissions in the British service, but had lost them by court-martial or by selling out.

'Some few were now on half-pay ; about twenty were young men who had served as midshipmen, but had not passed ; the remainder were runaway apprentices, clerks, sons of petty tradesmen, and a set of scamps who had tried every way to keep their heads above water.

'It was as well after all that our ship carried neither wine nor spirits, as no doubt this prevented dangerous disturbances ; but the rugged sons of Neptune, who in the worst times had been accustomed to their allowance of grog, grumbled terribly, and curses both loud and deep were often heard.

'Their spleen found vent in quarrels, and daily scenes of boxing were exhibited even on the quarter-deck ; and it required a full exercise of philosophy to avoid being drawn into the universal wrangle! Language was used I had no conception of, and thieving was carried on to a large extent, and I lost all my towels and pocket-handkerchiefs!

'No order of any kind was observed at meals ; and such a general scramble took place when anything at all good appeared at the table, that I was daily thankful that you were not present.'

After a few more details of that miserable voyage, Vignoles

informs his wife of his present occupation, but does not mention the passage in the schooner which the Consul of St. Thomas had provided for them; nor does he say a word about the filibustering army of Sir G. McGregor.

He continues :—

'Let me tell you that I have found here a situation which will afford me independence, and I trust you are prepared to come out to meet me in February.

'The fever here is gone, and the place is quite healthy.'

He must have had strong reasons for avoiding all these various warlike undertakings—viz. the United States expeditionary forces on the one hand, and the Independent movement of the Spanish settlements on the other.

We hear nothing of the armaments that must at this time have been collected in the magnificent harbour of Cumberland Sound, a sort of rendezvous formed by Amelia and the other adjacent islands on the Florida coast, where sometimes three hundred sail were in those days collected. The noble beach of the island, now guarded by a single sergeant, the sole tenant of the old crumbling brickwork of Fort Church, must at that time have been a busy parade-ground for Sir G. McGregor's troops; but though the struggle then beginning lasted for at least four years, and Vignoles's head-quarters were all that time, and up to the year 1823, chiefly at Charleston, we hear scarcely anything more of public events.

The simple truth is that the young Benedick, having nothing but his half-pay, which indeed he well-nigh lost,[1] and being compelled to work for a subsistence, began to turn to some good account his own eminent abilities, and thus unwittingly to prepare himself for the prominent part he was destined to take in the great engineering epoch soon to be inaugurated in his own country.

[1] This will be explained in one of the letters from his wife given in the next chapter.

CHAPTER VII.

Life at Charleston, U.S.A.—Birth of his daughter and eldest son—Correspondence with his wife—Letters from Professor Leybourne—Vignoles's claims on property in Florida—Description of Southern States—Changes in the military and scientific world—Visit of his wife and self to England —Vignoles returns to Charleston—Moves to Florida—Various surveys— Dangers incurred—Difficulties in his civil employments—He visits New York.

1817–22.

IT was some time in the month of November that Vignoles's wife received his letter from Madeira. The state of her health rendered it impossible to attempt the voyage to America; and she confesses that the lamentable death of the Princess Charlotte [1] had produced a profound impression on her mind. It is not necessary, however, to quote from her long and anxious letter more than the postscript, which must have been a very bitter morsel to her husband :—

'In my last I warned you that after Christmas the half-pay would be taken off[2] in case of the non-appearance of officers in his Majesty's service who had neglected to report themselves ; but I am shocked to read in to-day's papers a proclamation to recall all British subjects who had any intention of serving on either side in your part of the world, under the utmost penalties the law can inflict.'

Vignoles, in entire unconsciousness of this impending danger, writes in a very cheerful strain to his wife on Christmas Day :—

'The state of South Carolina has just elected a civil

---

[1] This occurred November 17, 1817.

[2] Vignoles's half-pay was suspended for a time, but was resumed on his making proper representations to the military authorities in London.

engineer, whose duties are to survey the country, project canals, roads, and such like. I arrived from Amelia Island, and was at once recommended for the post of assistant. My salary in cash is to be 1,000 dollars per annum, with permission to make as much more as I can by private practice. All this has resulted from my being the grandson of Dr. Hutton, and through the friendship of a gentleman in this city. The name of my chief is Major Wilson.'

It was well that he took such precautions to secure the transmission of his numerous letters by alternative routes, for his wife writes early in January 1818 to say that it was only the triplicate of those he sent from the West Indies which had reached her; and, moreover, that she had despatched several letters to him, one addressed to Jamaica, and two to the Post Office, Charleston. Incidentally we gather that his letter had been forty-six days on its way; and, from what he says subsequently, we find that this communication from his wife had been nineteen weeks in reaching Charleston.

His wife also informs him of what he might have anticipated :—

' Our marriage has been made known to Mr. Leybourne in a very singular way. Miss Hutton and the doctor have also heard of it through him. I know not how your family received it; but the result was to put Mr. L. in a great rage, though of all this I must reserve particulars for the next packet.'

In answering this letter he shows great anxiety to hear of his wife's embarkation, and he gives her many directions, and warns her that prices are five or sixfold above those of London; instancing the cost of a Leghorn bonnet in Charleston as *fourteen guineas*, and that he had just paid ten pounds for a blue frock coat!

It is not without a pathos of its own that, after a lapse of nearly seventy years, there are seen along the margin of this letter to his young wife entries of the various items noted down by the expectant mother, referring to articles required for the use of the little girl stranger who, three months later, was to be born into the world.

As these lines are penned the memory of that sister is vividly present with the writer, who was one of those—they were many, both relatives and friends—that laid her in the grave in November 1883.

One or two more letters from Vignoles's wife written at the beginning of 1818 have been preserved. They are full of the tenderest affection, but also of seasonable admonitions; the chief burden of which is prudence in money matters and self-restraint amid the temptations of genial society. She felt keenly her isolation, and it is clear that nothing but her then state of health kept her from an effort to join her husband in Charleston.

The kind feeling displayed by the Leybournes is seen in the following letter, which the Professor sent to Vignoles, dated April 6, 1818 :—

'I am writing to forgive the concealment of your marriage previous to quitting England, and I hope I shall have reason to rejoice in doing so. Let me intreat you to take care now that you have so good an opportunity of doing well. In addition to all my former advice, is this, that you will always, and under all circumstances, behave well and kindly to your wife, who is far too good for you! However, now that you are a husband, and as before you get this you will probably be a father, I look with confidence to your future good conduct. Mrs. L. joins me in wishing you all happiness.'

Vignoles writes to his wife in May :—

'I was distracted as I perused your melancholy letter, and my reflection on your position made me pass a sleepless night.

'I see that one of my letters was lost in the brig "Thames," which was wrecked on the Goodwin Sands, and all on board perished. Another vessel put back in distress to New York. Heavens! when I reflect a moment, what a series of misfortunes! But we must hope that all will end well. Thank God, I am now independent of everyone, and each spring of talent shall be put in motion to attain my end, for in this land of freedom industry alone is wanting to make our fortunes. . . .

'This country is now in its most beautiful state : all the pro-

ductions of England in July and August we have had this
month past, but they have only made me regret that you were
not here to enjoy them.'

A fortnight later he writes again :—

'Charleston: May 31, 1818.

' You see by the date that I am addressing you on my birthday. Yes, this day I am twenty-five, and the anniversary has
filled me with serious thoughts. Five years have I now been a
wanderer on the wide world. During that time the horizon of
my life has been overclouded; and had not you, at an early
period of my misfortunes, become my tutelar angel, I scarcely
know how the events of my existence would have turned. I
now look back with astonishment, as a traveller at the dawn of
the rising day views the gloomy and fearful path along which he
has pursued his course through the dark and tempestuous night ;
he wonders how he could possibly have escaped, and so, my love,
do I ! Now I am comparatively at rest, and have but to pursue
my way with steady determination. During the daytime I am
fully occupied in compiling and drawing out such of the surveys
of the state of South Carolina as have been already completed.
Some of these were done by myself; and the portion of the map
I have engaged to finish is about fifty square feet, and I hope by
the time you arrive I shall have nearly completed it. The
ladies here have good taste in dress, and the Englishwomen
who come out in the country fashions of home are only laughed
at. I cannot persuade the Carolinians that the real London
belles dress as simply and more elegantly than themselves.

' By the way, Mrs. H. has just arrived here with a guinea
in her pocket—her passage not paid—and her husband absent!
With the utmost delicacy and caution I informed her of his
proceedings. She seemed hurt, but not much surprised ; and
she then had the modesty to expect I should pay her passage
from England! This I declined, but I lent her some money, and
paid her passage to Boston, in all about eighty dollars, besides
what I had already lent her husband; but she did not seem in
any way sensible of her obligation. I was altogether disap-

pointed with her manner, which was rusticity without interest, and *mauvaise honte* without modesty.'

An extreme liberality to friends in pecuniary matters distinguished Vignoles through life, and, as may well be believed, he often severely crippled himself and others by an unwise generosity. What he had already begun to do at twenty-five years of age he continued to do half a century later; with this difference, that the unit of measure for such disbursements grew from tens to hundreds, and, in by no means solitary instances, to thousands of pounds.

In a paragraph of this letter he says:—'I anticipate not only reputation, but wealth—yes, wealth;' and he had largely obtained both before he was fifty years old. But his power of retaining the second of these desiderata was by no means proportionate to that by which he acquired the first.

Just in the height of the summer, with the thermometer at 100° in the shade for days together, Vignoles was offered free quarters in Fort Moultrie, on Sullivan's Island, off Charleston Harbour. Whilst there he received the welcome tidings of the embarkation, on August 9, of his wife and infant daughter on the "Robert Edwards," the vessel being bound to Charleston. The friend who gave him the information had previously written him a sad account of his wife's illness at the time his little daughter was born; and that when convalescent, she with her child had been invited to Sandhurst, and had been received and treated with most affectionate care by the Leybournes. There is a curious confusion in the names given to the baby by the writers on either side of the Atlantic. She is sometimes called *Camilla*, after his mother, and sometimes *Isabella*, after his aunt. The former name clave to her all through her life, and survives in the name of her only daughter;[1] and this was her ordinary appellation in her own family in after years. But the fact is, that when she was christened at St. Margaret's Church, Westminster, her mother being too ill to leave the house, the

---

[1] Miss Camilla Croudace, Lady Resident of the Queen's College, Harley Street, London.

only relative who was present at the ceremony (her mother's sister) was at the time unaware of the parents' wishes in this matter. It thus happened that after the names of her god-mothers (who were only friends of the family) the child was baptized by the name of ' Anna Hester.'

Leaving, then, in our narrative mother and babe to find their way across the ocean, we may make brief reference to a claim Vignoles believed himself able to establish to some lands in Florida, of which his family had unquestionably become pro-prietors during the few years of ownership of that peninsula by ' Great Britain—viz. 1763–83 ; but extant letters show that Vig-noles, though thoroughly convinced of his proprietary interests, did not succeed in vindicating them to the satisfaction of the authorities at Washington. There was just then no small risk of war between the United States and Spain, as, although the Floridas had been ceded by the latter to the American Govern-ment in 1810, the negotiations were not formally completed till 1820–1 ; and, at the time we are now writing of, the United States Government were becoming impatient. Captain Ratten-bury, one of Vignoles's fellow-voyagers, had also a claim on some property which his father had purchased in Florida some years before, and this gentleman had gone to Washington to look after his interests, and he writes to Vignoles :—

' I have been introduced to the President [1] and Mr. Quincy Adams, and have no doubt but that my grants will be confirmed. I have met in every direction the kindest attention, yet am I so ungrateful as to dislike the country and the Government. It is not like our own dear little island. I remained in Philadelphia three days. It is a handsome city. Thence to Bristol, where my Spanish friend gave me a letter of introduction to the Duke of San Carlos, the Spanish Minister in London, and I have been sniffing the air of diplomacy ever since!

' Here (New York) I have dined with the British and Spanish Consuls, and altogether have not realized the proverbial cold character of the inhabitants of this city. As I find I must remain in the neighbourhood two or three weeks longer, I

---

[1] James Monroe, who was re-elected in 1821.

intend visiting the springs of Saratoga and Ballaton. To-morrow I am to witness a " camp meeting" in Connecticut. I think of going on to Boston and thence to Halifax when I am done with affairs here, and hope to return home by the " Iphigenia " frigate.'

In a letter dated September 1818—about the time of Mrs. Vignoles's arrival—Professor Leybourne writes many interesting details of home news, but he also gives one more item of intelligence which his correspondent must have read with mingled feelings :—

' Perhaps your wife may have told you that General Gordon had got you placed on full-pay in a West India Regiment soon after your departure from England ; but of course I was obliged to ask him to cancel it.'

Looking back on what has been narrated in the previous chapter, we can see how the exercise of a little patience would have secured to Lieutenant Vignoles the career of continued active military service which he had been at the time so anxious for, and which his influential friends—H.R.H. the Duke of Kent above all—had done their utmost to regain for him on the conclusion of the war. It is useless now to speculate what his career as a soldier might have been, for, on the one hand, he had excellent abilities and was full of energy and daring ; whilst, on the other, he had no strong leaning towards a military life, promising though his prospects in that line undoubtedly were.

He had certainly been unfortunate in not being able to make more of the very good chance opened to him in the military profession, but, as it was, there was nothing then left him but to ' rough-hew ' his arduous way to competence and success the best way he could as a civil engineer. The struggle with him was long and severe ; but when his opportunity at last came he was well prepared to make the most of it.

It was not till twelve years later that Vignoles formed the habit of keeping a regular journal, and thus it happens that there is hardly any trace left on record of his early married life in Charleston. In one or two of the letters from which we have quoted he had begged his wife to engage the services of an old soldier named Jameson, who had been in his own regiment, or, failing that, to pick up a little negro boy. The cost of a regular servant (he says) out there averaged about 25l., besides board, lodging, and clothing. All we can glean of their domestic arrangements is that his wife brought out an English servant-maid as nurse from Sandhurst, and beyond that the story of their home life in Charleston is a complete blank.

In a letter to a friend, about the end of 1818, he gives some insight into the mode of travelling in the Southern States, and the general good feeling shown to 'Britishers' by the better class of the inhabitants :—

'Wilmington is a dismal sand-hill, and the place was only endurable by the kindness of our friend B. and his handsome wife. Thence we proceeded to Newtown, through the pine woods of North Carolina, a distance of a hundred miles, which took us two days. It is a very pretty little town on the river Neuse. At three o'clock in the morning we embarked in the steamboat for Elizabeth City, passing through the Pamlico and Albemarle Sounds up the river. . . . The city is in its infancy, but anticipates growth from the expected commerce with the States. Thence our course lay for twenty-two miles through the 'Dismal Swamp;' but the gloom expected was only in the name, as a canal is cut through the centre, and the trees on either side relieve the monotony by the beautiful magnolia and the yellow jessamine.

'The country round Norfolk is pretty, and we had a very agreeable visit there owing to our letters of introduction and the acquaintance of some charming ladies who were our companions from Newburn. I left Norfolk with reluctance, and we were to have gone to Richmond; but an injury sustained by the steamboat obliged us to direct our course to Baltimore, the sail up Chesapeake Bay being very pretty. Baltimore is a handsome city, and twelve days fled very agreeably there. The Carolinians may boast of their hospitality, but here the people possess it! I have more invitations than I can accept. I leave on Monday for Mount Vernon, and Alexandria.'

His old friend, the Professor at Sandhurst, wrote to Vignoles again in September 1819, to announce the sudden death of Mrs. Leybourne, who had been so kind a friend to the young couple under every vicissitude of their fortunes. He tells him that his grandfather's health is better than ever, but mentions no other member of that family. At Sandhurst, Sir Algernon Hope had been succeeded by Sir George Murray as Governor of the College. In the world of science he refers to the death of Professor Playfair at Edinburgh, and the appointment of Professor Leslie as his successor in the Chair of Natural Philosophy.

One matter of domestic interest, however, should be mentioned here—viz. that a son (Charles Ferdinand) had been born to Vignoles at Charleston in August of this year (1819).

In the spring of the year 1820 Vignoles undertook a surveying expedition on the banks of the Savannah River and in the neighbouring islands. Part of his professional labour was for the State authorities of Carolina; but it is plain that he was permitted to take work on his own account also, and he has preserved an item of special ' charge of $177 against the United States.'

Altogether his earnings—though for how long a period there is nothing to show—on this expedition amounted to upwards of $3,000; but, judging from the many and bitter complaints in his letters to his wife at different times, it is very doubtful whether he often got paid for his services.

Early in April 1820 he wrote to his wife from 'Coosawatchie,' and then from Hilton Head Island, where he had been on a short visit to a General Pinckney; and towards the end of the month he sends a fuller description of his tour from the Savannah River, on which (as he says) 'I have been travelling up stream, surveying as I go; but on Saturday I hope to be on Edisto Island,' to complete my public surveys there and in the rest of the parishes of this neighbourhood.'

His next halt was at Beaufort, (as he says) 'tempted by a large bribe to make the survey of an extensive tract or island

---

[1] This island is about two miles in length, formed by the two branches of the river of same name.

here, a very essential one in my survey. I hope also to pick up a small job or two on Edisto to help me on.'

His straitened circumstances are pretty evident from his remark—

'Had the Governor (of the state) only advanced me $500 in December, I should have been able to finish all my work without assistance from anyone. In fact, had not the composition of the people in this part of the world been made of very hospitable materials, I should have been badly off.'

Then, referring to his previous letter, he adds :—

'Decide quickly between a voyage to Europe and a tour through Tennessee! I think we ought first of all to go to England, that I might settle about my half-pay, and at the same time give Sir Willoughby Gordon, the Quartermaster-General, and Sir Henry Torrens, who is now Adjutant-General, the plans of this coast as finished.'

The story of Vignoles's first sojourn in the States ends here abruptly, and for six months there is no record of any kind of himself or his family.

From his next letter, dated London, October 3, 1820, we find that he, with his wife and children, had been in England for some little time, and that he was already meditating a return voyage to Charleston.

We get a glimpse of a visit to his old friends at Sandhurst in the same letter :—

'I got to the Leybournes at half-past twelve o'clock. All the Lawrys were there to dinner. Stewed leg of lamb and sweet sauce, veal pie and a fat goose, with apple pie and rice pudding. Plenty of wine and brandy! You see " Tommy " can launch out now and then, and all this in honour of me!'

Referring to the prospect of another separation from his wife, he says :—

'Perhaps I may leave London on Saturday night by the seven o'clock coach, and be at Andover by four o'clock on Sunday morning. But I am not sure whether we ought to renew the miseries of parting.'

We may conclude that the meeting took place, for his next

letter, also from London, is five weeks later, and in it he speaks
of a somewhat discouraging reception from many of his former
friends, with the exception of Mr. Hansom, who had behaved
very kindly to him, and that he had met the Earl and Countess
of Portsmouth [1] at that friend's house. He adds :—

'Mr. Hansom will act as my agent in this country, and will
receive the half-pay for me, and he will advance you any money
you may want. I hope to see my aunt to-morrow to say farewell, as we sail from Gravesend the next day.' [2]

We have a characteristic letter dated 'Ship "Elizabeth,"
November 14, 1820,' in which he says :—

'We are now under way with a fresh breeze and squalls of
rain and snow, giving freezing symptoms of an English winter.
We are fortunate in getting clear of Margate Roads, especially
when you learn that on Thursday night last a fine West Indiaman
of 400 tons was lost on the Margate Sands, and not only did every
soul on board perish, but not even a plank of the ship has since
been seen, so totally was she lost. He also tells her that he' had
just learned from his aunt,[3] the wife of Captain Wills, that his
grandfather had advanced him 80*l.* (through Mr. Leybourne) for
his outfit on his first leaving England after his marriage in 1817.
This shows that after all the old man was not quite so obdurate
as he had seemed, though it must be borne in mind that he and
all the family were at the time ignorant of his grandson's marriage.

He writes to his wife : 'Ship "Elizabeth," at sea ; lat. 37 N.,
long. 22 W., Tuesday, November 28, 1820,' and the letter is in
the form of a diary which is spread over seven weeks, the voyage
being prolonged at first 'by rough weather and latterly by a
heavy gale, almost a hurricane ; and then by our being disappointed in not finding the trades till last night.'

That was on December 10, but soon after this last entry he
began to perceive that the thirty days he had calculated on

---

[1] The latter was Mr. Hansom's daughter.
[2] This was his fifth voyage across the Atlantic.
[3] She was the second daughter of Dr. Hutton, his aunt Isabella being the
eldest and his mother the youngest.

would not see their voyage terminated. His entry on December 15 is :—

'Since Sunday, however, it has blown a fine prosperous gale, and we have averaged two hundred miles a day.'

This letter was posted at Charleston on January 3, 1821, and it concludes with a hurried postscript, telling of his having already seen many friends, including his chief (Major Wilson), and a M. Petitvale, who is often referred to in his subsequent letters, and who was his *collaborateur* in the South Carolina surveys.

He adds that a Mr. Graves required his services at once to survey a plantation ; and that Major Wilson and Mr. Poinsett had spoken to him about considerable undertakings, as many plantations were changing hands.

In the beginning of February 1821 he writes again in very good spirits :—

'I have plenty of work, and have already been busily engaged on a fine plan of the racecourse here for the Jockey Club, and am hard pressed to get it done, as the races begin to-morrow. Major Wilson has been turned out of office, but M. Petitvale and I are doing well, and keeping bachelors' hall together. I have concluded a bargain with the city of Charleston for a complete set of plans for $500, having now finished the map of the state of South Carolina.

'I am straining every nerve to make your present situation as comfortable as possible.'

In his inquiries after them all he asks concerning the possible arrival of 'baby,' who was then in fact a few weeks old, and had been christened 'Thomas,' although as yet his father knew nothing of these facts ; but he speaks much of the two elder ones, and adds :—

'I shall never be able to endure my children away from me when they are old enough to receive instruction. Should circumstances not enable me to return to England, you must all come back to Carolina. At present fortune seems to favour me, and I could not have done better than return to this country.'

He resumes the subject in a letter only two days later :—

' I am pleased to inform you that my success is great beyond all my best hopes. I am continually called upon, and have already made some very large surveys, and I expect in a year or two to have the whole important business of the country. Thus my professional reputation will be quite fixed. Petitvale and I spent six weeks on one plantation with Admiral Graves and the old lady, and he took a great fancy to us both. He goes to London in a few days, and I shall ask him to call on my grandfather, and let him know how I am going on.'[1]

In his letter of July 3, after going carefully over all items of his receipts and expenditure for six months, he puts the former at $2,000, ' out of which Petitvale has of course had his share of the profits ; ' and he calculated his expenses at $750. He informs her that ' the Floridas are about to be given up to the United States, and I have serious thoughts of going there. It is very healthy, and there is plenty to do, so perhaps we may meet in a grove of citron and orange trees.'

He continues : ' I am now making a superb plan of St. Augustine ; and, à propos of plans, I must tell you that Petitvale and myself are much improved in our drawing. I made a magnificent title to the Graves' plan, and the map was the admiration of all who saw it.'

On August 21 he writes from St. Augustine :—

' Almost immediately on my arrival I was nominated Surveyor and Civil Engineer for this city ; but the incessant heavy rains which have fallen in the southern parts of America have rendered the country very unhealthy.'

But at the end of this letter he gives a fuller insight into some of his professional disadvantages :—

' At present everything promises success ; but these Americans are so jealous of any acknowledged Briton succeeding among them, that I never feel sure. Were I to throw up my commission and become one of their fellow-citizens, I should soon be patronised, but that I will never do.'

We give here verbatim the copy of the certificate Vignoles

---

[1] *Vide* the beginning of Chap. VIII.

seems to have procured from Charleston, but, as will be seen, it is dated from Florida :—

'St. Augustine, East Florida : August 28, 1821.

'These are to certify—

'That Mr. Charles Vignoles was, during the latter end of the year 1817, and the whole of 1818, employed under the sanction and orders of his Excellency Andrew Pickens, Governor of the State of South Carolina, as an assistant engineer, surveyor, and draftsman to the State Engineer, for which he received a fixed salary.

'That during the year 1819 he was engaged by his Excellency John Geddes, Governor of that State, as a surveyor on behalf thereof, to make surveys and maps of the sea-coast of Carolina, at a stated salary of $2,000 per annum. That during the year 1820 he was engaged under a special contract, to the amount of $3,700, to make surveys and maps of the south-western section of the State of South Carolina, from the mouth of Combahee River, including the harbours of Port Republican, Dawfuskie, and Tybee,[1] the left bank of Savannah River, and sixty miles into the interior of the country.

'That the said Charles Vignoles has also acted as a private surveyor, and his plots and returns have been recognised by the courts of law and equity in the said State of South Carolina.

'Certified by the subscribers, resident during the aforesaid period in Charleston.

'(Signed by) COLONEL CHAMBERS.
JOHN GEDDES, Esqre.
CHARLES ROBINS, and the
FRENCH CONSUL (*sic*).'

Early in October 1821 Vignoles again writes in a very sanguine tone as to his position and prospects of work. The people of St. Augustine were kind, and the climate was delicious and agreed with his health, although the heat was very great even then. He had sent her papers which spoke of his appointment as ' city surveyor and engineer,' and he adds :—

---

[1] An island (with a lofty lighthouse) at the mouth of the Savannah River.

'I am here at the head of my profession, but the public caprice is uncertain. I am likely, however, to make money as land agent as well as surveyor.'

In a letter dated January 1, 1822, Vignoles encloses to his wife a copy of a communication he had received from Captain Bell, of the United States Artillery, ' Acting Indian Agent for the American Government.' It is worth while giving this at length, for it brings out clearly one of the most marked features in Vignoles's character—viz. his too disinterested zeal for his profession.

Letter from Captain Bell to C. B. Vignoles.

'St. Augustine: December 19, 1821.

' Sir,—In acknowledging the receipt of your letter of yesterday, accompanied by a map of East Florida from the Georgia line to the twenty-seventh and a half degree of latitude, together with a report on the geography and soil of the country, which at this time is very interesting and important information for the Government authorities at Washington, permit me, Sir, for myself and in behalf of the head of the War Department, before whom these papers will be placed, to tender you thanks for the signal services you have rendered me in the discharge of the various duties I have been called upon to perform in the affairs of this province. Also to express to you the sense I feel of the great value of your talents and accomplished acquirements, as thus rendered to the Government of your adopted country, with the sincere hope on my part that a more solid remuneration may be offered you for these services by the liberality of the Secretary of War, who, I believe, is not slow to reward the meritorious who devote their services to the State.

' Believe me, &c., &c.,

' R. BELL,

'Capt. 4th Regt. U.S. Artillery, and
Acting Indian Agent.'

This was neither the first nor the last of many instances in which the generosity of the engineer went considerably ahead of the prudence of the man.

Writing from St. Augustine early in February 1822, Vignoles says :—

'The dreadful malady [1] which devastated this city had the
effect of stopping all business, and I have scarcely done more
than pay my way. I set out to-morrow to Capes Sable and
Florida, thence to the Tortugas,[2] and up to Tampa Bay,[3] and
back to this place overland. I shall be accompanied by General
Scott, of the U.S. Army, and his staff, the surveying portion
being under my control. All this is part of my original
plan of making a new map of Florida, to be published with a
memoir in June next.'

A still more buoyant letter follows, dated March 31, 1822 :—

'I have extended my acquaintance to the principal towns in
the United States, and my reports upon this country are published, and are considered a standard authority. But for the
uncertainty of postage, I would send you a Boston newspaper,
in which I am spoken of in the highest terms. I have been
continually travelling since Christmas, and in a few days shall
again set out on a two months' journey. On my return I shall
complete my map, which is to be published immediately afterwards. In the meantime, however, I have a hard struggle.'

This last sentence finds its counterpart in a very pathetic
letter from his wife, dated March 22, 1822. She was then living
at Carisbrooke, in the Isle of Wight, where her stay had been a
series of misfortunes, scarlet fever in the village having found
its way into her little home, and all the children had suffered.
As may be supposed, she had hardly obtained any rest for herself; and, worst of all, her youngest child Thomas, after many
weeks of suffering, had expired on March 15.

This depressing communication reached Charleston on May
21, and seems to have been in her husband's hands early in June.
Meanwhile the roughing which was inevitable in his surveying
expedition had proved too severe even for his iron constitution.
He writes from St. Augustine on July 2 :—

---

[1] This was no doubt the yellow fever.
[2] A group of islands in the Gulf of Mexico.
[3] The largest bay in the gulf, on west side of Florida.

' The exertions and the hardships I have had to undergo, travelling through the wild woods and uninhabited regions, laid me up on my return here with a severe bilious fever, from the effects of which I am scarcely yet recovered.'

He then goes on to express his feelings of sorrow and sympathy with the sad tidings his wife had written to him :—

' I will try to speak of the painful topic which has marked the first inroads of death into our little family. But oh! how can feeble language, weakened by distance, console the distracted mother for the loss of her babe! Let me trust that the soft hand of time will by this have soothed the first keen anguish of your aching heart.

' Thank also, on your bended knee, the Great Creator that a deeper affliction has been spared you. Since I last wrote I have narrowly escaped destruction. In swimming my horse across a rapid river, the restive animal plunged me into the current, encumbered as I was with a heavy shot-pouch and other articles. With great difficulty I gained a mud bank in the middle of the river, and there, with the waves beating against me and scarcely able to maintain my footing, I had to endure for an hour a pitiless hailstorm which arose at the moment, accompanied by furious gusts of wind, so that the attendant Indians could not stem the swollen stream to relieve me. Twice I sank under the water, and only with a desperate effort rose up again to the surface. The following night I had to pass without fire, covering, or provisions, my party having in the confusion lost everything but our saddles. The fever was only the natural consequence of this exposure.'

Referring to her inquiries about the Hutton family, he says :—

' I have given up all idea of correspondence with my own family. The flinty obstinacy of my octogenarian grandfather, and the cold apathy of my maiden aunt, freeze every germ of affection in that quarter, and turn all my thoughts and feelings to my own small domestic circle.

' After long debating the subject, I have finally resolved to abandon England ; but I do so with regret, for only those who,

like myself, have drunk from the cup of refinement, and enjoyed the charms of cultivated society, can judge how I deplore
the necessity which drives me from her smiling land.'

It is sad to record that the hopes which Vignoles now so
eagerly and justifiably cherished of advancement in the land of
his adoption were again and again disappointed. Or rather,
as the readers of this memoir cannot fail to have perceived,
the recompense which the unwearied labours and undoubted
abilities of the young engineer had honestly earned was continually withheld; while he at the same time had made fresh
difficulties for himself by carrying out expensive surveys undertaken on his own account, chiefly with a view to the publication of his elaborate map of Florida, of which we shall speak
more in the next chapter. This enterprise certainly brought
him considerable local fame, but neither state nor private aid
was forthcoming in the time of his most pressing necessity ;
nor were his debtors at all forward to discharge obligations
actually incurred. His professional pride (and it was the same
all through his life) never allowed him to ' ban or contend ' for
his dues ; whilst his sanguine temperament caused him too
readily to forget the troubles of the past, and to under-estimate
the difficulties of the future.

The person best able to judge of the ill-effects of this course
of action was his wife, whose disposition, if not very hopeful,
was at any rate intensely practical. She writes early in
November 1822 :—

' I see plainly the difficulties by which you are surrounded,
from which you can only be extricated by the greatest economy,
caution, and prudence. In everything which may occur to
enlarge your occupations, endeavour to have some security
beforehand.'

This letter reached New York just before Christmas 1822,
at which city her husband had already arrived, and where this
narrative must now follow him.

CHAPTER VIII.

Unsettled state of things in Florida—Vignoles at New York—Publishes his
Map, &c. of Florida—Returns to England—Practises as a civil engineer.

1822-25.

VIGNOLES was evidently hard pressed at the time he quitted the
Southern States and took himself to New York, with a view to
publish his map of Florida and a brief account of that province,
in which he had for several months carried out many arduous
and ill-requited labours. His American employers were ready
enough to praise and commend him and his work, but they were
not willing to advance money towards the carrying out even of
national enterprises undertaken by a 'Britisher,' and they
evinced an unjust reluctance even to pay for work performed by
him at their own request. One typical example will suffice.
Admiral Graves, the officer referred to in the previous chapter,
was at this time on a visit to England, and had volunteered to
call on Dr. Hutton, but was unable to carry out his purpose; so
he wrote to the Doctor, mentioning his grandson in highly lauda-
tory terms, speaking of 'his diligence, his great abilities, and
his behaviour as a well-informed gentleman.'

Yet this officer had not sent the expected remuneration for
the very considerable amount of work done for him by the
gentleman whom he thus commends, nor is there any record of
the payment afterwards.

To exhibit the generally unsettled state of affairs in this part
of the world we give brief extracts from some letters which have
been preserved, the first being that of a gentleman who writes
from Pensacola, September 22, 1822 :—

'I was sorry not to find you here. You might have got the

appointment of secretary to our board very easily. The place
is now, however, permanently filled.   The head engineer is
dead and his papers locked up, so I cannot get you any certain
information for your book, but I can tell you a few things.
(Then follow some details of topography). The Council to make
laws have played the d——.   They have taxed the people
$15,000 to create offices for themselves.   All go home with an
office.   We have more judges, and attorney courts, and clerks,
than you can imagine.   You may consider me good for half a
dozen of your valuable work.'

Another letter is from a Dr. Mitchell, of New York, who says
amongst other things :—

'Thank you much for the good service you have rendered to
science by your collection of plants from Florida.'

We find a solitary instance of actual payment in a laconic
note from a Mr. Eakin, of the Treasury Department, Washington,
informing Vignoles that a requisition for $55 had that day been
issued in his favour!   It seems to have been an item of claim
on the estate of some person deceased.   Another extract throws
light upon the unsatisfactory social condition of affairs.   The
writer was Mr. Thomas Murphy, of Charleston :—

'I have just arrived here from the "Land of Promise" (i.e.
Florida), which unhappily overflows more with gall than with
milk and honey!   Pecuniary distress and disorganization are
increasing, and there seems no immediate prospect of improvement.   I find the impression has been very unfavourable as
regards settlement in Florida; and the crude laws of our
Legislative Council require the sanction of Congress, which
many of them will not obtain.   I hope you are likely to receive
encouragement in your publication.'[1]

The last attempt Vignoles seems to have made to procure
work in this 'Land of Promise' is recorded in the shape of an
elaborate and clearly drawn 'Schedule of Rates of Charge for
Surveys on Hackley's Lands, in October 1822.'   The document,

---

[1] Two or three very interesting and ably written articles on South Carolina, Georgia, and especially on the recent rise in the value of lands in Florida,
appeared in the *Times* in April 1884.

which is now before the writer, is in Vignoles's own hand, and is as clear as if engraved on copper-plate. The whole project, however, in all probability came to nothing; nor need we wonder at the general unsettled and unsatisfactory state of the newly-acquired territory when, so recently as December 22, 1884, we read in a letter of the 'Times' correspondent :—

'The magnificent forests of the Southern States and the excellent grass lands of Florida are still biding their time. A great deal of solid work is now being done in the South, but there is still far too much talking.'

Early in September 1822 Vignoles had arrived in New York with his map of Florida, and accompanying manuscript observations all completed. He took up his abode in Bleecker Street (No. 52), and at once put himself in communication with a map engraver of eminence, named Tanner, in Philadelphia, by whom the work was ably carried out. A framed copy of this map of Florida is now hanging up in the writer's study. The drawing is perfect, and the entire work is an admirable specimen of hydrography.

We give a brief account and analysis of this the first of Vignoles's published engineering labours.[1] It is a good-sized octavo volume of 219 pages, including an appendix, bearing the description on its title-page : ' "Observations on the Floridas," by Charles Vignoles, Civil and Topographical Engineer, 1823. New York: Published by E. Blois and E. White, 128 Broadway. The title duly registered on 1st day of March, in the 47th year of the Independence of U.S.A.'

The author begins by a brief introduction, in which he betrays his half-formed determination to remain in the United States by the expression ' the approach to our interior,' and referring to his own frequent journeys he remarks : ' On the map, almost the whole sea-coast from St. Mary's River to Cape Florida is from my own actual survey.'

He further observes on the paucity of inhabitants, especially on the west coast, and the extreme difficulty of getting exact

---

[1] The only extant copy known to the writer is in the Library (*Catal.* i. i. 5) of the Institution of Civil Engineers, London.

local information of the names of places, &c.   Indeed, many of
the settlers were as ignorant on such points as passing visitors
mostly are in any land, or as the British rustic is almost invariably found to be in his own.   Further on he says :—

'I was anxious to obtain the names of the original *grantees*
of estates in Florida, but have been unable to get permission to
search the archives after the departure of the Hon. Edmund Law
to Pensacola.'

He then proceeds to give a brief sketch of the history of
Florida, claiming for St. Augustine (founded in 1565)[1] the title
of the oldest town on the North American continent, except the
Mexican settlements.   He states that the Floridas came into the
possession of the English in 1763, but that after twenty-one
years of our improving and civilising rule they were ceded again
to Spain, and the towns (so the old inhabitants said) then soon
began to resume their former aspect of squalor and decay.
After the lapse of more than half a century, Florida was ceded
to the United States in February 1819.

This epitome of provincial history is followed by a series of
methodical observations on the soil and its culture, and also on
the climate ; the details being carefully followed out, with many
suggestions of practical utility appended.

Vignoles's book then gives observations on the native Indian
inhabitants, and notices the various titles to the land, which he
terms 'a subject of great complexity and fruitful of litigious
dispute.'

But there is not a word to show that the author had any
serious intention of reviving the long abandoned and now hope-
lessly extinct claim of his own ancestors, to which reference has
already been made.

Things were no better with the author when he had launched
his publication, though he feels assured that he is laying the
foundation of future emolument, and that the production of his
book and map had increased his professional reputation.

---

[1] This is disputed by some authorities, who give the priority to a small
town of less than 3,000 inhabitants, called Yleeta, situated on the Rio Grande,
in Texas.   The date of its foundation is ascribed to the year 1545.

At this time, however, a change was impending of which he as yet knew nothing, for on January 27, 1823, Dr. Hutton had died, full of years and honour. Mrs. Vignoles writes immediately on receipt of her husband's long letter of New Year's Day, and tells him the eventful news; but at the time this letter arrived Vignoles was absent in Washington, where he had gone to present his new publication to the authorities, who had received him very courteously. His wife states that she had left her husband's relations in Hants, and had found her way to the 'village of Littlehampton,' which she had heard of by advertisement; but, strange to say, in answering her communication he shows that he had not even then resolved to return to Europe. He says :—

'Without knowing the particulars of Dr. Hutton's will, I feel sure that he has not left me a shilling. But I shall write a letter of condolence to my aunt, and beg her once and for all to send you money sufficient to bring you and the children to join me, and when you leave England you must say "farewell" to it for ever. I find I must abandon one side of the water or the other, and old England presents not the resources of the United States for *me*. I must become altogether an American, but with a heavy heart. It is for your sake and that of my children I make this last sacrifice of all my youthful hopes and ambitions.'

What brought about so entire a change in his plans we do not know, but by the end of May 1823 Vignoles had arrived in England, and gone direct to Littlehampton; and a few days later he had called upon his aunt Isabella, then living in the metropolis, in Bedford Row. Miss Hutton, although she received her nephew with all kindness, at first gave him no encouragement to remain in England; and the advice of other kinsfolk was to the same effect, all trying to induce him to return to America without delay. This, however, he had now determined not to do, regardless of the decision he had come to three months before; and indeed, situated as he was, almost penniless, and with his wife and two children entirely dependent on him, it was only natural that he should appeal to the compassion of his aunt for temporary help, till he could secure some professional employment.   He was obliged to make a clean breast of it, and produced several of his wife's letters ; and no doubt the sad privations she had endured and the melancholy position in which she was now placed served to strengthen the husband's appeal, to which his aunt's affectionate disposition had already favourably disposed her.   It may be as well to let him tell the story of the first interview with his aunt in London.

The letter is dated June 3, 1823 :—

'On my arrival in town it was five o'clock, and by the time I had got rid of the dust of my journey and made myself decent, it was late in the evening.   When I came into the drawing-room my aunt looked as black as thunder, which, however, I would not mind.   She did not ask me many questions, but lectured me for half an hour on my having borrowed 5l. of Mr. M. and an umbrella from Mr. G.   But very soon I was "dear Charles," and it ended by her ordering my old room to be got ready for me, and she spoke most kindly to me when I retired for the night.   All to-day she has been even kinder ; and I cannot tell you the numberless marks of affection she has bestowed on me, although in some things she still looks upon me as a boy.'

Miss Hutton evidently had already become reconciled to her nephew's remaining in England if any kind of employment could be found ; and meanwhile he was helping to arrange his grandfather's papers, &c.   His aunt seems to have been sole legatee, but her income was much curtailed by the sinking of a sum of 25,000l., which the old Doctor had not very wisely invested in the Iron Bridge at Southwark, erected by his intimate friend the elder Rennie.   As the month progressed some of Vignoles's friends came forward with suggestions of help, George and John Rennie amongst them, and a very warm testimonial in his favour was also written by Dr. Olinthus Gregory [1] to Mr. Walker, the engineer.   In this document Dr. Gregory says :

[1] This gentleman had succeeded Dr. Hutton as Professor of Mathematics in the Royal Military Academy, Woolwich.

'I do not suffer my judgment to be influenced by my unalterable feelings of attachment and veneration for my late excellent friend in writing this. I have known his grandson, Mr. Vignoles, from his infancy, and have no hesitation in saying that his information is varied and extensive, and capable of wide application to practical purposes. As a military man he has often been successfully engaged in the engineering and topographical department, and is also conversant with computations of various kinds.'

Mrs. Vignoles was anxiously waiting for the opportunity to rejoin her husband in London, as soon as he could obtain some engagement, and be able to set up 'a snug little home' for themselves. In the village where she had taken up her abode, the London letters were so late in the delivery that there was hardly time to write a reply before the evening post was closed. Littlehampton, which has scarcely yet attained the repute it deserves, must have been in a very primitive condition in those days, when (as the letter from which we quote complains) not even a pair of shoes could be bought there! Meanwhile her husband seems to have gained a strong foothold once more in his aunt's home and heart, and was preparing her to receive his wife and children with affection. He gives a good sketch of Miss Hutton's character :—

'My aunt is fond of appearances, but when the eye of the world is not upon her she is economical almost to parsimony. Her principle is never to spend a farthing needlessly, in order that for better purposes she may have a store. She is kind-hearted and charitable, more so than I ever thought, but she is a decided enemy to waste under any circumstances. She detests noise of all kinds, and has a great dislike to litter or disorder. She is very fond of *small* society, and delights in anecdotes and conversation. She is also extravagantly fond of music, and since my return has begun to play again. She takes great pleasure also in going to the theatre, but, as the expense alarms her, she seldom gratifies herself.

'Like many economical persons, she is fond of bargains, and has many things by her, formerly purchased cheaply, which have

never been used. Lastly, her affections are confined to very
few.'

Meanwhile, her nephew had secured what he calls 'a
fatiguing job in Essex,' for which, including a large plan, he
was to get sixty guineas. He adds, that exertions were being
made in all quarters to establish him, but that must take some
time.

The letters now cease, and we lose sight of all family matters
for some months; but from other sources we learn that, after a
short stay with Miss Hutton, Mr. and Mrs. Vignoles took a house
in Kentish Town, where another son, named 'Hutton,' was born
to them in November 1824.

As Vignoles at this time had also engaged offices at
108 Hatton Garden, we may conclude that he was rapidly
getting into active employment; but he also found leisure for
literary work, which had always been to him an object of some
ambition. The following is from an autograph letter by the
Rev. E. Smedley, the first editor of the 'Encyclopædia Metropolitana:'—

'Wandsworth: October 7, 1823.

'The canals of America (more rather contemplated than
executed I should think) are only slightly touched upon by an
able engineer, who has contributed the article (in a very condensed form) on "Canals." He is quite willing to cancel the
little he has said on that part if you will favour us with any more
information in a compass proportional to the remainder of the
article. I feel assured your materials are all before you, and on
receipt of your contribution I shall more easily be able to take
into consideration the remaining subjects which you propose.'

Vignoles fell in with this proposal, and the correspondence
was fruitful in results; for several articles were eventually
contributed by him to the 'Encyclopædia,' the principal of which
are—'North American Geography,' 'Cuba' (in conjunction with
Dr. Bonnycastle), both printed in vol. xvii. In vol. xviii.
are found articles on 'Dock,' 'Dominica,' 'Dredging,' and
'Embankment,' all exclusively from his pen. In vol. xix. he

contributed (with Dr. Bonnycastle) the article on ' Florida,' and on his own account the articles on 'Georgia' and 'Guadaloupe,' and probably some others.[1] It is gratifying to add the encomium the editor was able to bestow on his new ally for what he had done :—

' Mr. M., I know, feels as much indebted to you as I do (and he cannot feel more) for the very obliging assistance you afforded us in the last part of our publication.'

In the course of the year 1824 Vignoles was engaged in various engineering works in or near London, but very few details are recorded. One reminiscence, which may serve as a specimen, is a ' receipt for payment from Captain Samuel Browne and James Walker, Esq., Civil Engineers, for forty-three days' employment upon the surveys and plans for the iron bridge of suspension (sic) at St. Katharine's (Dock), at the reduced rate of half a guinea a day and expenses.'

This is a glimpse, at any rate, into the day of ' small things' in the engineering world.

It was in the year 1825 that Vignoles began the custom of keeping a diary, a habit he persevered in till nearly the end of his life. On New Year's Day he enters : ' Forwarding the article " Cuba " for the " Encyclopædia Metropolitana." Mr. Terry engaged in a drawing of the iron cranes for that article.'

No more worthy name than that of Terry, found in the above extract, could be mentioned in the class to which he belonged. He was a faithful and able assistant to his chief for half a century.

Early in the year Vignoles received a friendly intimation from Mr. Walker, that he would be invited by the Collier Dock Committee to prepare some estimates. The entry in his diary on February 9 is that he and the clerks worked at this job from 9 A.M. to 9 P.M. ; and three days later he notes : ' Rose at three o'clock, and continued my calculation till 10 A.M.'

The same day information reached him that Mr. Rennie

[1] In February 1825 his diary shows that for several consecutive days he attended at the British Museum to obtain information about the ' Mexican Canal.' In his diary he also mentions having completed and despatched articles on ' Cumberland,' ' Curaçoa,' ' St. Croix,' ' Creole,' ' Crane.'

would be entrusted with the carrying of the Bill through Parliament, although that gentleman's plans were not to be adopted. His journal also notes: 'Sir Edward Banks has offered to employ me on a hundred miles of railroad.' But *where* is not stated.

He received from his professional work in the Collier Dock the sum of 127*l.* 10*s.*, which he paid into Gosling's bank.[1] This was the largest amount of money he had then received at one time as a civil engineer. About the same time he had received overtures from the 'Mexican Company' to go out to that country for them. A copy of his reply is preserved, in which he assures them of his competence to 'undertake the investigation and execution of all works relating to the improvement of the roads, canals, &c., in Mexico; but my pursuits have not qualified me as a mineral engineer, nor could I advise in doubtful cases, where the object was the discovery of the precious metals.'

A great part of the spring was occupied in an engagement under Mr. Walker in levelling on the banks of the river Witham, where it flows into the Wash, also in prosecuting various surveys of Lynn Harbour and the vast drainage system of the neighbourhood, especially on the 'Eau Brink' Cut, which the elder Rennie had constructed some years earlier; Vignoles at this time carrying out his system of levels as far as Cambridge. He was also engaged in laying out the improvements made soon afterwards in Cheltenham.

It was under the orders of the younger Rennie that, in the end of May 1825, Vignoles first entered upon a practical acquaintance with the system of railway communication newly commenced in England.

But before entering on the second part of the narrative in which the subject of this biography is seen amongst the very few eminent engineers of that day, the writer must bring to a conclusion that portion of Vignoles's earlier history, in which the faithful partner of his fortunes had borne her share bravely and

---

[1] He continued to be a customer to the old and respected firm of Goslings and Sharpe to the end of his life.

patiently, amid many trials and privations induced by the severe difficulties through which her husband had to pass in order to hew out for himself a new opening in life at the close of his military career. It is evident, from many letters found amongst family papers, that his wife's health had been seriously impaired by the changes and anxieties she had experienced in her twelve years of married life, and that after the birth of her youngest son (named after his godfather, Dr. Olinthus Gregory), she was a confirmed invalid.

But earlier than this, both before and during the time of their residence in the Isle of Man, Mrs. Vignoles was in a weak and infirm condition, which was of course aggravated by the increasing cares of her family, three children having been added to the household (one, a daughter, born in London, and two sons in the Isle of Man) subsequent to the birth of her fourth child, Hutton, referred to in this chapter.

At the beginning of 1826 Vignoles had established his family in Craven Street, Strand, the cost of a London house in those days presenting a marvellous contrast to the enormous rents now demanded in that neighbourhood. It was here that many of the engineers—such as Walker, John Rennie and his sons, and the elder Brunel—were visitors; Dr. O. Gregory being also one who frequently joined the family group, more especially when Vignoles's aunt, Miss Hutton, was one of the party. This relative (as we have shown) was deeply attached to her nephew and his children, taking especial notice of her godson—the little 'Hutton'—of whose childish self-possession, coupled with a quiet but keen observation of all that was going on around him, many amusing instances are recorded in extant letters. Vignoles's wife remained in London during her husband's engagement on the Liverpool and Manchester Railway, narrated in the next chapter, and he himself (as will be seen) was for several months detained in town during the renewed struggle to obtain Parliamentary powers for the projected Liverpool and Manchester line in the autumn of 1825 and the early part of 1826. It is only from an occasional entry in his journal, in which he rarely mentions family matters, that we get any con-

tributory touches towards filling in the picture of the domestic
group of these early days; but many letters of Miss Hutton are
in existence, some also written by Dr. Gregory, and these help
to show the incessant energy and activity of the husband, whilst
they point plainly to the increasing disability of his wife to
perform the work of domestic and social supervision inseparable
from the duties of a mother.

It was partly with a view to the re-establishment of her
health that early in 1828 Vignoles gave up his London residence, on his appointment to the Government survey of the Isle
of Man, and took a house at Douglas.

The change seemed at first beneficial to the invalid, but
after the birth of her son Henry, in November 1827, her health
perceptibly declined, and it was naturally not improved by
nursery cares, the baby being at first a delicate child. But a
more serious demand on her time and strength was soon made
by an accident to her eldest son, when he was about nine years
old. He fell from his pony on his head in Douglas Bay, and
was carried home insensible, and though the mishap did not
seem at the time to produce any serious consequence, it had a
detrimental influence afterwards, the boy being of a very excitable temperament. · In the case of most children this might not
have taken a severe form, but on returning to the school at
Douglas where the lad had been placed, his illness was quickly
renewed. We find from his mother's letters that he had been
a good deal knocked about by the boys, the older ones occasionally amusing themselves by throwing books at his head,
with other rough usage not uncommon in schools! This might
not have mattered with some lads, but in young Charles's case it
aggravated his nervous disorder, which in later years assumed a
chronic form, and has entailed a whole life-time of suffering.
This sad result is the more to be deplored as the boy grew up
to early manhood showing indications of great talent, and had,
moreover, received both in England and Hanover a thorough
education; so that the engineering profession has thus been
deprived of one who gave bright promise of future eminence.

Vignoles himself was often compelled by the necessities of

business to be away from home.   He had obtained constant
work, but had no important engagement beyond the Manx
survey, which he had quickly organised, as related in Chapter X.
He made frequent voyages from Liverpool to the island and
back, as he was anxious to be with his family as much as possible, and more than once between the years 1828–30 he
brought his wife over to the mainland, and eventually established her in a house at Liverpool, always, however, keeping an
office in London, which city, after his wife's death, became his
chief place of residence.   Just before leaving the Isle of Man,
Mrs. Vignoles (her husband being then away) lost her daughter
Isabella, aged six years, after a very brief illness.   The shock
was severe, and, as might be expected, the result was a serious
aggravation of Mrs. Vignoles's sufferings.   Her eldest daughter
Camilla (who lived until the year 1883) was at the time a girl
of eleven, and was her mother's constant companion, remaining
at Liverpool until her removal to a school in Paris in 1832, but
returning home twice a year for the usual holidays.   Soon
afterwards her mother's health was even more seriously affected,
in spite of constant change of air and the skilful attention of
eminent medical men, and she gradually became weaker until
her death, which took place on the day of the opening of the
Dublin and Kingstown Railway in 1834.

The writer thinks that the entry from Vignoles's diary at
the time we refer to may serve as the most fitting close for this
melancholy chapter in Vignoles's history, the sad issue of which
left an enduring mark on his career, for he then lost the faithful
and wise companion of his early manhood, and the devoted
mother of his children, who by her death were deprived of their
home—that sacred source and centre of human nature's best
and purest affections.

The writer has no personal recollection of those sad days,
yet he can vividly recall the opening scene at the Dublin terminus of the new line, and of his being hurried along between
his father and his nurse to catch the first train of passengers
that ever ran upon an Irish railway.

Mrs. Vignoles's surviving daughter was for many years

almost the only person who preserved a definite remembrance of her mother, and it was to her the brothers were indebted for a distinct portraiture of their deceased parent, whom as their best friend, though in course of years they less deplored, yet they never forgot.

> 'Dec. 17, 1884.—This day, at three minutes before one o'clock in the afternoon, my dear wife Mary died. Her long illness of twenty months terminated in dropsy, in her forty-seventh year. We had been married seventeen years and four months, and she has left me four sons and one daughter. One son and one daughter died in their childhood.'

His daughter Camilla, now in her fifteenth year, had left her school in Paris in the previous August and returned to Irelai d, and with her little brother Olinthus was left in the care of kind friends in Dublin, whilst her father and his three eldest sons were performing the funeral obsequies for her mother.

Mrs. Vignoles's grave is in the St. James's Cemetery at Liverpool, about a hundred yards from the mausoleum which encloses the tomb of Huskisson.

We give a short extract from a note of Dr. Olinthus Gregory, written to his friend on this occasion; the date is December 30, 1834 :—

'. . . I was in truth gratified by your writing to me on such an occasion, because it proves to me that you rightly and kindly appreciate the sentiment of esteem and regard which I cherish for you, and which makes me feel a lively interest in all that concerns your welfare, your reputation, and your happiness.

'I have been rejoiced to learn from various sources how auspiciously your great Irish work has commenced operations.'

Vignoles rarely spoke of his wife; but he bitterly felt her loss, which rendered still more arduous the steep up-hill climb to fortune and celebrity that still lay before him. He remained a widower for fifteen years.

PART II.

INTRODUCTION OF RAILWAYS INTO ENGLAND.

VIGNOLES ON THE LIVERPOOL AND MANCHESTER AND ON
SEVERAL OTHER ENGLISH RAILWAYS; CONSTRUCTS
FIRST IRISH RAILWAY; EARLY SURVEYS
IN WALES, ETC.

————

1825–1845.

CHAPTER IX.

Introduction of Railways into England—Vignoles on tl e Liverpool
and Manchester Railway.

1825–27.

In the surveys which Vignoles had carried out in Surrey and
Sussex in the summer of 1825 for the Rennies may be traced
the first germ of railway enterprise in the southern counties of
England.[1] In the autumn of this same year was opened the
Stockton and Darlington line, memorable in itself as the first
English railway—in the ordinary acceptation of the word—carrying both passengers and merchandise, and worked by the
'locomotive' engine; but even more remarkable as having led
immediately to an undertaking of far greater importance and of
national interest—the Liverpool and Manchester Railway, to
which enterprise may rightly be ascribed the parentage of all
other lines of railway throughout the world.

At this time the chief means of carriage for heavy goods
were the canals, wherewith a considerable portion of England,
but more especially its northern districts, were now intersected;
the engineering of these waterways having been in great measure
carried out by Brindley and the brothers Rennie. At least 3,000
miles of canals had been finished, at a cost of some fifty millions
of money, and these had proved (notably in the case of the Bridgwater family) a very rich source of revenue to the proprietors.

This method of locomotion had largely developed the in-
dustries and the resources of the country, so much so indeed
that the merchandise awaiting transport had far outgrown the
means of transit, and at the great ports of the North, especially

[1] The author in his earliest MS had traced this interesting survey in some
detail; but he has not here inserted it, in order better to preserve the unity of
the narrative.

Liverpool, an enormous mass of foreign produce was kept in a chronic state of delay, owing to the congested condition of the traffic on the canals. Similarly there had been continuous and steady increase in passenger traffic, by all sorts of conveyances, to and from various parts of the kingdom; and it is certain that at least from twelve to fourteen hundred coaches were despatched from the metropolis every day in all directions.[1] It was reserved for railway locomotion to supersede, to an enormous extent, both these great systems of traffic, and most opportunely was the invention applied to relieve them of demands which all their efforts were unable any longer to supply.

The general history of railroads has been so often touched on in different ways and by so many authors, that it is quite beyond our province to enter upon such a wide field in these pages. But it fell to the lot of the subject of this memoir to take a leading part from the first in the development of railway enterprise, and he had no inconsiderable share in the early stages of the formation of the line from Liverpool to Manchester. His connection with this undertaking is noticed somewhat briefly in the account of it found in the attractive pages of Dr. Smiles's work; but in all probability that eminent writer was not aware of the active part taken by Vignoles in the earliest stages of this important railway, and it must also be said that Vignoles in his declining years never took the trouble to do himself justice in this respect. But the records—both public and private—of his share in the work have fortunately been preserved, and it is of these that we desire to speak briefly in the following pages.

It seems highly probable that the earliest survey of the proposed line which was to connect Liverpool with Manchester was made by Vignoles at the request of Mr. Joseph Sandars,[2] a partner in a banking firm at Liverpool. He has been called the ' Father of the Liverpool and Manchester Railway,' although it is well known that his attention was first drawn to the subject by William James, a surveyor practising in London. There are

[1] *Railway Times* for 1888, p. 281.
[2] The authority for this statement is Bethell's *History of the Rise and Progress of the Liverpool and Manchester Railway, &c.*, published in Liverpool on the day of the opening of the line. It is in the Free Library, Liverpool.

no data by which the time or character of this first survey can be accurately determined; but a gap of several weeks in Vignoles's letters, and also in his diary, enables us to fix an approximate date in the early part of 1824. Mr. Henry Booth omits all reference to this in his more elaborate work published in 1830; but Vignoles's engagement as first resident engineer on the line, both under the Messrs. Rennie and for a time under George Stephenson, quite falls in with the statement given by Bethell.

The first prospectus was drawn up and issued by Mr. Sandars on October 29, 1824, and George Stephenson was at the same time invited to make a complete survey and estimate of the line, and to prepare a scheme for Parliament. It was a prodigious

PLAN OF STEPHENSON'S FIRST ROUTE FOR LIVERPOOL
AND MANCHESTER RAILWAY.

piece of work to have undertaken at such a short notice; indeed, it is highly probable that Stephenson must have been engaged upon it early in the autumn, for the date of his first complete plan and section is November 24, 1824.[1]

The accompanying map is from a later copy of the above, and it is interesting to notice that the proposed line was to enter Liverpool from the north, and the sharp turn at Vauxhall hardly gives the impression that the engineer had then seen his way clearly to introduce traction by any kind of locomotive engines.

---

[1] The writer has seen this document, which is preserved in the engineer's offices at Euston. It bears the autographs of George Stephenson and his surveyor, Thomas O. Blackett. The original is on a scale of four inches to the mile. Vauxhall is close to the intended terminus.

There were many serious errors in the plan, which were mercilessly exposed in the memorable conflict in the House of Commons in the spring of 1825, and these were fatal to the Bill. A minute examination of the plan seems also to show, or at least to suggest, that Stephenson, in his well-known horror of steep gradients,[1] at first had an intention to traverse Chat Moss on an embankment. If this supposition be correct, and had such an idea been persevered in, it is not unlikely that the confident assertion of Mr. Giles would have been verified, that it was impossible to carry a railway across Chat Moss.[2] As Dr. Smiles has related, it was the limited portion of embankment that was found absolutely necessary on this work that swallowed up so much both of money and material in that troublesome morass, and almost drove the directors to despair.

It is needless to dwell on the particulars of Vignoles's work as principal resident engineer on the Liverpool and Manchester Railway from the summer of 1825 to February 1827. The few extracts from his diary which follow, and his own letter to Mr. Riddle, from which a full quotation is given, will sufficiently elucidate (for our present purpose) his share in the modification of Stephenson's first scheme, as well as his brief connection with that eminent man.

But it may be mentioned that Vignoles was examined at considerable length in the Committee of the House of Lords in April 1826, when application was made to Parliament for a new Act, the company having been reconstituted, with the Earl of Lonsdale as chairman; and the engineer's evidence distinctly implies that the actual surveys, sections, and general profile of

---

[1] On one occasion George Stephenson expressed himself thus: 'It would be more economical to carry a load over six additional miles than to raise the same 174 feet in one mile.'

[2] The writer is disposed to think that it was rather the method by which Stephenson hoped to be able to cross the bog than the impossibility of the thing itself which brought down such denunciations of the proposed attempt in the first Parliamentary contest. Strong testimony, from their own large experience in Ireland, was given by the well-known engineers, Josiah Jessop and Alfred Nimmo, as to the extreme feasibility of the line over Chat Moss. One query and its answer may be quoted here:—Q. 'And you say that a railroad can be carried over that bog (Chat Moss)?' A. (by Mr. Nimmo): 'Yes, or over any other bog.'

the new line were his own.[1]   If the evidence of George Rennie
be carefully compared with that of his surveyor, the conclusion
is irresistible that Vignoles's employers gave him a *carte-blanche*
when they despatched him to Liverpool to lay out the line; to
the absolute accuracy of which work he was called upon to testify
in Committee; nor was his evidence in any way shaken or dis-
credited.   In the same Committee he was asked point blank if
he had ever undertaken work on his own account anywhere up
to that time, to which he answered in the negative.   This was
erring on the side of modesty, for he might very fairly have
adduced the work he had done in Florida, and have shown the
map and pamphlet we have described, illustrative of his labours
in that region.

A noticeable point in the evidence [2] is the studied way in
which the 'locomotive' question was kept in the background.
Fully half the battle in the Committee on that occasion was as
to the limit of load that horses could draw on a railroad.   Dr.
Smiles gives only a passing reference to this.   There can be no
doubt that it would have risked the success of the Bill if the promoters had laid any stress on the possibility of steam becoming the
traction agent; but it is tolerably evident that the Rennies, in
such good company as the Messrs. Telford, Walker, Rastrick, and
many others, had no confidence in the absolute success of the
locomotive.   But, so far as Vignoles was concerned, it must be
stated that there is not a line of his, in letters or diary, to show
any distrust in the power of that remarkable invention; whilst
his eager and liberal support, afforded to Messrs. Braithwaite and
Ericsson in their persevering efforts to construct an efficient
machine, prove that he was one of the very earliest believers in
the future of the invention itself.   The most characteristic distinction of the proposed new line from that of Stephenson was
the method of entering Liverpool by a tunnel at Edge Hill.
This cannot be separated from the general scheme which Vignoles

---

[1] The two engraved plans for the Bill of 1826 in the London and North-
Western Company's offices at Euston are countersigned by 'Charles Vignoles'
as the surveyor for the Messrs. Rennie.

[2] The writer has searched in vain in the libraries of the Institution of
Civil Engineers, of that in Liverpool, and even of the British Museum, for a
copy of the evidence given in the Committee of the House of Commons on

had evidently formed, and which the Rennies approved and
sanctioned. That he had matured this part of the plan is evident,
and quite falls in with his cross-examination in the Lords' Committee as to the stratification of the ground to be bored through,
of which he had made many trials.   It is somewhat amusing,
then, to notice in the explanatory letter which is given in this
chapter that Stephenson had endeavoured to fix a trifling error

OPENING OUT OF THE EDGE HILL TUNNEL.

in the matter of this very tunnel survey upon Vignoles as a
heinous mistake, which charge, to say the least, was not very
generous treatment of a young man who had been specially
selected by the eminent engineers whom Stephenson had superseded.   But the absurdity of the thing becomes more marked
when we know that it was in the details of this tunnel that
Stephenson had allowed some most serious errors to remain un-

the Liverpool and Manchester Bill for 1823. Probably that part of the evidence has never been printed.

detected, which, had they not been courageously pointed out to the directors by Locke, some years later, would have resulted in an engineering *fiasco*! Locke's biographer relates that this engineer showed conclusively that several portions of the tunnel from Edge Hill to Lime Street would not have formed, when joined, a continuous line ; and that in one place particularly two portions of the intended tunnel would have passed each other, and have never met at all![1]

Many minor defects were also laid bare during the recent opening out of the tunnel (see engraving, p. 112), the works of which were ably carried out under the London and North-Western Company's resident engineer, Mr. H. A. Dibbin, who has kindly supplied to the writer several details. It seems but just, therefore, to show that even the great Stephenson was not infallible; and, moreover, Vignoles's vindication of himself, and this attempt at his justification more than sixty years later, are not out of place, seeing that it was this unwished-for disagreement with his chief that so materially reduced his chances of immediate success in his profession. Stephenson could never brook the least opposition from his subordinates, as is proved by many incidents which have been related to the writer; but the best proof is that afforded by his subsequent serious disagreement with and opposition to Locke, which resulted in the latter superseding Stephenson as engineer-in-chief of the Grand Junction Railway in August 1835.

According to J. Rennie's instructions, Vignoles travelled down from London to Liverpool in the first week of July 1825, taking at the same time a large part of his household goods and chattels, which were to be transported by the canal.

The coach fare (inside) for himself amounted to four guineas, and he was twenty-four hours on the way; although, as we shall see farther on, this rate of progress was gradually accelerated as railways began to assume the appearance of a practical success. It should be particularly borne in mind by all who are interested

---

[1] See Devey's *Life of Joseph Locke*, pages 94 and 103. Mr. Locke had himself laid out for Stephenson and completed the smaller tunnel which connects Edge Hill Depôt with the railway wharf and warehouses at Wapping.

in Vignoles's career that his appointment as resident surveyor
and engineer to the newly projected line was at the hands of
the directors, on the recommendation of the Messrs. Rennie,[1]
who had just been called in by the reconstructed board.
Vignoles's appointment is duly entered as having been officially
confirmed on August 12, 1825.   He notes in his journal
that he had an interview with Mr. Charles Lawrence, the chairman, and received from him the necessary instructions, which
he proceeded at once to carry out.   His diary shows that the
first week was spent in examining the plans of the ' old line,'
as well as the ground over which it was to pass, and in suggest-
ing various imprcvements.   He seems rapidly to have matured
the project for the ' new line,' and in a few days more was prepared to state his views fully, which he sustained in detail (as
related in his journal) at a meeting with the directors on
July 18.   Mr. John Rennie was present, and the next day he
accompanied Vignoles over the ground, ' comparing the old line
with the proposed new one, which in many respects was considered more favourable,' as his diary states.[2]

For several days after Rennie's departure Vignoles was
occupied in the detailed surveys and section of the improved
project.   He spared neither himself nor his assistants, and all

---

[1] The Rennies paid Vignoles three guineas a day, which the directors increased to four guineas. Cf. the Blue Book ' Parliamentary Report of Evidence
before the House of Commons Committee, Dublin and Kingstown Railway
Deviation Bill,' May 1838.

[2] It was on one of these numerous excursions that George Rennie, in company with Vignoles, first met Mr. Bradshaw, the Duke of Bridgwater's well-
known agent, with whom Vignoles afterwards became very intimate. The
place of meeting was a wayside inn called ' The Little White House,' where
Brindley had met Bradshaw and the Duke many years previously, when no
money was forthcoming for the canal, and the first-named predicted the ultimate success of that enterprise. Mr. Bradshaw discussed the proposed railway
with the two engineers, and offered terms from the Duke to become sole proprietor of the concern. The alternative was to be uncompromising opposition,
and the agent had not the least doubt as to the Duke coming off conqueror in
the contest between him and the railway company, should war be declared
between them. Sir John Rennie, in his *Autobiography*, says : ' Owing to the
fall I had from London Bridge I was completely disabled, and the chief
management of the Bill in Parliament was left to my brother George and
Mr. Vignoles.' Cf. the work quoted, p. 236.

were kept hard at work together without a day s intermission.

On July 24 he writes:—' Levelled over Chat Moss and across the river Irwell to Lostock, 6¼ miles.'

In later times Vignoles occasionally referred to the work of those days, and always asserted that he was the first to construct a pathway across that vast and troublesome morass, whose contents have been estimated at sixty million cubic yards.

It was an anxious time for all concerned, but especially for himself, on the success of whose labours the future passing of the Bill must in great measure turn.

It is evident that the pressure on all engaged to complete the plans before November 30, 1825, was very great, but the work was done,[1] as the result proved; for in the following session the Bill passed both Houses of Parliament, the memorable division in the House of Commons on the night of April 26, 1826, showing a majority of 47, the numbers being 88 to 41.

The full details of the strenuous efforts made at this time, first in the field and the drawing office, and then in Parliament, have only been partially preserved to us by the subject of this biography. His diary stops abruptly on September 5, 1825, and the only subsequent entry for that year is on December 4, when he simply states: ' Left Liverpool for London.' But the date of this visit to the metropolis, and his sojourn there till the early summer of 1826, coincide with the transfer of the scene of operations from Liverpool to London, where Vignoles's continued activity in connection with this business did not leave him (so it seems) any leisure for entries in his journal, the keeping of which he did not resume till the beginning of 1830. Vignoles, on his return to Liverpool in the summer of 1826, was the only engineer on the spot in the employment of

---

[1] It should here be stated that the railway, as actually made, was on the lines of this survey conducted by Vignoles, except in the subsequent modification of the inclined plane at Huyton. This was originally laid out with a view to the train being hauled by a stationary engine. The Company afterwards obtained supplemental Acts for increase of capital to carry out improvements on the line, and for an extension of the Salford terminus across the Irwell into Manchester.

the new Liverpool and Manchester Railway Company, his former chiefs—the Messrs. Rennie—having resigned their connection with it.   The new Board of Directors (as every one knows) had insisted on George Stephenson's nomination as Chief Constructive Engineer, and thus it came about that Vignoles was unwillingly left as first resident engineer under 'old Geordie' when that gentleman returned to his former post.   The letter we are about to quote from will show that, although Stephenson's clear brain and practical genius enabled him to force his way in competition with many of the leading civil engineers of that day, they on their part did not conceal their want of sympathy with the rude untutored art of the old 'colliery brakesman!'   But it is equally evident from our present knowledge of the attainments of most of them, and of their general antecedents, that if Stephenson had not occupied the advantageous position he had then reached, there would have been no effort to force steam locomotion to the front, and thus possibly the real practical success of railways might have been indefinitely postponed.

Letter from C. B. Vignoles to Mr. Edward Riddle.[1]

'January 14, 1827.

'The following outline of my connection with Mr. Stephenson must have the first place.   After the royal assent had been given to the Railway Bill I was employed independently of any-one else to commence operations by marking out the line on the ground and preparing the drains on Chat Moss.   In June Mr. Rennie, who had been previously engineer to the company, having absolutely refused either to consult with or to participate in the slightest degree with Mr. Stephenson, vacated his appointment, in consequence of the directors making this co-operation a *sine quâ non*.   Mr. Stephenson was re-elected principal engineer in the early part of July 1826, and when he came to Liverpool he found me sole acting engineer.

'Soon after this I delivered your letter, which, from Mr. S.'s

---

[1] This gentleman was Mathematical Professor at Greenwich Hospital Naval School.   He was an intimate friend of Dr. O. Gregory.

subsequent expressions, I found gave him mortal offence, inasmuch as your friendly recommendations were construed by him as admitting me to be his *partner* instead of his *assistant*.

'Mr. Josias Jessop, civil engineer (since dead), was soon after called in as the consulting engineer, and he differed absolutely in many points with Mr. Stephenson. This was another cause of offence. I also acknowledge having on many occasions differed with him (and that in common with almost all other engineers), because it appeared to me he did not look on the concern with a liberal and expanded view, but with a microscopic eye ; magnifying details, and pursuing a petty system of parsimony, very proper in a private colliery, or in a small undertaking, but wholly inapplicable to this national work.

'I also plead guilty to having neglected to court Mr. S.'s favour by crying down all other engineers, especially those in London, for, though I highly respect his great natural talents, I could not shut my eyes to certain deficiencies.

'All these circumstances combined gave rise to a feeling of ill-will on his part towards me, which he displayed on every occasion ; particularly where I showed a want of practical knowledge of unimportant minutiæ, rendered familiar to him by experience.

'I now proceed to answer his accusations. It is true there was an error in the survey of the tunnel made by me, but it was one which might have been rectified without trouble or expense ; and it was one which would not have originated if I had been here alone.'

Here follows a long detailed statement of the whole matter, which cannot now possess any public interest.

He goes on further to explain the circumstances from his own point of view, stating that long after this misunderstanding had occurred Stephenson had commended him for taking a house, and for arranging that his furniture should be sent from London, by which he was put to the expense of 100*l*. He then continues :—

'The liberality of the directors will, however, indemnify me for this loss, and I trust I may quote this as a set-off against Mr.

S.'s charges; for, had I given any solid or serious cause of complaint, or any reason for dismissal, I should not be repaid an expense like this, nor should I receive (as I have done) expressions of regret from the directors individually that the queer temper of Mr. Stephenson will not allow of my remaining in Liverpool.'

He concludes his long letter (certainly honestly and ably written) by informing his correspondent of what had just passed between Mr. Marc I. Brunel and himself. Brunel, though naturally anxious to appoint his own son to the post of assistant engineer to the Thames Tunnel, had reason to fear that this step would not meet with the approval of the directors; and on hearing that Vignoles was about to leave the Liverpool and Manchester Railway had written at once to offer him the appointment. Subsequently the required permission was given, and Mr. I. K. Brunel (afterwards the engineer of the Great Western Railway) became his father's assistant. Mr. Brunel senior wrote at once to Vignoles explaining the whole matter, and added these words :—

'The directors have resolved to appoint my son : you must, therefore, consider the object of my last communication at an end. Be assured at the same time that you were the only person I thought I could have applied to on the occasion, from the reliance I had on your qualifications for so arduous an undertaking.'

In a letter to him from Miss Hutton, dated January 21, 1827, that lady says :—

'Dr. Gregory was here on Friday ; he told me he had seen your letter to Mr. Riddle, and thought that you had been very shamefully treated.'

On February 2 Vignoles wrote to Mr. Lawrence, chairman of the Liverpool and Manchester Railway, resigning his appointment as 'resident engineer, though with much regret.'

This letter was accompanied by a private communication, summing up briefly the points of disagreement between the engineer-in-chief and himself, in which matter it is evident that the chairman had in a very kind manner intervened.

Vignoles remained a short time in Liverpool forming various

projects of undoubted utility, though not at the time commending themselves to those most concerned in their adoption. One of these was a tunnel under the Mersey, which he boldly sketched out in a letter to the Liverpool ' Albion ' in March, 1827.

He states the fact of ' a few opulent inhabitants being already associated for a project which would formerly have been thought chimerical—viz. a tunnel under the river Mersey from the Cheshire shore to Liverpool.'

In discussing the subject he very properly adduces the case of the railway tunnel on the Liverpool and Manchester line, which was then in course of construction on the east side of Liverpool:—

' When it was first broached by the late engineers of the railway, it was received with distrust even by the directors; and when the intention became public, with alternate feelings of ridicule and fear by the inhabitants at large. The water-works talked of their supplies being cut off, and learned counsel employed against the Bill seemed to suppose that all the wells in Liverpool would be tapped, and that the water would filtrate diagonally into the tunnel ! How groundless all the outcries of the alarmists have proved is demonstrated by the operations now in hand.

' But I would especially refer to the tunnel under the Thames, at present advancing with rapidity and success under the able management of that eminent engineer, Brunel.'

Thereupon Vignoles enters on a bold sketch of the probable cost of the proposed Mersey Tunnel, and of the revenue which it was estimated to produce. Into such details it is now needless to follow him: the fact remains that, with the power he possessed of looking far ahead beyond the immediate future, Vignoles gave in this case a striking proof of the professional foresight which was one of his marked characteristics. He has often been heard to say, and it was felt to be true by many, that he lived half a century too soon. In this particular instance, the project which was then so speedily snuffed out was triumphantly accomplished fifty-five years later.

Before closing the brief account of Vignoles's work in

Liverpool at this time, we give a short extract from a letter of Mr. James Mawdsley, one of the most respected of the citizens of Liverpool, and a firm and faithful friend of our young engineer.

Speaking of the projected tunnel under the Mersey, he says :—

' In the event of the plan receiving a tangible shape, I feel sanguine that there will be no one so likely to be connected with it as yourself. Your success with the Liverpool and Manchester Railway (which would never have been a railway but for you) puts this beyond all doubt.'

CHAPTER X.

The Institution of Civil Engineers—Government survey of Isle of Man—Improvements of the Oxford Canal—Proposals for completing the Thames Tunnel—Controversy with elder Brunel—The locomotive question—Ericsson's 'Novelty'—The competition at Rainhill—Vignoles's notes made at the time—Success of the 'Rocket,' &c.

. 1827–29.

VIGNOLES was elected a member of the Institution of Civil Engineers on April 10, 1827, and continued to belong to it for more than forty-seven years, up to the time of his death in 1875.

In his interesting sketch of the early days of civil engineering, delivered from the presidential chair in 1870, he tells us that very few rallied to the support of the first president, Thomas Telford, when he founded the Institution in 1818; and even ten years later, when the charter of its incorporation was obtained, the number enrolled in all classes of membership was only one hundred and thirty-seven. The society was for many years contented with the very rudest accommodation in Buckingham Street, Adelphi, and it was not till 1839 that it secured the building in Great George Street, Westminster, which it still possesses. At the time of Vignoles's presidency (1870–71) there were affiliated to the Institution 1,632 members and associates, and 170 students.

In 1886 the number of the former (divided into three classes) amounted to 4,417, and of the latter 934; and there is a steady yearly increase.

Telford continued president till his death in 1834, being succeeded in the chair by James Walker, who held the office for ten years. On the accession of the late Robert Stephenson in 1845, the tenure of the presidency of the Institution was restricted to two years, and this rule prevailed up to 1882, from which date the president has been elected annually.

The well-known and commodious head-quarters at 25 Great George Street, on which considerable sums of money have been spent from time to time in enlargements and improvements, are becoming once more inadequate to the wants of the Institntion; and a supplemental royal charter was obtained in August 1887, authorising an augmentation up to the higher sum of 10,000*l.* yearly value in the property that may be acquired by the managing body of the association.

Probably few outsiders know the precise point of view held by its first founders, who in their petition for incorporation defined their object as follows :—

'The Institution of Civil Engineers is a society established for promoting the acquisition of that species of knowledge which constitutes the profession of a civil engineer, whereby the great sources of power in Nature are converted, adapted, and applied for the use and convenience of man.'

Early in the summer of 1827 Vignoles (as already noticed) had obtained an order from the English Government to make a new survey of the Isle of Man, which may be accepted as a proof of his increasing reputation; but he still kept on his offices in London, and also took care to maintain the professional connection he had formed with Liverpool.

Vignoles seems at first to have been considerably hampered in his work in the Isle of Man by the presence of surveyors who had been employed at the expense of the Duke of Athol, who was at that time the hereditary owner of the manorial rights of the island; but these persons soon received imperative orders to leave the coast clear, and Vignoles set to work, only to discover in the first instance that the triangulation of such parts of the island as had been surveyed was very imperfect, and the computations incomplete. He had in the island a limited but very efficient staff of assistants and pupils, with Mr. J. E. Terry at their head; and, owing to the entire confidence which his chief was able to place in the discretion and ability of this gentleman, Vignoles was at liberty to undertake engineering work in other parts of the kingdom.

During some portion of the year 1828 Vignoles was en-

gaged on improvements in the Oxford Canal. That this work
helped to advance his professional repute is sufficiently proved
by extracts from two letters here given. The first is to his
wife in March 1829, referring to the ceremony of opening the
St. Katharine's Docks, to which he had been invited. He had
met (he says) ' old Mr. Telford, who, in the interview, spoke very
highly to me of my improvements in the Oxford Canal.'

On the same subject George Rennie wrote to him in May :—

' It gave me great pleasure to find you usefully employing
your time and talents in the surveys and improvement of the
Oxford Canal.

' The field for engineers is but limited at present, but it is
still large enough for us ; and I trust that the experience you
have acquired at Liverpool of men and things will be found
useful on all occasions.'

Rennie was three years senior to his correspondent; but
neither they nor any of their contemporaries seem to have
dreamt of the marvellous epoch of engineering enterprise and
railway expansion on whose threshold they were standing.

The library of the Institution of Civil Engineers has a copy
of Vignoles's map, which is handsomely engraved, and his improvements clearly shown. The title is: ' Map of intended
Improvements along part of the existing Oxford Canal, from
Longford, in the County of the City of Coventry, to Walphamcote,
in the County of Warwick. Laid down from Surveys and Levels
taken by and under the immediate direction of Charles Vignoles,
Engineer: October 8, 1828.'

The improvements extend over upwards of thirty miles
between the points mentioned above.

After the completion of the Isle of Man surveys in 1828,
the metropolis became the centre of Vignoles's increasing business, which was now continually augmented, not only by his
acknowledged ability, but also by his great energy and vivacity,
coupled with most persevering and unflagging industry.

He was on very friendly terms at this time with all his
brother-engineers, and more particularly with the elder Brunel,
with whom, however, a rather serious professional conflict was

impending, which we proceed briefly to relate; but as an introduction to the story we first give an extract from a very pleasant letter written to him by Brunel, dated June 2, 1828, the reference being, of course, to the Thames Tunnel :—

' The papers, either by their silence or by their notice of us, convey sufficient information to give an idea of our situation. When they say nothing, you may conclude we are in a fair way ; when they take notice, it is of some sad occurrence ! I must now tell you that we are going on safely in the preparatory operations for the recovery of the work—a hard service, and of great precaution in every step.

' After our general meeting, which is to be held next week, we are to have another immediately afterwards, which is likely to be presided over by the Duke of Wellington. He said lately to a deputation from the directors that he would use his best endeavours to convince the assembly of the advantage of going on with the work; that he would subscribe again, and that the completion of the tunnel is coupled with the honour of the country. This is extremely flattering and encouraging. Now you must let me know how you are going on.'

Within twelve months from this date the friendly feeling subsisting between these two engineers was to receive a rude shock.

It was the time of the fatal influx of the river Thames into the works, which were suspended towards the end of 1828, and the tunnel was bricked up, and so remained for nearly seven years. There was thus an opening created for any competent engineer who could induce the directors of the enterprise to consider his suggestions. Vignoles had evidently formed plans and estimates for the completion of the tunnel, and had unquestionably induced the directors to give them favourable consideration. Sir C. H. Gregory (then in his boyhood) has a distinct recollection of visits paid to his father (Dr. Olinthus Gregory), at Woolwich, by Vignoles at this time, to consult him on his plans for taking up the tunnel works, in which operation the engineer proposed to dispense with the ' shield.' [1] The plan was referred to three eminent scientific

___
[1] For this ingenious contrivance, which we need not here explain, I. M·

judges, Messrs. P. Barlow, Walker, and J. Rennie, whose verdict was adverse to the adoption of Vignoles's proposals, and he at once withdrew from the field.

Whether or not they were really impracticable there is nothing now to show. A geologist has suggested to the writer that if Vignoles's proposal was to penetrate the London clay at a greater depth below the bed of the river than was intended by Brunel, it is highly probable that most of the difficulties encountered by the latter would have been readily overcome by Vignoles's plan. It was a matter, however, which involved at the time, and probably even in subsequent years, a great deal of heartburning; and there is undoubtedly room for wide diversity of judgment on the attitude of the disputants, and especially on the merits of the various plans proposed to rescue the affairs of the tunnel from a perilous condition, which at the time threatened to result in a total collapse.

The editor of Sir Isambard M. Brunel's 'Life' has written rather bitterly of this whole affair, and has pointed his keenest censure plainly, though anonymously, at the position taken up by Vignoles in this Thames Tunnel controversy. The writer of this biography does not feel himself qualified to pronounce any opinion on the disputed points ; but he cannot do less than allow the subject of his narrative to speak for himself. Vignoles writes to his wife in March 1829 :—

'We are in the very midst of all our Parliamentary bustle, and, moreover, I am engaged in a most serious treaty with the Thames Tunnel Company, and have a very important appointment on Monday with the directors, the result of which may possibly be my appointment to complete this great work instead of Mr. Brunel.'

He writes again on July 11 :—

'Since I wrote I have received the instructions of the directors of the Thames Tunnel to proceed with a new survey and examination of the river, and also to take fresh sections; and nothing but the continued heavy rains has prevented me from

Brunel received the 'Telford' Medal from the Institution of Civil Engineers in 1839.

commencing that business without a day's delay.   You may conceive what time, trouble, and vexation I have had in bringing
about my plan for finishing the tunnel, and in combating with
Mr. Brunel.   The show of hands against him at the meeting was
in the proportion of three to two, and if he had demanded a ballot
I should have polled four to one against him.   Two days ago
Mr. Brunel had a long interview with the Duke of Wellington,
and yesterday the Duke went down for the first time to see the
tunnel, and Mr. Brunel, jun., accompanied him.   Even if the
Duke would interfere (which we all doubt), he cannot do. anything for him, because his Grace has already publicly declared
that in his capacity as Minister he knows no difference between
Mr. Brunel and Mr. Vignoles; and he added that, if Mr. Vignoles's plans could be effected for 100,000*l.* less, he was the man
for him.   You will see this in the " Morning Herald " of the 1st
July.   Indeed, my friends here, when joking with me, call me
" *His Grace's man* "!'

This page of private history reveals, at any rate, something of
the keen competition for engineering business at the dawn of
the railway era ; but it also throws fresh light on the tremendous difficulties which, as is well known, Brunel had to contend
with in the completion of the Thames Tunnel.

The alienation between the two engineers was complete, but
it was happily not perpetuated by the younger Brunel, with
whom Vignoles renewed his intimacy in later years, and for
whom he carried out some important surveys.

To resume our chronological sketch, we find that at the end
of August 1829 Vignoles was in Ireland, and after a brief stay
in Dublin had made his way to Wexford.   He had been invited
by the trustees of the Earl of Portsmouth to carry out some
improvements in the navigation of the river Slaney, and surveys
of the estates on both its banks.

His principal assistant was the late Mr. John Collister, a
gentleman of high attainments as a practical engineer, and of a
very genial disposition.   He carried out the work in hand with
complete success, and (like Mr. Terry) he proved in after years
to be one of Vignoles's most able, zealous, and faithful assistants,

and continued to work with him and for him during the great
epoch of railway engineering which had already set in.

The era of railway development had now begun, and in it the
subject of this memoir was about to take an important if not a
very conspicuous part. In common with a few other young engineers, he had already perceived how much would depend on the
means of traction that should be finally adopted; but he had more
firmly grasped the subject than most of them. That he was
distinctly in favour of the 'locomotive' is shown by many entries
in his diary, and an additional proof is afforded of his practical
interest in the solution of the problem by the fact that at this
time he threw in his lot with Messrs. Braithwaite and Ericsson [1]
in their attempt to bring this momentous question to a favourable issue, taking a considerable pecuniary share with them in
their patent 'caloric' engine, the 'Novelty,' on which they were
now busily at work, to be ready for the approaching trial of
'locomotives' in October 1829.

One of the drawbacks in connection with the competitive
trial of this invention was the insufficiency of time (only six
weeks) the makers had allowed themselves for the construction
of the engine, of which we shall have more to say presently. But
Ericsson, its ingenious originator, was also materially hampered
—handicapped, we may almost say—by the want of any rail-

---

[1] It is with sincere sorrow that we are unable to speak of this eminent and
gift d man as being still alive. Mr. Ericsson was in his eighty-sixth year,
so that when engaged on the 'Novelty' he was only about twenty-two years
of age. From that day to this, his inventive powers have never slackened,
and the list of his varied contrivances in the mechanical arts of both war
and peace make up a catalogue of prodigious length and interest, his dis-
coveries ranging over the whole field of dynamics. It must suffice here to
mention the extended application of 'caloric' as a motive power, and the still
more daring achievement of utilising the sun's rays by means of gigantic
lenses, and collecting the motive force thus produced in a practical form by
ingeniously constructed machinery. The well-known fact of the "Monitor"
system of arming vessels of war having been invented by Ericsson scarcely
needs to be stated. Full information of what Mr. Ericsson has done during
his long sojourn in the United States of America can be readily obtained from
his representative in England, Mr. S. Boyd Browning. The news of Mr.
Ericsson's death in New York on March 7, 1889, has just been announced.

way line in or near London on which the 'Novelty' could be tried.

So far as Vignoles was concerned, in the first place mechanics were not his strongest point, although for several consecutive years he was secretary to the mechanical section of the British Association. Moreover, his work in the Isle of Man and his constant engagements in other parts had scarcely permitted him to keep touch with the marked progress which George Stephenson and his partners in the Newcastle works had made, and the gradual improvements they had introduced into their manufacture of 'locomotives,' which culminated in the great success of the 'Rocket' at Rainhill in October 1829. The whole scientific world was at this time watching intently for the result of this trial, and there were several competitors for the 500l. prize offered on certain conditions by the directors of the Liverpool and Manchester Railway.[1] The contest was nominally to prove which out of five machines was the best; but, in reality, it was the crucial test of the practical value in the matter of speed and power of the railway system itself which was then to be applied; and this (as we all now know) was absolutely dependent on the successful introduction and development of some kind of locomotive engine.

George Stephenson had fully grasped this great problem at the time of which we write; and it is undeniable that his mechanical skill, dogged perseverance, and unswerving faith in the invention which he had done so much to perfect, contributed at once to its immediate success and to his own undying fame.

The writer's excuse for travelling to some extent over well-trodden ground must be the extreme interest taken in that trial by the subject of this memoir. We must premise that a special account of the trial was written by Vignoles, and appeared in the 'Mechanic's Magazine' soon afterwards.

We may also just note in passing that Vignoles was caterer for the group of engineers assembled on this historic occasion, for a letter from Mr. Rastrick says:—

[1] The writer has purposely omitted all reference to the three other engines, which with the 'Rocket' and 'Novelty' completed the competition.

'Our best thanks are due to you for the vast trouble you have had in providing our dinner, and settling all the accounts.'

The famous 'Rocket,' painted yellow and black, with a white chimney, was ready early on the first day of trial, October 6, 1829; but the 'Novelty' put in an appearance very soon afterwards, and the impression it produced was extremely favourable. The machinery was of much more finished workmanship than Stephenson's engine, and as it was brought to view, burnished with copper and dark blue paint, it evoked universal admiration.

Mr. Locke told a friend of the writer's that George Stephenson at once regarded the 'Novelty' as the only possible rival to

'ROCKET' LOCOMOTIVE.

the 'Rocket,' and gave immediate orders to those about him to look well to the purity of the water in the cask placed upon the tender attached to his own engine, and to the quality of the coke for fuel; and with this agree the local chroniclers,[1] who described Ericsson's machine as 'exhibiting by its beauty and compactness the very *beau-idéal* of a locomotive engine.' It was very light—under three tons—and at its first trial (without a load) 'it seemed to the spectators to fly, as it shot by them at the unprecedented rate of twenty-three miles an hour.' This, how-

[1] Vide *Liverpool Mercury* of that date and other papers.

VIEW OF THE 'NOVELTY' WITH A TRAIN OF ENGINE AND 'COACHES' IN 1829.

(From Pen-and-Ink Drawing by C. B. Vignoles.)

ever, was but for a few minutes, for on its reverse journey, over the one mile and three quarters of the 'Rainhill level, the exhausting fan, used for creating an increased draught, gave way, and the 'Novelty' came to a standstill. It was then that George Stephenson exclaimed to Locke in the broadest Doric, ' Eh! mon, we needn't fear yon thing; it's got no goots ' [guts].

Meanwhile the ' Rocket,' with a load of twelve tons behind it, performed more than its maker had ever promised, running fourteen miles in sixty-nine minutes, and without a load from nineteen to twenty-two miles per hour; attaining even a greater pace when the formal trials (which were spread over several days) were concluded. It fairly won the 500*l.* prize; but, as is universally admitted, the secret of its success lay in its multitubular boiler, the undoubted suggestion of Henry Booth, and in the contrivance of the steam-blast. With regard to this latter, it seems to the writer that Dr. Smiles rather implies than asserts that George Stephenson was its inventor; but Mr. Locke has often told the story of its being a pure accident, originating from one of 'old Geordie's' workmen at Newcastle, who advised his master to allow the escape steam, which generally surrounded the engine-driver with its dense mist, to go off through the chimney, instead of from underneath the boiler, the suggestion being strengthened by the man's declaration ' that it would look so much better! ' [1]

The steam-whistle [2] was not then invented, and when trains first ran regularly a railway horn was blown by the engine-driver or guard to signal their approach ; indeed, the writer can distinctly remember that a few years later the horn was always blown by some official as the sign for the train to start from the Victoria Station at Manchester.

At the time of the trial, in October 1829, Stephenson had nearly completed his short line from Bolton to Leigh, and it was on that railroad that one of his locomotives was first used for passenger traffic. This was the ' Lancashire Witch,' which had a double boiler, and weighed nearly twelve tons.

To return to the ' Novelty.' It was again tried at Rainhill on October 7, when, with a load of about ten tons, it ran for a short distance at the rate of twenty-eight miles an hour, but was soon disabled by a mishap similar to that of its first trial. A day or two later it was again brought forward, and ran without a load, but for a short time only, at the rate of nearly thirty-five miles an hour.

The ' caloric ' system, which was its chief characteristic, was afterwards successfully applied by Ericsson to some of the Irish steam-vessels, and to one of the (American) Atlantic steamers, which unfortunately was wrecked on its second voyage.

Of the various and admirable modifications it afterwards received at the inventor's hands, and of the numerous improvements effected by him in mechanical science generally, the writer unwillingly abstains here from any further notice. Such a subject must yet receive full and adequate treatment from some thoroughly competent pen.

---

[1] This can be attested by a living witness, Mr. Wellington Purdon, who was afterwards Vignoles's resident engineer at the Woodhead Tunnel, on the Sheffield line, and was subsequently engaged by Mr. Locke as one of his principal engineers. [Mr. Purdon has since died, February 1889.]

[2] The steam-whistle was suggested to Stephenson by a Mr. Bagster, the then manager of the Colliery Railway from Leicester to Swannington, at the end of the year 1832. It was immediately introduced into general use.

We give here a few of the rough notes, first hand, which Vignoles actually made on the spot, during the memorable trial at Rainhill from October 6 to 14, 1829. They bear undoubted evidence of fairness, though naturally leaning with some partiality to the side of the 'Novelty.'

'LIVERPOOL AND MANCHESTER RAILWAY LOCOMOTIVE COMPETITION.

'*First Day, October 6, 1829 (Tuesday).*

'Place: Manchester side of the skew bridge at Rainhill, on the level of one and three-quarter miles, on which each competing engine was to make ten double journeys, or thirty-five miles in all, rather more than the distance between the two towns. Vast numbers of people were present. The "Rocket" first to try: it drew 12 tons 9 cwt. at exact rate of ten miles four chains per hour; without load it ran eighteen miles per hour. Its velocity was very unequal, and it did not at first thoroughly consume its own smoke.[1]

'The "Novelty" started off next without a load, and did one mile in one minute fifty-three seconds, running the mile and three-quarters at the rate of twenty-eight miles an hour. A delay then ensued caused by an insufficient supply of water and coke, and its trial with a load was deferred.

'*Second Day, October 7.*

'"Novelty" drew 11 tons 5 cwt. at twenty miles per hour, smoke consumption being perfect. [The report omits to say how far it went: we believe only the one and three-quarter miles.]

'Operations suspended in the afternoon owing to rails being clogged with mud, &c.

'*Third Day, October 8.*

'Some revision in rules was enforced. Each engine was to be timed as to interval between furnace being kindled and steam pressure reaching 50 lbs. on the square inch. "Rocket"

---

[1] This was one of the conditions of the trial; it was also prescribed by the Act of Parliament.

first appeared, and went thirty-five miles (ten journeys) in three hours and ten minutes (or at the rate of more than eleven miles per hour) with a load of thirteen tons. After sixteen minutes' delay for fresh water and fuel, &c., it again ran the thirty-five miles in two hours and fifty-two minutes (or more than twelve miles an hour), including stoppages.[1]

'On the fourth day, October 9, " Novelty " declined to try, so that was a *dies non.*

'*Fifth Day, Saturday, October* 10.

' " Novelty " appeared, got up steam in fifty-four minutes and started, but at end of its first trip of one and a quarter miles a small pipe gave way. No forge was at hand, and a message had to be sent to Prescot (two miles off) to procure what was necessary for repairs.

' Meanwhile the " Rocket," without its tender—" stripped for the race," as some spectator said—again proved its powers by running four times over the measured course (seven miles in actual distance) in fourteen minutes fourteen seconds, or, allowing for reversing, upwards of twenty miles per hour! As it carried neither fuel, water, nor load, it was not pretended that it was to be considered a competition trial ; but it was considered a convincing proof of the qualities of the engine.

' It was three o'clock when the " Novelty " was again fit to run, and her performance also was not deemed competitive. She drew a total weight of 10 tons 6 cwt. and one quarter, inclusive of her own weight. I rode on the engine [2] and carefully timed her performance. She went her first distance at seventeen and a half miles per hour, and then discarded the load for a waggon full of forty-five passengers, which she whirled along at upwards of thirty miles an hour.' [Original notes end here.]

It is plain that the ' Novelty ' [3] was too light in construction,

---

[1] The 'Novelty' was under repair this day. The next day its owners protested against the newly-revised conditions.

[2] His own weight was given at 9 stone, Ericsson's at 12 stone, J. Braithwaite's at 10¾ stone, and the engineman's at 12 stone.

[3] Her actual weight was only 2 tons 15 cwt. That of the ' Rocket ' was 4 tons 6 cwt.

however attractive her compact and finished aspect may have made her.   She was not a weight carrier; rather might she be compared—as some one said at the time—'to a Galloway pony instead of a road teamster.'   The apparatus of the bellows (pouring compressed air into the furnace) was always giving way, and the cement on the flanges of the boiler was continually yielding to the effect of the enormous heat produced, a temperature of upwards of 300° Fahrenheit.   It was a mishap of such a kind that occasioned the final breakdown of the 'Novelty' on the seventh day of the trial, Wednesday, October 14, when the patentees at once withdrew her from further competition, and the prize of 500*l.* was rightly adjudged to Stephenson's 'Rocket.'

Still there was nothing to show that Ericsson's 'caloric' principle was in fault; the successive mishaps of the 'Novelty' being sufficiently accounted for by her defective workmanship. Difficulties equally formidable were constantly developed by Stephenson's earlier locomotives, and it was only through the experience learnt in such failures, coupled with the increasing skill of the workmen employed by Stephenson, that his machines were little by little raised to the requisite standard of power and efficiency.

An extract from a letter of Ericsson will form a fitting conclusion for this chapter :—

To O. B. Vignoles, from J. Braithwaite.

'December 19, 1829.

' . . . I have this morning received a letter from Ericsson, who is now at Liverpool.   He says :—" We have been at work steadily the whole day (December 17), and everything has gone extremely well.   We have only had occasion to take in fresh supplies of water and fuel twice, and the bearings have not been oiled since we started this morning.   By these I mean the crank couplings, the eccentrics, and the four axle-tree brasses.   The spectators appeared highly delighted with our mode of conveyance ; and later on we rigged out some of the waggons for passengers (our *friends* having sent away the passage waggon), as the ladies were quite distressed at not being able to get a ride!

' " We went at various speeds during the day, sometimes with and sometimes without passengers, and the steam was kept up in wonderful style.

' " The engine did not exceed two hundred and sixty strokes per minute, not quite forty miles an hour; and I am confident that if I dare trust the *force pump* at such a rate I could have done *one mile in one minute!*

' " As the engine passed on in its velocity the spectators cheered in a glorious manner. I will send the particulars of more experiments to-morrow." '

CHAPTER XI.

Letters from America—Vignoles's engagement on the St. Helens, Newton, Wigan, and 'North Union' Railways—General condition and working of early lines—Opening of the Liverpool and Manchester Railway.

1829—1830.

NOTWITHSTANDING the formal severance of Vignoles's connection with the Liverpool and Manchester Railway, he had received so much encouragement in his profession during his stay in Lancashire that he determined to keep up and extend his provincial business, and accordingly he purchased the lease of a house in Liverpool, and also engaged offices in Bold Street,[1] one of the leading thoroughfares in that town.

In his address from the presidential chair of the Institution of Civil Engineers in 1870, Vignoles refers to his share in the laying out of a line from Barnsley to Goole in 1830 ; and about the same time he was nominated engineer to a projected line of railway from Liverpool to Birmingham, on which a large amount of preliminary work had been completed, when a formidable opposition sprang up in the proposed 'Grand Junction' line, which was powerfully supported by the Stephensons and their friends, and with which the promoters of the earlier scheme found it necessary to combine.   Vignoles's position was not then sufficiently assured to enable him to compete with such influential rivals, and thus the engineering of the Grand Junction was at first entrusted to the elder Stephenson, but eventually Mr. Locke became engineer-in-chief,[2] and carried out the undertaking which was designed to connect the two great termini of the Liverpool and Manchester Railway with Birmingham and the South.

[1] His private residence was 5 Bedford Street, Abercrombie Square.

[2] It was in this affair that a serious and lasting estrangement took place between Locke and his former chief.   Stephenson in a bitter moment said of his subordinate : 'Ay! that's the mon that can wrax a lee!'

We may here take the opportunity of glancing at the early
condition of engineering matters across the Atlantic, where in the
United States the impulse of the railway movement in England
had been already felt [1] and undoubtedly received a new impetus
from the accounts of the memorable ' locomotive ' competition
which had by this time crossed the Atlantic, as is shown by
passages in the following letters. The first is from Mr. Baldwin,
C.E., of Boston, U.S., in June 1830 :—

' I should like very much to have a run on your Manchester
and Liverpool Railway : but the accounts show with what
frightful velocity you move. Will it do to go at the rate of
fifteen or twenty miles an hour ? '

Vignoles's old friend and chief, Major Wilson, also wrote
about the same time from Philadelphia :—

' In several communications from Liverpool, which have
lately appeared in the Baltimore papers, your name has been
mentioned on the subject of the results of the experiments of
locomotive engines on the Manchester Railroad. It is now many
years since I heard anything of you, and you were then engaged
with Mr. Walker in surveys and plans for suspension bridges.
My own health was much impaired by exposure in the public
works, so that in 1825 I removed from Charleston to this place ;
and in 1827 I entered the service of the state, as engineer on
the contemplated railway between Philadelphia and Columbia,
on the Susquehanna River. . . . Professional men in America
are indebted to Britain for what is valuable both in railroads
and canals ; and the late results on the Liverpool and Manchester road have given an increased interest and impetus to
similar enterprises in this country.'

We now proceed to speak of two independent engineering
works carried out by Vignoles in Lancashire, not unimportant
in themselves, but to him of the highest moment as their engineer-in-chief, since he was thus afforded an opportunity of show-

---

[1] The first American trunk line, the 'Baltimore and Ohio,' was begun in
July 1828. The first English locomotive for Transatlantic use (the 'John
Bull '), was made by Stephenson for the Camden and Amboy Railway in June
1831. It was in use forty years, and is preserved as a relic in the Smithsonian
Institution at Washington. It weighed ten tons.

ing his power of original thought and constructive ability in
this newly-opened field of practical science. One of these
railways was to connect the town of St. Helens with Runcorn
Gap, on the river Mersey ; the other was to run from Parkside
to Wigan, but was afterwards extended to Preston. The first
enterprise was undertaken in the autumn of 1829, and the
second at the beginning of 1830.

Vignoles's appointment to carry out these new projects was

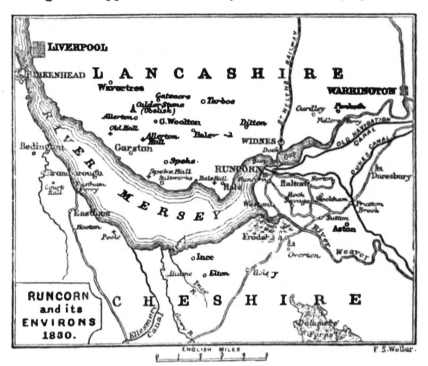

RUNCORN AND ENVIRONS.

by no means a matter of course, as considerable pressure was
brought to bear by Stephenson and his party on the promoters
of the lines, with a view to secure the post of engineer-in-chief
for one of their own people, but without gaining their point.
This was one out of many professional contests which our engineer had to wage at this time, and he may well be pardoned a
little exultation when he met with success in the strong competition that had already sprung up in the engineering world.

He had fortunately secured the goodwill and warm admiration of several of the directors of the Liverpool and Manchester Company, as well as of other leading men in Liverpool, amongst them being Mr. John Whitley [1] (with whom he formed a life-long intimacy), who was the solicitor to the St. Helens Railway, of which we have now to speak. This line was mainly projected by the coal proprietors resident in and about the important town of St. Helens, and several of these gentlemen were on the first board of direction, the chairman of which was Mr. Peter Greenall.[2]

The means of communication for heavy goods traffic between St. Helens and the river Mersey, a distance of twelve miles, was at that time only by the Sankey Canal, which abuts on the river at the 'gap,' or narrow bend of the stream opposite Runcorn. This canal is the oldest in the kingdom, having been made in 1775; and the railway scheme was to be completed by the construction of a dock at Widnes (then only a village),[3] on the Lancashire side of the river, where the terminus of the railway was to be. Vignoles's ambition even then was to construct a railway bridge across the Mersey at Runcorn Gap, perhaps incited by the half-formed project of a suspension bridge at that point, for which a very handsome design [4] had been made by Telford sixteen years before. Any idea of a railway bridge of such dimensions would have been deemed chimerical in those days; but Vignoles often returns to the conception of such an enterprise, which, however, was only carried out many years afterwards by the construction of the magnificent lattice girder bridge [5] of the London and North-Western Railway Company.

[1] Father of Mr. Edward Whitley, now M.P. for Liverpool.

[2] This gentleman retained his position till 1845, and was then succeeded by his brother, now Sir Gilbert Greenall, Bart., M.P. for Warrington. Mr. Whitley, sen., was brother-in-law to the Greenalls.

[3] Ten years later (1840) Widnes had not increased in population. Now it has 20,000 inhabitants, and its alkali and soap manufactures are the largest in the United Kingdom.

[4] The drawing for this—showing a proposed central opening of 1,000 feet, with two others of 500 feet each—is preserved in the 'Binns Collection' at Liverpool. The design was with a view to connect this route with the new high road from London to Holyhead, which Parliament had sanctioned.

[5] Completed in 1880. Brindley had also proposed a bridge (or rather an aqueduct) at the same place.

The collieries were the mainstay of the town of St. Helens in 1830, and there were more pits worked then than now, nearly sixty years later. But of the many important manufactories, chiefly glass and chemicals, now established in the place there were at that time only the works of the British Plate Glass Company, erected in 1775; the then newly opened Crown Glass Works; and one small establishment for copper-smelting. The first of the many chemical works, which now abound in the town, had been commenced only the year before (1829).

When the project of the Runcorn Railway was started the whole of the capital was promptly subscribed in the district. It may be said eagerly subscribed, for Mr. Arthur Sinclair, J.P., a gentleman now resident in St. Helens, has recently related to the writer the description given by his father of the scene at the ' Fleece ' Inn, where the first subscriptions for shares were received; how some of the eager applicants who could not get near to sign their names soon enough crept cleverly *under* the table, and emerging between the knees of those who surrounded it thus secured the chance of having their names enrolled as proprietors in the lucky scheme.[1]   This was in January 1830, and we learn from the diary that early in February the ' petition ' of the Bill had passed the Committee of the House of Commons; and on the 15th of that month Vignoles particularly records an interview (on the subject of the land to be scheduled) with the then Marquis of Salisbury at Hatfield.

It was on the affairs of this railway that the engineer (after three years' estrangement) was happily thrown once more into conference with George Stephenson,[2] as to the crossing of the

---

[1] Whilst penning these pages the attention of the writer was drawn to the launching of the new scheme—the St. Helens and Wigan Junction Railway inaugurated by Lord Derby twelve months ago. [Cf. *Times*, January 30, 1888.]   His lordship was able to recommend strongly the new line as an investment, and he referred to the vast development of railway enterprise since the opposition of his great-grandfather to the proposals of the first promoters of the Liverpool and Manchester Railway sixty years before!   The new line will virtually unite the two railways made by Vignoles, of which this chapter speaks.

[2] It was at this time that Vignoles first saw Robert Stephenson, who had recently returned from South America   Cf. Dr. Smiles's *Life of George Stephenson*.

St. Helens line over the Liverpool and Manchester Railway.[1] After a good deal of negotiation this question was solved by determining on a handsome stone bridge, which was in due time erected; and that it was worthy of its position may be seen by the annexed drawing of the original design on a smaller scale.

Very soon after this railway was taken in hand, the proposal for a short line from Wigan to join the Liverpool and Manchester Railway at Newton Junction, near Parkside, had been launched by some influential residents and coal proprietors of Wigan, and Vignoles was nominated the engineer. It may be remembered that in the case of the Liverpool and Manchester line the original

BRIDGE ON THE ST. HELENS RAILWAY.

grievance of the mercantile and industrial world was the exceedingly high rate charged for the transit of cotton by inland navigation; but in the case of the Wigan, as in that of the St. Helens line, it was the cost of carriage for coals. The distance

[1] An anecdote of the early surveys of this line has been preserved by one of Vignoles's assistant engineers. His chief was on the ground, and had with him a theodolite, which was to be carried by a chain-bearer, who had never seen an instrument of the kind before. It was a very valuable one, and Vignoles laid many charges on the man as to the care required in carrying it about, speaking to him in the quick and peremptory tone of voice which was habitual to him in busy moments. 'Is it all right now?' said the man, eyeing the instrument ruefully. 'It is,' replied the engineer, 'and on your life don't let it fall!' 'Aye! very well,' says the man, laying it carefully down, 'but as it's all right now I'll be d—— if I have owt to say to it, and you may just carry her yoursel'!'

from Wigan to Liverpool by canal was thirty-five miles, for which the Duke of Bridgwater's trustees charged 3s. 8d. per ton for coals; but by the proposed railway the distance would be reduced to twenty-three miles. To Manchester the shortening of distance would be only one mile, but the saving on the carriage, whether of minerals or merchandise, would in each case be enormous. The first public meeting had been held at Wigan on November 29, 1829, and the shares were rapidly taken up, the capital at first being fixed at 60,000l. for a line of six miles and three-quarters; afterwards considerably increased, proportionably with the extension from Wigan to Preston, which cost 30,000l. per mile. Vignoles had prepared all that was necessary for submitting both these lines to Parliament, and they went through the usual legal ordeal almost *pari passu*. His diary notes that the Wigan Bill passed the Committee of the House of Commons on March 31, 1830,[1] and that he was formally appointed engineer-in-chief to the two lines on June 15 and 16 respectively. In each case his salary was 650l. per annum. It will be of interest here to trace the development of the lines from Parkside to Preston, as these were important links in the early system of railways in Lancashire.

The first promoters were almost exclusively the Wigan coal proprietors; but before long the cotton spinners of Preston perceived the extreme importance to them of becoming connected with the two great towns of Liverpool and Manchester, which

[1] In a long letter to a friend, dated December 4 in the previous year, Vignoles describes the race against time in preparing for this line:—'You have no idea how we were driven to get our plans ready for lodging at Preston before November 30 (1829). The hurry and anxiety were five times greater than with the Liverpool and Manchester line. For three nights none of us went to bed, and when all was finished every one was completely knocked up. I have, however, accomplished my task; but it has left me full of nervousness, and I am reduced to a skeleton. The worst is that I can see no end to it, for the public estimation and enthusiasm for new railways and locomotive machines is daily augmenting; and I find that my opinion and service are in constant requisition. It seems as if Liverpool would be my scene of action for some years to come. I want nothing but good tools to have any amount of work under my control. My staff here, Charles Forth [he died in Ireland at an early age] and Mr. J. K. Terry, and my excellent assistant, Mr. John Collister, have all acted with the utmost zeal and devotion to duty.'

would of course require the extension of the line from Wigan to Preston. This was soon determined on, and the combined lines eventually received the name of the ' North Union Railway,' the completion of which occupied just eight years.

At first the centre of gravity of this little system was to be found in the town of Wigan, which was the residence of Mr. (afterwards Sir Hardman) Earle, the chairman, and of Mr. Part, the solicitor to the company;[1] but, as the lines progressed, Preston was considered the chief station, and has since become a very important railway centre. Canal traffic between Preston and Wigan had been established in 1802 ; but for about five miles out of Preston a tramway, to join the Liverpool and Leeds Canal, for colliery purposes, had been running for some few years at the time we speak of, the haulage up the steep Avenham Brow, now the summit of the very pretty park which overlooks the valley of the Ribble, being worked by a stationary engine. This tramway continued in use till about 1858, and a local publication states that the last person employed upon it was still living in 1882. It has been calculated that in his thirty-two years of employment, ' man and boy,' walking or riding, this *employé* had travelled over about 199,000 miles. The prospect of railway communication to and through Preston soon began to tell on the coaching traffic. The number of coaches running was gradually reduced from eighty-one to twelve between 1830 and 1837 ; and in 1842 the clatter of the northern and southern mails, which had long formed a part of the daily and nightly routine of this flourishing town, finally ceased to reverberate in the streets of Preston.[2]

The railway from Preston to Bolton was not opened till 1846, and it also became incorporated with the North Union ; but the Preston and Lancaster was an independent concern, opened in 1840 ; and some years later was completed the Preston and

---

[1] Sir Hardman was the father of General Earle, who was killed in the Egyptian campaign of 1885; a statue to his memory is now erected on the pediment of St. George's Hall, Liverpool. Mr. Part, of Wigan, died in the same year at an advanced age.

[2] Cf. Anthony Hewitson's *History of Preston* (published in 1883), pp. 197, 198, &c.

Wyre Railway, opening up communication with Fleetwood, a town created out of a rabbit warren by the energy and enterprise of Sir Hesketh Fleetwood.[1]

Most of the locomotives used on these two lines made by Vignoles in Lancashire were of very limited power; and the same may be said of all the early lines, and, incredible as it may now seem, it was sometimes a matter of difficulty to start them on an average gradient, when only drawing a moderate load. The writer can recollect the time when on the rather stiff incline from Cophull to Euxton, on the North Union line, the guard of the train would call to some of the men in the third-class open carriages (or *trucks* rather, for such they were), ' Come, my lads, lend a hand to give a shove to the train just to start the engine ! ' In rough weather, too, the effect of a strong wind dead ahead of the train had often a decidedly negative influence on the starting power of the locomotive. Something of the same sort was often witnessed on the St. Helens line, when the train leisurely moved out on its way to Runcorn. The line was then (as now) chiefly used for the transit of minerals, but there was generally a carriage or two for passengers; and occasionally, when some of the travellers would reach the booking office a little behind time, the station master, handing them the paper slip which in those days served as the ' ticket,' would say to them : ' Now hurry yourselves—she's not long started, and if you look sharp you'll catch her up ! '

On this line, about a mile or so from St. Helens, was an exceedingly stiff incline of about 1 in 70, which Vignoles felt himself obliged to adopt, and which he speaks of as the ' Sutton Inclined Plane,'[2] in length about a mile and a half. This was worked by ropes drawn by a stationary engine, the house for which stood on the bank to the south-west of the present St. Helens Junction station.[3] This house remained—a dilapidated remnant of early railway history—for many a long year, even

---

[1] Vignoles was intimate with this gentleman, and always visited him when in the neighbourhood, and advised him in the development of his property.

[2] Called locally the ' Sutton Bank.'

[3] On the Liverpool and Manchester line, which runs here under the St. Helens line, as before explained.

after this line, together with the North Union and numerous others, was absorbed in the London and North-Western Railway.[1] The writer was shown the spot (to him of some interest), in the summer of 1886, where the last remains of this engine-house had been buried a foot or two under the ballast of the present line, on which the gradient has been considerably improved during the last few years, and a girder bridge of plain appearance substituted for the handsome stone structure of which we have already spoken. About three miles farther, on this same line, may still be seen the very handsome red sandstone bridge, of five elliptical arches,

BRIDGE OVER THE ST. HELENS RAILWAY.

which carries the old road from Liverpool to Warrington over the St. Helens Railway.[2] By the kindness of Mr. Arthur Sinclair a sketch of this bridge is here given.

Both these lines of railway—following the then universal custom—had at first granite or other hard stone blocks for sleepers;[3] but on the North Union line the permanent way on

---

[1] Baines, in his *History of Lancashire*, says that 'the St. Helens line, which only forms one-fortieth of the London and North-Western Company's mileage, conveys annually 2,000,000 tons of minerals and goods, or one-seventh of their entire merchandise traffic.'

[2] The 'oldest inhabitant' informed the writer that ''e'd 'eared it 'ad been put up by a Mr. Vivian!' Not a bad shot at a name always difficult to the uninstructed ear.

[3] One of the steeples of a church in Preston was largely built of these

the embankments was laid on transverse wooden sleepers, which was probably a very early example of what has now become almost universal on the English railways, with light rails, on which the carriages bumped and jumped as they ran in a very uncomfortable fashion.   Even in the first-class 'coaches'[1] the journey was very tiring, whilst the wretched traveller by the third class, scarcely so good as cattle-trucks are now, generally without seats and always open at the top and the upper portion of the sides, had a woeful time of it, as the writer can testify! There was some compensation, however, in the numerous stoppages for rest and refreshment.   Nobody was in a hurry, for the craving for quick transit or express trains did not then exist. Long and frequent halts for refreshment were the rule absolute, and the few passengers who did not leave their seats had their wants attended to by men carrying trays with foaming pots of porter and other requisites for the inner man.   In many of the early prints and sketches of railway travelling scenes like these are extremely common, with the additional feature of the passengers and the people at the station being represented as all intermingled in a free and easy fashion ; the whole grouping being simply the transfer of what had been seen at every posting house on the arrival of the mail-coaches to this new mode of travelling by railways.   The station-houses were mostly mere sheds at the smaller stopping-places, and level crossings were of course the almost invariable rule.   Even the *termini* were poor structures, not for a moment to be compared with what we now see at even second- and third-rate stations.   The well-known one at Lime Street, Liverpool (for example), has been continually enlarged, both laterally and longitudinally towards the mouth of the tunnel, the whole of which has been (as we have already

stone blocks, a few of which may still be seen on the banks of the London and North-Western line, on the south side of the Ribble Viaduct.

[1] The first-class conveyances were all built on the inside 'mail-coach' system, with an outside seat for the guard.   The luggage was placed on the top of the carriages, with little room to spare beneath the bridges under which the trains passed.   Luggage vans were not introduced till many years later. The writer and his brother, on their way from Manchester to Repton School, in 1840-41, used constantly to ride outside with the guard, and many a time were they pulled down flat on the roof of the carriage as the train approached a bridge.

observed) sliced away at different times.   The church of SS.
Simon and Jude, which may be seen at the west end of the
deep cutting as the train debouches from it on the approach to
Lime Street, has been thrice taken down, removed, and rebuilt,
stone by stone, to make room for the successive enlargements
of this terminus of the London and North-Western Railway.

A WAY-SIDE RAILWAY STATION IN 1832.

From the ' Binns Collection,' Liverpool, by permission.   Reduced scale.

Another excellent example of enormous enlargement of area and
of entire renovation is to be seen at Preston station.

Vignoles speaks much in his diary both of the expense and
difficulty encountered by the directors and himself in the approach
to Preston from the south.   By sheer force of will he prevailed
on the Board to sanction the erection of the magnificent stone
bridge over the Ribble, on five elliptical arches of 125 feet span,
one of the handsomest structures of its kind in England ; and he
had an equally stubborn fight to get the directors to agree to a
moderate-sized station being built.   One of Vignoles's [1] staff,

[1] Mr. John Watson, one of the ablest and most faithful of Vignoles's
fellow-workers.

who happily still survives, distinctly remembers the look of horror
on the face of the chairman, Mr. Earle, when their engineer
came into the board-room with the proposed plan in his hand
to show to the directors.

'What!' exclaimed the chairman, 'spend 6,000*l.* on the
station! You want to make it three times too large.'

'Well, sir,' answered Vignoles, 'I can only say that I hope
we may both live to see this station, when it is built, ten times
too small for the traffic.'

This has been more than verified; and the proof is seen in the
erection of perhaps the finest railway station[1] in the kingdom
out of the metropolis; and the bridge over the Ribble, which
we have referred to, has also been doubled in width during the
last few years, allowing space for *four* lines of rails, which improvement already extends for a few miles north and south of
Preston, and is being gradually introduced over the whole trunk
of the London and North-Western system. This widening of
the bridge[2] was carried out, happily, on the scale of the original
design, and has preserved the same character of masonry. It
forms a very pleasing object when viewed from the slopes of
Avenham Park, or from the windows of the handsome 'Park'

[1] This station was built and is used in common by the London and North-
Western and the Lancashire and Yorkshire Railway Companies. Nearly 500
trains pass through it every week day. Its total cost, with approaches, was
about 500,000*l.*

[2] This seems the best place to introduce the following letter :—

'Office of Public Works, Dublin : December 19, 1837.

'Sir,—At a meeting of the members of the Civil Engineers' Society of
Ireland, held in Dublin on October 7 last, it was unanimously resolved, "That
the thanks of the Society are justly due to you for the very munificent present
of a splendid model of the Ribble Bridge, which you so kindly bestowed on
their infant Society; and I have been directed to convey to you their thanks
for the same."

'In doing so, allow me to add that it is with no ordinary feelings of admiration for the genius displayed in designing, and the judgment necessary to
carry that great work into execution.

'I have the honour to be, Sir, your very obedient servant,
'EDWARD RUSSELL, Secretary.'

One of Vignoles's inveterate and most expensive hobbies was the construction of *models*. Of this more will be told in subsequent chapters. The society
referred to is now the 'Institution of Civil Engineers in Ireland.'

Hotel, which the London and North-Western Company have recently built on the crest of the hill.[1]

It is worth while here to introduce a remarkable case of oversight on the part of a contractor, which may easily raise an incredulous smile, but of the truth of which the writer is well assured.

Mr. McMahon had tendered for the first length of line out of Preston, including the construction of the fine stone bridge over the river Ribble already mentioned, which was to be on five elliptical arches, each of 120 feet span. The contractor made his calculations founded on the estimate for *one* arch. The figures were duly entered in the formal tender, but the clerks, or the contractor's engineer, forgot to multiply those particular figures by *five* ! The error was discovered after the formalities were complete, but no alteration could then be made. McMahon stood to his bargain manfully, and on that part of the work of course lost heavily. But it is said that on the whole contract his eventual gains were not inconsiderable.

The North Union proper was opened on May 31, 1838, as Vignoles records :—

' The formal opening of the North Union Railway took place to-day, trains running from 7 A.M. Everything went off without any mishap, and I dined with the directors in the evening at a public entertainment given by the inhabitants of Wigan.'

Vignoles's diary for the previous day gives the last mention of the ' Novelty ' engine found in his journal :—

' This day for the first time I went with a locomotive on the rails just laid over the new Ribble Viaduct. The engine used was the " Novelty," which was conducted by my son Hutton, who also regulated the steam : proud exploit for a boy of fourteen ! '

Our record of Vignoles's life in order of time calls us away once more to the affairs of the Liverpool and Manchester Railway, which was now approaching completion. He had entered in his diary the experimental trip of some of the directors in

---

[1] Mr. Crosbie-Dawson was the Company's engineer for the enlarging of this bridge, which, however, narrowly escaped disfigurement. The Company wished to avoid the serious expense of having it *all of stone*; but there was a great outcry from the inhabitants and the municipal authorities of Preston, and the Company very liberally agreed to this plan as now carried out.

June 1830, and all the scientific world was then in eager expectation of the formal opening, many no doubt distracted between fear and hope of its success.

An amusing reference to the general suspense as to the result is found in a letter from Mr. J. Braithwaite to Vignoles, dated London, July 30, 1830, from which we give a brief quotation:—

' I am, with hundreds of others, all anxiety for the results of the great experiment on your Liverpool Railway. Some persons here are specially on the alert for information, but whether for

OPENING OF LIVERPOOL AND MANCHESTER RAILWAY.
From the 'Binns Collection,' Liverpool, by permission. Reduced scale.

the purpose of drawing comparison of the respective engines, or for railway *share-jobbing*, I cannot tell. The reports here are beautifully exaggerated, and some actually say that goods are to be carried from Liverpool to Manchester for nothing!'

Vignoles had received a cordial invitation for himself to meet the directors and their friends at the banquet, as well as permission to bring a party with him to the opening of the railway.

That opening day—September 15, 1830—is still remembered as one of mingled joy and sorrow ; but, at the moment, the full significance of the great conquest achieved for civilisation and science was perceived by few, if any, of those tens of thousands whose hearts were shocked and saddened by the terrible and untimely death of Mr. Huskisson.

The entry in Vignoles's diary here given is in its brevity characteristic of the soldier in the presence of some great calamity :—

'Opening of the Liverpool and Manchester Railway. Procession went from Wavertree Lane to Parkside Bridge, fourteen and three-quarter miles, in an hour. Here Mr. Huskisson was killed by the " Rocket " engine passing over him. The procession went on to Manchester. In returning the procession occupied five hours —viz. two and a half hours from Manchester to Parkside Bridge, with three engines and twenty-four carriages, and two and a half hours from Parkside to the tunnel head, with five engines and the same load. N.B.—All the gentleman passengers had to *walk* up the inclined plane.'

The newspapers of the day [1] record the poignant grief evoked by the tragic death of a leading statesman at the moment of reconciliation with his great political adversary ; but it remained for history long afterwards to estimate at its true worth the great success which had been won on that memorable evening— a victory in the realms of practical science which was prophetic of unnumbered benefits to mankind. It was the dawn of an epoch whose duration no one can foresee, during which there has been already wrought that enormous augmentation of national wealth and enterprise which Great Britain is now enjoying ; and, so far as any material agency is a factor in moral and social blessings, the railway era seems still to hold the ' promise and potency ' of a continuous increase in the welfare and prosperity of all civilised nations.[2]

We conclude this chapter with some notes made at the time

[1] The *Times* of September 17, 1830, has not a single paragraph descriptive of the opening of the Liverpool and Manchester Railway, or the slightest reference to the event, except as having occasioned the untimely death of Mr. Huskisson. Indeed, for several days afterwards the railway is still unnoticed by that journal.

[2] Mr. W. H. Lecky says: 'It is probable that Watt and Stephenson will eventually modify the opinions of mankind almost as profoundly as Luther or Voltaire.' Cf. *History of Rationalism in Europe*, Introduction, p. ix.

by Vignoles on the opening of the Liverpool and Manchester
Railway.

The story of that eventful day has been admirably told by
Dr. Smiles; but the notes now given are from Vignoles's own
pen,[1] and of circumstances of which he was an eye-witness,
and in which from his connection with this railway he felt the
deepest concern.

' *Notes on Opening Day of the Liverpool and Manchester Railway.*

' Vast crowds had assembled from a very great distance, but
there was no confusion, as the arrangements were excellent.

' The " Northumbrian " (one of the eight [2] of Stephenson's
engines used on this occasion), with the state car, and the carriages in which the directors rode, was on the south or right-
hand line; on the other were the following engines in order,
each drawing passenger waggons filled with invited guests—
viz. " Phœnix," " North Star," " Rocket," " Dart," " Comet,"
" Arrow," " Meteor."

' The procession started at twenty minutes to eleven o'clock.
The brilliancy of the *cortège*, the novelty of the sight, considera-
tions of the almost boundless advantages of the stupendous
power about to be put in operation, gave to the spectacle an
unparalleled interest.'

After further description of the triumphant progress to Park-
side—the maximum speed being twenty-four miles an hour—
Vignoles goes on to give some details of the terrible accident to
Mr. Huskisson, who, after shaking hands with the Duke of
Wellington, was about to recross the line to be out of the way
of the approach of the ' Rocket' on the opposite set of rails :—

' When the cry of danger was raised several gentlemen succeeded in regaining the state carriage, but Mr. Huskisson, who
was in a weak state of health and one of whose limbs was some-

---

[1] These notes were evidently prepared for the *Mechanic's Magazine*. Cf. the
number of that journal *in loco*.

[2] New engines made by Ericsson and Co. for this occasion—viz. ' Queen
Adelaide' and ' William the Fourth '—had been contracted for by the Liverpool
and Manchester Directors, but they had not reached Liverpool in time to be
' proved' before the day of opening.

what tender, became flurried, and after making two attempts to cross the road upon which the " Rocket " was moving, ran back in a state of great agitation to the side of the Duke's carriage, the door of which was open, and thus hung considerably over the opposite line of rails. This was owing to the great width (eight feet) of the state car, which projected over nearly half the space (of four feet) that separated the up from the down line. The door itself was three feet wide, and this was under the circumstances a fearful source of danger. The perilous position of Mr. Huskisson was immediately perceived. Mr. Littleton, M.P. for Staffordshire, had just sprung into the car, pulling after him Prince Esterhazy; but Mr. Holmes, M.P., was unable to get in, and thus he found himself standing close by Mr. Huskisson, and, seeing his bewildered condition, he cried out to him, " For God's sake, Mr. Huskisson, be firm ! "

' But the unfortunate statesman had just tremulously grasped the handle of the door, which at that moment was struck by the advancing " Rocket," and he was thrown upon the opposite rails, and his leg and thigh fearfully crushed, causing his death (at Eccles) a few hours afterwards.'

Vignoles describes the intervening circumstances pretty much as Dr. Smiles has done, except that he dwells upon the protracted delay at Manchester,[1] where the procession arrived at a quarter to three, but whence the bulk of the invited guests did not start on the return journey till twenty minutes past five.

He says :—

' The Duke of Wellington and his friends, with a train of four carriages, had departed an hour previously, and the twenty-four remaining vehicles thus left behind were now formed into one continuous line, drawn by three of the eight engines. But

---

[1] Vignoles merely refers in passing to the luncheon which was prepared at Manchester in the new warehouse sheds, but of which none of the leading persons invited to be present, nor the directors, partook. Vignoles in a letter mentions Mr. Ogden, the American Consul, as being one of those who sat down to luncheon. He also referred in after days, not unfrequently, to the fact of his own health having been drunk on the occasion, and how in responding he provoked an incredulous laugh from the company by predicting that in the course of years the railways would bring much more coal to London than could be carried by all the sea-going collier-vessels. This has been amply verified.

these had not the power to drag double their former load at a greater rate than five to ten miles an hour (only once did they for a few minutes reach twelve miles an hour), and it was past eight o'clock before we reached Parkside,[1] the scene of Mr. Huskisson's lamentable accident. Proceeding onwards—after another delay in watering the engines—we were met on Kenyon Embankment by two more engines. But for all this additional help--if it can be so called—we crept on at only snail's pace till we reached the Sutton Inclined Plane,[2] where the greater part of the company were compelled to alight, and to make use of their own legs. It was ten o'clock before we reached the station in Crown Street, having accomplished the distance of thirty-three miles in four hours and forty minutes.'

In another entry Vignoles has ascribed the delay to the foul condition of the rails, encrusted with gravel and mud from the traffic of the day, and still more from the vast crowds which everywhere surged over the track as the procession of engines and carriages passed on. The rails used on that and other early lines were known as the 'wedge-rail,' the patent of Mr. Birkenshaw. They were supported at intervals of three feet on stone blocks, weighing about four hundredweight, each block having two holes drilled in it six inches deep, with an oaken plug wedged in ; and into these were firmly driven the spikes which held the iron pedestals (or 'chairs,' as they have ever since been called) that supported the rails. On the embankments, however, the rails were laid on oaken sleepers.

A very interesting model of these wedge-rails,[3] and of the far-famed 'Rocket' engine upon them, full size, formed an attractive feature in the Liverpool Exhibition of the year 1886.

[1] A marble tablet let into the wall at this point records the melancholy occurrence.

[2] Now a greatly reduced gradient. This is not to be confounded with the inclined plane at Sutton Oak, on Vignoles's St. Helens line, spoken of on p. 144.

[3] The equal top and bottom rail was first introduced by Locke in the construction of the Grand Junction Railway.

CHAPTER XII.

Vignoles elected member of Athenæum Club—Its library—First introduction of 'atmospheric' system of traction—Letter on early railway work in U.S.A.—Vignoles's activity and readiness as consulting engineer—Value of his opinion—Proposed 'London and Paris' Railway—Visit to France— Letters from Paris--Interviews with King Louis-Philippe and M. Thiers— Accompanies latter on English tour—The project of line to Windsor, &c.— Vignoles's surveys in Gloucestershire.

1831–34.

EARLY in the year 1831 Vignoles was elected a member of the Athenæum Club, to which he continued to belong for nearly forty-five years. He seldom passed a day, when in London, without paying this club an afternoon visit, and having a chat with some of his brother-members (especially those of his own standing), by whom he was held in great esteem. There are many who can yet recall his form and figure, as he sat reading in his favourite corner, always, as dusk drew on, with an extra pair of candles when his sight began to grow dim. He greatly prized the privileges of the valuable and comprehensive library of which this institution is justly proud; and he had the highest esteem for the principal officers, especially the secretary, Mr. J. Claude Webster, and the well-informed and courteous librarian, Mr. Hall, who predeceased Vignoles (by four months) in the year 1875.

With regard to Vignoles's railway business in 1832–33, and up to his engagement in Ireland early in 1834, as related in the next chapter, it must be remembered that his chief work was in Lancashire on the lines spoken of in the previous chapter. These occupied a considerable portion of his time, but left him ample opportunities for visiting other parts of the kingdom, to advise as to various matters of engineering, on which his opinion was now beginning to be sought after.   He was very energetic, and an unwearied traveller, and always readily responded to each demand made upon him, so far as it was possible, with military promptness.   Thus about this time he was summoned to Ireland to give his advice to a few landed proprietors in the South and West, who were eager to promote some kind of railway communication between the towns of Cork, Limerick, and Waterford, a scheme entirely premature then, but which took shape some twelve years later, as will be related in its proper place.

He was also consulted by the Earl of Rosse as to a proposed canal from Birr (Parsonstown) to the Shannon, along the course of the Bresna Valley.   He made a stay of two days with that nobleman, who entertained him hospitably at the Castle, and held long conferences with him as to the navigation of the river Bresna and other local improvements.

An incident which occurred just after the conclusion of this visit may be told here, as illustrative not only of Vignoles's activity and promptness in all such emergencies, but of the high value which was already set upon his capability as a Parliamentary witness in the railway contests that had become so frequent, and which were such potent factors in deciding the fate of early engineering projects.

His journal says :—

'On July 2 (1832) received a sudden and urgent summons to London, whilst engaged on the Widnes Dock.   I immediately crossed the ferry at Runcorn, and posted thence to Northwich, thence to Sandbach.   Gig from there to Lawton Gate, where I was taken up by the "Red Rover" for some distance.   Posted on for the rest of the day and through the night.

'*July* 3.—Posted on right through to London, and arrived at the House of Lords exactly at noon, and was immediately sworn.'

Nothing can be more characteristic than this record ; but why this hot haste on the occasion we refer to ?   The question is best answered by citing a brief passage from a letter to his wife on July 12 :—

'On my return from Dublin to Liverpool I received a sudden summons to London in order to support the London and Birmingham Railway Bill, on account of Mr. Robert Stephenson having broken down in Committee, but I am now on my return to Liverpool.'

That Vignoles rendered efficient aid to the promoters in this emergency is plain from a special memorandum in his journal :—

'My acccunt furnished to the London and Birmingham Committee and *paid*:

	£	s.	d.
Posting expenses, 210 miles	21	0	0
Travelling expenses, 210 miles back . . .	5	5	0
Expenses in London	4	4	6
Seven days at 7 guineas	51	9	0
Total . . .	81	18	0 '

A few months previous to this time Vignoles had entered into negotiations with some proprietors in Staffordshire on the subject of water power. He had visited Consall, and closely inspected all the hydraulic machinery at Mr. Leigh's works, and he refers to the matter pretty often in his journal. A month or two later, when in London, he took the opportunity of consulting his kind and firm friend Dr. Gregory on the matter, and his answer is given in the following letter :—

'Royal Military Academy, Woolwich: December 27, 1831.

'Your two letters, which reached me together last Monday morning, have remained unanswered much longer than I could wish. If I were a man of leisure I should enter with great avidity on your questions about water-wheels. It is now some years since I have paid any attention to this especial department of scientific application, so that my mind is quite off the hooks in reference to it ; and it is better to be frank and say so, than to lead you astray by an appearance of knowledge where the reality is wanting. All our books are, I think, exceedingly defective as to those matters. You should see Gray's " Mill-wright," a Scotch book; and Oliver Evans's, an American book. Neither of them contain any theory, but each may convey some useful practical hints. Evans was a fine fellow in his day, and in his way. You should see also the new edition of Belidor's "Architecture Hydraulique," by M. Navier. It will give you the best information on these subjects now possessed by the French. There is a work of M. Fabre on hydraulic machines, which contains a good deal about mills. Thus you will perceive that I have nothing to communicate but the merest hints; if they shall prove of any value I shall, however, be thankful.

'I remain, with much esteem,

'Yours very cordially,

'OLINTHUS GREGORY.'

But the most interesting of all the engineering schemes entertained by Vignoles at this epoch was the proposal made by some influential English capitalists to the French Cabinet to use their influence towards the construction of a line of railway from Paris to Havre and Dieppe, as a link in the project of improved communication between London and Paris. Vignoles had previously (in 1832) drawn up full reports to the Bureau of Ponts et Chaussées on the subject of railways in France, and this seems to have been the first step in that direction; although, as the issue of the later proposal shows, the French Government, or rather M. Thiers, could not be induced to consider seriously the great importance of the new system of locomotion, either for internal or international traffic. It was not till eight years after the circumstances detailed in the following letters that the first line of railway in the North of France was constructed by an English engineer, Mr. Joseph Locke, and an English contractor, Mr. Thomas Brassey.

Early in the year 1832 Vignoles (as we have said) had been engaged on the question of railway communication in France. The scheme was informal, and he generally alludes to the subject as the 'proposed railway from London to Paris.' The persons who sought his advice were, however, connected with the French Government, and Vignoles's diary shows that by the end of

June he had completed a preliminary report. He notes on July 6, 1832 :—

'Engaged in drawing out further particulars of public works in England, and transmitted same to the chief of the *Ponts et Chaussées* in Paris.'

But the matter slumbered till the summer of the next year, when Vignoles paid the visit to Paris which we are now about to speak of.

His course of procedure may be introduced by a brief series of extracts from his journal :—

'*Ramsgate, July* 22, 1833.—Engaged from an early hour in completing the prospectus of the London and Paris Railway. Writing a long letter to Mr. Montefiore,[1] which Mr. Peirce Mahony took up to him at East Cliffe Lodge (Ramsgate). An hour afterwards I had a long and satisfactory interview with Mr. Montefiore, when it was agreed that he should communicate with Mr. Rothschild in London.'

The day following, after first sketching a lithographic plan with his own hand, ' to be circulated privately,' Vignoles, on his return to London, visited Rothschild and other influential persons in the City, and on August 8 his diary records :—

'Wrote to the Duke of Richmond, enclosing the prospectus of the Paris Railway, and also a letter from Colonel Burgoyne. Long conferences with Mr. Cubitt[2] on the proposed railway, when it was agreed that he should be considered as engaged thereon.'

It was soon arranged by Messrs. Montefiore and Rothschild, and other capitalists who had taken up the scheme, that Vignoles should at once set out on a mission to Paris, and he accordingly left for Brighton, and crossed the Channel the next morning to Dieppe by the steamer " Mountaineer." The diary notes :—

'Ten hours in reaching Dieppe ; the weather perfectly calm and the sea smooth. Steamer had two thirty-five horse engines ; twenty-five revolutions of the paddle-shaft per minute. The

---

[1] Afterwards Sir Moses Montefiore, whose death at the age of 100 years took place in 1885.
[2] Afterwards Sir William Cubitt. This eminent engineer died in 1861.

" Dolphin " would have made the voyage in seven hours easily, probably in six.'

The cabin fare, it seems, was thirty shillings, for which now-adays one can go (second class) all the way from London to Paris. The next day he left for Rouen on the top of a diligence, which journey, he remarks, only cost him eight francs, including eighty pounds of luggage. The same evening he went on to Paris in the diligence, arriving there early in the morning of August 12.

To Peirce Mahony, Esq., London.

' Paris : August 13, 1833.

' My dear Sir, — I arrived in Paris on Sunday night, having had the advantage of one night's rest at Brighton, and another at Rouen, which I conceive to be one of the easiest journeys in equal time ever made from London to Paris, and I shall consider it as a forerunner of what may happen hereafter.

' I first visited my friend and brother engineer, Major Buissin. An hour's conference determined our mode of proceeding, and at two o'clock yesterday we saw M. le Comte le Grand, the Director General of the French Board of Works (Ponts et Chaussées), to whom I presented my credentials and the numerous printed documents which you had procured for me respecting the public works of Great Britain and Ireland, as well as the large collection of maps and drawings which I had brought over for him respecting the English railways.

' This paved the way for introducing the subject of the railway communication from London to Paris, when a very long and satisfactory interview of *an hour and a half* ensued, the result of which I will endeavour to embody in the following conclusions.

' 1. That the railway project from Paris to Calais is *not* entertained by the French Government,' and as a sequel of this conclusion that Mr Stephenson's name was not once mentioned.

' The explains the absence of any suggestion in these letters of a shorter route to be established between England and France. M. Baptiste le Grand was, it is said, about one of the most eminent engineers of that day. The

' 2nd. That the French Board of Works, acting on the strength of the hints given in my reports of last year, are now actually engaged, and their engineers are now on the ground levelling the country between Paris and Dieppe, with a view to the railway and with a branch to Rouen, and that these surveys will be finished in a few months, certainly before Christmas.

' 3rd. That the French Government almost despair of obtaining French capital for the whole of any such project, and that the shortest line to the coast must be preferred as the one most practicable from the less difficulty in raising the funds.

' 4th. That there are at present 500 passengers passing daily between Paris and Rouen—viz. 250 each way—and that the number has increased gradually of late, having been only 400 per day a year or two since.

' 5th. That the tonnage from Havre, Rouen, Gisors, and Pontoise to Paris is nearly 1,000 tons daily at the least; the official returns make 400,000 French tons annually, which is equal to nearly 450,000 tons English.

' 6th. That the whole of the 4,000,000*l*. sterling which was voted by the French Chamber last session for public works was specially appropriated to purposes named by the Chamber; but that fresh appropriations are to be brought forward for next year.

' 7th. That one-fourth of the sum voted by the French Chamber for the surveys of new lines of communication, particularly railroads, has been appropriated for the survey of the railway line from Paris to Dieppe, with branches to Rouen and Havre, now going on as stated in No. 2.

' To-morrow I am again to see M. le Grand, and on Thursday I am to have an audience of M. Thiers, the Minister of Public Instruction.

' This gentleman was to have visited England, but his journey is postponed for the present. Both M. le Grand and M. Thiers are men of public spirit and enterprise; but I am informed that it is only through M. de Montalivet that we can

year following Vignoles's visit M. le Grand was made Commander of the Légion d'Honneur, on the recommendation of M. Thiers.

succeed eventually.   He is the Minister of the Interior and a personal friend and favourite of the King, who always calls him by his Christian name (Camillus). I have, therefore, to request you will forward me without delay some introduction to him, which can only be procured from some of our own Ministry, and which I trust you will endeavour to do if possible by return of post.'

To the same.

'Paris: August 14, 1833.

' Yesterday I had a long interview with Mr. Blount, jun., who confirmed all I had been told about the scheme of Stephenson respecting the railroad from hence to Calais.   He informed me that Mr. Stephenson, jun , had gone down to Lyons to look out a line from thence to Paris ; this is another part of my original project, but one which we cannot expect to see accomplished during our lives.   However, I have gathered from another quarter the real object of Mr. Stephenson's visit to Lyons—namely, to see what could be done towards putting in order a small railway there lately opened, but whereon they had made the rails too light and the blocks too small ; and the locomotive engines furnished by Mr. Stephenson had quite knocked the road to pieces, and the directors wished to remedy the defect, either by lightening the engines or repairing the road.   Notwithstanding these disadvantages, this road was paying the subscribers 15 per cent.

' I shall not have much to write to you about until after I have had an audience of M. Thiers.   I have only to urge you to get me some powerful letter to Montalivet from some of the official persons in London, for the reasons assigned yesterday.'

To the same.

'August 15, 1833.

' Your letter of the 10th inst. has come to hand, but I have not the letter from the Duke of Richmond nor some others which I expected, and which I hope to get in a few days.

' Baron Rothschild is at Aix-la-Chapelle, and so is the British Ambassador, but Mr. Blount, jun., tells me that the Secretary of the Embassy will be very serviceable, and that I must present the letter to him.

'I will avail myself of the Duke of Richmond's hint. I know the country very well, and the railroad might be made for 10,000*l.* or 12,000*l.* a mile very easily, particularly with the assistance of the Dukes of Richmond and Norfolk, who are still the principal landowners on that line also. [This reference is no doubt to the English South Coast line spoken of in Chapters IX. and XVIII.]

'My letter of Tuesday will have anticipated what you have stated as to his Grace's objections in other respects, and I hope you will show it to him and endeavour to send me the letter for M. Montalivet.

'I have nothing to add to my last two letters at present except that every person here to whom I have mentioned the matter views it favourably. I have seen Hottingner, the banker, on the matter.'

To the same.

'Paris: August 20, 1833.

'I have been working very hard since I wrote last, and hope before I leave Paris to get such written and official documents from the French authorities as will satisfy you and our friends also on the matter.

'Owing to some political movements my appointments to see M. Thiers have been put off from time to time, but I have now a certain interview for to-morrow at half-past ten, when I will write you the result.

'Your letter for me from the Duke of Richmond to Lord Granville only reached me the night before last. I have seen Aston, the Secretary of Legation, who, in the absence of Lord Granville, will introduce me to Montalivet. I have hopes also of seeing the King. I have seen M. de la Hachette,[1] Baron Prony,

---

[1] De la Hachette was then only in the beginning of his fame as a French *littérateur*, being at this time thirty-two years of age. He afterwards published (amongst many other works) a *Bibliothèque des Chemins de Fer.* Baron Prony was the architect of the beautiful bridge over the Seine near the Place de la Concorde. He was made engineer in-chief to the Republic

and Girard, the three most influential scientific men and
engineers in France, who have all promised to support the
measure when it comes before them officially, as it will as a
matter of course.

'I am to dine to-day with M. le Grand to meet a large party
of official people. I have also engagements for the rest of the
week. Among others, I have seen the Count Rambuteau, the
Préfet (Lord-Lieutenant) of the metropolitan district, who
approves of the scheme.'

To the same.

'August 21, 1833.

'I have just returned from a two hours' audience with M.
Thiers, the Minister, and I find your letter of Sunday. I am to
return to dine with him at six, and I have just time in the
interval to give you an account of the interview, which I must
premise was of the most favourable character.

'I was introduced by M. le Grand, who had paved the way
for my reception, and the conversation began by a full explanation on my part of the system of public works in England, as
well as of the manner of obtaining Acts of Parliament, and
monies from the English Government by way of loan. We
then entered into the details of the system of internal communication in England, and especially on the rivalry between canals
and railroads. Many other subjects were started, which I have
not time to write by this post. M; Thiers will introduce me to
M. Montalivet and also to the King.

'We have thus far concluded: That the French Ministry
will make the whole of the surveys at the Government expense,
and procure an Act of Incorporation for the Company by next

in 1791, and in the same year he produced his *New Trigonometrical Tables,*
adapted to the Decimal Division of the Circle, which remains an enduring
m nument of his industry and skill. He died in 1839. M. Pierre Simon
Girard was in the highest rank of French engineers. After some years spent
in examining and improving the bed of the Nile, he was called upon by
Napoleon Buonaparte to form a navigable canal from the river Ourcq to
Paris, to augment the water supply of that city—a formidable undertaking,
which occupied eighteen years. At the time of Vignoles's visit M. Girard had
been made Chevalier of the Légion d'Honneur. He died in 1836.

December; that they will grant the powers to a mixed corporation of English and French capitalists, without putting the matter up to biddings in their usual manner; and that they will grant every encouragement possible. My next suggestion was that the French Government should make a grant or loan, which I have every reason to believe will be acceded to as far as the Ministry can pledge themselves; but we shall discuss this matter again this evening, and I will write you thereon more fully to-morrow.

'I shall also avail myself of Mr. Blount's hint about iron coming in free of duty. I hope you will press him more strongly on the subject of the railway on the other side.

'The good people of Paris look upon the railway scheme with great interest; and I am assured in all quarters that if it becomes a Government question, and a few leading English capitalists give the tone, there will be no difficulty in inducing the French to come forward largely; but they must take the tone from the English people.'

To the same.

'August 22, 1833.

'I wrote you a few hurried lines yesterday in the short interval between my two long interviews with M. Thiers, the French Minister, and I will now endeavour to give you a more deliberate account of what I consider the results concluded upon in the long conference of last evening.

'After the dinner, which you know in France occupies but a short time, we entered again into the consideration of the railway communication between Paris and London. The question of its great importance in all the relations we have ourselves considered was at once admitted; and the other points—of surveys, grant of act or charter, incorporation, and power to take land, &c.—were at once undertaken to be made by the French Government. We then proceeded to the more important matter of how far a new mode (to the French) of encouraging public works by loans or grants would be palatable to the Chamber of Deputies; and it was a long time before

I could bring Thiers to fully understand that no English
capitalists would embark in the scheme unless the French
Ministers promised to come forward with a grant, or at least
a loan of not less than one-third, and rather the one-half, of the
estimated expense of the railway from Paris to Dieppe. I had
on my side M. le Grand, who is not only celebrated as an ad-
ministrator, but, being highly educated and having practised as an
engineer, it follows that his opinions, particularly when strongly
urged, have great weight ; and M. le Grand, as I know both from
himself and from the private communications of Hachette and
Baron Prony (for whom Dr. Gregory sent me letters), has set
his heart upon this railway, and I think M. Thiers would be
glad to seize so striking a scheme to make himself popular.
Besides Le Grand, there was present M. David, the head of the
Commercial Department (an office similar to the one held by
Mr. Poulett Thompson), and another of the heads of departments. Before leaving I took Le Grand on one side and desired
him to press M. Thiers to come to a conclusion on the subject.
M. Thiers has appointed me to be with him again to-morrow on
the subject as early as eight, and, after having discussed the
matter with him *alone*, to take breakfast with some of the heads
of departments. In the interim he will sound certain parties
to know how far the King or royal family may be disposed to
unite with the measure ; and, at all events, I think I shall be
presented to the King on Saturday.

'Lord Granville is at Aix, as also Baron Rothschild. I will
see the latter's nephew, but I fear nothing can be done by me
in that quarter ; and even if I succeed to the utmost with the
French Government it will require Mr. Montefiore's personal
conference with the Baron to bring the matter about ; and the
sooner you begin to hint this to Mr. Montefiore the better, as
I am certain nothing whatever will be effected here by any but
those who can get confidential admittance to the *sanctum sanc-
torum* of Baron Rothschild.[1]

---

[1] Mr. J. Sebag Montefiore (who has favoured the writer with these letters
of Vignoles) remembers a remark of Baron Rothschild (grandfather of the
t Lord Rothschild), made to his uncle, the late Sir Moses Montefiore.

' Mr. Aston, the Secretary of the English Embassy, has been very kind, and has promised to do what he can for me. I have also interested General Bertrand. The object of my visit is already whispered in some of the highest circles of society here, and obtains the most favourable reception. I am assured, if the French Government grant a loan, or promise to do so, that there will be no want of capital from the Paris bankers. The people at Rouen and Dieppe would also largely contribute ; but, after all, the lead must be taken by the English capitalists.

' I must not omit the most important part of what I have to communicate—viz. an official invitation from M. Thiers to accompany M. le Grand, M. David, and himself on a tour of inspection of all the principal works in France. I should not hesitate a moment but for the pledge I have given your friend, Mr. John Drew Atkins, of Cork, to be there on September 2. I told M. Thiers of my engagement, and he was good enough to say he would put off his journey for a week if I could get back in time. They would leave Paris on the 10th of next month, and the first point would be to accompany the King on the long-talked-of visit to Cherbourg. For the moment I have determined to come to London, as I had originally fixed, and if I can persuade one of the engineers of my acquaintance to take my place at Cork and you can pacify Mr. Atkins for the exchange, I will accept the invitation.'

To the same.

'August 23, 1833.

' I have yours of the 21st, delivered exactly forty hours after its departure from London ; thanks to the new Post Office arrangements for expresses.

' It is with the utmost satisfaction I have to announce to you that after four hours' interview with M. Thiers this morning, from eight to twelve, he has fully concluded to do all I have proposed.

It was to the effect 'that what both English and French *royageurs* cared most about was not the distance by land to be traversed between London and Paris, but to obtain the *shortest sea-passage.*'

'It is really astonishing to remark the lamentable ignorance which exists in the minds of all the principal functionaries of France relative to the public works of Great Britain, as well as of the manner in which our Government gives assistance and encouragement to them.

'I first attacked M. Thiers on the great honour which would attach to his name as the promoter of such an undertaking, and the immense popularity it would bring to the Government, particularly if the King and the royal family subscribe to it. I pointed out the effects the communication would have on the political, commercial, and social relations of the two countries ; and I then argued that the success of this measure would give an impulse to many similar works in France, particularly towards Lyons, Bordeaux, and perhaps Lille ; hinting also at the ultimate advantage in a military point of view, which would enable the army to be stationed centrally and yet troops be carried by rapid movements without fatigue to parts of the kingdom threatened by commotion or invasion. M. Thiers at last gave in to my suggestions, and has promised, upon my writing him an official letter stating my conditions, that he will reply thereto *officially*, letting the letter pass through the hands of M. Talleyrand, the French Ambassador in London. I am to receive from him on quitting Paris a letter of introduction to Prince Talleyrand, to confer with him on the subject ; and we are to present to him the principal people concerned in promoting the measure. The terms are what I wrote you yesterday—viz.:

' 1st. That all the necessary surveys and plans and all preliminaries of that kind shall be made at the expense of the Government, they advising with the English engineers as to the principle on which the railway shall be constructed.

' 2nd. That the Government will undertake in December next, at the meeting of the Chamber, to pass an Act incorporating the company to make the railroad from Paris to Dieppe, having a branch to Rouen, with the assurance of no interference from any other parties.

' 3rd. That the Government will recommend to the French Chamber either a loan or grant of at least one-third, and as much more as may hereafter be arranged, of the amount of the estimates of the railway in France.

'4th. That they will use their influence in raising among the capitalists of France at least one-third of the estimate, looking to the English capitalists for the balance. . . . .

' M. Thiers is to see the King to-day and explain all matters to him, and on Sunday I am to be presented and am to have the honour of a private audience with his Majesty Louis-Philippe. It is further arranged that after the King's return from Cherbourg M. Thiers, the Minister of Public Works, M. le Grand, the Director-General, another official officer, and myself are to make an inspection of the principal harbours, canals, and roads of France, including their solitary railroad near Lyons. About the first week in October, M. Thiers will come to Dublin, thence he will go to Liverpool and Manchester, see the Menai Bridge and the other great works, then to the iron manufactories, and thence to London, where he will spend a day or two and see M. Talleyrand and confer with him. I am particularly invited to attend them; or rather M. Thiers comes over at my special request and on my promise of accompanying him as interpreter and *cicerone.*

' I hope to be with you on Wednesday, but I am not quite sure, and I should like to have time to fix something with you, and to write out a new prospectus which will embody all the new lights and information I have acquired. I shall ask M. Thiers's permission to make known the result of our arrangements, without waiting for the formal letter to Talleyrand. In the meantime, let me suggest that you should at once see the Duke of Richmond and get him to talk to Talleyrand. Mr. Aston, in the absence of Lord Granville, has broached the subject to the Duc de Broglie. You should see Lord Palmerston.

' I think the only effectual way of getting the Baron (Rothschild) to join will be to induce Mr. M. Montefiore to take a voyage to Aix to confer in person with him; and when the Baron finds how much this matter is patronised by the French Government, and that there are English capitalists ready to pour in their funds, I think he will not like to be the last in the field.'

[The original of this letter, sent to M. Thiers, was written in French.]

'Paris: August 23, 1833.

'Sir,—I have the honour of submitting to your Excellency a statement of what I have already been permitted to explain personally on the subject of a railway communication between London and Paris *viâ* Brighton and Dieppe.

'Referring to the prospectus which M. le Grand laid before you in its translated form, I beg to state that the capitalists of London are prepared to apply at once for an Act of Parliament authorising the construction of the railway from London to Brighton, the surveys for which are now nearly completed. In this Act the Loan Commissioners of England will be authorised to lend money to the English company on the usual terms and in the manner I have already had the honour of submitting to your Excellency.

'The English capitalists will also undertake the establishment of a set of steam packets between Brighton and Dieppe of such power as will reduce the time of transit to seven or eight hours on the average.

'A large amount of English capital is also ready to be brought forward in aid of the French capitalists for filling up the subscriptions for forming the railway from Paris to Dieppe, with a branch to Rouen, on the understanding that the French Government will undertake the surveys, inquests, &c., in France, will procure the Act of Parliament, and recommend to the Chamber of Deputies a loan of at least one-third of the estimated expense. Also that the French Government will use their influence with the capitalists at Paris, Rouen, Dieppe, and other points on the line, to contribute funds to this undertaking ; with the hope also that the members of the royal family of France, in their individual capacities as possessors of disposable means, will unite with the French and English subscribers.

'On receipt of your Excellency's official answer to this communication, a meeting of the capitalists will be held to form the detailed features of the measure, and to confer with Prince Talleyrand.

'According to the standing orders of the British Parliament, all the surveys and detailed plans, sections, and estimates for the line from London to Brighton must be lodged on or before the 1st November next; which will be undertaken to be done, and the Bill presented to the British Legislature the day after the meeting of Parliament next Christmas.

'I have the honour, &c.,

'CHARLES VIGNOLES, M.I.C.E., F.R.A.S.

'4 Trafalgar Square, London.

'To his Excellency M. Thiers, Minister of Public
Works and Instruction, &c., &c., Paris.'

To P. Mahony, Esq., London.

'Paris: August 25, 1833.

'My dear Sir,—After a great dinner of ceremony at the Minister's yesterday, where I met most of the principal attachés and heads of departments and the leading engineers, I went about nine o'clock with M. Thiers to the King's evening party at St. Cloud, which is about five or six miles from Paris, and had the honour of about half an hour's private audience with Louis-Philippe.

'The King assured me that he felt the warmest interest in the matter, and would support the measure to the utmost. His Majesty told me that he would take a personal interest in it, as would also the other members of the royal family; and he desired M. Thiers to pay every attention to have the matter brought in the strongest possible manner before the Chamber of Deputies, with a proposal for a loan or grant after the manner of the public works in England, with which his Majesty was quite familiar. He told me he was convinced that it would be exceedingly profitable to subscribers, but that it was not possible in his mind to measure the importance of the affair in its political relations. He mentioned as a matter of personal interest that he had a *château* close to Dieppe, and all the royal family were fond of bathing; and that when four hours would take the Parisians to Dieppe, it would become as fashionable a watering place as Brighton. He dwelt on the necessity of having very powerful steamers.   In fact, it is impossible for me to convey to you in writing the warmth and even eagerness of his manner for the promotion of the scheme.

'I have not quite fixed a time for leaving Paris.   I had thought of going to Dieppe to-day to cach the steamer which sails for Brighton to-morrow morning at seven o'clock ; but the Minister has again sent for me, and as the Post Office closes on Sunday at one o'clock I merely scribble this to show you the extent of my success.

'Yours with great regard,

'CHARLES VIGNOLES.'

[M. Pierre David was a well-known diplomatist under the Empire, and after the Restoration was entrusted by M. Talleyrand with several important missions to Naples, Smyrna, and Greece. He died in 1846.   The Duc de Broglie was at this time Minister of Foreign Affairs.   He was the son of Claud-Victor Prince de Broglie, who had been guillotined in 1794.   He was married to the daughter of the celebrated Madame de Staël; his wife died in 1838.   Her husband occupied a prominent place in the Republican Government of 1848, but retired into private life after the *Coup d'Etat* of Louis Napoleon in 1851.]

Soon after his return to London, M. Thiers, accompanied by Count le Grand and others of his suite, arrived in England, Vignoles meeting them at Dover.   On the morning of September 7 they posted to Chatham, and called on Colonel Pasley at Brompton Barracks, thence proceeding to Woolwich.   The diary states :—

'From Blackheath went to the Thames Tunnel, and after an inspection of this work accompanied the party to Mivart's Hotel. Afterwards went with the Préfet of the Department of the Pas-de-Calais over a part of London, and in the evening saw him off by the Dover mail.'

Vignoles now gives an interesting account of a tour he made with M. Thiers.   On September 9 his diary says :—

'This night left town with M. Thiers and M. David on a tour of inspection of the public works of England.

'*September* 10.—Reached Birmingham about noon. Visited the establishment of Sir Edward Thomason, also the rolling, slitting, and wire mills. Afterwards proceeded to view Mr. Telford's great excavation on the old Birmingham Canal. Thence through Dudley to Mr. Foster's works at Stourbridge, and afterwards proceeded through the night to Wolverhampton, Shrewsbury, and Oswestry.

'*September* 11.—Arrived about noon at Bangor. Visited the Menai Bridge and approaches. Afterwards went over the grounds and residence of Mr. Dawkins-Pennant, of Penrhyn Castle. In afternoon examined bridge at Conway, and on through the night to St. Asaph, Holywell, and Chester, arriving at Birkenhead long after midnight.

'*September* 12.—Crossed over to Liverpool and inspected all the docks—the works of Mr. Bury—and the Leeds and Liverpool Canal termination. Went on the Exchange, and then called on the Mayor. Visits to M. Thiers from many gentlemen, and particularly the railway directors. Inspected Mr. Forrester's works, the Wapping station, the great tunnel, and went by railway to the foot of Sutton Incline. Also on the St. Helens Railway to Widnes. Returned to Liverpool, and in evening went with M. Thiers and M. David to the Mayor's dinner.

'*September* 13.—Left Liverpool by the first train. Inspected the station at Manchester, particularly the coal, cotton, and dry goods warehouses, also the canal termination, and the warehouses there; went to the spinning mill of Birley and Kirk, *but we were refused admittance*! After *déjeuner* left Manchester for Congleton, and saw the silk-spinning and weaving. Then on to the Potteries and inspected Mr. Meigh's establishment, also Mr. Wedgwood's at Etruria. Supped at Newcastle, and proceeded through the night to Stone, Stafford, and Wolverhampton. There saw the flowing of the metal from the blast furnaces. Thence through to Birmingham.

'*September* 14.—Reached Warwick early this morning and viewed the Castle. Afterwards posted rapidly to London, arriving before seven in the evening. Dined with M. Thiers, and afterwards went with M. David and M. Delmer to view the streets of London by gaslight.'[1]

The next day Vignoles accompanied some members of M. Thiers's staff to places in the neighbourhood of the metropolis, interviewing Mr. Clark, the engineer of the West Middlesex Waterworks at Richmond, and afterwards examining the mode of supplying the private houses in London with water, a subject of considerable interest at the time to the visitors from Paris, who were deliberating as to the best method of providing similar accommodation for their own capital. The last day of their visit is noted as follows :—

' Conferences with the French deputation and Mr. Palmer on the prospectus of the London and Paris Railway.[2] With M. Thiers to see the Spitalfields silk-works, the East India Company's warehouses, the Custom House, the Treasury, &c. Lunched at the London Tavern.

' Procured several Acts of Parliament, reports, &c., and in evening dined with M. Thiers and his staff, and at night saw them off in their carriages on the route to Dover.'

An amusing passage from Vignoles's ' Presidential Address ' many years later may be given here as a humorous summary of M. Thiers's visit :—

'. . . . Mr. Vignoles (said the accomplished statesman), I am infinitely obliged to you, and I think you a very clever fellow; but, do you know, I did not believe a word of what you told me (in Paris) before I came over, and even now I cannot see the great advantages you were constantly dwelling on. You have good canals, but very small, and ours in France are much superior. As for your roads,[3] they are very good, but I have

---

[1] Vignoles to the end of his life pronounced the word as he spells it here.

[2] Up to 1842 the total length of the lines sanctioned by the French Government only amounted to a little more than six hundred miles. The authorities then began to regulate subventions on a better system, and in that year alone concessions were granted for upwards of fourteen hundred miles; and rapid progress in railway constructions soon began to cover France with a network of useful and profitable lines. The first concession to any railway company from the French Government was in 1823. It was a line of twelve miles, from St. Étienne to the Loire : a tramway no doubt.

[3] M. Thiers could hardly have said as much now under our present manage-

not met a merchandise waggon on them in the whole course of our journeys! As to railways, I do not think them suited to France ; and, as to your vaunted posting, we go quite as quickly in my own country.'

' Perhaps,' added Vignoles, ' this last remark was not to be wondered at, as M. Thiers had insisted on bringing over to England his own heavy lumbering vehicle, quite *à la* Louis Quatorze, with immense lamps, like the old Paris reverberators, at the four corners on the top of the carriage, which also carried heavy imperials, and eight or nine persons, outside and in, requiring six horses most of the way.'

The result was that M. Thiers, on his return, made several violent speeches adverse to the introduction of railways ; and thus the benefits to France of that new mode of progress were postponed for eight or ten years.[1]

Early in the year 1834 Vignoles was occupied in the consideration of various English projects in the engineering world, on which he was either actually engaged or concerning which he was consulted by the promoters.

Amongst other enterprises he had taken a very active part in the contemplated London and Windsor Railway, with an extension to Reading and the West. He made a personal survey of the country to be traversed, and prepared comparative estimates of this and of the rival line proposed by the younger Brunel ; and in due time gave his evidence in committee, when the struggle had reached the Parliamentary stage. His diary is full of interest with reference to his constant journeys of inspection in Berks and Gloucestershire, posting here, riding there, and walking for miles over any difficult country where a choice of lines presented itself.

ment of highways. They are not to be compared to any of the great *chaussées* in France or Germany, which are not only (like many of our own) well laid out, but also (unlike ours) admirably kept up.

[1] When the first great trunk line from Paris to Orleans was made by Mr. Locke, many years later, English ' navvies ' were brought over by the late eminent contractor, Mr. Thomas Brassey. It was then (as Mr. Locke tells us) the French bystanders used to exclaim : ' Mon Dieu ! les Anglais, comme ils travaillent !

But it must suffice here to take one page only, that of March 29, 1834, by which it is clear that he then foresaw what has only recently been carried out—the necessity of crossing the Severn at Sharpness Point :—

'Explored the line from Stanley Park to Sharpness Point. by threading the lanes, &c., surveying the situation, and the probability of forming a passage across the Severn, which appears quite feasible with a bridge of twenty arches, each of 130 feet span, with suitable piers. The roadway to be elevated about twenty feet above the level of high water spring-tides. Probably a drawbridge on each side. If a rocky bed is to be found, I think—at a rough guess—such a bridge might be constructed for a moderate sum.'

A few years ago the Midland Railway Company erected a noble bridge over the Severn at this point, at a cost of about 200,000*l*. There are twenty-two arches, the widest of these having 327 feet span. There is a swing bridge 200 feet wide over the Gloucester Ship Canal, which has its terminus at Sharpness, on the left bank of the estuary. The length of the railway bridge across the stream is 4,162 feet, the roadway being 70 feet above high-water mark.

In the matter of the railway project Vignoles was considering in 1834, a compromise was eventually effected between the promoters of the rival schemes, and in the next session he gave evidence in favour of Brunel's line, by which the inhabitants of Windsor were able to find entire satisfaction in a branch from Slough, leaving them in their much-desired isolation from the main line.

The Great Western Company, however, adopted the idea, which (according to Vignoles's diary) was originally started by the rival scheme—viz. to have their terminus at Paddington instead of Brompton or Vauxhall, as they at first intended.[1]

---

[1] The writer has, however, been assured by a competent authority that the circumstances which led to the selection of Paddington as the terminus were purely accidental, and that the original intention of the Great Western Railway Company was to join the London and Birmingham line at Euston, the tunnel near the terminus being widened for the purpose.

CHAPTER XIII.

Dublin and Kingstown Railway.

1832–34.

In April 1832 Vignoles received his first summons to Dublin by the projectors of a line of railway from that city to the old harbour of Dunleary, which at the time of George IV.'s visit to Ireland in 1821 had received the name of Kingstown.

Vignoles's diary of April 7, 1832, says :—

' I arrived here this morning, and find that Mr. Killaly, the Government engineer, has died suddenly, which leaves the way entirely free to me. Made conditional arrangements with the directors of proposed Dublin and Kingstown Railway, by which I am to be appointed their engineer at a salary of eight hundred a year ; thus superseding my old friend Stephenson, which is of itself worth a thousand more.'

A brief retrospect of local history may not be without interest here. The royal harbour at Kingstown (or Dunleary as it was then called) was begun by the elder Rennie in 1816, under an Act of Parliament authorising additional harbour accommodation at this point of the coast; Mr. Rennie having reported that it was impossible to improve the port of Dublin, so as to be fully adequate to the increasing commerce of the Irish metropolis. It was, however, deemed requisite in those days that a waterway should exist between the city and its new harbour, seven miles away, and the intention was to connect them by a ship canal from the inner basin of Dunleary Harbour to the Grand Canal Docks at Ringsend. This canal was to be twenty feet deep, to have a width of 160 feet surface, and of eighty feet at the bottom, and its total cost was estimated at little less than half a million sterling. Nothing like this amount of capital could then be raised from private

N

sources, and, as the harbour had already cost a like sum, the scheme was voted impracticable.[1]   That something in its place, however, was still thought desirable fifteen years later is evident from the fact that Rennie's son—Sir John—revived the project in 1833, after the Dublin and Kingstown Railway had been commenced, his object being to obtain an Act empowering the Irish Government to pay for the canal out of public money.

But this proposal received very little support, for in 1831 the promoters of the railway had obtained Parliamentary powers, and Mr. Alexander Nimmo had been appointed engineer.

The Act was entitled ' An Act for Making and Maintaining a Railroad from Westland Row, in the City of Dublin, to the Head of the Western Pier of the Royal Harbour of Kingstown.'

There was a clause empowering the Irish Board of Works to advance money to the company on certain conditions ; but there was also a clause—considered very formidable at the time—that in the event of the ship canal being constructed the railway company was not to be entitled to claim compensation.

The Act also restricted the width of the land to be acquired to 100 feet, except in a few places, and the two principal landowners—Lord Cloncurry and the Rev. Sir Harcourt Lees —were specially exempted from the compulsory sale of their property.

The promoters estimated that all outlay and contingencies would be covered by a capital of 150,000l., a fair proportion of which had been subscribed before going to Parliament.

Mr. Nimmo (the engineer) died in January 1832, and thereupon an urgent application was made by the directors to Mr. Telford to visit and report on the line, but he declined on the plea of ill-health.

Early in February a like request was made to George Stephenson, then at Liverpool, to which he acceded, and he visited Dublin with Mr. Joseph Locke, and examined the plans and sections.   He had an opportunity also of discussing the

---

[1] The harbour of Kingstown was not entirely completed till 1859, under Sir John Rennie, but it was available for its purpose many years earlier.

subject with Colonel J. F. Burgoyne, the chairman of the Irish
Board of Works, which body had provisionally granted the
railway directors a loan of 75,000*l.*   In March, Stephenson sent
in an estimate of something over 90,000*l.*, with an additional
sum for offices, &c., of 20,000*l.*   He also made many useful suggestions relative to the traffic with England, and, as a detail of
considerable importance, he calculated on a diminution of three
shillings per ton in the price of coal delivered in Dublin.

His report is said to have been favourably received by the
directors, but no further steps appear to have been taken ; and
on the suggestion of the Commissioners of the Board of Works
their engineer (Mr. Killaly) was appointed to make an independent report.   Before this gentleman had time to complete
his task, he died quite suddenly, and it was then the first
application was made to the subject of our memoir, as already
noticed in his journal.

Vignoles commenced active work immediately after his appointment.   He was constantly over the five or six miles of the
projected line, in company with the chief promoters, especially
Mr. James Pim, of Monkstown, who became his fast friend ;
and cordial relations continued to exist between them and
their families during many subsequent years.

On April 10 Vignoles was asked by the directors to make
a special report on the proposed line, to be laid before the
' Board of Public Works,' of which many of the most influential persons in the city were members, including Sir William
Gossett, Mr. Ottley, and Colonel John Fox Burgoyne, R.E., who
had been with Vignoles in some of his military campaigns, and
between these two officers there was maintained a life-long
intimacy.   Vignoles now became acquainted for the first time
with Mr. Dargan, afterwards the contractor for the line, in
which enterprise he won great repute for the skill and celerity
with which the works were completed ; and in many ways also
he proved himself a permanent benefactor to Dublin in subsequent years.   Vignoles drew up more than one report to the
Irish Board of Works and also to the company, the value of his
suggestions and the clearness and ability of his observations

being highly commended by both these authorities. His estimate was in close agreement with that of Mr. Nimmo, being
at least 30 per cent. higher than Stephenson's.

It might have been expected that Vignoles would recommend a broader gauge than that which had been hitherto
adopted on English railways.[1] But the narrow gauge of 4 feet
8½ inches was prescribed by the Dublin and Kingstown Act,
which settled the matter, even had any debate arisen on the
point.   At the same time there is evidence to show that
Vignoles considered the accepted gauge too narrow, and on this
head he was in accordance with Mr. Brunel, although the broad
gauge of 7 feet subsequently introduced by that eminent man
was deemed faulty in the other extreme. His evidence before
the Parliamentary Committee on the subject of ' gauges,' many
years afterwards, shows that amongst civil engineers Vignoles
then stood alone in advocating an intermediate gauge between
the ' broad ' and ' narrow,' whilst objecting to any ' break of
gauge.'[2]

Vignoles's diary, through the summer of 1832, shows how
much time and toil he expended not merely on the work of the
specifications, &c., for the contractors, but in negotiating with
the landed proprietors. His genial manners and unfailing tact
gave him many advantages in this kind of diplomacy ; and his

---

[1] The origin of the 4 feet 8½ inch gauge is said by Mr. W. Wilson, C.E., to
have been simply this : Stephenson was advised that the width of his Stockton
and Darlington line should not differ from the general measurement of the
country carts in the district. To this the engineer was quite agreeable, and
forthwith he took the required dimensions of about a hundred of the carts
used by the farmers and others in the neighbourhood. Their average width
between the wheels was just 4 feet 8½ inches, and that was the gauge generally adopted on all the early lines of railway from 1825 onwards. But this
does not account for the fact that several years earlier the colliery tramways
had been laid on the same gauge, which may have been reached by a similar
process.

[2] In 1846 Parliament forbade any alteration of the 4 feet 8½ inch gauge
in English railways constructed after that date, with a few specified excep-
tions. The Irish gauge was fixed at 5 feet 3 inches, on the recommendation
of General Pasley, R.E. The Rennies proposed a gauge of 5 feet 6 inches,
and they rightly affirmed that if then adopted no contention on the subject
would ever have arisen. Mr. R. Mallett thought that a 3 feet gauge in many
parts of Ireland would be advantageous.

friend Mr. James Pim generally left to him the chief part to
play in such matters, whilst the former was employing all his
acumen in battling with the thousand and one objections which
arose in Dublin from all sides. The commercial world in that
city seemed at the time to have very little faith in the success
of the new enterprise as a feeder of the business of the metropolis; whilst the public press, almost without exception, de-
nounced and ridiculed the scheme. But beyond all this, it is
evident that without Mr. Pim's perseverance in combating the
scruples of the Irish Board of Works, and his skill and industry
as exhibited in negotiating with them on the part of the
company, they in all probability would not have advanced the
large sum of 75,000*l.* previously referred to; and indeed the
eulogium won from that board, in their last letter on the
subject to the directors, may be taken as a personal tribute to
Mr. Pim :—

 'The Dublin and Kingstown Railway is an example of what
may be achieved by an active and spirited proprietary when
assisted by public credit.'

 Vignoles had great difficulty in obtaining the consent of the
two principal landowners already mentioned, whose property
reached to the sea-shore between Blackrock and Monkstown.
For a long time Lord Cloncurry in particular remained obdurate,
and in October 1832 he had written to the Board :—

 'I continue to believe that the proposed undertaking does
not hold out such national or other probable benefits as should
induce me to make the contemplated sacrifice.'

 But it is evident from the diary that the new engineer gave
him and Sir Harcourt Lees no rest; and he not only submitted
designs of a very ornamental character for the masonry on the
portion of the line running through their estates, but he also
had models made to illustrate the effect of this in their case, as
well as for the works on the Trinity College property through
which the railway would have to pass; and these he personally
exhibited to the respective proprietors, enforcing arguments
addressed to the ear by those which appealed to the eye. Vignoles, all through his career, was a thorough believer in Horace's

motto,[1] and spent much good money at different times in exemplifying and enforcing it.

The chief landowners at last reluctantly yielded, but not without a handsome *solatium*. Lord Cloncurry received 3,000*l.*, with fishing and bathing lodges, and a pier and harbour; the company also agreed to throw an iron latticed bridge over the cutting which severed the portion of the grounds near the sea from the rest of his lordship's demesne.

The whole of the buildings were executed in the best Italian style of architecture, and to this day travellers on the line cannot fail to notice with admiration the strength and elegance of the masonry which characterises that part of the railway works. Sir Harcourt Lees also received 7,500*l.*; all these items making necessarily formidable additions to the general estimates.

Mr. Dargan's contract for 83,000*l.* was accepted in January 1833, and the works on the whole line of nearly six miles were vigorously and rapidly carried out by this enterprising man. The exact length to the temporary station at old Dunleary Harbour was 5 miles 43 chains and 4 yards.

Fortunately the contractor made a good bargain for the iron work; some of the rails, in lengths of eighteen feet, and weighing 45 lbs. to the yard, being supplied by Messrs. Bradley at 7*l.* 10*s.* per ton.

There were very stringent clauses in Mr. Dargan's contract with the company, but these did not prevent that gentleman claiming and receiving in due course an extra sum of 26,000*l.*

Vignoles's diary relates that on one occasion, during the autumn of 1832, the directors of the Dublin and Kingstown Railway, together with Mr. Radcliffe, of the Irish Board of Works, accompanied Vignoles to England, and made a close inspection of his own two lines then in progress in Lancashire, and also of the Liverpool and Manchester Railway; the Board of this company having in the most courteous manner given permission to the directors in Dublin to lay down upon the English railway 100

---

[1] 'Segnius irritant animos demissa per aurem,
  Quam quæ sunt oculis subjecta fidelibus.'—*Ars Poetica*, 180–81.

yards of the permanent way they had adopted for their own line. This experimental line was laid, as usual, on stone blocks, according to the rigid system then in vogue, to the defects of which Vignoles soon afterwards became keenly alive. He candidly states, in a report drawn up some years later, that the cause of the breakage of rails, and of the heavy shocks resulting daily to the engines and carriages on most parts of the line, was ' the fruitless attempt to obtain a perfectly non-elastic railway.'[1]

He adds :—

'This error I have to lament in common with many other engineers, few of whom are even yet convinced of the false step taken. . . . The proximate cause is partly from the play the bar (rail) sustains throughout its whole length, by the action of the chair and block or either of them. If the chair remains fast to the block, the latter is lifted and hangs on the rails, and ultimately is rammed until its bed is too low to allow the block to take any bearing, and finally the heads of the chair pins are fairly jerked off. If the chair is loosened, the same effect takes place, and adds to the continual rattle and the wear and tear of the line.'

He further remarks :—

'The best remedy is the simple one of laying the whole line upon kyanized longitudinal timbers, and placing between each chair an iron bearing-piece.'

Vignoles always claimed to have been one of the earliest to introduce the fish-plate joint.

We must observe here that, although Vignoles had at this later date (1837) pretty well made up his mind as to the form of rail he preferred (afterwards called by his name), which dispensed with the ' chair,' he does not seem to have pressed it

---

[1] *Report to the Directors of the Dublin and Kingstown Railway,* June 1837, quoted by Mr. T. B. Grierson, C.E., of Dublin, in his admirable paper read at the Institution of Civil Engineers of Ireland, fifty years later, June 1887. Of Vignoles's candour in acknowledging his error as to the non-elasticity of the road Mr. Grierson remarks: 'It was well for subsequent railway companies that this error in the method of constructing the permanent way was discovered so soon, and that such an eminent engineer as Mr. Vignoles had the courage to condemn it.'

upon the notice of the directors; indeed, it is doubtful if any of the rolling mills had up to that time produced rails of this pattern.

. During the years 1832–33 Vignoles visited Dublin constantly, sometimes spending only a single day there, and returning by the evening boat, and again, after a short stay in Liverpool or a hurried visit to London, recrossing the Channel to the Irish metropolis. On one occasion, when speaking to the writer about the increased speed and comfort of the passage from Liverpool to Dublin fifteen years later, he remarked :—

'It is absurd to complain of an occasional rough passage! I, at one time, for six consecutive weeks spent most of my nights in the steamboat sailing between Liverpool and Dublin.'

Occasionally in the autumn season he came in for several long and stormy passages of from eighteen to twenty hours; but it was only the loss of time which troubled him, as he was always a capital sailor. He seems to have paid upwards of forty visits to Ireland in the course of the year 1832.

Vignoles naturally felt the very deepest interest in the success of the Dublin and Kingstown Railway; and on the plea of its being the first line constructed in Ireland he had some hopes that her Royal Highness the widowed Duchess of Kent, and her only daughter the Princess Victoria, now her most gracious Majesty the Queen and Empress, might be induced to go to Dublin for the purpose of opening the railway. Vignoles accordingly availed himself of his father's former connection with the Duke of Kent, and obtained a presentation to the Duchess, of which he speaks in the following extracts from his diary :—

'*July* 1, 1834.—Called on Lord Lansdowne, when he gave me a letter to Sir John Conroy.[1]

'*July* 8.—Visited Kensington Palace with Mr. Peirce Mahony,[2] when we had a long interview with Sir John Conroy

---

[1] For many years equerry to H.R.H. the Duchess of Kent. He was made a baronet by H.M. the Queen in July 1837.

[2] Mr. P. Mahony was the legal adviser of the Dublin and Kingstown Railway Company.

on the subject of the opening of the Dublin and Kingstown line.

'*July* 9.—Received a letter from Sir John Conroy, in which H.R.H. the Duchess of Kent commanded my attendance on Saturday next.

'*July* 12.—This day at Kensington Palace I had the honour of being presented to their Royal Highnesses the Duchess of Kent and the Princess Victoria. I gave a description to the Princess of the railway system, and particularly of the Dublin and Kingstown line, and I also enlarged on the probable future benefits to Ireland. H.R.H. the Duchess was pleased to allude to my late father's connection with the Duke [cf. Chapter I.], as well as to my having held a commission in the " Royals," the Duke's own regiment. No positive answer was given as to the royal party opening the railway, on account of political embarrassments.'

During the rest of this year (1834) Vignoles was closely engaged on his work in Dublin, where the directors had intended to open the railway early in October, but the works were not sufficiently advanced, and the event was postponed.

An entry of some interest is found in his journal for November 1 :—

'Went with a train of carriages drawn by a locomotive engine, and found the spring buffing apparatus of Mr. Bergin most successful—quite destroying all concussion on starting and stopping, and freeing the carriages when in motion from all unequal oscillatory movement. Tried the speed of the new engines, and went one quarter of a mile with the " Hibernian " and her tender (made by Sharp and Roberts, of Manchester), at the rate of sixty miles an hour! Mr. Bergin, on another engine, went at the rate of forty-eight miles an hour, with a carriage holding forty passengers, for three-quarters of a mile. Owing to bad coke, the " Vauxhall " engine, made by G. Forrester and Company, of Liverpool, did not attain a higher speed than thirty-six miles an hour.'

Mr. Bergin's contrivance is the subject of so much notice in the diary throughout the year, that it seems as if it must have been an original invention.   The springs and the mechanism generally were made in Liverpool, but the only patent recorded in this year having reference to the end designed is in the name of Mr. Henry Booth, treasurer of the Liverpool and Manchester Railway.   Whatever the fact of priority may be, the thing itself was so obvious an improvement that it was almost immediately adopted on every line in the kingdom. Another help to railway locomotion was the peculiar lubricating composition for carriage axles, with whose appearance we are all familiar.   A patent for this was also taken out by Mr. Booth in 1834.

It should be mentioned that a deputation from the London and Birmingham Railway, including Henry Booth and Robert Stephenson, visited Dublin in July 1836, and made a careful inspection of the structure and working of the Dublin and Kingstown line.

But another unlooked-for cause still further delayed the public opening of the line, as Vignoles records on November 7:—

' Early this morning the river Dodder, swollen by yesterday's incessant rain, overflowed its banks, and a flood rose greater than has been known for half a century.   Two wooden bridges up the country had been swept away, and, with other wreckage, came down upon the centres of the new arches of Ball's Bridge; and the upstream half of our railway bridge was lifted bodily by the weight of the great mass of timber resting upon it, the by-stream acting as a lever.   The railway itself was also much damaged by the flood rushing across it.'

In Mr. Bergin's account he states that he saw a torrent, three or feet deep in places, rushing down some of the principal thoroughfares; and that it was not without difficulty that the lives of some of the residents were saved.   A wooden bridge, suggested by Mr. William Cubitt, was rapidly constructed instead of the stone one thus swept away, and it was of course only intended to serve its purpose till a new one of some other material should be erected.   But the temporary structure stood so well that it remained in use for ten years without any repairs; and it was not till 1851 that an iron bridge resting on stone piers was designed by Mr. Gibbons, the contract being taken by Mr. William Fairbairn, of Manchester, and admirably carried out within the stipulated price—viz. 1,500*l*. One of Vignoles's most notable designs for a bridge was that over the Grand Canal Docks near Dublin, where a very handsome skew bridge on three arches was erected, the material being granite, with the spandrils and parapets of limestone. One of the local papers described it as ' a bridge of peculiar construction well known in England, but introduced for the first time in Ireland, and it is the admiration of all operative mechanics.'

Opening of Dublin and Kingstown Railway.

The actual inauguration of this first of the Irish railways took place on December 17, 1834. Vignoles's diary records :—

' This morning at nine o'clock the first train for passengers started from each extremity of the line. The opening to the public was very successful; and immense crowds continually assembled during the day, so that it was impossible to convey the numbers applying. Upwards of 5,000 persons were carried, and at times the crowds burst through the barriers. Nine trains were run from each end, and an extra one from the Dunleary station at 5.30. Six trains had nine passenger carriages, the rest eight; and all of them full to overflowing each trip. In the evening I dined by invitation with the directors at the Salt Hill Hotel, Monkstown, which was opened that day to the public.'

On Thursday, 18th, he also notes :—

' Crowds still continued to flock to the railway carriages throughout the whole of this day, and up to the hour of my departure. The directors appeared to derive great satisfaction, and it is to me a delightful reward for two years of incessant anxiety.'

On Vignoles's return to Dublin a few days later he found the traffic over his new line as brisk and regular as could be desired. From the day of opening to the end of the year they carried 35,000 passengers, the gross receipts being rather more

than 1,000*l.* The line was a success from the commencement, the shares rapidly rose in value, and the dividend on
the subscribed capital was never less than 5 per cent., and
eventually reached nearly 10 per cent. The early returns of
traffic receipts on the line compare favourably with those of that
most memorable and successful of English railways, the Liverpool and Manchester. On the Dublin line the receipts from
passenger traffic were 2,000*l.* per month on less than six miles ;
which on thirty miles, at the same rate, would amount to 10,000*l.*
per month, or largely in excess of any of the Lancashire lines.
The goods traffic on the Dublin and Kingstown line, however,
has always been a much smaller item than was anticipated.

The rails on the Dublin and Kingstown Railway were
altered to the accepted Irish standard of 5 feet 3 inches when the
line was leased to the Dublin and Wicklow Company in 1850.

A few remarks on the character of the line in its course
along the shore of Dublin Bay may add to the interest of the
narrative.

From the outskirts of Dublin to Merrion the line was carried
on an embankment, the slopes on the sea side having layers of
sods, and also the upper half of those on the land side, the
lower half being faced with stone.

Between Merrion and the now important and flourishing
town of Blackrock the line was carried on embankments built
upon the strand, the outer portion of these being formed of
indurated clay or tenacious gravel. The space intervening was
filled in with sand taken from the shore at each time of dead
low water, this sand being raised to within five feet of the level
of the rails, and then covered in with gravel, all surmounted by
the pitching and ballasting on the top. On the sea side of the
embankment a layer of granite chips, or rough shingle, mixed
with refuse tanner's bark or waste flax, was laid to the depth of
eighteen inches underneath the granite pitching. This latter was
made of large blocks, the bottom rows formed of stones each not
less than a ton weight ; and this was terminated by a rough
low parapet made of heavy stones.

This portion of the works was at first a cause of some

trouble from the sinking of the embankments between the high retaining walls. On the other side of the account an advantage, not previously in the calculation, resulted from the construction of foot-paths along the top of the sea embankments, which the directors at first intended to be used as a marine promenade, and to be lit with gas.[1] This attractive programme, however, so far as the public were concerned, was not carried out; but for all that the footpaths were of great service to the stability of the embankments, thereby helping to falsify the predictions of some morbid prophets who had foretold the destructive effects of the winter storms upon the infant railway. To this day some of the old discarded granite sleepers, with the oaken plugs and iron spikes still firmly fixed in them, may be seen in the paving of these foot-paths, the weight of the blocks adding immensely to the resistance of the whole structure against heavy seas.

By the advice of Colonel J. F. Burgoyne the parapets were materially strengthened and also raised in height, after some damage from the storm of October 1836; since which time the embankments have been well maintained, and have proved an effectual barrier against the fierce assaults delivered every winter by the stormy tides of Dublin Bay.

Beyond Monkstown the line was carried to the end of the old Dunleary Harbour, at which point a temporary station, inconvenient but inexpensive, was erected, which served till the extension[2] of the line to its present terminus, near the wharf

[1] The charge for gas supplied by the Hibernian Gas Company was 12s. per 1,000 cubic feet.

[2] This extension was strongly opposed by Sir John Rennie in the Parliamentary Committee, of which Daniel O'Connell was chairman, in the spring of 1833. On that occasion a rather severe altercation was held between this gentleman and Vignoles on the subject of the estimates, which (as reported in the Blue Book) certainly reads to the advantage of the latter, who kept his temper—no easy task for him—and whose answers are couched in a very courteous form, contrasting agreeably with the fierce onslaught made on him by the excitable orator, then M.P. for Clare, whose conduct was evidently out of harmony with the general feeling of the committee. During the sitting of a similar committee some years later, a more genial and amusing scene between the same 'combatants' was witnessed by Mr. P. Sewell, when O'Connell pressed Vignoles for an answer on some point, which the latter only fenced with, and with his usual *sang froid* skilfully evaded a direct reply.

which accommodates the mail steamboats running twice daily throughout the year from Kingstown to Holyhead. It was not till 1837 that this half-mile prolongation of the line was completed and a temporary station erected; the present terminus, a handsome and commodious granite structure, not being completed till 1853. Previously to this the Dublin and Kingstown Company had obtained powers to extend their line to Dalkey, a distance of one and three-quarter miles. This extension, completed early in 1844, acquired considerable notoriety, as the directors had been induced to lay it down on the 'atmospheric' system, which was there successfully carried out, and was an object of great interest to scientific men, who came from all parts of the kingdom, many also from abroad, to inspect the line. There can be no doubt that the success obtained in this experiment largely influenced the late Mr. Brunel to attempt a similar undertaking on a larger scale in the case of the South Devon Railway in 1844.[1]

The little line to Dalkey was altered in gauge and adapted to the locomotive system in 1856, when the Dublin and Kingstown line became the property of the Dublin, Wicklow, and Wexford Company. In 1865 the agreement was enlarged into a lease in perpetuity, the Dublin, Wicklow, and Wexford guaranteeing a fixed interest of 9¼ per cent. on the Dublin and Kingstown Original Stock, forming an annual payment of 36,000l.

But our brief notice of Vignoles's work on this earliest of Irish railways would be incomplete without speaking of the far seeing views he held on the subject of the connection between the city terminus of his line and those of other lines, which, ' in his mind's eye,' he clearly perceived.

His idea was broached in 1833, placed before the public in a maturer form in 1835, and still more completely developed in 1838, when the second Commission on Irish Railways was

At last the chairman said, ' I think, Mr. Vignoles, I may conclude that you have no intention of giving any answer to my question?' A bow and a smile formed the only response, on which a laugh ensued, which being joined in by the chairman and the witness culminated at length in general merriment.

[1] Cf. *Life of I. K. Brunel*, chap. vii. p. 139. Cf. also Ch. XVIII., *infra*.

holding its meetings in Dublin. It was a scheme for a high-level railway through the city from Westland Row terminus to Barrack Bridge, where Vignoles proposed that the central terminus should be placed, to which all the chief trunk lines entering Dublin should converge; and he predicted that there would thus eventually be performed a direct journey (by rail and steamboat), from London as a centre to the western extremity of Ireland at Valentia, which should be completed within four-and-twenty hours!

His proposal (of which we only give the barest outline) was to construct a railway running upon a grand iron colonnade from Westland Row, to be carried at the rear of the houses in Great Brunswick Street, and crossing D'Olier Street and Westmoreland Street to Aston's Quay, where it was to run along the footpath on the river-side, with one row of the supporting columns on the kerb-stone and the other rising up from its foundation on the river-bed, about twenty feet from the quay wall; the railway colonnade to terminate at the Central Station. It was an ambitious as well as a beautiful design, as the superstructure was to be of the Ionic order of architecture, the intercolumniation with thirty feet centres, and the rails at a general level of twenty feet above the streets. The project created a great sensation, and would have been highly popular in Dublin; but the expense of such a design was alone sufficient to ensure its rejection in a poor country like Ireland.[1]

Within the last three years—in November 1886—the Postmaster-General pressed strongly upon the various railway companies the importance of having their Dublin termini connected by a railway through the city, in conformity with the Act obtained in July 1884, for an undertaking termed the 'City of Dublin Junction Railways,' the purpose of which was stated to be 'to connect Westland Row with the termini of the Great Northern of Ireland and the Midland Great Western of Ireland on the north side of the Liffey.'

---

[1] In the first Report of the Irish Commissioners they say: 'We submit this plan, which would undoubtedly serve a very useful purpose, but we do not recommend its present adoption.'

The Liffey has not yet been crossed as thus proposed, but a very convenient branch line has been formed from the terminus of the Belfast and Northern Counties lines in Amiens Street to the Steamboat Quay near the Custom House, which is now the place of embarkation for the powerful express steamboats belonging to the London and North-Western Railway Company.[1]

In concluding this chapter we cannot refrain from once more quoting the words of Mr. Grierson, in his admirable and exhaustive paper already referred to:—

'It is not too much to say that but for the great courage, determination, and sound judgment of the promoters of the Dublin and Kingstown Railway, who so bravely led the way, Ireland would not have enjoyed the benefit of railways at so early a period of their history; and this fact brings out in clearer light the public spirit of these men, when we find that for exactly ten years there was no other railway in Ireland till the opening of the 'Dublin and Drogheda' in 1844; the 'Great Southern and Western' being completed to Carlow in 1846, and the 'Midland Great Western of Ireland' opened in 1847.'[2]

---

[1] Early in 1887 the writer observed in the *Times* an offer from some of the leading Dublin merchants of the sum of 35,000*l.* towards a railway connection through Dublin, between the termini of the Northern lines and that of the Dublin and Wicklow Railway in Harcourt Street.

[2] Some interesting remarks of Vignoles are found in his article on Ireland, written for the *Dublin University Magazine*, and quoted in Chapter XVII.

CHAPTER XIV.

Visits Hamburg, Hanover, and Brunswick—Proposed railways—References to Mr. Walker, Mr. Brunel, Mr. C. H. Gregory—Letters from Dr. Gregory, Sir John Burgoyne, M. Poussin, &c.—Gives evidence on various railway schemes — The Vignoles Rail—Appointed Consulting Engineer of Eastern Counties Railway—Reminiscences of this line—Rival projects of London and Brighton Railway—Early surveys in Wales and Ireland for the first Irish Railway Commission—Various letters—Professional visit to Scotland.

1835–37.

IN February 1835 Vignoles was invited to visit Hamburg and Hanover on the subject of a proposed line of railway to connect those cities with Brunswick.

The scheme had been placed in his hands a few months earlier, and a good deal of preliminary work had been accomplished by his staff towards the close of 1834.

A few friends interested in the proposed railway, including Herr Hübbe, the State Engineer of the city of Hamburg, were awaiting him when the vessel arrived, and the next morning he began a careful examination of the river banks, in order to fix on a suitable and accessible terminal site for the line.

Several days were occupied in this inspection, and it is plain that he had also in view the purpose of testing the practicability of his own proposal to cross the river by a monster railway bridge.

Many of us remember the inconvenience of this passage across the Elbe to Harburg, when the steam ferry-boat was in use ; but in 1835 *voyageurs* were at the mercy of the wind and tide, and this is well illustrated by our engineer's own experience on February 21, when he notes :—

'After clearing the harbour with difficulty, and tacking across the stream for more than an hour, we had to land on an

o

island and shelter from the storm. We got into the boat again at one o'clock, but did not reach Harburg till three o'clock P.M. Pretty specimen this of the present mode of communicating across the Elbe!'

This was when Vignoles was on his way to Hanover; and his diary shows that during several days he examined carefully the whole route, exploring most of the ground on foot, and roughing it with his son and a couple of servants.

On one of these days he notes :—

'After crossing the river at Lükmallen and procuring a guide, we got at night to Welzen. Here the people refused to take us in, and we were obliged to go on in the dark to Marzen, where we got shelter. Our own provisions and the brandy were of good service, for the people only brought us some straw to sleep on. Poor Charles's first night of bivouac!' [This was his eldest son, then in his sixteenth year, whom he was about to place at school in Germany.]

He notes also their first night in Hanover :—

'*February* 24.—Went this evening in my Court dress to attend the great party given by H.R.H. the Duke of Cambridge [1] on the occasion of his birthday. I had a very gracious reception, and was also presented to the Ministers of the Duke of Brunswick, with some of whom I had an opportunity of speaking fully on the railway business.'

During the next few days he was chiefly engaged in examining the district between Celle and Brunswick, a distance of thirty-two miles, of which route he remarks :—

'I never found a tract of country so favourable for a railway, which I believe may be made for a minimum of expense.'

Vignoles received every information at Brunswick from Colonel Pratt, the Quartermaster-General, and M. Krabé, the State Architect, but was unable to make Herr Amsberg (the Duke's principal Minister of State) a convert to his views, though he received every encouragement from the Duke himself. Eventually he found the Railway Committee of both

---

[1] Father of H.R.H. the present Commander-in-Chief. The Duke was then acting as Viceroy for King Ernest of Hanover.

Governments opposed to the direct line between Hamburg and Hanover, and a circuitous route *viâ* Lüneburg and Celle was chosen.

It is only recently that this direct railway has been made between Hamburg and Hanover, following closely the line of country so earnestly advocated by Vignoles at the time we speak of; and several years also elapsed before the inconvenience and delay of crossing the river ferry was remedied by the erection of the two large railway bridges which now span the Elbe over its northern and southern branches.

The line to Bremen, and thence by direct route to Paris, was only undertaken at the end of the Franco-German war, when the little Hanoverian kingdom had been swept away.[1]

Vignoles, on his return to Hamburg, held long consultations with the Burgomaster and the principal merchants on the subject of the improvement of the harbour and of the river navigation, over which project he spent a great deal of time in that and subsequent years. His attention later on was drawn to the same subject, more particularly after the great fire which devastated Hamburg in 1842 ; and he forwarded at intervals several reports to the authorities there, with estimates, &c., as appears from many extant letters. In most of the points on which his opinion was then sought, time has proved that Vignoles's perceptions were correct although his ideas were considerably in advance of his age.

On the eve of his return to England he was entertained at a public dinner by the principal people of Hamburg, of which banquet he gives a lively sketch.

He returned to England on March 20, and his diary for March 24 says :—

'Attended the meeting of the Institution of Civil Engineers for the first time since the election of Mr. James Walker as President.'

Another entry three days later may serve as an illustration of a good trait in Vignoles's character previously touched on—

---

[1] Five years after Vignoles's visit, a proposed railway from Hamburg to Lübeck was *vetoed* by the King of Denmark.

viz. his wish to be on friendly terms with his professional brethren :—

'Present at the examination of Mr. I. K. Brunel in Committee on the Great Western Railway Bill. On this occasion I tendered him my hand, which he accepted cordially ; thus, 1 hope, closing a long open breach, originating seven years since, in my interference with his father's work on the tunnel under the river Thames.'

There are no entries in his journal during the year of any great interest, until the first mention of his definite engagement as engineer-in-chief of the Midland Counties Railway ; and some portion of a letter from Dr. Olinthus Gregory may be given here, containing the earliest notice of this appointment of his friend. The doctor's son ' Charles,' referred to in the quotation, is the eminent engineer now so well known as Sir Charles Hutton Gregory, K.C.M.G. :—

'Woolwich Common . September 26, 1835.

' My dear Friend,—I very sincerely congratulate you on the result of your professional excursion in the Midland Counties. Your talents and reputation are rapidly working their way to eminence, and will eventually raise you, I trust, to complete independence. We all feel, and Charles not least, the great kindness of your proposals with regard to him, whether for Leicester and Derbyshire, or for the Continent. Indeed, I should avow not only regret but vexation at my inability to accept your offer, did I not feel that his engagement with Mr. Bramah will be permanently valuable to him in his profession.

' He has been well employed in the initiatory drawings ; and I think that a good acquaintance with the actual construction of machinery of various kinds, at the Pimlico works, will doubtless lay a good basis for usefulness. I am just now overwhelmed with proofs from Stationers' Hall, so you must excuse this hasty note as an acknowledgment of all your kindness, which I do indeed feel very much.

' Take care not to overwork yourself, if possible, and believe me ever, my dear friend; cordially yours,

'OLINTHUS GREGORY.'

We also give here a few extracts from two letters to his eldest son, whom he had left with a tutor at Brunswick but afterwards transferred to the care of Mr. Taylor at Hanover, where he remained about two years. The first letter is dated March 29, 1836 :—

'. . . . I hope you are going on steadily with your lessons in German, also in ancient and modern history. Your French should also be kept up, and I am glad to hear you are to take riding lessons ; but you must not omit your visits to the drill-sergeant once or twice a week.

' I am worn out with work. The chief struggle hitherto has been on the Midland Counties Railway ; but to-day the principal decision has been in our favour, and I think after Easter we shall obtain our Act of Parliament without much further fighting.

' I will write to Mr. Taylor as to your Easter holidays, but no holidays for me ! I have to make an extensive tour to look out *new* railways, and in looking after *old* ones, and probably I shall not stop more than a few hours in any one place.

' Mr. Denis, the engineer of the Nuremberg and Fürth Railway,[1] and my friend, M. Hübbe, will accompany me to Ireland. Mr. Taylor will be glad to hear that I have just despatched the first half of my report on the Hamburg Docks, and that the rest, with a general plan, and explanatory transverse sections, will follow immediately. After Easter I shall have time to finish the discussion of the improvements on the upper part of the river, also as to the inundations of the town, the forming of the steam-boat quay, &c.

' Just now I am so much overworked that I have scarcely time to eat my meals, and am every night obliged to sit up to a late hour.'

In the conclusion of this letter Vignoles mentions that he had just been appointed engineer of the ' Cork and Passage ' Railway, six miles in length.

Another letter to his son, from which we give some brief extracts, was written in December 1836 :—

[1] The first line completed in Germany.

'You are now growing older, and I hope wiser, and will understand the importance of giving serious attention to the composition as well as the writing of your letters. An engineer has always a large correspondence to keep up, and nothing more distinguishes the character and ability of a professional man than the facility and clearness with which he can express himself in letters and reports.

'I also wish you to enter into society as much as Mr. Taylor may think it good to introduce you to it. The Duke's [i.e. of Cambridge] party of the 12th will be a proper commencement for you, and I hope you will present yourself with becoming grace and propriety to his Royal Highness, to whom (if you have the opportunity) you may talk freely about railways, in which the Duke takes a great interest.'

The following extract from a letter to Vignoles about this time on the education of his eldest son will be read with interest :—

From Sir John Burgoyne to C. B. Vignoles.

'In your son Charles's new employ he will require a thorough knowledge of the precise meaning in both languages [1] of all technical terms, which I should think could not be carried too far, or into too great minutiæ.

'Every description of timber, stone, &c., as well in their first rough state as in their progress through each conversion, tools, materials, artificers' expressions and the like, should all be known to him. Dictionaries do not give these, and the sooner he commences the long operation of collecting them the better.

'A few years hence, when his collection is abundant, it will (with needful explanations) be valuable to the world at large, and bring him into prominent notice, for I imagine there is no such thing now. If he would also add the French terms, it would embrace what I have long sought for in vain.'

---

[1] Referring to English and German. Vignoles at first thought of placing his son on one of the Continental lines, but eventually found him employment in England, and afterwards he was appointed one of the engineers on the Shannon Commission.

Vignoles also kept up about this time a brisk correspondence with Major Poussin, the eminent French engineer; and the extracts here given are from letters written by that gentleman to the subject of this memoir in 1835–36 :—

'My recent works on internal improvements in this my native country have been well received, and also consulted by those in office, as they were advised to refer to me for practical counsel; but notwithstanding the reputation I have already acquired in America, the ' hierarchy ' here are very shy of their patronage. The grand scheme so long talked of to connect London, Paris, and Brussels, has again been brought to light by your distinguished countryman, Dr. Bowring; but before he had fully unfolded his plans he was obliged to leave Brussels to return to his Parliamentary duties.

' At the first association for that object I was promised to be the engineer of the Company.

' Do you know that I despair completely of having anything to do for our French people? The corporated engineers of this country will not suffer any one who has not received the baptism of their sacred congregation even to swim through the waters of our common country.

[This last phrase is, no doubt, an allusion to Vignoles being also of French descent.]

' Let me know what you will next do, now that your railroad from Dublin to Kingstown is completed. You, on the other side of the Channel, do not remain so long contemplating what is better to be done, but you go to work at once. In fact, *you* say, " I have been doing so-and-so; " here *we* are obliged to say " I wish I could do so-and-so." '

We now give two or three detached earlier entries from Vignoles's diary of 1836 before relating in detail his more serious engagements :—

' *January* 5, 1836.—We were three hours going from Liverpool to Manchester, owing to the slippery state of the rails.

' Attended public meetings at Manchester to-day, and at Sheffield yesterday, on behalf of a proposed line of railway between these two towns. Lord Wharncliffe was in the chair.'

'*March* 4–8.—Engaged several days in examining the proposed "Cheshire Junction Railway." Carefully looked at both lines from Manchester to Stockport; branch lines from Macclesfield Canal to Cheadle, and also the main line from the banks of the Mersey to where it meets the Grand Junction Railway at Crewe.'

By way of illustration of the value of Vignoles's services as a witness we may notice some entries in the same month :—

'*March* 9.—I was invited to support Mr. Robert Stephenson's line (Western entrance) to Brighton. Remuneration to be one hundred guineas retaining fee and ten guineas a day in committee. The same for attendance and evidence on the following—viz. Cheshire Junction Railway, Cheltenham and Great Western Railway, London and Blackwall Railway, Dublin and Drogheda Railway.'

In an entry for May 12 he notes :—

'Mr. Gibbs called to inform me that the directors of the Croydon Railway wish to retain me as their consulting engineer. Received an official letter from the secretary to the same effect. The preamble of the Eastern Counties Railway passed the House of Commons.'

'*May* 20.—Agreed with Mr. Gibbs to adopt my flat-bottomed form of rails for the Croydon line, to be laid on wooden "sills" 8 × 5 longitudinally, and tied transversely every five feet.'

With reference to the entry concerning the original Eastern Counties Railway in the diary of May 12, a brief account is all that we can give here of this line, which was projected in 1834, Vignoles being the consulting, and Mr. John Braithwaite the acting engineer. The chairman was Mr. Henry Bosanquet, with a strong board of directors, including Sir Robert Harvey, of Norwich, who was also vice-chairman. Mr. Tite (afterwards Sir William) was the surveyor for the Company, and Mr. J. C. Robertson the secretary.

The capital was 1,600,000*l.* for a line from Whitechapel to Norwich and Great Yarmouth. Not a single tunnel would be required, nor any embankment more than thirty feet high, and the steepest gradient would be less than 1 in 400.

The largest number of shares was taken in Liverpool, and two proprietors from that town were on the directorate; but we can see from an observation of Vignoles, found in his diary for January 30, 1836, that by that time financial difficulties had made their appearance. At the first half-yearly meeting in July of the same year, many of the shareholders indulged in very sanguine anticipations, but the chairman was satisfied with a more sober view of the future, remarking: 'The Board consider it quite enough at present to launch our vessel, but we will come to you again when we feel we want more of the sinews of war. Our motto shall be—*Festina lente!*'[1]

THE 'VIGNOLES RAIL.'

The entry in Vignoles's diary for May 20, 1836, is of considerable interest, as being the first mention of an improvement —or at any rate a modification—in the form of rail for the permanent way, which he first introduced.[2]

Other entries show that at this time the matter here referred to was constantly before him, and that he gave to it very earnest and serious consideration. Indeed, it may be said that a decision as to the best form of rail had then become a subject of general importance, and, together with the kindred question of 'sleepers,' was largely occupying the attention of engineers. Vignoles's diary shows that at first he was disposed to adopt the form of rail he describes as 'equal top and bottom, and equal sides,' with 'longitudinal sleepers.' This last idea he seems to have retained (in common with Mr. Brunel) in subsequent years; and indeed its superiority, both for ease of

---

[1] Nothing is said in the prospectus about a line to Cambridge; but a ' Norwich and Leicester Branch' (which would not be far short of the original Eastern Counties line in length) had been surveyed by the spring of 1836; Mr. Braithwaite undertaking the portion from Norwich to Peterborough, and Vignoles that from Peterborough to Leicester. These details are taken from some early documents in possession of the Great Eastern Company which they have recently reprinted.

[2] It has not been thought necessary to give here an illustration of this form of rail, so well known to engineers. A drawing of it (from Vignoles's pen) will be found in Chapter XV., in the account of the Midland Railway.

travelling and security, is amply borne out at the present day. But at the time we speak of Vignoles had definitely fixed upon the form of rail of which a rough sketch will be found in the next chapter, and which has been almost universally adopted on the Continent and in many British Colonies, also largely in India and in the United States of America. In Europe it is known as the 'Vignoles rail,' but across the Atlantic it is generally termed the 'American rail.'

RIVAL PROJECTS FOR LONDON AND BRIGHTON RAILWAY.

In the early summer of 1836 Vignoles was actively engaged, in common with other engineers of high repute, in seeking to establish railway communication between London and Brighton, on which subject his diary has many notes. In June 1836 a passage in his journal says :—

'The Committee of the House of Commons decided by twenty-nine to sixteen in favour of Robert Stephenson's line to Brighton.'

There were no less than four of these rival lines suing for Parliamentary favour in this session, besides the scheme which Vignoles himself had in some measure prepared, and which was (with the others) laid before the Town Council of Brighton, but which was not sufficiently matured to be brought before a Parliamentary Committee.

These four lines were as here stated ; viz. :

1. Sir John Rennie's, 'the Direct' line, from Ken-
   nington Common to Park Crescent   .   .   . 47 miles
2. Mr. Gibbs's, with Western entrance at Brighton, to
   start from South-Western line at Vauxhall . . 51 ,,
3. Mr. Cundy's, ' the line without a tunnel '   . . 54 ,,
4. Mr. R. Stephenson's .   .   .   .   .   . 53 ,,

This first decision (noted in Vignoles's diary) was by no means final ; but the case had been pretty well threshed out in Committee, and Vignoles had given very strong evidence in favour of Stephenson's line, in company with some of the ablest members of the profession, including George Stephenson.

The struggle between the rival lines was renewed in the

House of Lords, where Stephenson's proposals were again sub-jected to a fierce opposition by the competitors. His project was weakened very much in the estimation of the Brighton supporters by its intended terminus at the west end of the town, the approach being from Shoreham. Vignoles, as we have seen, had a high opinion (to which Stephenson also inclined) of the capabilities of Shoreham to be the port of embarkation for Dieppe; whilst Rennie was more disposed to favour Newhaven, as being nearer to the east, and vessels entering it would have more advantage from the prevailing westerly winds.

It is worth remark that Stephenson seemed never to have heard of Vignoles's surveys of this part of the route in 1825; although Mr. Bidder [1] showed his acquaintance with them.

Stephenson's line was intended to start from Nine Elms, using the South-Western line as far as Wimbledon. Thence it was to go by Epsom and Dorking to Horsham; and from that town to West Grinstead, and to reach Shoreham on the east side of the valley of the Adur; thence by Kingston to West Brighton.

Sir John Rennie's line was at first planned to utilise the South-Western line as far as Wandsworth, and then to strike into Gibbs's line at Croydon; but afterwards it was determined to apply for running powers from Croydon to London Bridge, the original terminus of the Greenwich line (opened in 1836), to which point, eventually, after another long and costly fight in Parliament, the South-Eastern line was also to have access. This was of course long before the present railway bridges over the Thames were even dreamt of; although, as we shall see in Vignoles's diary for 1845, he at least had then clearly grasped the idea of a terminus for his Chatham and Dover line on the City side of the Thames.

---

[1] Mr. Bidder's words are: 'It is notorious that Mr. Vignoles, who had surveyed the line through the valleys for Sir John Rennie in 1825, had prepared himself during the last two or three years to go to Parliament for a line to Brighton, and had deposited plans with the Clerk of the Peace. But he had found it quite hopeless to try to obtain the consent of owners of ornamental property in the Vale of Mickleham.' This is a fair statement of the case. Mr. Stephenson had not considered the question of a line to Brighton before 1833.

We must content ourselves here with two more passages from his journal in 1836, in the matter of the Brighton lines : [1]—

' *July* 8, *Dublin.*—In consequence of an " express " message requiring my attendance in London for the promoters of Stephenson's line to Brighton, I sailed at once for Liverpool, and reached London early in the morning. Proceeded to the consultation held at Mr. Serjeant Merewether's, and was received with great joy.

' *July* 11.—Examined by the Committee of the House of Lords for upwards of six hours for Stephenson's Brighton Railway. The promoters considered that I had rendered them good service, which was not impaired by cross-examination.[2]

' *August* 13.—Interview with Mr. Young, the secretary, and Mr. Moxon, the chairman of the Croydon Railway; also with Mr. Duncan, the solicitor for the opposing Brighton line. I proposed a union of their forces; and that a branch from Stephenson's line, south of Dorking, and by Reigate through Smither's Bottom to join the Croydon Railway, would be the most effectual plan of uniting all interests. I fully explained my views, but at the same time distinctly disclaimed any intention of interfering with other engineers. In the end it was agreed on all sides that I should be considered as a mutual friend.'

Welsh Surveys: Port Dinlleyn, &c.

It was in May 1836 that Vignoles was first engaged on the surveys in Wales, in connection with the inquiries then being made by the Board of Works in Ireland for the best route between

---

[1] Some very interesting and amusing recollections of this struggle, and of the famous coaching feats between London and Brighton just about that time, may be read in Bishop's *Brighton in the Olden Times*, published in 1880. The last Brighton coach running to London was courageously started by the late Mr. T. W. Capps, the spirited coach proprieter of Brighton, after the opening of Rennie and Rastrick's line in September 1841. It was called the ' Railroad,' and continued to run for two years. Mr. Capps died in December 1887 in his eighty-eighth year.

[2] The House of Lords Committee did not recommend any of the lines; but the next year, as the competing companies could not come to an agreement, the Government appointed a special commissioner, Captain Alderson, R.E, to

London and Dublin. His attention was chiefly fixed upon Port
Dinlleyn, half way up the north-western seaboard of the *Lleyn*
promontory in Caernarvonshire, that sheltered spot being considered by naval men, as well as by many engineers[1] of eminence,
the most promising port for embarkation for the steam transit
to Kingstown. Vignoles was much impressed by its capabilities,
especially in connection with the railway route he so strongly
advocated *viâ* Shrewsbury, and through the Welsh valleys to
Dolgelly and Portmadoc, and thence to Pwllheli, and across the
peninsula to Port Dinlleyn. But he also considered an alternative
line to Holyhead by Llanberis and Carnarvon ; and generally
broke ground in this direction (so far as the writer can discover)
before the question had been examined by any other engineer.

Seven years afterwards he went over the same country with
the same object on behalf of Mr. Brunel ; and his diary for the
year 1843 affords materials for a more extended notice, which
will be given in Chapter XVII.

THE FIRST IRISH RAILWAY COMMISSION.

Early in 1836, at least two great trunk lines for Ireland had
been projected by private capitalists, but the Irish Commissioners
considered them both as premature, nor did they in any way
commend them to the notice of the Government, or deem them
worthy of public support.

On this point it is necessary to remember that the Commissioners were bound to consider the whole question of trunk
lines with great seriousness ; as the basis of them, in the point
of view entertained by the Government, was the idea that
Valentia and Galway were the ports best suited for Transatlantic
packet stations. There was nothing but vagueness and uncertainty both about the merits of the two ports in question and

report on the subject. This officer decided that Rennie's ' Direct line ' was the
least objectionable, and on July 15, 1837, the Bill for this scheme received the
royal assent. The Brighton Railway was thus entitled to keep its fiftieth
birthday in 1887, our gracious Sovereign's Jubilee year.

[1] E.g., Mr. Wm. Cubitt said that ' he believed Port Dinlleyn to be in the
best position of any for a transit between England and Kingstown Harbour.'
(Cf. the *First Report of the Irish Railway Commissioners*, 1836-38, page 84.)

as to the possibility of raising capital to render either of them
adapted for steam navigation to America; and the investigation
of this and all kindred questions was very properly entrusted
to the first Irish Railway Commission, of which Colonel John
Fox Burgoyne, R.E.,[1] was the most influential member.

Colonel Burgoyne was (as we have seen) an intimate friend
of Vignoles; but it is evident that this fact produced no bias at
all in his favour, and the copious letters to him from this officer
show that his friend was rather a severe though kindly critic on
the sayings and doings of the subject of our memoir.

From two of these letters we here quote :—

Colonel J. Fox Burgoyne to C. B. Vignoles.

[Letter dated June 23, 1836.]

'I am glad to hear you are coming over soon, for I have
always looked to you as one proper to be consulted by Government on the *general* policy of lines of railway [in Ireland]. You
should be able to act ministerially, without regard for local or
partial interests. I hope to find you untrammelled and independent.'

Colonel J. Fox Burgoyne to C. B. Vignoles.

'Dublin: September 30, 1836.

'I am going across to Liverpool to pay a short visit to
Knowsley, and I shall take the opportunity to see your Preston
line works [North Union Railway], particularly the Ribble
bridge and embankments. I shall be anxious to have you
engaged on our Government investigation ; but I do not exactly
know yet what may be the feeling of the various Commissioners,
of whom I am to be one. I advise you that there ought to be
no coquetting with parties who may wish to employ you on *trunk
lines* in Ireland. Remember that I am your friend.'

In November 1836 the first Irish Railway Commission
assembled at Dublin, Captain (afterwards General Sir Harry)
Jones, R.E., being the secretary, and Vignoles was at once

---

[1] He became Sir John Burgoyne, K.C.B., in 1838, and was created a baronet
in 1856. From 1831-45 he was Chairman of the Irish Board of Works.

nominated one of their principal engineers. Mr. John Mac-
Neill was directed to examine the North of Ireland, and he
had the assistance of the Ordnance maps ; but these were not
completed for the southern counties, which were entrusted to
Vignoles. He began by an examination of the country between
Kingstown and Bray, round the rocky edge of the coast, and
thence to Wicklow and Wexford. He then traversed Kildare
and Queen's County, of which district he notes in his journal of
December 8 :—

'This line of country I found to correspond as nearly as
possible with my original design and ideas, as promulgated for
the Valentia Grand Trunk' [Railway].

His route then took him through Templemore and Thurles
to Cashel, and as far south as Mallow, and thence to Cork, where
he arrived on December 11.

On the following day he records his exploration of the
valley leading to the coast at Bantry Bay ; and thence by the
headlands of Glengariff, where he speaks with rapture of the
grand scenery formed by the amphitheatre of lofty rocks, to
view which he embarked in a small boat, and a storm coming
on he had a narrow escape with his life. From Glengariff he
went north-east to Macroom, and examined the valley of the
Lee ; and thence across the mountain ridges northwards near
to Mill Street, and down into the valley of the Blackwater.

His journal continues :—

'From Mill Street posted to Killarney, and then on through
the night by Castle Island and Listowel to Tarbert. After an
early breakfast at Tarbert, and receiving the maps [1] and instructions from the Commissioners, proceeded to examine the line by
the south shore of the Shannon, through Glinn, Mount Tren-
chard, Askeaton, &c., to Limerick—an exceedingly easy line,
and capable of being laid down with good gradients. It follows very nearly the course marked out by Mr. Griffith on the
tracings sent us, but which line I had previously suggested to
the Commissioners, and had also marked it on the map of

[1] He often speaks of the great hindrance to his work occasioned by the
absence of Ordnance maps for this district.

railways, as projected and published by me during last year.'
[No trace of this map can be found.]

The line of exploration followed brought him back to the adjacent county of Tipperary, and as his diary says :—

' Thence northwards to the crossing of the river Suir, thus confirming my ideas on the former survey ; and finally tracing the modes of connection, and also establishing the division of the lines to Limerick and Cork.'

Vignoles had evidently kept his friends *au courant* of the progress of his work, as is seen by the following letter :—

John F. Burgoyne to C. B. Vignoles.

' Dublin : January 8, 1837.

' With regard to your reports, &c., I feel persuaded that your labours for the Railway Commission will do you credit, and I think you deserve it for the exertions you have made, but for which you will hardly obtain the usual remuneration. That, however, I believe, is with you not a primary considera-tion.[1]

' An extract from one of your papers shows the following dis-tances for possible lines of railway—viz. :

London to Port Dinlleyn, *viâ* Birmingham, Bala, Bar-mouth, &c.	260 miles
London to Holyhead, *viâ* Chester and Bangor . .	272 ,,
Orme's Bay, *viâ* Chester	230 ,,
Liverpool, *viâ* Grand Junction	200 ,,

I should be glad to know how far these are correct, to the best of your judgment, of lines that have been only cursorily surveyed as yet.

' I also want to know whether the result of the late Committee on Post Office Communication for Railways has produced any uniformity of opinion as to the rates for which the mails will be conveyed, &c. How are the different opinions to be got at, and what is yours ?

---

[1] Vignoles was certainly making money rather rapidly about this time ; but it was entirely his own fault that his eager disposition and his insatiable appetite for hard work often put him at a disadvantage where pecuniary re-compense was concerned.

'The 200 miles distance from London will be all *night-work*. Is that for or against rapidity? Under good arrangements, I think it ought to be favourable.'

The report which Vignoles made is referred to in the following letter:—

John Fox Burgoyne to C. B. Vignoles.

'Dublin: July 20, 1837.

' I have most carefully read through your report, and think it very satisfactory. As regards the South of Ireland, it seems that general principles may be adopted, and that a vast degree of railway intercourse may be obtained by moderate means if worked on one system.

' There is in your report, however, occasionally an indistinctness that *you* might overlook, but which strikes *me*, who come fresh to it.

'I think the number and extent of your difficulties very legitimate subjects for observation ; but I think they might be better put forward in a few pithy sentences than all enumerated.

' I would also recommend your collecting all general observations regarding the facilities afforded by the country—the best levels, the freedom from great bridges, embankments, &c., the inferior value of the land or property invaded, &c. If you group these observations either at the beginning or end of the report, they would attract more attention, and be more generally read.'

It is highly probable that it was an early, or, at any rate, not the final draft of the report, on which the General comments.

Two other letters of somewhat later date may be given in this place, as referring to events connected with the first Irish Commission on Railways:—

Colonel Harry Jones, R.E , to C. B. Vignoles.

'Dublin : August 16, 1838.

' Your proposal respecting the presentation of a copy of the Report of the Commissioners to the British Association was instantly agreed to, and Mr. Griffiths will bring you over a box containing the report. But there never was such a blundering piece of business as the distribution of that document. I am beset with applications, some civil, some authoritative, some impudent, and nothing to give to any of them! Mr. A. indignantly demands the return of his papers, of which (as he says) "no notice whatever has been taken, and they seem to have been thrown aside." Sir John Burgoyne returned last Friday, highly amused with the newspaper squabbles, which are daily continued with greater scurrility!'[1]

Sir John Burgoyne to C. B. Vignoles.

'Dublin: July 8, 1838.

'I have nothing to add to what I mentioned in my letter of yesterday. . . . I do not quite understand upon what grounds of probable success you can apply to the Government for *honours*, which I suppose is what you refer to by the words "not pecuniary." If you mean *general merits*, I fancy that is one of the best qualifications on which to found a claim; but such affairs are usually a matter of interest, added to some accidental circumstance.

'As my friend Major Wells remarked, when some person rather rudely said to him, "I cannot understand what they gave *you* your majority for," "My good fellow," was the cool reply, "we get what we *can* in these days, not what we *deserve*!" The question is, What have you besides *deserts* to assist you? Have you any offers of service from men of influence or rank?'

It may be asserted, without fear of contradiction, that Vignoles never made any direct application to those in authority on his own behalf for formal recognition of his services. Whether his acknowledged ability and high standing did or did not entitle him to favours, which in so many cases had been granted to his contemporaries, certainly not more distinguished than himself, the writer will not venture to inquire. An extract from the *naïve* letter of Vignoles's daughter to her eldest brother

---

[1] In a short letter from Sir John Burgoyne to Colonel Jones (amongst Vignoles's papers) the former writes: 'I think Mr. Vignoles has written a very excellent report.'

on the occasion of her father's return from this Irish tour is worthy of insertion here. It is dated London, December 31, 1836:—

Miss Vignoles to her brother Charles Ferdinand.

'I assure you I never spent a happier Christmas Day than last Sunday. Papa had been absent for six weeks in Ireland, but he had promised faithfully to be with us for the Christmas dinner.

'It was a dreadful snowy day—indeed, such severe weather has not been seen for years; all the roads are blockaded, and the mails stopped.

'Well, all the morning and afternoon passed away without any signs of papa, and we had at last sat down to dinner in despair; when lo! all of a sudden a tremendous rap-tap-tap made the hall resound, and in walks papa! He had posted day and night through the storm from Holyhead on purpose to eat his Christmas dinner with us. We were all so delighted; and as soon as papa was unpacked—for you may guess how he was muffled up—we all sat down to dinner, and I do not know when I spent such an agreeable and delightful evening.

'To-morrow will be New Year's Day, and I hope it will be as pleasant. Papa has brought a great number of pretty things from the Killarney Lakes.'

In January 1837 Vignoles visited Glasgow and Edinburgh, by invitation from the directors of the proposed railway between those two important places. He made an inspection of the whole country to be traversed, and, as usual with him, sketched an alternate route wherever difficulties presented themselves, the chief of which was to decide upon the best mode of entering the Scotch capital. He met Mr. J. U. Rastrick on this occasion, and also had long and friendly conferences with the Scotch engineers, Mr. R. Stevenson and his son, who had been already appointed to carry out the enterprise. His report was distinctly in favour of the line they proposed, with some few modifications.

During his short stay he records with great delight an unexpected meeting with Colonel George Wright, R.E., whom he had known so well in Canada more than twenty years before :—

' Our meeting was very agreeable.   He has grown old, but is still the same frank, jovial person, and the sincere friend who showed me such kindness in Canada.'

No one more valued or more warmly reciprocated deeds of kindly fellowship, whether in social or professional life, than the subject of this memoir; and we may remark in passing his own geniality and courtesy to everyone—engineers especially—who called on him for friendly advice or help.   For such he would always make time, exerting himself to give them proper introductions, making out for them routes of travel, or drawing up plans to facilitate their tours of inspection and inquiry. Examples of this are scattered freely throughout his diaries; but those who really knew Vignoles's kindness and generosity do not require any written records of these traits in his character.

CHAPTER XV.

The Midland Counties Railway.

1835–39.

WE proceed now to give a brief sketch of Vignoles's work as engineer to the Midland Counties line, extending over nearly four years, from the summer of 1835 to May 1839. The origin of this great trunk railway in the Midlands, which has now reached such gigantic proportions, has been generally ascribed to George Stephenson, and this eminent man certainly broke ground in that portion of the virgin soil, and was afterwards engineer to two other lines in Derbyshire and Warwickshire. But we shall see that his earliest work in Leicestershire was rather a single and detached enterprise than an integral part of the Midland Railway system proper.[1]

The first constructed railway in this part of England was a colliery line from Leicester to Swannington, in many respects analogous to the Stockton and Darlington line, on which the carriage of passengers was subsidiary to the bringing of coals into the market. The main object was a purely local one—viz. to open up facilities to and from the Snibston pits, near Swannington, in the district which is now called 'Coalville.' The purchase of the ground where these pits were afterwards sunk had been made by Stephenson from Mr. Joseph Sandars[2] and Sir Joshua Walmisley; and it was a signal proof of that engineer's practical knowledge of geology that he predicted that the coal measures would be met with in a formation where,

---

[1] It is announced that the Midland Railway Company will celebrate their 'jubilee' in May of this year, 1889. This corresponds with the date of the opening of the first portion of the line we are describing as engineered by Vignoles.

[2] The 'Father' of the Liverpool and Manchester Railway. Cf. Chapter IX.

prior to the deposition of the Trias, intrusive igneous rocks have broken through and overflowed the Carboniferous series.[1]

Swannington lies some fifteen miles north-west of Leicester, and the railway (a single line) was begun soon after the opening of the Liverpool and Manchester line in the autumn of 1830, and was opened for traffic on July 17, 1832. There was a very steep gradient near Bardon Hill, where passengers used to get out and walk; and there was also a tunnel partly through the shoulder of syenite rock one mile in length. This tunnel could not be widened, and in 1846, when the line was purchased by the Midland Railway Company, it was determined to work this branch by locomotives and dispense with rope traction altogether; and thus it became necessary to make a loop line to Leicester, so as to avoid both the tunnel and the stiff incline up Bardon Hill, these portions of Stephenson's first line being then entirely abandoned.[2]

[1] In sinking these Snibston pits, Stephenson had reached a depth of 166 feet when the greenstone (called ' Whinstone ' locally) was met with; and it was found that the igneous rocks had in some places actually calcined the edges of the coal-bearing stratum. Stephenson said ' it was only the boiling over of the pot,' and he ordered the boring in the shaft to be continued through the solid rock. At the depth of twenty-two feet lower his perseverance was rewarded by striking the coal measures. Cf. the new and improved edition of *Lives of George and Robert Stephenson*, by Dr. Smiles, p. 353 (edition of 1868).

[2] Professor Bonney, F.R.S., has kindly furnished the writer with the following note on the geology of this district :—

' Charnwood Forest mainly consists of slaty rocks, volcanic breccias, lavas (probably), with some masses of intrusive syenite and hornblendic granite. The exact geological age of the former group is uncertain ; probably it is a little older than the Cambrian. On the western flank of this upland district lies the Leicestershire coalfield, under which would be the millstone grit, and possibly a representative of the carboniferous limestone; beneath this, probably, we should find a prolongation of the Charnwood rocks. The Carboniferous period in most parts of England was closed by considerable disturbances which lasted a long time, and during this epoch, in several places (*e.g.* Staffordshire, Shropshire, the North east of England, &c) masses of igneous rock were ejected into or poured out above the coal measures. One such sheet has flowed over this series on the west side of Charnwood Forest, and at Snibston Colliery it was found to be sixty feet thick. This or another sheet has since been struck (I am told) at a neighbouring colliery more distant from the hills. The rock here, as in most places, is a basalt (some would prefer to call it a dolerite). Its microscopic structure is described by Mr. Samuel Allport (*Quarterly Journal Geological Society*, xxx. p. 550). Over this comes the New

Exactly one month after this pioneer line was opened in Leicestershire, the real foundation of the Midland Counties Railway was laid, and the circumstance has been graphically narrated by the late Mr. Williams in his interesting ' History of the Midland Railway.' The mainspring of this, as of all the early lines in England, was to afford cheaper and quicker transit for merchandise, and to open here, as in other mineral districts, access to the collieries from distant centres of commerce and industry. In the case we are detailing a meeting of coal proprietors was held at the village inn of Eastwood, in Notts, on August 16, 1832, when it was decided that a line of railway should be constructed to connect Leicester with the coalfields in the counties of Derby and Nottingham.

A committee of seven was appointed, and on October 4 following the first public meeting was held in the town of Leicester, and Mr. Jessop was provisionally entrusted with the preparation of the plans for Parliament. In February 1833 the engineer reported that he could not complete the needful work in time to apply for powers in the session then opening ; but he laid before the local committee his sketch of a line that would connect the three towns of Derby, Nottingham, and Leicester, with the northern terminus of the proposed Erewash Valley line at Pinxton, but on the south to form a junction with the London and Birmingham Railway at Rugby.

Mr. George Rennie was then called in to co-operate with Jessop, and the usual Parliamentary plans were deposited in November 1833. No progress was made during the ensuing twelve months, and the required plans, &c., were again lodged in November 1834 ; but somehow the enterprise hung fire, and at the close of the latter year the total amount of shares applied for was only 125,000*l.* This was deemed very discouraging, and the scheme fell into abeyance ; or rather, as was asserted by Mr. John Fox Bell,[1] ' the former company, which had its birthplace

Red Sandstone (i.e. possibly some Permian and the Trias). We thus conclude that this basalt is much more recent than any of the rocks (of which we know the age) in Charnwood Forest. Still it is a rock of Palæozoic age.

[1] For many years the able and energetic secretary of the Midland Counties Company.

CAST-IRON RAILWAY BRIDGE OVER THE TRENT, ERECTED BY C. B. VIGNOLES, 1838–39.

in the little inn at Eastwood, now wound up its affairs and
died.'

Mr. Williams thinks, however, that the continuity of the old
and the new scheme was unbroken; but as a matter of fact it
was determined in 1835 to look for another engineer-in-chief, and
it was then that Vignoles, who had just completed the Dublin
and Kingstown Railway, was appointed to the important post.

Vignoles had acquired many friends in Lancashire since his
first employment on the Liverpool and Manchester Railway, and
these persons were foremost in strongly urging that he should
now be called in; but it was also well known that he was then
engaged in constructing two lines of railway in Lancashire, both
of which at this time were rapidly making favourable progress.

The upshot of the matter was that, in August 1835, Mr.
Babington, the chairman of the proposed Midland Counties
Company, met Vignoles in Liverpool; and a month later he was
formally appointed their engineer, with a commission to find
out the best possible line of railway for the requirements of the
promoters, and this he agreed to do (to use his own words), 'as
though no other engineer had been engaged upon it.'

It is evident that this appointment was a strong testimony
to the high reputation Vignoles had already acquired, for he
virtually superseded his old chief, George Rennie; and though
the elder Stephenson had constructed the line to Swannington,
there is no trace in the negotiations of any overtures to the
veteran engineer to help the Midland Counties committee out of
their early difficulties.

Vignoles's first official report is dated November 12, 1835,
and we give here a few extracts from the document, which commences by thanking the directors for having entrusted him with
' full powers to exercise his deliberate judgment ' in adopting
or rejecting the proposals of the engineers who had been previously engaged.

He recommends, in the first instance, 'a total alteration in
the course of the railway between Rugby and Leicester—(1) to
get rid of the long tunnel proposed near Ashby Parva, and (2)
to avoid the sharp rise of twenty-one feet in the mile between
Blaby and Leicester.'

He proceeds to explain that ' by the new summit pass a better gradient will be obtained, ruling a little more than 400 feet per mile, between Rugby and Leicester ; and, moreover, that much private property would be spared.'

He shows himself in accordance with the opinions of George Stephenson when he adds :—

' I consider it a point of much importance, whenever practicable, to obtain the greatest possible uniformity of gradient.'

According to his proposals the gradient from Leicester to

REDHILL TUNNEL BETWEEN LOUGHBOROUGH AND DERBY.

the river Trent would not be more than six feet per mile ; Langley[1] to the Trent a uniform gradient of twelve feet per mile, from the Trent to Derby a rise of six feet per mile, and to Nottingham a fall of two feet per mile.   Between Leicester and Derby there would be one tunnel necessary, though of no great length.   It is chiefly through the Triassic red marl, and its general architectural appearance is shown by the above woodcut.

We give on p. 216 an admirable drawing of the very handsome

[1] This was near Pinxton, on the projected Erewash Valley Extension.

cast-iron bridge over which the line still runs from Leicester to Derby. The structure is a striking as well as a very early example of a railway bridge of this description, and is considered by the engineers to be in as sound a condition as when Vignoles first erected it half a century ago. Vignoles also urged on the

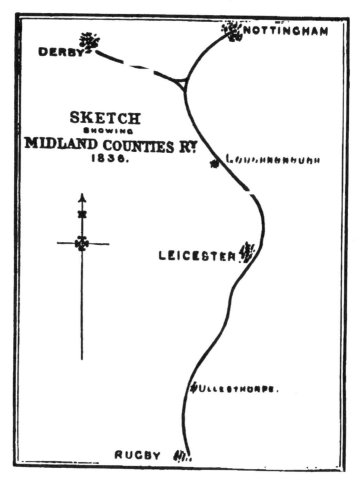

SKETCH MAP OF MIDLAND COUNTIES RAILWAY.

Board the necessity of augmenting their capital from 600,000*l.* to 800,000*l.*; and, with reference to any northern extension, he advised that it should be 'effected from Derby through the valleys of the Derwent and Amber by Clay Cross, and by the valley of the Rother to Chesterfield.' And he my opinion, the promoters of the Midland Coun should consider their undertaking as a section of a great travelling line from London to the North.'

It is worthy of remark that about the same time Vignoles brought before the directors the question of a direct line from the river Trent to Sheffield, which, however, was much too formidable an undertaking to be then thought practicable. It was many years indeed before this was carried out, but Vignoles felt all along how necessary it was that the isolation of that town, in the system of railways then being developed, should be removed ; nor was it long after this date that he himself was chosen as the engineer of a line that was to unite Sheffield with Manchester.

As a proof of the confidence of his Lancashire backers in the newly-appointed engineer, we may observe that out of a total amount of 785,000*l.* of shares taken up before application to Parliament was made, no less than 356,000*l.* was subscribed in the County Palatine, which thus shifted the financial centre of gravity from Leicestershire to Lancashire. One result of this was that the Erewash Valley Extension was eliminated from the Midland Counties scheme, of which at first it formed the prominent feature. The northern subscribers in fact cared little or nothing for the colliery facilities which the early project promised to confer on the Midlands, but they cared a great deal for a through route to the South ; and so the Erewash portion of the scheme had to be given up, to the great disgust of its original promoters, who (to use the new engineer's words) 'were cruelly left out in the cold.'

Did our space permit, we could give many curious particulars of the imperfect means of communication in those days between the Midland towns and other parts of the country ; and of the heavy tolls levied upon the carriage of goods and merchandise, which impeded the development of trade throughout the kingdom, and in fact rendered any great improvement in commercial traffic impossible. That railways were destined to remedy this we all know now ; but it required great faith and no small self-sacrifice on the part of the first projectors of the new system of communication to hold to their purpose through all difficulties, and against the most persistent opposition.

Fortunately, in the case of the Midland Counties Railway, the estimates had been so carefully made by Vignoles that the entire works were completed within a small amount of the sum specified, and the shares rapidly rose to a premium.[1] Vignoles had again scored a great success, which proved the fertility of his scientific resources and the soundness of his judgment ; and to him thus belongs the credit of laying the foundation-stone of that vast fabric of railway enterprise in this part of England, which has now assumed such colossal proportions.

It should be noted, however, that the Leicester and Swannington Company opposed the Midland Counties Bill in Parliament; but, as an engineer (happily still living) puts the case, 'they had not a leg to stand upon,' and an entry in Vignoles's diary for April 14, 1836, records :—

'The Committee of the House of Commons decided this day in favour of the Midland Counties line against the opposition of the Leicester and Swannington Railway.'

No doubt the success of their line so far would have encouraged the directors to extend it both north and south in due time over ground which has since formed part of their amalgamated property. But other projectors had no intention then of allowing them to occupy more territory than they could help ; and so, in the very same session (1836), George Stephenson had brought forward his own line, the 'North Midland,' which was to run from Derby through the successive valleys of the Derwent, Amber, Rother, Calder, and Aire, to Leeds. Vignoles, as we have seen, had been on the alert for an opportunity for the extension of the Midland Counties scheme north of Derby, and across the ridge by Clay Cross, Chesterfield, and Dronfield, so as to reach Sheffield directly, and not merely by a lateral branch —a concession which Stephenson had found himself compelled to yield in order to silence the outcry raised in Hallamshire. Accordingly Vignoles supported to the utmost of his power the

---

[1] The two chief contracting firms were Messrs. McIntosh and Messrs. McKenzie and Co. The contracts for the whole fifty-seven miles of railway were taken at 566,000*l*., being only 5,000*l*. in excess of Vignoles's estimate. The gradients were asserted by the public papers to be superior to almost every other line. Cf. *Railway Times*, March 10, 1838.

strong opposition offered in Parliament to Stephenson's line, and a severe struggle ensued. The outcome of all this was that the 'Midland Counties' opposition was unable to upset the 'North Midland' project, and thus Stephenson's Company obtained their Bill, and the line from Derby to Leeds was begun and vigorously carried on almost *pari passu* with the Midland Counties line, which, however, kept the start it had obtained, and was opened twelve months before its rival. The more extended southern development of the Midland Counties line was anticipated by the construction of a railway from Birmingham to Derby, also engineered by George Stephenson, which obtained its Parliamentary powers without much difficulty, and was partially opened for traffic in August 1839, about three months later than the first portion of the Midland Counties line.

It is worth noticing that in September 1836 Vignoles seems to have suggested to his directors the advantage of building a station at Derby, to be used in common by the three companies of which we have been speaking. It is more than possible that he foresaw the amalgamation between them which was brought about in 1844, the complex details and incidental difficulties being surmounted successfully, in great measure owing to the strenuous advocacy of a young man who was then rapidly coming to the front in the railway world, Mr. (now Sir James) Allport, to whom also the Midland Company is largely indebted for the gradual development and eventual prosperity of its whole system. The celebrated Mr. George Hudson, the 'Railway King,' who had been chairman of the North Midland Railway, became the first chairman of the three amalgamated companies, the new corporation being from that time known as the 'Midland Railway Company.'

It is quite evident that from the very first Vignoles was anxious to have the rails for the permanent way upon his own line laid on wooden sleepers instead of the stone blocks which had wrought such havoc on the Dublin and Kingstown, and indeed on every other line;[1] but he was unable to convince the directors of the Midland Counties Railway on this point, although

[1] Cf. Chapter XIII.

he obtained their consent to a trial of the 'longitudinal timbers' on the London and Birmingham line, near Harrow, the requisite permission being granted by that company.

The following extracts from his reports refer to these matters:—

'Every day's experience convinces me of the propriety of laying the rails altogether on baulks of wood placed longitudinally; and by rolling a rail of 50 lbs. weight into the annexed form,[1] I dispense with the use of chairs, and obtain a better fastening, simple and less expensive. A railway thus laid will cost about 1,000*l*. per mile less than one laid on stone blocks with cast-iron chairs; the repairs would be very much less, and a great saving would accrue in the diminished wear and tear not only of the railway itself, but principally of the engines and carriages passing over the same, from the smoothness of the motion and the absence of vibration. I have been studying this subject at every available moment for a long time, and from the experience of eighteen months on the Dublin and Kingstown line I am more and more convinced that the true principle of forming the upper works of a railway is by placing the rails sustained throughout the entire length on wood.

'Mr. Stephenson having informed me that an order has been made for taking up the experimental rails laid on longitudinal wood sleepers near Harrow, I have, with the assistance of Mr. Woodhouse, made a minute examination of the state of the parts of the road so laid. The part north of the Harrow station, which was laid on timbers of small scantling and on soft sand ballast, without any precaution being taken to consolidate it, I found to be in an indifferent state of repair; and although that might have been prevented had the same care been taken in repairing and adjusting it as the other parts of the line have had (for I am informed it has not been adjusted since laid), I do not wish to raise any unreasonable objection to your order being carried into effect, so far as regards that portion of the line. On examining the part laid south of Harrow, I found it to be as perfect, if not more so, than any other length of the road;

[1] See wood-cut on next page.

and, having ridden over and also observed a train pass over it, I satisfied myself that there is less motion in the engine and carriages on it than on the greater portion of the line.   I, therefore, beg to protest against it being taken up, upon the representations at present before you, but suggest that your engineer-in-chief and managing directors should visit and travel over this piece of the road themselves, and thus suffer the experiment to be fairly tested.   It is necessary to state that the part south of Harrow is laid on timbers of larger scantling than the other, and the ballast is of a more dense and solid description; and I submit the experiment on that portion has fully borne out all I stated or expected from it.   Moreover, the extreme facility and of course economy of repair, and particularly of adjustment, are evident to the humblest workman.'[1]

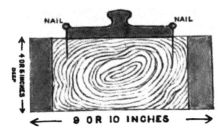

THE EARLY FORM OF THE 'VIGNOLES RAIL.'

Vignoles states, as the result of his observations and of the experiment thus made on the London and Birmingham line at Harrow, that the 'actual cost was 22*s.* 6*d.* per lineal yard on a single track of 534 yards.'

On this he bases his estimate of 3,500*l.* per mile of double line for a railroad constructed as he proposed.   This of course must have had reference only to the expense of the permanent way.   In a subsequent report he estimates that if the lines were laid on continual bearings of larch wood, with wrought-iron rails of 48 lbs. to the yard, the cost would be 4,664*l.* per mile; whilst if laid on stone blocks, with rails of 62 lbs. to the yard,

---

[1] Vignoles adds to his description of the timber to be used: 'The wood should be of the best Baltic timber, either charred on the surface or impregnated under hydrostatic pressure with coal- or gas-tar, or else kyanised in the tanks prepared, according to the process now patented.'   The Midland Counties Board had voted 500*l.* towards the carrying out of the experiments at Harrow.

the cost would be 5,456*l*. per mile.   It is evident, however. that in those early days engineers were always much too sanguine in such computations.   On this point we may notice that in Mr. Locke's Biography it is stated that of the two lines, the 'Grand Junction' and the 'Lancaster and Preston,' made by that engineer, the former cost 25,000*l*. and the latter 20,000*l*. per mile.   Locke declares (but gives no data) that Vignoles's 'North Union' cost 30,000*l*. and Robert Stephenson's 'London and Birmingham' 46,000*l*. per mile.

Vignoles did not succeed in convincing the directors of the value of his suggestions.   They persisted in laying their line on stone blocks,[1] which in a very few years had entirely to be discarded.[2]

The entries in Vignoles's journals for 1837–38 are largely occupied with details of the work and progress on the lines from Leicester to Derby and Nottingham, on which there were occasional mishaps, but none of a serious character.[3]   He

---

[1] The outer side of the platforms at some of the wayside stations near Derby is faced with these blocks.   Just south of Chesterfield a building is still to be seen, composed entirely of the same materials, and was formerly the residence of Mr. Oliver, who was a contractor for the maintenance of the permanent way ; it is called 'Stoneblock House.'

[2] Mr. I. K. Brunel, who had at first advocated the use of stone blocks for sleepers on the Great Western Railway, began about this time to substitute 'timber continual bearings' (as he then termed them), which were afterwards known as 'longitudinal timbers,' the same as those which Vignoles recommended on his own lines.   But Brunel did not agree with our engineer as to the form of rail to be used, as he preferred that peculiar shape which was called the 'bridge rail.'   In Brunel's system, piles were driven in between the rails, and their heads were bolted to the cross-transoms, the ballast under the longitudinal sleepers being well rammed down.   The permanent way, however, was not found satisfactory until heavier rails and longer timbers were used.   In later years, transverse wooden sleepers have been substituted for longitudinal bearings over the whole of the Great Western Railway system.   The last addition in this department of engineering is the introduction of *steel* sleepers.

[3] A portion of a tunnel fell in not long before the opening, and a bridge collapsed, owing to the giving way of part of the foundations.

An amusing record of a conversation on a similar subject heard by a living engineer of the highest eminence has been communicated to the writer.   The letters A, B, C, must suffice to stand for the names of three engineers of the greatest repute in those times, some fifty years ago.

Mr. A. related that, on reaching his London offices one day, he received a

received the greatest possible assistance from Mr. Thomas Woodhouse, whom he had appointed resident engineer (with the full consent of the directors), and who had filled a similar position with honour and success on the Dublin and Kingstown Railway.[1] Mr. Woodhouse was of the same opinion as his chief on the subject of the permanent way, and in the course of the next five years he induced the directors to lay a portion of their line on longitudinal timbers. The company had bought their experience, like so many other railway corporations, at a dear rate, whereas a large saving might at once have been effected if they had listened to the advice of their engineer-in-chief, to whom belongs, as we have seen in Chapter XIII., the credit of being amongst the very first to perceive and own his error in trying to make railway lines inelastic.

Opening of First Portion of the Midland Counties Railway.

The Midland Counties Board had all along been put to great trouble and expense in the renewal and repairs of their line, and it may be as well to state here that in the summer of 1842 they contracted with Messrs. Smith and Holland for the maintenance of the permanent way between Rugby and Leicester for three years at 240l. per mile per annum.

report that another bridge had fallen. The sub-engineers in the department hearing of this, held a conference amongst themselves, and began to bet on ‘whose bridge it was.’ Heavy odds were laid on its being one superintended by a Mr. X., who had earned a grim notoriety in this respect. But Mr. X. confidently denied it, and declared he would accept odds to any amount; and as this cooled the ardour of his brother engineers, he quietly explained: ‘I knew right well it could *not* be mine, as my last fell in a couple of days ago!’ In the course of the same conversation, Mr. A. acknowledged to ten bridges that had failed on his (a very important) line. Mr. B. owned to fifteen or more, on another equally important line. On Mr. C. being asked how he had fared in this respect, he being the engineer of a line as notable now as it was then, replied: ‘I really can't undertake to say how many bridges of mine have fallen down, but one has certainly failed *six times over*.’

[1] Mr. Thomas Woodhouse left the service of the Midland Counties Company in 1842, with the strongest possible testimony from the Board of Directors to his ability and zeal. He was succeeded by Mr. W. H. Barlow, who has long since risen to the highest point in the profession. Mr. Woodhouse died a few years ago.

The arrangements for passenger traffic were much the same as on other lines, the third class in particular being no better than those already described by the writer. A proof of this may be found in a recommendation from the Board of Trade, dated January 1842, impressing upon the directors the importance of 'raising the outside panels of the third class from 3ft. 9in. to 4ft. 6in., and also of introducing the *spring buffers* into that, as had already been done* in the other classes of carriages.'

They also inquired into the number of passengers who could be seated, but they say nothing at all about the carriages being *roofed*!

The formal opening of the first portion of the Midland Counties line took place on May 30, 1839. Vignoles notes in his diary that the first train ran from Nottingham to Derby, performing the distance of sixteen miles in forty minutes. The passengers' fares were, according to class, 3s., 2s., and 1s., for the single journey.

Such was the first of three independent lines, having no original connection with one another, from which, when amalgamated, there has been developed in later years the great system of the Midland Railway, with its nearly 1,400 miles of metallic highway, its combined capital of upwards of eighty millions, and its central metropolitan terminus at St. Pancras, covered by a vast and lofty roof of 240 feet span, larger than any other of its kind in the world. This roof has an elevation of a hundred feet from the metals to the soffit of the Gothic arch, itself a striking and probably unique feature in structures of this character.

It seems quite worth while to step aside for a moment to give a few technical details on this point. The writer, partly from choice and partly from inability to do justice to such treatment, has generally avoided statistical minutiæ, or at any rate reduced them 'to their lowest terms.' But in the story of the completion of the St. Pancras terminus, by a pleasing coincidence, Vignoles occupied the presidential chair at the meeting to which Mr. Barlow read his account of the structure we are referring to, which had been rendered necessary by the extension of the Midland Railway from Bedford to London.[1]

In consequence of the height of the rails above the ground level, a large area was available beneath the station. Columns and girders were adopted in this space instead of brick piers and arches, and the engineer perceived that the floor girders of the station formed a ready-made tie sufficient for an arched roof over the station of a single span. All that was required in this case was to obtain an arch that would be the upper member of the truss, of which the floor girders would form the lower member, and, by adopting this plan, the height from the tie beneath the rails to the crown of the arch became the effective depth of the truss. This height being about two-fifths of the span, all the horizontal strains arising from the dead weight of the roof, with possible accumulations of snow, &c., would be about the same in the arch of 240 feet span, with an effective depth of truss of 100 feet, as in an ordinary truss of 120 feet span, with a depth of 24 feet. Another advantage resulting from such an arch was that, as the weight of the roof would be carried at the floor line, the usual great thickness of the side walls would be rendered unnecessary. Again, in the expansion or contraction of the arched roof, the ties being beneath the ballast, the variation of temperature would be insignificant ; and in the arched part of the roof the only change would be a slight rise or fall in the crown. As a matter of fact, the greatest depression in any rib of the arch, when the centre was struck, proved to be (on an average) $\frac{8}{10}$ths of an inch. The area within the walls covers 169,400 square feet.

The noble hotel which forms the magnificent façade of the St. Pancras station was designed by Sir Gilbert Scott.

Mr. Williams[2] gives a full account of the opening of the earlier portion of the Midland Counties Railway in his work, and adds these words :—

[1] The paper was read at a meeting of the Institution of Civil Engineers in March 1870.

[2] *History of the Midland Railway*, by Frederick S. Williams, 2nd edition, pp. 30-31 (London: Bemrose & Co.). The writer is indebted to this work for a few points of detail in the earlier portion of this chapter.

'Thus one of the earliest, and as it proved one of the most important, lines of railway in the country was completed. The cost fell within the amount of capital authorised by the Act, and the line was (as the directors remarked) one of the lowest in cost per mile of any similar work of the same extent.'

It would have been an agreeable task to the writer to dwell more at length on the remarkable development of the 'Midland' lines, at which he has merely glanced in this chapter; but such details are not within the province of this memoir.

But there is one feature in the traffic arrangements of that company which is exclusively due to the initiation of Sir James Allport, and this point the writer cannot but notice.

In May 1850 this gentleman, then general manager of the Manchester, Sheffield, and Lincolnshire Railway, obtained the consent of the directors to run certain trains each way daily with first and third-class carriages only. This was carried out on the section of their line from Lincoln to Great Grimsby and New Holland, opposite the port of Hull. The experiment met with immediate success, but was not extended to other trains on that railway, nor was it adopted by any other company. After Mr. Allport's return to the Midland Company in 1853 as general manager, he from time to time pressed upon the directors the importance of trying the same experiment on their line; but it was not till 1875 that he prevailed on them to have *only* first and third-class carriages on all trains, and at the same time the first-class fares were reduced to the scale of the old second-class, which was then abolished. But previously to this—viz. in 1872—Mr. Allport had carried out (for the first time in railway management) that important simplification of passenger traffic which now prevails on most lines in the United Kingdom. This was the adoption of the 'Parliamentary' third-class fare of one penny per mile for *all* trains, including mails and expresses.

To these improvements, by which a range of scale that virtually embraced *six* different grades was reduced to two classes only, a large measure of the present prosperity of the Midland Company, as well as the corresponding advantages accruing to the public, are unquestionably due.

CHAPTER XVI.

The Sheffield, Ashton-under-Lyne, and Manchester Railway.

1835-40.

SUCH was the first title of this remarkable line, which from the boldness of its engineering, the expense and difficulty of its construction, and the sorrow and disappointment which it brought to its original designer, render it notable as a history of railway enterprise, and for many years made it sadly memorable to Vignoles himself, as well as to his friends and admirers, as a stage in his career.

His connection with the company began, as we have seen, in 1835, and at first it seemed to be attended with the brightest auspices. The promoters of this line, with Lord Wharncliffe at their head, had invited Vignoles and Mr. Locke to draw up full reports upon the undertaking, with an approximate estimate of the expense. Heavy works, involving serious outlay, were inevitable; and this not even Locke's favourite 'undulating' system (as it was called) could avoid, though one of his chief claims to belong to the great 'triumvirate' of civil engineers[1] was his skill in subordinating distance to expense in the laying out of his lines. The reports of both engineers lie before the writer, and have very much in common; nor do they appear to differ materially in their ultimate conclusions; but of the two it will be manifest from the narrative that Vignoles's scheme more thoroughly commended itself to the promoters as a whole. His diary records on January 5, 1836 :—

---

[1] So the *Times* classified him in its obituary notice; the others being Stephenson and Brunel.

'Attended the public meeting on the subject of the Sheffield and Manchester Railway, when the principles of the same were fully admitted, and the resolutions for the formation of a company were all carried. I was also appointed as engineer.'

It was an additional important victory for him, and his letters own that he was proud of his success, and determined that the affair must and should prosper. The minutes of these meetings entered in the company's books show that Vignoles's report on the line he proposed from Manchester to Sheffield, along the course of the rivers Etherow and Don, with branches to Glossop and Staleybridge, and also to Ashton-under-Lyne, was unanimously adopted, and the route suggested was pronounced 'a very eligible one.' A company was at once formed, with a capital of 800,000*l.*, which was very soon increased to one million sterling. Amongst the more prominent members of committee--in addition to the chairman of the company, Lord Wharncliffe—were the then Master Cutler, Mr. John Spencer, together with Messrs. Hugh Parker, T. A. Ward, John Rastrick, and others. Many influential names of Manchester men are also recorded, and of those in the neighbourhood of Mottram and Dinting Vale, on the borders of Cheshire and Derbyshire, we may mention the Messrs. William, James, and Joseph Sidebottom, names which were a tower of strength in the locality.

The strangest part of the arrangements was the formation of two centres of management, one at each terminal end of the proposed line. The Sheffield solicitors were Messrs. Parker and Wells; those at Manchester were Messrs. Hadfield and Gram. There was afterwards a special 'tunnel' committee, which met from time to time at Woodhead, where the first stage of the tunnel works was located. Of this formidable feature of the railway we shall give a brief account farther on; but it may be said here that Vignoles was from time to time brought into collision with the members of this committee, on which, unfortunately, were some gentlemen who almost from the first had been less friendly to their engineer than any other members of the Board; and these evinced a determination to interfere in

the purely technical part of the affairs of the line, which conduct, as is plain from entries in his diary, he strongly and justly
resented.   But we are now anticipating a little.   Notwithstanding all financial and personal difficulties, Vignoles, from the very
moment of his engagement, carried out the preliminary work
for the line with his wonted energy; and he also began to use
every possible means to stir up the zeal of his friends and
kindle the interest of the public in the proposed scheme.   The
dangers which thus beset so sanguine and unmercenary a temperament as his may be best illustrated from a contemporaneous
record of his history, where in his diary he refers to the difficulties (serious enough they were, and of long duration) of the
Eastern Counties Railway.   The date is January 30, 1836 :—

'Conferences with Mr. Bosanquet, the chairman, and my
co-engineer, Mr. John Braithwaite, relative to the mode of carrying this bill through Parliament.   The principal obstruction
arose from the want of willingness on the part of the solicitors
to advance the necessary funds.   *I offered to make myself fully
responsible.*'[1]

The italics are the editor's, for that passage is pregnant with
fateful meaning, as the sequel of this chapter will prove.

The Sheffield and Manchester Railway had not made much
progress up to the autumn of 1836, and some of the promoters
seemed from the first anxious for Mr. Locke's co-operation,
although there was not the least necessity for it.   Vignoles's
journal of October 14 says :—

'Posted to Peniston, where the provisional committee had
assembled to decide upon the comparative merits of the lines
as laid down by Mr. Locke and myself.   After hearing both of
us, they requested that we should confer together on the plans,
&c.; but it was privately intimated to me that my profiles of
the line were considered by the meeting as the best.'

On the next day he writes :—

'Engaged from an early hour with Mr. Locke in discussing
the line, and especially the gradients.   Each of us gave way,

---

[1] Cf. Chap. XIV.

but the general features of my line and its characteristic gradients were preserved.'

On October 22 Vignoles received definite instructions to prepare the Parliamentary plans; but here the friction between the Manchester and the Sheffield committees again becomes apparent; for while the resolution of the one states that 'the alterations suggested by Mr. Locke constitute a desirable improvement upon Mr. Vignoles's former line,' the minute of the latter, three weeks later, records :—

'A letter from Mr. J. Locke was read, declining on his part to subscribe to the joint report, in consequence, apparently, of some personal feeling between the two engineers. It was thereupon agreed that the chairman (Lord Wharncliffe) should meet both engineers at Manchester in a few days.'

Nine days later, however, smooth water was again reached, as we find this minute :—

'At a meeting of the committee in Manchester, Lord Wharncliffe stated the particulars of an interview which he and the deputy-chairman had held in Liverpool with Mr. Locke, on the subject of Mr. Vignoles's report, which was now confirmed by an additional report from Mr. Locke, which the chairman produced and read to the meeting.' [1]

This quite falls in with the impression produced by Vignoles's diary, and is borne out by a still living witness, Mr. Wellington Purdon—viz. that, of the two lines proposed, Vignoles's was certainly the better, especially in the matter of gradients.

It was not, however, till six months later that Vignoles submitted his first separate report as engineer-in-chief, but no actual commencement of the works was made because of the small amount of capital subscribed. He had already taken a considerable number of shares, and had induced some of his relatives to do the same. We also find that in the autumn of this year he called on many of the leading City men in London to induce them to become shareholders. Yet with all these exertions the financial prospects of the scheme were far from bright, and some attempts were made by the Manchester subscribers to

[1] Minutes of the Company, October 22 and November 14, 1836.

break up the concern altogether. It would have been well for Vignoles if at this juncture he had acted upon the well-known admonition of Talleyrand, 'Surtout, point de zèle;' for it was then that he began to buy up largely the depreciated shares of the company, thus entering upon a venturesome and dangerous course, which landed him at last in almost inextricable difficulties.

For the sake of clearness it is desirable here to quote again from the Company's minute-book :—

' At a meeting of directors at Peniston, held April 18, 1838, Lord Wharncliffe in the chair, it was unanimously resolved that Mr. Vignoles be elected engineer to the company, on the terms of his subjoined letter:

'That the engineer provide for the—

'(*a*) Staking out the line from minute level and transverse sections to be made under his supervision.

'(*b*) Plans and sections on a large scale of all the properties to be taken, and of the adjacent roads and diversions of same, with copies of same for the owners and for the contractors.

'(*c*) Working drawings to be made of all bridges, tunnels, and other masonry, and copies for the contractors and use of the directors.

'(*d*) General and detailed specification and estimates of all the works along the line, with copies for the directors and the solicitors.

'(*e*) The expenses of the engineer-in-chief and his assistants on the line to be paid by him; but the resident engineer to be paid by the directors. If the engineer-in-chief be summoned specially from London, his charges to be extra.'

Vignoles had agreed to carry out all this preliminary work for 5,000*l*., although he found afterwards that he had considerably under-estimated the cost. As usual, he threw his whole strength into the work he had undertaken, engaging a large staff[1] on the plans and field operations between Manchester and Glossop, and appointing Mr. Purdon to superintend the tunnel

---

[1] Amongst those who had been employed under him on some of the preliminary surveys, it is interesting to notice the name of Mr. (now Sir) John

at Woodhead—a very important, difficult, and expensive work, three miles and twenty yards in length.

At that time there were but two tunnels in the United Kingdom (only one of them being completed) which could be compared with this project of a tunnel to penetrate the backbone of England; these were the Box Tunnel, on the Great Western line, and the Kilsby Tunnel, on the London and Birmingham, and we give the respective lengths of each :

Woodhead Tunnel	5,300 yards long.
Box Tunnel	3,230 ,,
Kilsby Tunnel	2,425 ,,

But these last two were not nearly such tough work as the driving of the Sheffield Railway through the millstone grit of the Pennine Range ; by many, indeed, the project was deemed impossible, although a practical refutation of such prophecies had already been furnished in the construction of several very difficult lines, either already completed or approaching completion, in different parts of the kingdom.

The formal cutting of the 'first sod' on the Sheffield and Manchester Railway was performed by Lord Wharncliffe, at the west end of the tunnel at Woodhead, on October 1, 1838, and the sinking of the shafts on all parts of this work was at once begun ; for up to this date the operations had been only partial, as the financial difficulty was still stringently felt, and there was also very strong and serious opposition on the part of some of the principal landowners.

We have already adverted to the friction occurring from time to time between the engineer and a small minority of the Lancashire directors ; but it must be added that two or three of these carried their personal feeling quite beyond the limits of ordinary courtesy, even to the point of giving their own directions to the *employés* on the tunnel works, and otherwise interfering with the strict prerogatives of the engineer. Unfortunately, this was just the sort of conduct which Vignoles's

---

Fowler, who has lived to become one of the most eminent and distinguished members of the profession.

fiery temperament was unable to brook; and it can hardly be doubted that the leaders of the hostile party on the directorate purposely exasperated him, whenever occasion served, with a view to drive him to resign his appointment, and thereby afford themselves a leverage for aggressive action in the matter of the shares so largely taken by their engineer, on which calls were already due to an extent that he was quite unable to meet.

The minutes of the Board show that Vignoles's first report as engineer-in-chief was read at a meeting held on July 18, 1838. In this he specially mentions the introduction of a new boring apparatus, which he had procured from the Saarbrück mines, near Metz.

Three months later we find Vignoles successfully urging the directors to provide tents for the miners who were working on the tunnel shafts, there being then no accommodation at all on those bleak hill-sides, and no human habitation visible.

Even now, after the lapse of half a century, on the moors through which this picturesque line gradually climbs to its summit level, not a house is to be seen on the more elevated spots, save those for the railway pointsmen; nor can a sound be heard, after the passing train has dashed into the western entrance of the tunnel, but the splashing of the mountain streams as they rush down into the vast basins spread along the upper parts of the steep valley sides, between which (on a still lower level) repose the huge reservoirs that supply the city of Manchester with water, although the collected streams have still twenty miles to flow westward before their needful and salutary mission is accomplished.[1]

Vignoles had taken a country residence at Dinting Vale (two miles from Glossop), to which he removed his two youngest children from London, engaging a resident tutor for them; and he also brought home his eldest son, Charles, from Germany, to initiate him into practical engineering on the works of the Sheffield line. His second son, Hutton, had not then returned

---

[1] The supply has for some time proved inadequate, and Manchester is now about to draw additional resources from Thirlmere Lake, in Westmoreland.

from his school at Menars, near Blois, where he had spent five years.

His sons still cherish bright and happy memories of the charming home which they enjoyed (alas! only for two brief years) a mile or so away from the steep and wooded glen through which runs the brawling river Etherow, whose stream there forms the boundary between Derbyshire and Cheshire.

It was over this romantic valley that the handsome viaduct at Broadbottom was afterwards erected, and the company's books record on April 24, 1839, that 'the engineer's plans for a stone bridge over Dinting Vale were adopted.' This, and every other salient feature of the proposed line of railway, was eventually carried out by Mr. Locke according to his predecessor's designs, with a few modifications rendered necessary by the shortness of funds.[1]

A very lengthy report by Vignoles, on the subject of the Woodhead Tunnel, was laid before the directors at their meeting on April 19, 1839. This report occupies nearly six folio pages in the minute-book of the company, but the interest of it hardly warrants our giving details of a work now so well known. In this document Vignoles does not venture even on an approximate estimate of the cost of such a formidable work, but considers that four years at least would be occupied in its completion. He also expressly leaves it to the directors to decide whether there should be a single or double tunnel.

The tunnel occupied seven years in construction, and was made for a single line of rails. Many years afterwards it was doubled, an indispensable though expensive undertaking. The first contract for the early works was taken by Messrs. Warwick, Smith, and Enderby.

The following letter may be introduced here with propriety; it has the acumen that characterised Burgoyne's intellect, and displays also the keen interest he took in all matters of civil

---

[1] Several of the bridges were built of timber, and have proved serviceable for many years. The late Mr. Alfred Gee, C.E., referred in some of his extant reports to the admirable nature both of the designs and of the material of which the bridges were constructed.

engineering.   Of his eminence as a military engineer it would
be an impertinence for the writer to speak :—

From Sir John F. Burgoyne to C. B. Vignoles.

'Dublin: October 12, 1839.

'I see no early prospect of being able to visit your tunnel
works, but let me ask you for an idea of how they are getting
on.   What are your dimensions, and how relatively situated?
Are you driving a double drift, and do you require them to keep
pace together?   To what extent are they carried from the Manchester end, which I believe is the only one you have commenced
upon?   What is the rate of driving these drift-ways, and what
the nature of the material met with?   Does any of it work
with picks and crowbars, or does it require to be blasted entirely?   Is any want of ventilation experienced yet, or any great
quantity of water found, either in shafts or galleries?   To what
depth have you got in boring?   what is the material, and at
what rate does it proceed?   what also is the diameter of hole
bored?   I am asking all these questions as I would in a conversation.'[1]

Things seemed to be running pretty smoothly in the summer
of 1839, for the minute-book has an entry, dated August 28,
recording a resolution of the directors 'that thanks be given to
Mr. C. B. Vignoles for his valuable services.'   It is rather
amusing (though charity requires us to construe it *post hoc non
propter 'hoc*) to peruse the diary of Vignoles just at this time,
and to read the animated account of a splendid banquet given at
his residence in Dinting Vale, in honour of the coming of age of
his eldest son, on August 17, 1839.[2]   All the gentry for miles
round were asked, and of course the directors of the company.
The festivities were spread over two days, both of which were
wet, and at the principal feast there was a downpour of rain

---

[1] The tunnel is through the millstone grit, and all but about 1,000 yards
was lined with masonry.   The deepest of the five shafts is 579 feet.   The total
cost was 200,000*l.*   The parallel tunnel is close to the earlier one, on the up
side, but is quite distinct, and their dimensions are the same.

[2] In reality he was only *twenty* years of age.

that soaked through the large marquee on the lawn during the progress of the banquet, and made everything and everybody extremely damp and uncomfortable, as the writer well remembers. The provisions, decorations, waiters, and the whole ' paraphernalia' of the feast were supplied by Mr. Towers, then a well-known caterer for such entertainments, and proprietor of the Angel Hotel, Liverpool.

The festal gathering on this occasion marks the boundary line which separates the story of Vignoles's earlier life as an engineer from the many troubled and chequered years which he was destined to pass through, before the sun of prosperity once more cheered and brightened the period of his riper age.

In the month of September 1839 Vignoles had determined to make an appeal to the directors to relieve him of some of the liability he had incurred on the large number of shares standing in his name; and his diary for September 20 records :—

' To-day, in company with Mr. Sidebottom [1] and Mr. Michael Ellison, I waited on Lord Wharncliffe at Wortley Hall, and fully explained to his lordship about the shares, and the part I had taken in the matter; and I said that unless some satisfactory arrangements were made I should resign my situation as engineer-in-chief.'

' *October* 3, 1839.—Occupied till a late hour in looking over the state of calls upon shares, &c., and on the outlay I had incurred to support the railway.'

A week later the directors informed him that they were about to summon a special meeting, which took place on the 24th of the month; and we give an extract from the speech of the chairman, Lord Wharncliffe, on that occasion, as it affords the clearest exposition of the case, and vindicates the honourable motives which actuated Vignoles in his disastrous financial operation.

Lord Wharncliffe said :—

' One circumstance has placed us in considerable difficulty.

---

[1] The father of Mr. W. H. Sidebottom, now M.P. for Staleybridge. He was always a firm and kind friend to Vignoles.

There are no less than 1,402 shares held by one person, with a liability upon them of 140,000*l.*

'This gentleman, in August 1837, being very anxious that the threatened break-up of the company should be avoided, thought fit to buy up this vast number of shares, and distribute them to his various friends in small apportionments, under a guarantee that they should not be called upon to pay up. . . . . A short time ago he was advised by a friend to take advantage of a momentary rise and sell some of the shares. You will agree with me that one individual is little likely to be able to pay up such a heavy liability.

'Indeed, I know that this gentleman can no more pay the 140,000*l.* than I could pay the national debt.'

On the motion of Mr. Hugh Parker, M.P. (who was afterwards chairman of the company), the meeting agreed to leave the matter in the hands of the directors. Vignoles was not present at this meeting, but in his journal of the next day he says :—

'Long interview with Lord Wharncliffe and the other directors appointed to confer with me, when they agreed that all the shares I had bought or subscribed for should be forfeited.'[1]

On November 15, 1839, he placed his resignation as engineer to the railway in the chairman's hands, at his lordship's London residence, and adds in his diary :—

'Thus ends my connection with the Sheffield and Manchester Railway, after great attention bestowed on it for nearly four years, and having sustained on its account, in one shape or another, an actual loss of 10,000*l.* in hard monies.'

---

[1] Vignoles's meaning is that he was willing to lose all the money—about 15*l.* per share—he had already paid upon the shares referred to in the remarks of Lord Wharncliffe just quoted. But though this compromise was agreed upon by himself and the chairman, and (we believe) by the principal members of the Sheffield Committee, it was not formally put to the whole body of directors ; and it would appear that the full Board afterwards repudiated the promise made on their behalf by the chairman, that they would not exercise their strict legal-claim upon their engineer to enforce his payments in full of the monies due on the shares as calls were successively made. Vignoles's actual losses when the matter was at length closed, some years later, amounted to upwards of 80,000*l.*

On June 19, 1840, his diary records :—

' Received a letter from Lord Wharncliffe, stating that the directors had refused to respect his pledge; that his lordship and most of the Sheffield directors had resigned; and that I and my friends must take such steps as might appear best.'

On June 30, 1840, Vignoles records :—

' Conferences with the secretary and with Messrs. O. Randall and D. Waddington, two of the directors, on the subject of the shares. In consequence whereof I wrote a letter to the Board offering to assign over the whole of my property to meet the calls, provided my friends were released from their liability.'

An entry of a very precise character on this painful subject is found in his diary for July 22, 1840 :—

' This afternoon went with Mr. C. C. Macaulay and Mr. W. H. Smith to meet Lord Wharncliffe by appointment at the House of Lords, when the following conversation took place. His lordship was asked whether, before he made the communication to Mr. Vignoles in October last, a concurrence was expressed on the part of the whole Board in the arrangement he was about to propose to that gentleman.

' Lord Wharncliffe answered: "I certainly conceived that to be the case, or I should not have made the proposal."

' Lord Wharncliffe was then asked if, when he returned into the (Board) room, he communicated to the Board what had taken place.

' His lordship replied that he did so.

' Lord Wharncliffe was then asked whether the directors expressed their acquiescence in the arrangement

' His Lordship replied : " I most certainly conceived that they did, but no minute was made of it at the time." '

Vignoles's intentions as to his property were not long delayed, and on July 25 the journal records :—

· This day I affixed my name and seal to a trust-deed, whereby I assigned the whole of my property of every description to four trustees—viz. Mr. C. C. Macaulay, Mr. R. S. Palmer,[1]

---

[1] This able and upright gentleman, the head of the respected firm of

Mr. W. H. Smith, Mr. Thomas Port—to repay all persons holding shares in trust for me in the Sheffield and Manchester Railway.'

Meanwhile the Board of Directors had determined to enforce their claims by an appeal to law. An unsuccessful effort was made by Vignoles's legal advisers to stay proceedings by application to the Vice-Chancellor for an injunction, and, this being refused, the trial came off at Liverpool on September 7, 1840.

The journal states :—

' Verdicts were taken for the railway company in all the cases (about nine), but several points of law were reserved on which counsel obtained leave to move the court above to enter a *nonsuit*. The cases were admirably conducted by counsel, and the harsh conduct of the directors was exposed in a very complete manner, and produced a great effect in court. It was agreed that nothing more could be done before next term, and until after the result of the bill in equity was known.'

Alas! Vignoles too soon found the shallowness of all hopes founded on this further appeal to the law.

On January 15, 1841, his diary records :—

' This day the Court of Exchequer gave judgment against me in the Sheffield and Manchester Railway cases, by which decision a great number of my friends will be utterly ruined, and the rest either cruelly embarrassed or obliged to go through the *Gazette*! Considering in what way 1 could assist some of them to meet the cruel pressure that will immediately be put on them. Half distracted at the frightful prospect before us all !

' Good God! that men whom I had served so faithfully, and for whose railway I had done so much, should act like this ! '

The editor has advisedly given these various extracts from Vignoles's journals. They are very distressing to read ; but what then must the weight of trouble and anguish have been which he endured, and that chiefly on account of his many

Palmer, Eland, and Nettleship, happily still survives. He was a firm friend and faithful counsellor to the end of Vignoles's life.

trusting friends and relatives who were innocently included in this terrible crisis !

The entry in his journal now given well illustrates the gravity of his position :—

'Had to-day an advance of 100*l*., which was voluntarily offered by a friend—the only one of many I had obliged who had the kind consideration of thinking that I had need of a few gold pieces at such a time.'

It is evident that for at least two years longer Vignoles carried on a severe and gallant struggle against overwhelming odds, and had he not been made of very tough material, and endowed with invincible hope and courage, he could hardly have sustained the strife.

For weeks together in 1841 his journal is a blank, and when he resumes it at the end of March his first entry is :—

'Much distressed at the receipt of a letter from Mr. S. that the directors of the Sheffield and Manchester Railway had thrown him into gaol at York Castle.'

This gentleman (now dead), who often in after years jocosely referred to the events of those days, which, however, were no laughing matter at the time, was only released from ' durance ' by an act of bankruptcy. Another of Vignoles's assistant-engineers—in his green old age—often relates the laughable account of his own escape from arrest by driving about in a gig between the borders of Lancashire and Yorkshire, and thus dodging the sheriff's officers of both counties.

In these and all similar cases, however, Vignoles made the only atonement in his power by stripping himself of every penny of his patrimony, and his whole accumulated savings of twenty years, to provide funds for the relief of his friends. His total losses were upwards of 80,000*l*.

It is not necessary to dwell further on this untoward event in the history of the subject of our memoir. He saw his own mistakes and bitterly condemned them ; but it must not be forgotten that they were the errors of an honourable and trusting mind. The fact of his having refused to sell one single share in the Sheffield and Manchester Railway when the market price rose in 1839 is demonstrative of his absolute sincerity and his simple devotion to the interests of the company; although it is impossible to approve of, and very difficult to understand, so daring and perilous a transaction on the part of their engineer. A fit conclusion to the story of this chapter of his life may be found in a page of his diary of two years' later date—viz. May 31, 1843 :—

'This is my birthday, when I complete my fiftieth year! Looking back at the twenty years that have elapsed since I returned to England from America, on the death of my grand-father, Dr. Charles Hutton, and entered on the practice of civil engineering, I find myself a poorer man than at my start; and yet, on reflecting, *the fault is my own*! I have gained money, but have never had the art of keeping it   I have brought up my family in a proper manner, and settled my only daughter and my eldest son.   My second son will soon be able to do well for himself, and my two youngest sons are nearly ready to leave school.[1]

' I have established for myself a first-rate reputation as an engineer, particularly so for railways—I hope justly.   Yet I am overwhelmed with difficulties! . . . . Still there is a bright prospect as to the future, and I have not yet to discard hope! With activity, prudence, and perseverance, I shall be able ulti-mately, I trust, to met all my obligations, repay the losses of my riends, set up my sons fairly in the world, and increase my pro-fessional reputation and connection.'

A paragraph on the same page affords the clue to this, the only hopeful entry in his diary for four years previously :—

'This day I got finally settled with the Sheffield and Manchester Railway Company, and obtained from the Board a handsome professional certificate.'

---

[1] They were then under Rev. Nicholas Germon, Head-master of the Man-chester Grammar School. Three years later they were placed as private pupils in the care of the late Rev. Thomas Tattershall, D.D., of Liverpool.

CHAPTER XVII.

Miscellaneous letters—The Second Irish Railway Commission—Vignoles's article on Ireland—Later Welsh surveys—Vignoles's dark days--Elected Professor of Engineering in University College, London.

1838-43.

WE have reserved for this chapter a few letters belonging to the time occupied by events narrated in the pages immediately preceding. They may still possess some interest for the profession, since they refer to the period of the ' romance of engineering,' as it has been well called, the memories of which have nearly faded away, save in the recollection of a very few veterans, some of whom the writer has been privileged to consult.

This chapter is also necessarily of a miscellaneous character, as the severe loss and disappointment spoken of in the last chapter proved to be a very serious hindrance to Vignoles, who, in fact, had at the age of fifty almost to begin the world again ; and although the reader has been spared all needless details of a painful kind, it was necessary to the truth of this biography that the outline of the story should, at any rate, be told ; nor will it be any detraction from the merit or interest of the tale if it be not quite in accordance with the form of narrative so much in vogue, which has by a caustic critic been termed ' the gospel of success.'

From Colonel J. Fox Burgoyne to C. B. Vignoles.

' Dublin : March 14, 1838.

' I regret to hear of the stone blocks anywhere outvoting longitudinal timbers ; but I suppose there are some sufficient arguments, and experience at least, to justify there being so strong a party for them. . . . . *Nous verrons* ! '

J. Fox Burgoyne to C. B. Vignoles.

'Dublin: March 25, 1838.

' Your account no doubt shows fair grounds for the charges you make, according to the present rate of railway engineers' payments.[1] Indeed, compared with some of these, they appear to be low. But I must say I think you are running a great rig in such expenditure. I was greatly startled the other day when I saw in the accounts of the London and Birmingham Railway the charges for engineering and surveying, 127,000*l.*

' Perhaps it might be justified; but I am astonished that such an enormous amount should be put in, without being thought worthy of one word of explanation.

' The more you detail the account, the more satisfactory it will appear, and the better you will bear out the reasonableness of the charges.'

Colonel Fox Burgoyne to C. B. Vignoles.

'Dublin: June 22, 1838.

' The expenditure on the leading railways hitherto, or at least up to a comparatively recent period, has shown an actual amount little short of 1,800*l.* or 2,000*l.* per engine per annum for rapid passenger traffic, and of 1,200*l.* for slow work of luggage traffic, the locomotives burning coke and not coal.

' The cost of wear and tear, and of establishment and all other charges, has amounted to nearly twice that of engines, making in the whole an enormous outlay for current annual expense, amounting on lines of very considerable traffic to nearly one-half of the gross receipts.

' As I understood from a conversation with you that you considered such expenditure unreasonable, I should be glad if you would explain to me the reasons for your opinion. It is to be expected that great improvements will be made in this respect, the present high rate of expenditure having probably arisen from the first imperfect experience in a business entirely new, and of great intricacy and difficulty.

[1] This refers to his professional charges as engineer to the first Irish Railway Commission

' Any absolute facts or positive proofs of the cause of so great expenditure, and how it may be remedied, will be for me far more valuable than any individual anticipations or reasonings.'

We hardly think that the hopes or wishes here expressed were ever realised in an appreciable measure.

This will be a convenient opportunity for referring to the sitting of the second Irish Railway Commission, in which Vignoles was one of the engineers consulted; and by way of introduction we give a letter of date just previous to this period written by him to the eminent mathematician, Mr. Peter Barlow, who was placed on this Commission, having also previously served in the preceding one referred to in Chapter XIV.[1]   The letter will stand as a connecting link between the two; and though Vignoles's work in the South of Ireland has been noticed under the year 1836, we have not yet spoken fully of his surveys of the Welsh lines, which were a subject of careful inquiry in both these Commissions.

For convenience' sake, the surveys just mentioned, which were resumed in 1843, are given in some detail in this chapter.

C. B. Vignoles to Professor Barlow, Royal Military Academy.

' R. M. Academy, Woolwich : November 15, 1838.

'. . . . My first instructions from the Commissioners did not extend to taking any line into Dublin ; but I am now preparing a special report on this matter, accompanied with plans and sections on an enlarged scale.   I will take the liberty of sending the report to you in the first instance, as Colonel Burgoyne and Major Jones, with Mr. Griffiths, are gone to the Shannon, and will be absent some time.   I will afterwards run down to Woolwich to talk the matter over with you.

' I may mention that it was always intended to consider at length, and separately, the important point of the entry into

---

[1] His brother Commissioners in 1838 were Sir Frederick Smith, R.E., the first Inspector-General of Railways, and Sir John Burgoyne ; but the latter did not take an active part upon the second Commission. Professor Barlow died in 1862, and Sir F. Smith in 1874.

Dublin; particularly as the Kilkenny Bill prohibits that company from moving between Naas and Dublin until the Commissioners have fixed the line. It is to be observed that the (proposed) terminus at Island Bridge is on the very out-skirts of the city and two miles from the General Post Office, in a vicinity where it is very inexpedient that the terminus of a great trunk line should be.'[1]

It will be remarked that the observations in the above letter refer to the first report of the Irish Railway Commissioners, which, judging from the remarks of Sir Harry (then Colonel) Jones, the secretary, was not very promptly either prepared or circulated. As a matter of fact, the second report was in print as early as July 1838, and must have trodden closely upon the heels of the first. The appendix to this second report shows that Vignoles's contributions to this document were as follow :—

'1. Report on the Irish Southern and South-Western lines of Railway.

'2. Ditto, on the practicability of connecting the terminus at Barrack Bridge (Island Bridge) with the railway terminus in Westland Row. [Dublin and Kingstown].

'3. Ditto, on the best mode of effecting a railway communication between London and North Wales.'

The preliminary surveys in Wales were made by Vignoles and Mr. Rastrick during the early autumn of 1835 and again by him-self in 1836 ; the work of the former year contemplating a line through Shrewsbury in connection with the Great Western system, and that of the latter year having reference to a junction with the proposed coast line from Chester to Holyhead. Vignoles's preference was for the former route, which later on was also strongly advocated by Mr. I. K. Brunel, for whom a fresh survey of the ground was made by Vignoles in August, 1843. The earlier surveys are referred to by the Commissioners

---

[1] The terminus was placed there, and is still a source of great inconvenience to travellers entering or leaving Dublin. Cf. Vignoles's proposed scheme of communication referred to in Chapter XIII.

in their first report on Irish railways, 1836–38 ; of the latter we shall speak presently.

Mr. Cubitt has already been quoted as one of those who gave favourable testimony to the value of Port Dinlleyn, asserting that 'it is in the best position possible for a transit between England and Kingstown ; ' but he acknowledged that the expense of a railway to that port and of the necessary improvement of the harbour would be very great.[1] Strong testimony also is found in a report to the Admiralty by Lieutenant Sheringham, after some weeks' examination of the various harbours along the coast. The date is June 14, 1838 :—

' Port Dinlleyn has an excellent shelter and clear anchorage ; and there is no other port on the west coast of Wales that is so well or so economically adapted for a packet station.'

Mr. Cubitt was of opinion that not less than twenty hours must be allowed for the whole journey, whichever port was chosen.[2] Vignoles's calculation was sixteen hours ; and, as a matter of fact, up to the time of the first Exhibition in 1851, the transit from London to Dublin was seldom less than fifteen hours. This has now been reduced to little more than eleven hours.

The general work done by Vignoles for the Commissioners is very favourably noticed by them ; and in an appendix they print the special report which he had made on the rival projects for the direct line from London to Dublin.

The two acting Commissioners carefully examined the section of the proposed line *vià* Shrewsbury, which was planned to go through Chirk, Corwen, Bala, Dolgelly, Harlech, and Pwllheli, to Port Dinlleyn, a great part of which route (all, in fact, but thirty miles from Shrewsbury to Chirk) had been surveyed by

[1] Sir J. Rennie and Mr. Page made a highly favourable report to the Government some years later on the advantages of this harbour; and in 1845 these two engineers planned a line, called 'The North Wales Railway,' to run from Bangor by Caernarvon, Llanberis, Navin, to Pwllheli, and thence to Port Dinlleyn. Mr. Assheton Smith was a director and Mr. Ormsby Gore was chairman.

[2] If the line should go from London through Birmingham, and thence *vià* Bala, &c., the distance to Port Dinlleyn would be twelve miles less than to Holyhead.

Vignoles. The Commissioners acknowledged that the proposed line was the best possible route through the difficult country it would traverse, and they added :—

' We are of opinion that the line so proposed by Mr. Vignoles has been suggested with much judgment; and we should have pressed on Government the great importance of completing the survey as recommended by that engineer, had we seen any reason to prefer an inland line.'

The Commissioners in their report gave preference to the coast line *viâ* Chester and Bangor to Holyhead; but they were strongly influenced by the fact that the line to Chester was already made, whilst according to the other proposal (though really the shorter by eighteen miles in direct distance), a considerable part of the railway which would be needed to connect it with the Great Western system at Didcot was not then in existence.

When the whole subject came before Parliament—not long afterwards—Robert Stephenson only carried his proposal to select Holyhead Harbour by the casting-vote of the Speaker.

We may say that Vignoles during several years clung with immense tenacity to the prospect of an intervention of the Home Government, with an accompanying vote by Parliament, for the extension of railways in Ireland according to the recommendation of the Commissioners. A momentary gleam of encouragement on his long-cherished hopes on this behalf is found in his diary for June 7, 1839 :—

' . . . . Met some members of Parliament, from whom I understood that my plans for the Irish railways were likely to be adopted with some variation in detail. Also that the opposition of Sir Robert Peel was modified, if not wholly withdrawn.'

Two noblemen who were anxious for the settlement of this question seem to have held frequent conference with him : one was the aged Lord Clive, Earl of Powis,[1] who was much interested in the projected Welsh line from Shrewsbury to Port

---

[1] He died in May 1839, but his son afterwards maintained an equal interest in the subject.

Dinlleyn; the other was the celebrated statesman, Lord Morpeth,[1] whose heart was set upon the development of the resources of Ireland, and who was also intimately acquainted with the oft-debated subject of her railways.

An entry in his diary says:—

'Discussed with friends the result of my interview with Lord Clive on the pending question of the Irish railways and the threatened opposition of the great Tory party.'

During 1840 and 1841 he kept the question constantly before him, and made many trips to Ireland with foreign visitors, who came over on tours of inspection, bringing with them letters of introduction to Vignoles, for in addition to his celebrity as an engineer, then (and perhaps still more *now*) widely appreciated on the Continent, he was known as a good linguist; whilst his readiness, even eagerness, to oblige such visitors 'goes without saying' to those who knew him.

The Russian General Tscheffkin, and his aide-de-camp Captain Ivanitzky, were amongst those who accompanied Vignoles on a tour of railway examination in England and Ireland. This was in 1840, and in the autumn of 1841 he records a special visit to Dublin to pay his respects to the new Lord-Lieutenant (Earl de Grey), to whom, in the beginning of a long spell of Tory rule, he communicated his earnest wishes and oft-expounded plans for the extension of railways in the sister island. Vignoles's opinions and reflections on this subject had been now matured, and at the close of that year he prepared a very long and carefully-written article for the first number of the 'Dublin University Magazine,' which appeared in that publication the following January.

This article was thought highly of at the time, and was reprinted in pamphlet form. The style is good, clear, and animated; and we quote a few passages illustrative of some of the points on which we have touched already; his observations being by no means inapplicable to the present state of home politics in Ireland:—

[1] Became Earl of Carlisle in 1848. Up to the year 1841 he was Irish Chief Secretary, and afterwards was twice Lord-Lieutenant of Ireland.

'*January* 1842.—The advent of a Conservative Government has naturally aroused the hopes of all who have long looked in vain for some well-digested and extensive plans of internal improvement to be introduced into Ireland ; not partial schemes, but comprehensive and practically useful undertakings, applicable to every part of the island, designed to develop the resources and arouse the energies of the nation by well-directed means.'

He next speaks of the fatality that had rendered incomplete or abortive the many plans proposed by Parliament.

The success of the Shannon navigation was held by competent judges to be problematical, whilst the ' general drainage ' and ' highway ' schemes had been sacrificed, as he expresses it, ' to the indolent whims and legal crotchets of one functionary after another.'

He continues :—

' While all other parts of the empire have been constructing railways, their extension in Ireland has been prevented by the conflicting discussion of various projects, the whole tendency of which appears to have been to neutralise each other.'

He argues that the only result of the much-talked-of Railway Commission had been to destroy all hopes of obtaining English, or of drawing forth Irish capital, even for the most promising undertakings. He then refers to Lord Morpeth's proposal in 1839 to appropriate two and a half millions to the making of the principal southern and western trunk line and branches, to be repaid by a sinking fund out of revenue, any deficiency below 5 per cent. to be charged on the county rates, to which plan he adduces the objection of Sir R. Peel, who had said that ' to advance money for the advantage of one locality was taxing the whole empire for that special object ; and that no plan ought to be sanctioned, the principles of which were not applicable to all parts of the country.'

Vignoles then goes on to argue that ' the raising money by Government for the construction of railways in Ireland must be considered as a proposition not to be taken into account ; ' and he continues :—

'Whatever attention might have been bestowed by speculative capitalists on railway projects in Ireland a few years ago, it is clear that, owing to the present state of the English share market, the serious disappointment of too sanguine expectations of profit, and, above all, to the ruinous, reckless, and unpardonable excess of expenditure over estimate in English lines, it is hopeless to expect any extensive embarkation of private capital on railway speculations in Ireland.'

Vignoles then quotes a passage or two from a pamphlet then recently published by Mr. James Pim, of whose great abilities we have already spoken : [1]—

'We do not want (says Mr. Pim) a grant of one farthing of English money. Having no separate exchequer of our own, we only ask for the aid of British *credit*, to enable us to raise the necessary capital, at the same time offering unquestionably good security to protect the State against loss.' [2]

Mr. Pim goes on to propose a modification of Lord Morpeth's plan, that the suggested grant of two and a half millions should be applied to the formation of three principal trunk lines having their terminal stations in Dublin.

A few more forcible remarks from the article may conclude our quotations from Vignoles's contribution ; we give but a brief extract :—

'The essential interests of Ireland require that English prejudice, so hurtful, so baneful to her, should be dispelled ; that mutual confidence be substituted in their stead, and for rival and injurious jealousies a feeling of reciprocity. Facilitate the intercourse between the two countries ; connect not only the island generally but also its remote parts as intimately as possible with England, and we shall in effect—without changing actual distance—bring all parts of Ireland within the influence of the Executive, giving each country the advantages of both. We shall thus introduce not only the muscle, but the mind, the

---

[1] Cf. Chap. XIII.

[2] Herein seems to lie the weak point of the argument, even in those days. In the present crisis of Ireland's history the objection applies with tenfold force. (January 1888).

enterprise, and the security of England, imparting to the sister country new objects, new feelings, and new interests; that thus, where Nature has been so abundantly bountiful, ingenuity and capital may have undisturbed scope, agriculture may advance, manufactures flourish, while industry, happiness, and civilisation may be largely extended. Railways and steam will effect a new economisation of life, of business, of government in Ireland, which neither ignorance can stop nor interest interrupt; they will be the true regenerators of the country. The occupation of the public mind, and the employment of the peasantry in such enterprises, and the increasing fruits of progress, would do more to pacify the fearful dissensions of the people, and ameliorate their condition, than any legislation of even the best-disposed British Parliament. The advantages to Ireland of such a state of things would open to her, as it were, a new world, whilst disclosing her resources to the enterprise and public spirit of England. It would, in fact, call into existence a UNION which nothing could REPEAL[1] short of a convulsion of nature or a moral revolution.'

Vignoles's Later Surveys in Wales.

To complete the account of the work carried out in 1835-38 by Vignoles in the matter of the projected direct communication between London and Dublin, his surveys for Mr. Brunel in this year (1843) must now be noticed.

The somewhat fragmentary record in Vignoles's diary gives so sketchy an outline, that it has been thought well to add here and there a few paragraphs illustrative of his original ideas on the subject, as well as a small outline map portraying the general features of the country traversed, all based on the actual railway communication through the district, as now completed :—

'*July* 8.—Long conference with Mr. Walker as to various lines through North Wales to Holyhead and Dinlleyn. Also

---

[1] So printed in the original.

with I. K. Brunel, and suggested to him a possible line for the
Great Western Railway by Oxford, Moreton-in-the-Marsh,
Worcester, Ludlow, Newtown, the Carno Pass, Dolgelly, Tre-
madoc, and Port Dinlleyn.

' *July* 12.—To-day Mr. Brunel asked me to undertake an examination of the line of country I had proposed. Had also an
interview with Earl Powis on the subject of the lines through
Wales.

' *Bangor, August* 1.—After much consideration I concluded
that the crossing of the Menai Straits *must* be at the point on
which Mr. R. Stephenson had also fixed, south of the suspension
bridge. I observe that Mr. Stephenson has followed exactly
the same route I had previously levelled from Llanfair to Lake
Coron. Indeed, there is no other line to be had.

[The village generally called Llanfair is noted for possessing
the longest name (when fully written) of any place in the
kingdom, probably in the whole of the British dominions. The
writer, having obtained the exact spelling of this portentous
name, cannot refrain from placing it before his readers. He
begs, however, not to be credited with the capacity either of re-
membering or of pronouncing it—' Llanfairpwllgwyngyllgogerb-
wllgertrobwllchwyrnbwll-cum-Llandysiliogogogoch.' We annex
a translation, kindly furnished by the Rev. W. C. Edwards, rector
of the parish: ' St. Mary's Church, near the pool of the white
hazel, opposite the whirlpool, the rapid pool, with the church
of Tysiliogogo, the red saint.' The name makes up a total of
seventy-one letters! Fortunately, it is deemed sufficient for a
letter destined for an inhabitant of that happy locality to have
as its postal address ' Llanfair, P. G.']

Vignoles spent several days in examining all the country
through which each of the alternative lines might run. He
enters in his diary very elaborate details, and remarks by way
of summary of his first impressions :—

' It must be confessed that great and unusual difficulties
surround the subject.'

'*August* 7 [*Diary*].—Breakfasted with Mr. Assheton Smith

at Plas-Newydd. Discussed with him the comparative merits
of Holyhead and Port Dinlleyn. Found he was a strong advocate
for the line from Chester to Bangor, Caernarvon and Port
Dinlleyn. Examined the site proposed for a bridge by Rennie,
and the oblique line across the Red Weir [1] as now proposed by
me.

'*August* 10.—Engaged all morning in plotting the work
of the last two days. Got exact position of the rocks at the
Red Weir. Find that a practicable and not very expensive
crossing could be had over the straits obliquely at that
place.[2]

'*August* 12.—Examined line by Holywell and Flint to
Chester. No alteration needed from line surveyed by me
several years ago. Went to Chester by boat and examined the
shore all the way. Also proposed modes of approaching station
at Chester, and connecting with lines to Liverpool and London.
I think the proper junction should be at 184th mile from
London. From Holyhead to Chester (by my proposed line)
would be eighty-four miles. Total distance from London, 268
miles. [By the London and North-Western it is now 264¼
miles.]

'*August* 15.—Reached Preston (with my son Hutton) and
discussing my proposed Holyhead line with Captain Chapman,
and Mr. Earle, and James Moss. Directed Mr. Coulthard to
prepare designs for a timber bridge of seven arches over Menai
Straits, the probable estimate for which is 105,000*l.*

'*August* 19.—Mr. Purdon and the rest proceeded with me
by the "Erin-go-Bragh" steamer from Liverpool to Caernarvon,
where we hired a four-horse omnibus on which we placed all
luggage and instruments, and drove off, reaching Tremadoc
between ten and eleven o'clock at night.

'*August* 20.—Mr. Purdon and myself, with some of the others,
examined the mode of crossing the two estuaries—the Traeth-

---

[1] The Welsh name is 'Gorad goch.' It lies between the suspension and
the tubular bridges.

[2] He gives a rough pen-and-ink sketch of a bridge of six arches, each of
250 feet span. Height of rails above high water (springs), 120 feet.

mawr and Traethbach, near Tremadoc.[1] Also completed the examination of the line generally, and examined the ground by Tremadoc, Criccieth, and Pwllheli and back. Shall try to keep line away from the coast.'

[His reason for this seems evident, for at that time the slub-land gained by the embankment across the estuary, about 7,000 acres in extent, was by no means fitted for railway works. The Festiniog Railway, with its narrowest of existing gauges (twenty-three inches), as well as the high road from Pwllheli to Tan-y-bwlch, run along this embankment, which is thirty feet wide at the top and 100 feet at the base.

The present Cambrian line crosses the estuary three-quarters of a mile farther inland. The land of the Traethmawr from the embankment to Pont Aberglaslyn is hardly even now quite consolidated.[2]]

'*August* 22.—In heavy rain went with Mr. Flanigan to Tan-y-bwlch, Harlech, Barmouth, and Dolgelly. Examined minutely the crossing of river Mawddach.

'*August* 23.—We explored from Mallwyd up eastward valley to the Pass of Bwlch-y-fedwen. Examined the Talgloch Valley, and walked back to Dinas Mawddwy, where the east end of the long tunnel should be.'

[It seems probable from this reference that Vignoles was un-decided as to his choice between the Passes of Carno and of Bwlch-y-fedwen, each of which presented great difficulties. The line, as now made by the Cambrian system, runs through the Carno Pass, and a very stiff gradient it is.]

'*August* 24.—Examined the south banks of the Mawddach, scrambling through the woods, the ground broken and difficult. Again examined the line from Barmouth to Harlech, and to the ferry at Portmadoc. Got to Tremadoc at dark.

'*August* 25.—Examined the country to Bodfean on foot. Also the fine harbour of Port Dinlleyn. Finally settled how to

---

[1] Since that time Portmadoc has grown into importance, in connection with the slate industry.

[2] Upwards of 100,000*l.* was spent in this reclamation scheme by the late W. A. Madock, Esq., M.P. The Festiniog Railway, fifteen miles long, was engineered by Mr. J. Spooner, and cost only 6,000*l.* per mile.

get from the cliffs round into the valley leading to the interior.
At Tremadoc remained up all night examining the surface
levels for the alternative lines as plotted. After repeated trials,
fixed the exact curve of the line chosen, and also determined the
gradients, &c.

'*August* 26.—Walked over the line with one assistant in
heavy rain. Determined how to cross the ferry at Traethbach.
Went over line to the racecourse,[1] and fixed exact route to be
followed. On to Harlech; traced line at the foot of the cliffs.
Considered the mode of crossing at Barmouth, and the way
behind the town, and the location of the railway up the valley.

'*August* 28.—Examined the report of Sir F. Smith and
Professor Barlow, and compared it with the line I had surveyed
in 1836. Confirmed in the opinion I had expressed to Mr. Brunel,
that a good line, without serious difficulties, was to be had.'

After three days' examination of the valleys and mountain
passes and the country generally from Llanfair[2] to Welshpool,
Vignoles proceeded up the valley of the Severn to Berriew and
through the western valleys to Manafon; thence to Church
Stoke, from which point he found an easy country to Snead.[3]
He then proceeded up the valley of Carno to the summit of the
pass (called Talerddig), and examined minutely the ground from
this point towards the Talglog Valley. Much of the ground
was very difficult, and he considered it probable that two tunnels might be required—one of three and a half miles between
Dinas Mawddwy and Dolgelly, and another of two and a half
miles through the head of the Carno Valley.

[Vignoles seems to have oscillated between a choice of the
two passes of Carno and Bwlch-y-fedwen, the latter bearing
more directly to the north-west, although both led from Montgomery.

A line from Craven Arms to Bishop's Castle (just south of
Snead) has been made by the ' Bishop's Castle Railway Company,'

---

[1] Two miles north of the present Harlech station.

[2] Llanfair is, of course, not the small village with the long name in Angle-
sea, already spoken of.

[3] The Cambrian line along the valley of the Severn now passes about equi-
distant from Manafon on the east and Church Stoke on the west.

which is unfortunately now in the hands of a receiver. We must here remark that, if the route as suggested by Vignoles half a century ago had been followed, this beautiful but almost unknown neighbourhood would probably long ago have become a favourite pleasure resort.

Of Vignoles's route as suggested to Mr. Brunel, the line now made from Oxford through Moreton goes only as far as Worcester. The link that should have joined Worcester to Newtown has never been made, the London and North-Western Railway and the Great Western Railway having joined the Cambrian system at Buttington Junction, near Welshpool, by a line from Shrewsbury. Vignoles's suggested route as far as the Pass of Carno has been followed, but not with the idea of making railway communication with Port Dinlleyn, to which place the nearest station is Pwllheli. There can be no difficulty, however, in identifying all the remainder of the route through this virgin soil (except between Llanbrynmai to Dolgelly) with that which is now traversed by the London and North-Western and the Cambrian Railways to Tremadoc, Pwllheli, and Bangor. The Cambrian line, after running south to the town of Montgomery, turns west to Newtown, and then runs north-west through the Carno Pass to Cemmaes Road, from which point a branch line has been made northwards to Dinas Mawddwy, and westwards by Machynlleth to Aberystwith. It was evidently Vignoles's purpose to run along the Dyfi Valley from Cemmaes Road, as he would thus have been able to break away westwards to Dolgelly by means of the 'long tunnel,' as he calls it.

Dolgelly is now reached by rail on the west coast from Barmouth, where the line crosses the estuary of the Mawddach and runs along its southern bank. This line then continues north-east by the southern border of the Bala Lake, and on to Corwen.]

'*August* 31.—Traced the lines on the Ordnance maps, which are here very correct, the hill shading having been put in with great accuracy and skill. Tried to obtain something like a diagram section. Greatly knocked up this night, having made through the day (with Mr. Cook) twenty miles over rocks and through woods and bogs.'

Vignoles went from Shrewsbury to Wolverhampton and on to Birmingham, and his diary says:—

'*September* 5.—At night met Mr. Purdon, and we carefully discussed the lines through Wales. Made him fully master of the leading features, and saw that he understood how the details were to be carried out.'[1]

MAP OF EARLY SURVEYS FOR RAILWAYS IN WALES.
made for first Irish Commission (1835-6); and for M.r I. Brunel, (1843).
by Charles B. Vignoles.

MAP OF VIGNOLES'S WELSH SURVEYS.

Having thus rapidly sketched Vignoles's contribution towards the much controverted question of direct railway communication between London and Dublin, and the close examination of

---

[1] Mr. Purdon was subsequently engaged by Mr. Brunel as one of his chief-assistant engineers. The writer notices with much regret (as these pages are passing through the press) the announcement of Mr. Purdon's death (February 1869).

North-Western and Central Wales as part of the proposed
scheme, the order of our narrative requires us to return to the
'dark days' of his history, from the termination of his engagement with the Sheffield and Manchester Railway Company until
the completion of his work in Würtemberg, of which we shall
speak in Chap. XIX. The interval was in great degree one continuous struggle, though mitigated by the comparative brightness
of the busy year 1845; and if the details of the whole period
found in his diary were given at full length, the picture would
be such as in ancient days the gods were said to contemplate
with satisfaction—that of a brave man struggling with adversity.

In a more practical form the lesson to be learnt by all young
engineers is that of the Trojan *Teucer*, which Horace has
familiarised us with : 'Nil desperandum.'

In Vignoles's case the struggle was at times almost desperate, and it may be truly said that it was only his sanguine
temperament united to an iron constitution that enabled him to
prolong the fight with Fortune which he bravely carried on for
many years.

The bereavement he sustained at the beginning of this adverse time is feelingly alluded to in his diary :—

'*May* 19, 1839.—This morning I received the melancholy news
of the death of my dear aunt Hutton, in her seventy-eighth year.
For forty-three years she has acted a mother's part to me : from
the time when, at two years of age, I was brought home from
the West Indies after the death of both my parents. It is an
irreparable loss to me.'

We have so often mentioned the proofs of deep affection
which subsisted between his aunt and himself, that it is needless
to add more on that subject ; but the writer of this memoir well
remembers the impression left at the time on the members of
the Vignoles family, all of whom had learned to look up to their
aged relative with feelings of deep reverence and attachment.

In October 1840 Vignoles received instructions to examine
the ground for a branch line from Tunbridge to Tunbridge Wells,
on the South-Eastern Railway, and on November 1 his diary
says :—

'Finally concluded that the best course would probably be a direct short line of four miles from the station at Tunbridge to the Camden Road at the "Wells." I also was of opinion that it was a capital opportunity for the introduction of the "atmospheric railway system."'[1]

The plans were not fully completed till the end of the following year; and, oddly enough, there is nothing to show for whom he was acting. The only clue in his journal is an entry for December 31, 1841, where he writes:—

'Mr. Pamler and others finishing off the fair copies of the map and sections of the Tunbridge Wells branch, with accompanying book of reference. Writing fully on subject to Mr. Decimus Burton.'[2]

About the same time Vignoles received from Sir John Rennie a request to prepare a design for the construction of a floating pier at the Southwark Iron Bridge. It was a small matter, but entirely successful, thanks in some measure to the careful supervision of Mr. F. Wentworth Sheilds, who has long since attained a high place as a civil engineer. This, and the surveys of the Tunbridge Wells branch line, were amongst the last of Mr. Sheilds's labours as one of the articled pupils on Vignoles's staff; for he soon afterwards sailed for Sydney, New South Wales, where he quickly took a leading part in the earliest railway works of that colony, of which his uncle was Attorney-General.[3]

In June 1841 Vignoles received a formal proposal from the Senate and Council of University College to allow himself to be nominated to the professorship of engineering. After some

---

[1] Vignoles's final estimate was for a line of nearly five miles at 14,000*l.* per mile; but he was not employed to carry it out. The evidence given before a Select Committee by the chairman of the South-Eastern Railway in June 1846, before the completion of the tunnel (one mile long), was that 'this line of five miles, on a gradient all the way of 1 in 100, would considerably exceed in expense the average of the main line.' This branch line was opened in September 1845.

[2] Mr. Burton was specially engaged by Mr. Ward, of Tunbridge Wells, to lay out the Calverley Estate, which occupied him twenty years. This gives a clue to the passage in the diary. Mr. Burton, at the early age of twenty-four, was appointed architect of the Athenæum Club.

[3] Mr. Sheilds returned to England in 1853, and is still in practice as a civil engineer of high repute.

consultation with friends he acceded to the request, which in his former busy period he would have been unable to do, and probably would not have thought it worth while. His inaugural lecture was delivered on November 10, 1841, the day after the birth of H.R.H. the Prince of Wales, which auspicious event Vignoles duly notes in his journal. For the 10th he records :—

'At 2 P.M., in the theatre of University College, I delivered my introductory lecture on civil engineering, largely from notes, correcting what I had written as I went on speaking. This was the first public lecture I ever gave, and it was very well received. There were about one hundred present.'[1]

His second lecture, and the others up to the sixth, were given at University College between November 24 and December 23, and on the delivery of his seventh lecture on December 29 he observes :—

'This lecture, like the last, was wholly on "earthworks," and the correct principle of computing cubic contents. I explained something that had been reported unkindly as to the earthslips which had occurred in the accident on Friday (December 24) on the Great Western Railway.'[2]

Vignoles retained his professorship up to the spring of 1843, delivering a course of lectures in each academic term. He had the intention of making these the foundation of a systematic treatise on engineering, and no doubt would have carried out his purpose if he had found leisure to devote to literature in the years of difficulty and depression through which he was passing. But he was so much straitened in circumstances at this period of his life, that all his time was required, as he expressed it, 'to keep the wolf from the door;' and he was compelled to undertake such work as he could get in any shape

---

[1] Many of these lectures will be found reported in the *Railway Times* of that and the following year.

[2] This occurred about 6 A.M. to a mixed train of passenger carriages and goods trucks, in the Sonning Hill cu·ting, near Reading, and was the most fatal accident since the opening of the line, eight persons being killed on the spot. It was caused by the train plunging into a mass of earth, three or four feet deep, which had fallen from the slope of the cutting. The jury (according to the then custom) brought in a 'deodand' of 1,000*l.* on the engine.

or dimensions not incompatible with his position as a civil engineer. In being thus crippled in the use of his pen, and debarred from the repose and 'leisured ease' needful for serious application to professional literature, he was only paying an additional penalty for the unwisdom and improvidence of his conduct in the matter of the shares of the Sheffield Railway—the *fons et origo* of all the misery and toil endured in these dark days.

It is impossible to detail the various miscellaneous work he was engaged on, but we may mention the very valuable assistance given by him to Mr. Clegg, the inventor of the 'dry meter' for the measurement of gas, on which Vignoles spent both time and money at the urgent solicitations of the ingenious but (at the time) somewhat impecunious inventor.[1] Both in this and the following year he wrote articles on the subject in the scientific journals, and a series of these, accompanied by carefully drawn illustrations, may be found in the 'Mechanic's Magazine' for 1842. He mentions in his journal that up to the spring of 1843 he had contrived (with some difficulty) to procure advances to Mr. Clegg to the amount of 1,000*l.*; but Vignoles does not appear to have secured any share in the ultimate profits accruing from the patent taken out by Mr. Clegg, which in after years must have amounted to a very considerable sum.

During some months in 1842 Vignoles was engaged on designs for a patent slip in the island of St. Thomas, which had been brought to his notice by Mr. (afterwards Sir William) Tite, always one of his firm friends. The slip was constructed in Glasgow, and afterwards put together *in situ* at its place of destination, under the superintendence of Mr. M. Matthews, and completed early in 1843. The work was entirely successful, and has contributed materially to the commercial prosperity of the island.

---

[1] In his presidential address of 1870 (pp. 42, 43) there occurs the following reference to Clegg:—'It is interesting to know that one of the earliest London thoroughfares lit by gas (in 1813) was a part of what is now Great George Street, where our Institution is placed. Our deceased member, the elder Clegg, confident in its practicability, proposed to light all London with gas, of which project Sir H. Davy, the great chemist, remarked, "Impossible, Mr. Clegg; you would want a gasometer as large as the dome of St. Paul's." "And why not ?" retorted this shrewd practical engineer.'

CHAPTER XVIII.

Sir Robert Peel and railways—Great development of railway enterprise—
Vignoles's various railways in England and Ireland, &c.—The North Kent
Railway—Projects in South of England—The atmospheric system—Vignoles
invited to become engineer for East Indian railways.

1845.

THE year 1845 is a very memorable one in railway history.   An
enormous impulse had been given to engineering enterprises by
some observations which had fallen from Sir Robert Peel in his
place in Parliament; and this encouragement from the Premier
augmented the flood which had been for some time steadily
setting in, and which this year reached its highest level.   Sir
R. Peel had said: ' If by the advance of science or the improvement of machinery you are enabled so much better to accommodate the public as, for. instance, to run a new line by the side
of an old one or by a turnpike road, then it is not because
parties have laid out their money in another speculation that
such improvements are not to be made for the public advantage.' [1]

The consequence was the sudden creation of a vast multitude
of railway schemes and projects of every kind, possible and

---

[1] But it is worth while also to quote a passage from the right honourable
baronet's speech made at the opening of the Trent Valley line in November
1845, when he remarked that ' railway directors must establish their claim to
a continuance of the privileges they possess by combining the highest degree
of velocity in travelling with the greatest possible safety to the traveller,
and in other ways showing that they have consulted the comfort of all classes
of railway travellers—the poor as well as the rich—thus encouraging that
love of locomotion on which the permanent prosperity of railways must
depend.   Their greatest claim for public support should be founded on the
proof that the privileges which have been conferred upon railway companies
have been exercised for the public advantage.'

impossible, and in almost every part of Great Britain, irrespective both of the utility or sufficiency of railways already made, and of the local circumstances of the various districts through which the speculative lines were to run.

Moreover, the revenue had been improving in a very marked manner during the previous two years, so much so that it was deemed worthy of especial notice in her Majesty Speech at the opening of Parliament on February 1, 1844. All through that year and up to the close of the next session these favourable symptoms continued, and the consequence was that upwards of three hundred new railway schemes were prepared by promoters who were ready to apply to the Legislature for statutory powers in the spring of 1845.[1]

This immense accession of railway business produced a corresponding amount of speculation, which in the end wrought its own cure by results more or less disastrous to over-sanguine investors, a few sober and long-sighted persons making, as usual, enormous profits.

Vignoles's diary fully reflects the state of prosperity which had arisen upon the engineering profession; but there is no indication of his being in any way infected with the prevailing speculative mania, though these pages prove how high his reputation stood as a railway engineer, and how large a share of work was put into his hands.

In this chapter we shall let his journals speak for themselves, generally quoting verbatim, but sometimes giving only a brief summary of their chief points. We shall notice (1) his English engineering business in districts north of London; (2) his occupations in Ireland; (3) and, lastly, those records which refer to London and the southern counties, more particularly the important project of the North Kent Railway.

(1) Lines North of London.

'*Feb.* 3–5, 1845.—Inspected the Sunderland, Durham, and Auckland Railway, in company with Mr. Rastrick, with a view

---

[1] The Railway Department of the Board of Trade had 248 schemes under their consideration at the beginning of this year.

to convert the same from being worked by stationary engines to traction by locomotive power. Had much consultation with Mr. Blenkinsop, the company's engineer.

'*Feb.* 8.—Mr. Eddison, the company's solicitor, engaged me to make an inspection of the Leeds and Thirsk line. This I did, being occupied till night and slept at Ripon.

'*Feb.* 10.—Had a consultation with Mr. Worthington, the solicitor to a proposed line to be called the "North-Western Railway," to go from Lancaster through Bentham, Giggleswick, to Settle and Skipton, with branches to Ingleton and More-cambe Bay.'

This is the first mention of that line, which is referred to more than once in subsequent quotations from Vignoles's diary of this year, and which he successfully completed.

On March 23 and two following days he was engaged in 'an inspection of the line of railway from Hawick through Dumfries to Carlisle.'[1]

'*March* 26 —Visited the ruins of Melrose Abbey, and went over the house and grounds at Abbotsford.'

Vignoles was closely engaged for some days in the inspection of projected lines on the Border, after which he returned to Lancashire.

'*April* 5.—Made a careful inspection of the whole of my old line from St. Helens to Runcorn Gap, in company with Mr. Arthur Sinclair. Found it and the canal and docks all in capital order. It only wants heavier rails on the permanent way.

'*April* 6.—Resting at Manchester,[2] after seventeen or eighteen days' consecutive travelling in the North of England and the Lowlands of Scotland.

'*April* 16.—Went over the proposed line of railway from Sheffield to Chesterfield, of which I had accepted the position

---

[1] The line connecting Dumfries with Carlisle is now part of the Caledonian system. Carlisle is reached from Hawick by the North British Railway.

[2] Vignoles had a house in Manchester at this time, which was a home for his second son Hutton, then a pupil of Fairbairn's, and also for his youngest son, who was a pupil at the Grammar School in that city.

of engineer-in-chief, with a view of making a report to the directors.'

On May 31 he notes that he had undergone a long examination in the Parliamentary Committee on this line, the Bill for which was, however, thrown out on June 9 following.

'June 12 and 13.—Reached Coventry at night, and rose at 2.30 A.M. next day. Closely engaged till nearly eight o'clock with some local engineers in examining the country for a competing line between Coventry and Nuneaton, and fixed same on the Ordnance map.[1] Greatly fatigued, on reaching town in the afternoon, from the exertions I had made, which I did under great pressure of time to oblige Mr. Glyn, chairman of the London and Birmingham Railway.

'July 21.—I was this day asked to become the engineer-in-chief of the Leicester and Birmingham Railway, and received an immediate advance of 500l., with instructions to proceed with the surveys at once.'

This line received the strongest local encouragement, the shares being subscribed for fivefold. The Earl of Hillsborough was chairman, and the project had the support of the Trent Valley and other sound railway companies. The line was to be twenty miles in length, saving eleven miles between Leicester and Birmingham. It was to form a junction with the Midland Counties at Broughton Astley station, and with the Birmingham and Derby line at Whitacre.

This district has been plentifully supplied since that day with railway communication; but the writer of this memoir does not attempt the almost impossible feat of tracing the surviving elements of rejected railway schemes of that epoch, in their revived form, as component parts of amalgamated companies in the present day.

'July 31.—Reached Sheffield, and attended meeting of the directors of the Manchester, Sheffield, and Midland Junction

---

[1] This was a proposed line from Coventry to Bedworth and Nuneaton which the London and Birmingham Company had agreed to lease. It was strongly supported at the time, and only thrown out on some technical informality.

Railway, who advanced 500*l.* with full instructions to begin the surveys at once, and make all arrangements to suit my own convenience.'

This line was strongly opposed by the Duke of Norfolk, and was thrown out in the Parliamentary Committee.

' *Aug.* 4 *and* 5.—Went down to Birmingham by the "express" train,[1] and inspected progress of the levels, &c. Proceeded next day to Nottingham and Leicester. Posted through the night to Grantham and Stamford with my youngest son, Olinthus. Pointed out to him Belvoir Castle by moonlight, the seat of the Duke of Rutland.

' *Sept.* 3.—A deputation from the Leeds and York Railway waited on me to-day. I agreed to become their engineer-in-chief.'

Amongst the many ambitious schemes of this year was that of a proposed line of railway from Leek to Buxton, and thence by the Peak passes and valleys to Sheffield. This line of communication was at the time deemed impracticable ; but the problem has been solved in recent years by the exertions of the ' London and North-Western ' and of the ' Midland ' Railway Companies.

Vignoles refers to this in his diary as here given :—

' *Sept.* 15.—Examined the country from Buxton to Baslow with a view to find the best way for the line to pass Chatsworth. Considered the question of tunnels through the summit into the eastern valleys. Also examined the plans and sections for the line as it passes through Sheffield, to avoid (if possible) the Duke of Norfolk's property. The line would thus come by Beauchamp Abbey, and from Chesterfield to Dronfield the gradient would be 1 in 165.

' *Sept.* 24.—Proceeded from Sheffield to Chatsworth. Had long conference with Mr. Paxton,[2] and explained the way the

---

[1] This is the first time 'express trains' are mentioned by Vignoles. The writer has found amusing details of some of the effects of this most welcome innovation, including a complaint from the guards on their elevated outside seats, that they with difficulty kept themselves from being blown off the 'coaches.'

[2] Afterwards Sir Joseph Paxton, the co-designer (with Sir Charles Fox) of

proposed line would go.   Dined and slept at Chatsworth by invitation from the Duke.[1]   Quite a railway party!—Lord Morpeth, who talked to me about Irish railways ; Lord Jocelyn, about Indian railways ; Mr. Lascelles, M.P., about the North Kent ; and Mr. Talbot, the Parliamentary agent, about railways in general.   The Duke spoke chiefly about the Derbyshire lines.   His Grace showed me the waterworks, and the conservatory.

'*Sept.* 25.—Examined the environs of Chatsworth ; also the course of the line towards Bakewell and Ashford, and the proposed branch to Chesterfield.[2]   Returning to Sheffield, I fixed the levels of the line through the town.

'*Sept.* 27.—The ceremony of cutting the first sod of the Blackburn, Darwen, and Bolton Railway took place at Darwen to-day.   Attended a grand entertainment given by the directors in honour of the occasion.

'*Oct.* 6.—Attended meeting [in London] of the directors of the proposed "Grand Union Railway."   Also of the "Norfolk Railway."   The making of the Spalding and Boston Junction line was agreed to ; Messrs. Stephenson and Bidder, with myself, being joint engineers.'

This proposed 'Grand Union' line was launched favourably under a strong direction, Lord Rancliffe being chairman, and it was highly spoken of in the public papers of that day.   It was to start from Nottingham, and crossing the Trent to run through the fertile vale of Belvoir to Grantham.   Thence it was to connect with King's Lynn by Spalding and Long Sutton.   A separate line was also to be made from Nottingham to Ambergate.   A co-operation of the Midland Railway was hoped for,

the first Exhibition building in Hyde Park ; also of the Crystal Palace at Sydenham.

[1] An amusing incident occurred on this occasion, Vignoles being compelled to borrow from Paxton a suit of dress clothes much too large for him. This being noticed by some of the guests near him at table over their wine, Vignoles explained the reason of the misfit to the Duke and his friends amidst roars of laughter.

[2] No line has been made from Bakewell to Chesterfield.   To reach the latter place from the former it is necessary to go by Ambergate, and then due north on the line through Chesterfield to Sheffield.

and thus intercommunication was to be established between the Eastern Counties and Lancashire, Yorkshire, and the Midland Counties. These proposals had strong local support.[1]

The line from Spalding to Boston was made, and is now part of the Great Northern Railway.

'*Nov.* 12.—Skipton. Rose at daylight, and engaged all day till dusk, and afterwards by moonlight, with Mr. Watson inspecti ig the whole of the [Little] North-Western Railway.'

Mr. John Watson was principal resident engineer on this line, which was afterwards called the "*Little* North-Western" to distinguish it from the amalgamated system which began to take form in 1846, and is now so well known as the 'London and North-Western Railway.' This line now forms part of the 'Lancashire and Yorkshire Railway.'

'*Nov.* 13.—Engaged with Mr. Watson on the affairs of the Blackburn and Clitheroe Junction; also on the Blackburn, Chorley, and Liverpool lines. Settling all the gradients, &c. Agreed to meet at Derby.'

Vignoles's diary for December 15 shows that he had a long interview that day at Derby with Mr. Hudson (the 'Railway King'); but he has left no record of the circumstances connected with their meeting.

Of all these various projects to which we have made reference in the preceding extracts, only four were completed *exclusively* by Vignoles—viz. those that connected with Blackburn and the neighbourhood, and the line from Lancaster to Skipton. The others, to which he had been nominated as engineer, either perished altogether, or were absorbed by new companies, or passed into the hands of other engineers.

(2) RAILWAYS IN IRELAND.

The diary extracts next given refer to Irish railways.

'*Feb.* 17, 1845.—Received instructions to-day from a deputation in London to undertake the formation of a line from Kingstown to Bray.[2] Engaged all day in preparing a draft

---

[1] Cf. *Railway Times*, vol. viii. No. 21.

[2] This line was to have been on the atmospheric system. In former years

statement for the Board of Trade, and consulting with some of the chief promoters of the line.

'*Feb.* 27.—Engaged in preparing estimates of the Cork and Bandon Railway for lodgment at the Private Bill Office.'

At the first meeting of this Company in Cork on August 20, the chairman, Captain Belcher, remarked on the very rapid and satisfactory manner in which the Bill had passed through its various stages. He alluded in a highly complimentary manner to the reduction in the contemplated expense of laying out the line which their engineer, Mr. Vignoles, had effected. The chairman also expressed a hope that an amalgamation between their line and that from Cork to Passage might soon be carried out; and this was agreed to by the two companies in the following October.[1] Vignoles had constructed this last-named line in 1836.[2]

We find he paid a short visit to Ireland between the dates of these last two entries; and on April 10 Vignoles records the passing of the former of these two lines through the Parliamentary Committee of Standing Orders.

'*April* 26.—Attending at Lord Stanley's[3] with a deputation from the Waterford and Limerick Railway. Mr. Rendel conditionally agreed to become engineer to this line, in the case of my acceptance of a post in India.[4]

'*May* 9.—Received instructions from the Admiralty to report on the proposed drainage of the Tacumshin Lake in conjunction with Mr. Rendel, on my next visit to Waterford.[5]

'*May* 14.—Examined Tacumshin Lake. Four small boats on it, employed in securing seaweed! Met Mr. Dargan and went with him over the railway works. Met Mr. Bianconi, famous for his large jaunting cars.'

Vignoles had also sketched out a probable line by the coast all the way to Wicklow, which long afterwards was carried out by Mr. Brunel.

[1] Cf. *Railway Times*, vol. viii. No. 42.
[2] Cf. Chap. XIV. p 197.
[3] Father of the present Earl of Derby.
[4] See the remarks at end of this chapter, p. 287, *note*.
[5] A lagoon on the south-east shore of county Waterford, within a few miles of the well-known Tuskar light off that coast.

On July 8 Vignoles notes the passing of the Waterford and Limerick Bill through the committee of the House of Lords.

On August 18 he went to Dublin, and thence by steamer to Waterford.

His diary for August 19 says :—

'Occupied myself the whole day, on board the packet, in completing the design for a National Harbour of Refuge at Dover, with estimates, &c., which Captain Beaufort[1] had asked me to prepare.'

On August 23, in the midst of his Waterford Railway business, he notes that he had 'drafted a report to the Admiralty on the harbour scheme at Dover.'

'*Aug.* 20.—Attended the first general meeting of Waterford and Limerick Railway. Mr. Meagher, the chairman, presided.[2] Talked over the matter of Lord Clare's property with the directors. Conference with Mr. Dargan on the contracts.

'*Aug.* 25.—Dublin. Explained the working of the Dalkey Atmospheric Railway to Mr. Joseph Hume, M.P., and Captain Washington, R.N., the Harbour Commissioners.

'*Aug.* 26.—This evening attended a great banquet at the Salt Hill Hotel, given by the railway directors to Sir John Burgoyne on his leaving Ireland.'

Vignoles visited Ireland again about the middle of October. His diary for the 15th of that month says :—

'Got to Limerick at ten o'clock A.M. with Mr. Galway, one

---

[1] Afterwards Rear-Admiral Sir Francis Beaufort, K.C.B., for twenty-six years Hydrographer to the Navy. Vignoles enjoyed a life-long intimacy with him. Professor Romney Robinson, of Armagh, was a near relative of the Admiral.

[2] The chairman stated at the meeting that, under an agreement with the Great Southern and Western Railway, it was essential that the work on that part of the line between Tipperary and Limerick should be commenced within three months from the passing of the Act, as a rival company had also proposed to undertake it. At this meeting Vignoles made a speech, and said (amongst other things) that he had appointed as engineer over this part of the line a gentleman belonging to the neighbourhood, and that he had arranged that all the sub-engineers under that person should be Irishmen. (Cf. *Railway Times* for 1845, p. 1,393.) Vignoles was at this time also requested by the promoters to become the engineer of the 'Cork, Charleville, Limerick, Ennis, and Galway Railway.'

of the directors.   The Earl of Clare cut the first sod of the Limerick and Waterford Railway at Boher, on his own estate, seven miles from Limerick.   The usual entertainment given in the city.   Interview with Mr. Dargan, the contractor, and Mr. Osborne, the resident engineer.   At 8 P.M. left in carriage and four for Dublin with Mr. Riall, one of the directors.   We got to Dublin at 10 A.M. on the 16th.'

A final visit to Ireland for this year was paid by Vignoles in December.   His diary for the 18th says :—

'Reached Waterford before noon, and met the directors. They finally settled all accounts up to August, and we agreed on terms for all subsequent expenses in the engineering department.   Dined with the chairman.

'*Dec.* 19.—Left Clonmel, and with Mr. Osborne examined the site for the crossing of railway over the river Suir, and other points.   Posted through to Tipperary and on to Limerick. About twelve miles from that city we were overtaken by a terrible storm of wind and rain, with intense darkness, which detained us till a late hour.

'*Dec.* 22.—Dublin.   Dined with Colonel Jones, R.E., the new chairman of the Government Board of Works.[1]

(3) North Kent Line, &c.

We have now to speak of Vignoles's engineering occupations in London itself, or in the southern and western counties.   The first of these that claims attention is that of the 'North Kent Line,' on which project Vignoles lavished the best of his intellectual powers, and for the success of which he left no stone unturned.   It was a noble and much-needed enterprise, which was launched under the highest auspices, and worked out in all its details with great skill and care, as was very generally acknowledged, and with the practically unanimous—we might almost say enthusiastic—approval of the principal towns and districts through which it was intended to pass.

[1] Afterwards Sir Harry D. Jones, K.C.B. and G.C.B.   He was in Ireland up to the breaking out of the Crimean war; and in 1856 was made Governor of the Royal Military Academy at Sandhurst, where he died in 1866.

Its most strenuous opposers were the directors and share-holders of the South-Eastern Railway Company, who had hastily put forth a counter-scheme in August 1844, but whose keen hostility made up for their late appearance on the arena. This company beyond all question incurred an enormous outlay in the Parliamentary contest that ensued, which in its later stages assumed almost the proportions of a death-struggle; but the secret history of this bitter strife has never been revealed, and we may be sure never will be. It has been conjectured—nay, even strongly asserted—by many of those best informed in such matters, that the story of the ultimate overthrow of the North Kent scheme had a very dark background, especially as regards its defeat in Parliament; but so, no doubt, had many a similar enterprise, both before and since. Into such *apocryphal* records (using the word in its literal sense), it would be very unwise for the present writer to dig; but some of the untold mysteries of company manipulation would make a very interesting chapter in the investigations of a competent historian, and would throw a new—possibly a rather lurid—light on the hidden craft of company-mongering.[1]

We must not attempt to detail the many modifications which the original scheme of the North Kent line underwent from the time of its inception a few years earlier up to the session of 1845. From the first, however, the late Sir Isaac Lyon Goldsmid was the chairman, Mr. Stephens, of Bedford Row, the solicitor, and Vignoles the engineer of the company; and the original intention was simply to accommodate the towns in North Kent from Greenwich to Chatham, but without crossing the Medway. The greatest difficulties to be overcome were the passing by or near the Observatory of Greenwich and the Park itself, and as to the best mode of avoiding the parade ground at Woolwich.

But in 1844 or earlier the scheme had developed itself into an independent line to Dover, by crossing the Medway, and

[1] The writer has heard with pleasure that Mr. H. R. Tedder, the accomplished librarian of the Athenæum Club, has written an article for the ninth edition of the *Encyclopædia Britannica* on 'History of Learned Societies' (vol. xxii.). It is much to be hoped that this writer will one day favour us with a history of *Companies!*

passing (with tunnels) the Royal Engineers' quarters at New Brompton, and thence by Sittingbourne to Canterbury and Dover. Access was also to be had to Deal and to Ramsgate and Margate. In fact, the line to a large extent is now to be traced in the London, Chatham, and Dover Railway, shorn of part of its original route near London, from which it was ousted by the South-Eastern Company's North Kent schemes; but finding some compensation eventually in opening up access to Pimlico and the City from the flourishing suburban settlements in Surrey and Kent, in the vicinity of the Crystal Palace. Vignoles (as his diary shows) was anxious to make a City terminus, and for this object he at one time proposed the purchase of the Southwark Iron Bridge; or, failing this, he was anxious to cross the Thames to Hungerford Market, a suggestion which the South-Eastern Company carried out twenty years later. But the principal promoters of the North Kent Railway seem to have aimed at no more than a terminus in the Borough and a connection with the South-Western line at or near Waterloo.

Vignoles's diary for January 15 says:—

'A summary of the report on the North Kent Railway was despatched to all the newspapers. This, with a copy of the engraved plan, was also sent to the principal civil engineers and to the library of the "Institution." '[1]

Early in 1845, when the prospects of the North Kent Company looked at their brightest, the promoters learned to their dismay that the Railway Department of the Board of Trade had decided in favour of five lines put forward by the South-Eastern Company, and against all other lines, including the North Kent.[2]

---

[1] Vignoles notes that I. K. Brunel had declined to give evidence on the North Kent line: this was not from any hostility to the scheme, but was only following out the principles of action that engineer had laid down for himself in all such cases. (Cf. *Life of I. K. Brunel*, p. 94.)

[2] Amongst numerous other schemes—many of them to be worked by the 'Atmospheric'—Sir John Rennie had projected 'The Central Kent Railway.' Vignoles's diary for February 1845 shows that at a public meeting in Dover the decision had been strongly in favour of the North Kent line over the proposals of the rival company.

This led to a further and final modification of the last-named enterprise, and an influential meeting of the shareholders was held in London, when some important testimony was adduced in favour of the engineering skill which characterised the proposed line, and this was confirmed by the professional opinion of Mr. Joseph Locke. A brief extract from the published records of the enterprise may be given here with propriety, as reflecting credit on the subject of this memoir.

At a general meeting held in February, Sir Isaac L. Goldsmid said : ' We lay upon the table a full statement of all the engineering circumstances of our lines, together with a copy of all the plans and sections as placed before the Board of Trade. This line has not been hastily prepared, but is the result of full and matured consideration ; and we are certain that the plans which have been prepared by Mr. Vignoles are those which have met with the approbation of engineers of the highest distinction.'

The adverse opinion of the Board of Trade, which, however, carried no Parliamentary force, did not arrest the efforts of the promoters of the North Kent line ; and they were also encouraged by some important decisions in their favour by other far more qualified authorities.[1] Sir John Rennie had alleged that ' the North Kent line, as proposed by Mr. C. B. Vignoles, will prove disadvantageous to public property at Deptford and Gravesend, and will also prejudicially interfere with the practice ground of the Royal Horse Artillery on Woolwich Common.'

It was urged also as a formidable objection that ' this railway proposes to cross the Medway at Rochester, and to pass through the town of Chatham.'

But as a matter of fact the consent of the authorities had been already obtained to the mode by which the North Kent line proposed to pass through Greenwich and Woolwich and over the Medway ; and this is best shown by giving here a copy of

---

[1] Although the Board of Trade was overwhelmed with railway business at the time, it had only *one* engineer as an assessor. In fact, this special department had only been constituted in the preceding session.

the letter from the Admiralty which was addressed to the chairman of the company :—

'January 15, 1845.

'I am commanded by the Lords of the Admiralty to give their consent to the course proposed to be taken by the London, Chatham, and Dover Railway,[1] so far as concerns the passing of the Royal Observatory, the bridge across the Medway, the quay at Chatham, and the viaduct over the Swale; provided the position of the terminus at Sheerness be left to their Lordships' decision.

(Signed) 'JOHN BARROW.'

We may add that the consent of the Ordnance Department had been obtained to the mode of passing the fortifications at Chatham. The Corporation of Rochester, moreover, had unanimously approved of the proposed line, whilst a vast majority of the landowners had declared themselves favourable to the scheme.

That the South-Eastern promoters were by no means sanguine of the success of their North Kent proposals, which indeed were all rejected during the session, is plain from Vignoles's diary, to which we now revert :—

'*Feb.* 13.—Had a confidential interview with Mr. Robert Stephenson on certain offers [of a compromise] made by him. I was disposed to meet him half-way, but Sir Isaac Goldsmid was strongly opposed to it.'

This resulted in the rejection of Stephenson's proposals the next day; but Vignoles had another private conference with him on the 16th, the record of which shows, however, that the terms suggested 'did not include any beneficial interest to the North Kent Committee.'

'*Feb.* 22.—R. Stephenson and Mr. Fearon, the solicitor to the South-Eastern Railway, and I, with others on behalf of the North Kent Company, had an interview to-day with the bridge wardens at Rochester, when they made known to us

---

[1] This title is itself an historical link between the original scheme and the present admirably managed company whose assured prosperity is drawing nearer every day.

their terms [as to crossing the Medway by the railway]. We all dined as a party most amicably, and R. Stephenson and self posted together up to town.'

Vignoles records another 'confidential interview' with R. Stephenson on March 3, as to the mode and point of crossing the Medway; and on March 8 he says:—

'Went to Rochester, when after long discussion the bridge wardens came to an unanimous conclusion in favour of our North Kent design, and to support our plan.

'*March* 18.—Attended the Parliamentary Committee on the petition for the North Kent line, when not a single objection of engineering was suståined against us.

'*May* 30.—Four hours under examination in committee on the North Kent Railway. Late in the afternoon posted down to Chatham with Mr. Hawkshaw[1] and others, examining the line as we went along.

'*June* 17 *and* 18.—Messrs. R. Stephenson and Bidder were examined to-day in committee and gave evidence against our North Kent line. R. Stephenson's examination not concluded till 18th. Same day we received the approval of the Board of Trade to our proposed method of passing the powder mills at Faversham.

'*June* 29.—To-day Serjeant Wrangham[2] replied on behalf of the North Kent Railway Bill; but after a short discussion the committee declared the preamble not proved, to my great chagrin. The South-Eastern Company's bills for their Maidstone lines also rejected.

'*July* 10.—Held a consultation this day with Mr. Joseph Locke, as to the enlarged scheme for the North Kent Railway, to be started immediately, with a capital of three millions.

'*July* 25.—At a general meeting held in the City to-day, Sir Isaac L. Goldsmid in the chair, it was resolved to reorganise

[1] He became Sir John Hawkshaw in 1873. Sir John is still vigorous and active, and his latest work—the Severn Tunnel—will certainly add to his high repute as amongst the very first in the engineering profession.

[2] Mr. C. Austin, Q.C., was the leading counsel engaged by the South-Eastern Company. Both these legal gentlemen were very able pleaders, and in the front rank of their profession.

the North Kent Railway scheme, and go in for a direct line from Hungerford Bridge to Dover.'

[An extract from Vignoles's diary in this same year may be read with interest in connection with the Severn Tunnel :—

'*June* 28.—At the request of Mr. Brunel I went down to report on the mode of crossing the Severn for the South Wales Railway, and engaged all day with Mr. Miller (Brunel's assistant) in examining the line by the Severn at Fretherne, twelve miles below Gloucester, where it is proposed to pass under the river by a tunnel. Examined particularly the lias limestone rocks on the left bank, and also the rocky bed of the river. Laid down the tunnel section for a length of about 2,000 yards, with 600,000 cubic yards of excavation. At a rough estimate it ought not to cost much above 200,000*l.*']

Vignoles always claimed to have been the first to suggest that the terminus of the Dover line should be on the Middlesex side of the river. The directors of his North Kent line seem to have urged him to content himself with a site near Waterloo Station, and there are many records in his diary of explorations in Southwark with this view; but he never abandoned his preference for the western bank of the river. The two following extracts confirm this :—

'*Oct.* 20.—Attended meeting of directors of the North Kent Railway. Went with some of them as a deputation to the trustees of Southwark Bridge, when proposals were made to purchase the bridge for 300,000*l.*, or an annuity of 12,000*l.* per annum.'

The records of the time show that other projectors had made similar proposals, which, it must be remembered, were based on the then imperfect knowledge of iron in connection with the strain involved in locomotive railway traffic.[1]

---

[1] Cf. *Railway Times*, vol. viii. No. 45. From this reference it will be seen that the overtures of the North Kent Railway were the only ones which found favour with the bridge proprietors out of several other proposals. Much valuable information on the subject of the use of iron in bridge formation will be found in the full account given by Professor Pole of the memorable failure of the trussed-girder bridge over the Dee at Chester, which occurred on May 24, 1847. (Cf. Pole's *Life of Robert Stephenson*, vol. ii. pp. 46-63.)

A rather remarkable entry is found in the diary of Nov. 20 :—

' Mr. Jackson, of Birkenhead, was introduced to the directors of the North Kent Railway.   He proposed a scheme, to be called the "London Central Railway Company," which was well received by our directors, and the nucleus of the undertaking was at once formed.   I was to be the engineer, and some of our directors would join the Board.   Messrs. Stephens and Few were to be solicitors.' [1]

Throughout the month of November there are constant notices in Vignoles's diary of the terrible race against time which had become the normal condition of the engineering world in 1845 ; and he particularly observes on the tremendous pressure of work in his own offices at Trafalgar Square to get all the plans for the reorganized North Kent line (together with about twelve or thirteen other railways) ready for deposit in the Parliamentary offices by the night of November 30.   He remarks that up to that date for a week previously ' some of us were engaged incessantly on the various plans and sections for twenty-four hours at a time.   Indeed, for several nights not one of my staff went to bed. Many of them were completely knocked up.   My son Hutton, twenty-one years of age, on the last night of our work fell into a profound sleep with all his clothes on ; and, as he could not be awakened, they cut off his Wellington boots, and rolled him into bed just as he was ! '

But a very dismal entry, and one prophetic of final disappointment in the matter referred to, is found in his journal for Dec. 10 :—

' Attended with Mr. Stephens at a meeting of the bridge wardens at Rochester.   Found we were completely jockied by the South-Eastern Railway in the matter of the joint bridge over the Medway.   We must now either quarrel with the wardens or spend 100,000*l.* extra money on the bridge.'

This unexpected ' check' in the stiff contest between the

---

[1] A day or two later he refers to this project as the proposed ' Charing Cross and Mansion House Railway.'   It would be interesting to know what route the projectors intended to follow.

rival companies was ominous of the 'checkmate' which was to befall Vignoles when the strife was finally closed.[1]

We must now glance at the brief history of another project in the railway world which had an interest of its own, as it proposed to occupy much of the ground covered by the earliest railway surveys which had been made by Vignoles in 1825. We allude to those carried out in Surrey and Sussex for Messrs. John and George Rennie, already referred to.[2] This original project of a railway from London to Arundel and Brighton was now to be revived, but with an evident intention to work the line by atmospheric traction, that ingenious system having reached its zenith of popularity in 1845.

On September 1 Vignoles's diary states :—

' Had a conference this morning with the promoters of the London and Arundel Railway, and agreed to accept the office of engineer-in-chief, and to direct the laying out of the line. Messrs. Sherrard and Hall were appointed sub-engineers.

' *Oct.* 4.—Conference with the solicitors of the Brighton and Arundel Atmospheric Railway, and received 1,000*l*. on account of the surveys of the new line.'

This projected line from London to Arundel (followed long after, almost precisely as Vignoles then laid it out, by the Mid-Sussex line of the London, Brighton, and South Coast Company), was to have been worked by locomotives, but the portion from Arundel to Brighton (in part at least) on the atmospheric principle ; and this was then acknowledged to have a marked advantage over the locomotive system in the matter of gradients, which on Vignoles's proposed line were very different from the easy and almost dead level course pursued by the existing South Coast line west of Shoreham. Vignoles's line was intended to go up the picturesque valley of the Adur by Steyning, and along the pleasant vale at the foot of Chanctonbury, under the

---

[1] '*July* 1, 1850.—Had a conference with Mr. Stephens, of Bedford Row, in reference to a new concern, of which the plans and sections had been lodged. It appears that the line adopted is nearly that laid out and advocated in Parliament by myself several years ago. The line between Chatham and London is to take a new direction through the " Crays," and much nearer to Maidstone.'

[2] Cf. Chap. IX., p. 107 ; opening remarks, and *note.*

northern side of the chalk range of the South Downs. The
river Arun was then to be crossed, probably near Amberley;
and the line turning southwards was to force its way by a
tunnel under the shoulder of the hill which abuts on the Arun
on its western bank, and to come out nearly due south of
Arundel town [1] There was also to be a branch to Littlehampton; but the exact route of this part of the line is somewhat conjectural, as no maps or written records of the scheme
exist, save the notices in Vignoles's diary.

On October 18 he notes :—

'Surveyed the country from Brighton to Horsham, accompanied by Mr. Upperton and the solicitor to the company. At
Horsham we endeavoured to gather the opinion of the several
landowners. Also examined the ground particularly on each side
of Dorking.

'*Oct.* 23.—Engaged all day on the line from Arundel to
Horsham. Fixed the line to Pulborough, and thence to Bil-
lingshurst.

'*Nov.* 1.—Engaged all morning examining the ground for
the Brighton terminus for the atmospheric line. Inspected
closely the ground on both sides of the existing railway to
Shoreham. Went with Mr. Upperton to Steyning, and up to
the height of Bramber Castle. Found I could not bring the
line any nearer to Steyning.

'*Nov.* 2.—Posted from Brighton to Littlehampton, and
viewed site of proposed station there. Conference at Arundel
with Mr. Holmes, the local solicitor.' [2]

---

[1] The present awkward junction of the Mid-Sussex with the South Coast
line at Ford was forced upon the Brighton Company by the opposition of the
then Duke of Norfolk.

[2] The son of this gentleman still lives at Arundel, honoured and respected
by the whole neighbourhood. He was working under his father at the time,
and was also frequently with Vignoles at his offices in London, and during
his visits to Sussex. After a thorough search Mr. Holmes has been unable to
discover any papers or documents belonging to the project. He says everybody, attorney and engineer included, lost money by the scheme; but Vignoles's
third son has preserved one pleasing financial reminiscence of the transaction,
as he was paid 50*l.* for his share in the surveys, and this was the first money
that he had then received for engineering work.

On November 21 Vignoles's diary says :—

'Attended the meeting at Windsor on the Windsor Atmospheric Railway. Arranging the proper models and drawings for the inspection of her Majesty.'

A short digression is desirable in this place on the subject of the atmospheric railway. It is plain that Vignoles had felt a strong predilection towards that system from the first moment of its introduction to public notice. He had, moreover, formed a close intimacy with Clegg and his co-patentees, Jacob and Joseph Samuda, the first-named of the brothers being the mechanical genius of the firm; and there can be no doubt that his death (by a terrible accident) was an irreparable loss, occurring as it did in 1844, when Brunel had already resolved to try the atmospheric system on an extended scale for the South Devon line, which attempt on the part of that gifted engineer was destined to prove the crucial test of this ingenious invention.

In the year 1845, amongst the civil engineers of eminence, there may be said to have been at least three convinced advocates of the adaptability of the atmospheric system to lines of railway under certain conditions. These were Isambard K. Brunel, William Cubitt, and Charles B. Vignoles; but many others in the same profession were by no means disinclined to its introduction.[1] On the other hand, one engineer of the very highest position, Robert Stephenson,[2] was its uncompromising opponent. Many scientific theorists (e.g. Herapath), however,

---

[1] The subject was fully discussed at the Institution of Civil Engineers in February 1845 and in November 1846, when the most formidable of the theoretical opponents of the atmospheric system (Professor Barlow) read a weighty and lucid paper, founded on mathematical as well as experimental data. The arguments are well worth reading even after so long a time, especially in connection with the practical failure of the system on the South Devon line a few years later. Professor Barlow's calculations and his conclusions were strongly supported by the late Mr. J. Scott Russell. (Cf. *Mechanic's Magazine*, vol. xliv. pp. 519 and 617–622.)

[2] In only one known instance did this engineer admit an exception in favour of atmospheric over locomotive traction—viz. in the case of Brunel's line across the Apennines in a long tunnel between Genoa and Turin, with a very steep gradient. (Cf. *Life of I. K. Brunel*, p. 137.)

upheld, and by their literary skill helped to propagate the principles of the invention.

It appears from what we read in Vignoles's diary that he strongly advocated its introduction for such heavy gradients as could not then be overcome by locomotives; and as an auxiliary ou such stiff ascents, for example, as that of the Alb Plateau, near Stuttgart, so often referred to in his Würtemberg diary of 1843.[1]

But Brunel alone seems to have had the courage of his convictions in partly adapting a line especially to be worked by the atmospheric system, as tried from 1846–48 on the South Devon Railway, where one-fifth (=10¼ miles) of the whole distance would in any case have some kind of auxiliary tractive power, even if locomotives were used. The result of Brunel's decision, and the undeniable failure of the atmospheric system on that line, after about nineteen months' persevering trial, can best be understood by those who are sufficiently interested in engineering history to go carefully through the various reports and arguments of Brunel, as given in Mr. Froude's admirable and lucid account of the whole story in the 'Life of I. K. Brunel,' by his son.[2]

As that acute and gifted engineer intimated in one of his reports, it seems difficult not to believe that, if Jacob Samuda's life had been prolonged, he would have devised some sufficient remedy for the apparently simple defects which marred the working of the atmospheric apparatus on the South Devon line, and eventually caused its abandonment (in all but one or two isolated cases) over the whole of Europe. Who will venture to prophesy that the idea will not yet be revived, and that some unborn —or at least unknown—genius may not find a practical solution of the mechanical difficulties which so largely contributed to its failure forty-five years ago?[3] Its theoretical superiority in some respects to the 'locomotive' system was acknowledged

---

[1] Cf. Chap. XIX.

[2] Mr. Isambard Brunel, B.C.L. The life was published in 1870 by Longmans, Green, and Co.

[3] About 300 miles of railway on the atmospheric plan were brought before Parliamentary Committees in 1844–45.

by R. Stephenson and most of the great engineers of that day ; and the Parliamentary Committee before which its merits were pleaded considered it proved that a *single* atmospheric line was safer than a *double* locomotive line.[1]

Before referring to lines in foreign parts on which Vignoles was consulted, we may mention the project for a railway in the Isle of Wight, which was first suggested in this year, so prolific in such enterprises. His diary says :—

' *Oct.* 5 *and* 6.—Engaged in a minute examination of some lines proposed in the Isle of Wight. Mr. Thornton accompanied me. I tried the various heights and curves and sections already taken, and drew a series of possible lines. Much occupied with directions for levelling the new line proposed for the Isle of Wight. Writing a provisional report.'

Several foreign railway schemes were submitted to Vignoles's opinion in the course of the year, a few of which we here mention.

In the month of Feburary : a proposed railway in the Roman States.

In March he held a conference with Mr. Elmslie, the acting engineer of the 'Madrid and Lisbon Railway,' and agreed to become engineer-in-chief to this important line.

On June 26 he relates the account of an interview with Count Rosen, the Swedish Minister, on the subject of railways in that country.

On December 29 he notes that he had a long conference with Messrs. Schneider, Price, and other gentlemen connected with the ' Vera Cruz and Mexico Railway,' and that he advised them on various grounds, and as to the capital likely to be required.

By way of bringing this chaper to a close, we must now relate briefly an episode of some interest with reference to a proposal made by the Governors of the East India Company,

---

[1] The full report of the Select Committee of both Houses of Parliament, issued April 22, 1845, may be seen in Hyde's *Railway Register*, vol. l. p. 579. The Committee were largely influenced by the evidence of Brunel, Cubitt, and Vignoles.

which, had it been accepted by Vignoles, would have changed the whole course of his future life.

On April 8 his diary says :—

' Had an interview to-day with the Chairman, Deputy-Chairman, and the Secretary of the East India Company, when the formal proposal was made to me to go out to India for three years, to examine and report upon a railway system for India. I requested a week to consider the matter.'

Vignoles was at first inclined to entertain the proposal favourably, and his diary for April 22 says :—

' Had an interview with Lords Ripon and Dalhousie, and with the Chairman and Deputy Chairman of the East India Company, as to the principles on which railways in India should be carried out.

'*April* 26.—Attending at Lord Stanley's on a deputation from the Irish railways ; and also arranging with Mr. Cubitt [1] to be my successor in the case of my going to India.

' *May* 4.—Long interview with the East India Board, and afterwards had a confidential talk with Sir I. L. Goldsmid and other friends, who advised me not to go out except on very favourable terms.

' *May* 5.—Long conference with the Earl of Ripon, and an interview with the directors at the East India House, when I entered a series of objections [to their proposals], which to a certain extent only were explained away. But I also stated that I could not accept less than 7,000*l.* per annum for myself, besides 1,000*l.* per annum for my chief assistant, and all expenses paid. Salary to commence and continue from port to port until my return.'

Further conferences showed that the directors were not willing to accede to these terms, and a few days afterwards he was offered 4,000*l.* for himself and 1,000*l.* for an assistant, but this he declined, and the negotiations were finally broken off.

What we have now related of the year 1845 has been, of course, exclusively with reference to Vignoles's own share in the

---

[1] Mr. Cubitt soon afterwards declined the offer, which, however, was con-ditionally accepted by Mr. Rendel.

engineering enterprises of that *annus mirabilis* in the records of the profession.   But incidentally our narrative may help to throw light on a field of scientific, social, and commercial activity, that for complexity, rapidity of movement, and intensity of conflict, in which all the elements of national, personal, and public life were seething and commingling, has perhaps no parallel in the history of our country and of civilisation.

PART III.

FOREIGN ENGINEERING ENGAGEMENTS.

U

CHAPTER XIX.

EARLY in the year 1843 Vignoles received overtures from the Würtemberg Government to pay a visit to that kingdom with the view of advising the King and his ministers on the subject of a system of railways which had been projected by the State engineers, and for which two and a half millions sterling had been voted by the Parliament. Whilst these proposals were under consideration, the Crown Prince of Würtemberg,[1] accompanied by some of the chief ministers, paid a visit to England, and, after several interviews had taken place, Vignoles was invited to join the Prince on an excursion into Wales, a few particulars of which expedition are given here, taken from the diary :—

'*June* 1, 1843.—Went by appointment to see Baron de Mancler, and had also a short interview with H.R.H. the Crown Prince of Würtemberg. Found him less *arriéré* than I expected. Signs of much intelligence, and he evinced a good deal of interest in the objects of his visit.

'*June* 5.—I joined H.R.H. and suite at Clifton this evening, and the next day we went by steamer to Cardiff, where we met Mr. Crawshay, of Cyfarthfa, and Sir John James Guest.

'*June* 6.—After examination of Cardiff Docks and railway terminus, &c., I accompanied H.R.H. on a locomotive up the Taff Vale Railway to Merthyr Tydfil. I was much struck with the laying out of the lines, and especially the curves. The royal party thought the Taff Vale similar in character to the valley of the Neckar. In the evening we visited Mr. Crawshay's " Cyfarthfa " iron-works.

[1] The present King of Würtemberg.

u 2

'*June* 7.—Our party was conducted by Sir J. Guest over his Dowlais iron-works. Sir John explained to H.R.H. and party the complete process, from the first operations of the blast furnace to the finish of the iron for delivery. Rain in evening hindered us from visiting the Rhymney iron-works.

'*June* 8.—In company with H.R.H. and party, left Merthyr at 7.30 A.M. and crossed the hills to the Neath Valley, and then on to the Aberdulais tin-works, and examined minutely the whole process. Afterwards we visited Mr. James's alkali-works at Llandore, near Swansea. H.R.H. and party then walked on to the Hafod copper-works, belonging to Messrs. Vivian. Examined the process, from the first smelting of ores to the refining and rolling of the plates in the mills; also the copper-nail cutting process. Visited Swansea harbour and pier, &c. Received letters from London which necessitated my immediate return.'

This was an urgent request from Mr. Robert Stephenson to examine the Peterborough branch of the London and Birmingham Railway, and support it as a witness in the House of Lords, which he did in due course, and his diary for June 17 says :—

'Engaged from 4 A.M. till 10 o'clock in preparing report on this line. Much gratified at Mr. Robert Stephenson's entire approval of it, as coinciding altogether with his own views. My report likely to strengthen his case. Gave evidence for the Bill on the London and Birmingham Railway (Peterborough Extension), which Mr. Stephenson acknowledged to have been of good service.'

Vignoles did not rejoin the Crown Prince of Würtemberg, who continued his tour in Wales, and afterwards visited Ireland and other parts of the United Kingdom.

Meanwhile due preparation had to be made for Vignoles's visit to Würtemberg, as he foresaw it would not be a short one, and some weeks were spent in winding up his English business, although the year 1843 was rather a slack time for engineers generally.

It has been thought desirable to give a somewhat full account of this Würtemberg expedition, as Vignoles's diary is full of interest, and his various tours and journeys of inspection in

Southern Germany, together with his able and comprehensive reports, were no inconsiderable factors in the origin and development of the railway system in that country :—

'*Sept.* 7.—At noon to-day embarked on G.S.N. Company's boat "Soho" for Antwerp, accompanied by my son Hutton, my daughter Mrs. C., and her husband.

'*Sept.* 8.—Got aground in thick fog off island of Walcheren. Only reached Antwerp at 4 P.M. Saw the cathedral, &c. Left at seven o'clock; arrived in Brussels at 10.30.

'*Sept.* 9.—Obtained letters from the direction to view the inclined plane at Liège and the railroad from Liège to Verviers. Met by Mr. Hudson, the resident engineer, who took us in a special carriage by ourselves. Saw the very fine four 80-horse power [stationary] engines midway between the two places. Difficult line to Verviers. Eleven tunnels and sixteen crossings of the river. The same kind of line all the way to Aix-la-Chapelle.[1] Line will be opened through on October 15.'

Vignoles had an interview at Cologne with M. Beyser, a railway engineer of note. This gentleman had made surveys through some of the valleys of Würtemberg for a rival line to that of M. Bühler, the Government engineer.

Diary adds :—

'M. Beyser gave us a copy of his report translated into English, and explained his principle of strategy. Up the river to Coblenz, and there stopped the night. Steamer so shaky that I found it impossible to write. Enjoyed the scenery—weather delightful. Mr. Creed, secretary to the London and Brighton Railway, travelled with us up the river. Long talk with him as to Port Dinlleyn.

'*Sept.* 14.—We went by railway from Mannheim to Heidelberg, sending on the heavy luggage to Stuttgart. Drove to the Wolf's Spring, visited the old castle, &c. In afternoon went on by rail to Carlsruhe. Observed particularly the valley of the Neckar and the chain of hills dividing Baden from Würtemberg. This high ridge seems to have very few openings for a rail-

---

[1] In a note he adds: 'The line from Aix-la-Chapelle to Cologne (single line only) has cost 30,000*l.* per English mile.'

way. From Carlsruhe posted on to Rastatt, and thence on to Baden-Baden, arriving very late at night.

'Sept. 17.—We all went a long drive to visit the valley of the Murg. Got a glimpse of Schloss Eberstein.[1] The carriage road magnificently engineered through the pass between Baden and Gernsbach.

'Sept. 19.—Left Baden-Baden this morning and posted by Gernsbach to Forbach, and along the valley of the Murg some considerable distance. Passed the boundaries of Würtemberg at two o'clock. Climbed up the steep table-land to the head of the valley of the Enz, which we followed some twelve miles to Wildbad, in the depths of the Black Forest. Scenery magnificent. All day at Wildbad Charmed with the delicious walks on each side of the Enz. Thick woods clothe the steep hills to the top. We found the Queen of Würtemberg, with the Princess Royal, staying here.

'Sept. 21.—Our party reached Stuttgart in afternoon, and took apartments in the Hôtel Marquardt. I had interviews with Professor Machlen. Received cordially by Baron Mancler.

'Sept. 22.—Obtaining some insight into the state of affairs here. Delivered my letters of introduction to Sir George Shee, the British Minister, who gave me a most agreeable reception. In the afternoon Baron Mancler was kind enough to call with me on several influential personages, viz. :—

Count Beroldingen	Minister of Foreign Affairs.
M. de Herdigen	„ Finance.
M. de Schlayer	„ Interior.
M. de Prieser	„ Justice.
Count Sontheim	„ War.
M. de Gaes	Secretary of State.
M. de Köstlin	Chief Railway Commissioner.
President Von Goortner	Minister of Privy Purse.
M. de Louche	Councillor.

And some others.

'Sept. 24.—At 4 o'clock to-day I had an audience of the King, but I could not enter into any business, so conversation turned only on general matters. In course of to-day nearly all

---

[1] The romantic ballad of Uhland gives the legend connected with this castle.

the principal persons on whom I had called returned my visit. Several also came to our box at the Opera in the evening.

'*Sept.* 25.—Went to the railway offices and inspected the enlarged plan and sections of the projected lines from Cannstadt to Ulm. M. Bühler, Government engineer, attended me. Also had audience of H.R.H. the Crown Prince, who pleasantly recalled our meeting in England.

'*Sept.* 27.—Spent upwards of eight hours in examining the same plans as yesterday. In course of the day had confidential talk with M. de Louche, and hinted my idea that some English capitalists should be invited to execute the railway works for a payment reduced to a terminable annuity of forty or fifty years. Went particularly through the portfolio of working drawings prepared by Mr. B., none of which appeared to be of the least use! This being the King's birthday, I dined with a distinguished company at Count Beroldingen's, in full Court dress. Afterwards attended the Opera, where I was introduced to Count William of Würtemberg and other noblemen.

'*Sept.* 28.—This morning I examined the plans of the line projected from Ulm to Friedrichshafen, on the Bodensee. Considering the rise of 500 feet in four miles on proposed line between Cannstadt and Ulm. At particular request of some of the gentlemen of the Court, went to the races at Cannstadt. The day was stormy; but in any case very little amusement for an Englishman!

'*Oct.* 2.—Just about to set off for a tour of inspection when I received a visit from MM. Köstlin, Bühler, and Etzel, who appeared quite staggered at the formidable series of questions I had proposed; but I insisted on having them answered. At their request, agreed to postpone my journey till Wednesday. Examined the country round Stuttgart from the top of one of the churches. Also looked at proposed site for the railway station. It is evident that by adopting a steep gradient an exit from the town may be got towards Ludwigsburg.[1]

---

[1] Stuttgart is surrounded by vine-clad hills. The railway from Pforzheim Junction through Ludwigsburg now enters Stuttgart through a tunnel (on the eft bank of the Neckar) 954 yards long.

'*Oct.* 4.—Examined the ground at Berg (two miles or so S.E. of city), and the way in which the line would diverge from principal route to Stuttgart. We then followed proposed line along left bank of Neckar until opposite Plochingen, where we

recrossed the river;[1] the road not allowing us to travel along the left bank for two or three stages.[2] Then along the left bank of the Fils Valley and pursued the line to Altenstadt, and (as it was getting dark) got into our night quarters at Geislingen.[3]

[1] This place is on the right or east bank of the Neckar, at its junction with the Fils, which flows from the south-east.

[2] The line as made crosses the Neckar to the right bank at Cannstadt, two and a half miles from Stuttgart. Here the Neckar is joined by the little river Nesenbach.

[3] Geislingen is thirty-eight miles from Stuttgart, in a ravine at the base of the

It is clear to me that the right bank of the river ought to have been levelled and tried.'[1]

Vignoles criticises the two lines proposed for his consideration; one was very circuitous—' up and down both sides of the Fils Valley, which is too absurd; the other an oblique inclined plane with gradient of 1 in 30, which is ridiculous.'

' *Oct.* 6.—Our party left Geislingen and explored the Alb of Altendorf, partly on foot, for some miles. Followed the line closely from Dornstadt and Mehringen to the river Blau, when it grew dusk. The whole of the projects of M. Bühler across the plateau seem unadvisable. We got to Ulm about seven o'clock P.M.

' *Oct.* 7.—Inspected site of station at Ulm, and explored the high ground on the Blau river.[1] Examined the proposed line up the Kiesenthal Valley, went back through Albach along the Bavarian frontier.[2] The line as intended I deem preposterous. [No evidence of its exact course.]

' *Oct.* 8.—Left Ulm and examined proposed line as far as Waldsee.[3] This *détour* I think quite inadmissible. Towards evening saw one or two peaks of Alps and the Tyrol for a moment. Had some conversation at Ulm with Major von Prittwitz, the engineer who is constructing the fortifications.

' *Oct.* 9.—Left Waldsee and explored the return lines as proposed by M. Bühler as far as Ravensburg, to which place a cheap line can be constructed, but by a very different system of laying out. At a wedding festival held at the inn at Ravensburg fully

---

Alb [Swabian Alps.] The line [as made] here quits the valley of the Fils, and ascends the Geislingen Steig (a wooded limestone hill) to the tableland of the Swabian Alb, which is the 'Wasserscheide' between the Neckar and the Danube. The ascent is 1 in 45.

[1] After leaving Cannstadt the railway [as made] crosses the Neckar to the right bank, and after passing Esslingen quits the Neckar Valley. This latter town was once a free imperial city.

[2] The Blau joins the Danube at south-west side of Ulm, which city (on the *left* bank of the Danube) has belonged to Würtemberg since 1810. Ulm had been constituted a fortress of the Germanic Confederation in 1842.

[3] The line from Ulm through Mengen and Mosskirch to Rudolfzell, at the extreme north end of the Bodensee, now passes through the Albach Valley.

150 guests were assembled.   It gave us a curious insight into the customs of the country.

' *Oct.* 10.—Left Ravensburg and followed the line proposed by M. Bühler along the valley of the Schüssen.   This with some modifications may be made into a good line from Ravensburg, and along the valley above to Friedrichshafen, which we reached at noon.   In the afternoon went on to Lindau, examining the ground with a view to a branch line giving the Bavarians access to Lake Constance.[1]   Returned late to Ravensburg at night.

' *Oct.* 13.—After a heavy rain storm, which lasted till noon, examined the country south of Waldsee, and came along the valley of the Schüssen, now full to overflowing.   Ground much broken and full of springs.   M. Bühler's proposed way of bringing his line on the slope of the ridge here would be unsafe ; but it seems practicable to keep along the valley, and adopt higher gradients at the upper end.   The whole valley of the Schüssen is well adapted for a railway.

' *Oct.* 14.—Left Waldsee, proceeded to Aulendorf, and thence over the summit ground to Ingoldengen.   Traced a practicable railway from the waters of the Rhine to those of the Danube, and thus can avoid the *détour* to Waldsee.[2]   However, all the suggested lines require minute examination ; and the estimates of comparative cost relative to local accommodation must be the chief guide.   Examined the rest of valley of the Riss to Bieber-bach, and thence on to Ulm.   Gradients between these towns must be thoroughly altered, to reduce the needless extent of embankment.[3]   Grand hills, close to the proposed line, to within ten miles of Ulm, all the way from Aulendorf.   In after-

---

[1] The line from Lindau now reaches Ulm *viâ* Immenstadt and Memmingen, in Bavarian territory.   It is not clear from the diary where this proposed branch to Lindau was to run *from*, probably from Ravensburg.   This con-necting link has not been made.

[2] In the lines as made, the Waldsee is reached from Aulendorf, and from Kisslegg (some miles south of Waldsee) it bifurcates to Leitkirch and Isny eastwards, and to Wangen on the south.

[3] This line has been made.   Some of the embankments on the lines *origin-ally* proposed were to be 120 feet high.

noon attended public dinner given by Major P. in honour of the King of Prussia's birthday. My health also was drunk, and I had to make a speech ! Slept at Gersbach.

' *Oct.* 16.—Got on to Gunzburg, and by main road to Augsburg. The watercourses all filled by the incessant rain. I think a practicable line may be made for locomotives from Ulm to this place, as the valleys are wide and the ridges not very high. Possibly a tunnel through high ground nearest Augsburg, and a viaduct or two. No serious obstacles of difficulty or expense.[1] Caught the 4 P.M. train to Munich.

' *Oct.* 17 *and* 18.—Paid a hurried visit to the " Pinakothek " and " Glyptothek." Rather disappointed with both, though no doubt very interesting as historical collections. Got back to Augsburg, and thence posted on to sleep at Langweich, which we left at daylight next morning. Inspected the railway now being made from Augsburg to Donauworth. Went across country northward from Bieberbach. Walked to all the heights, and then recrossed the valley by Wertingen : very steep and difficult, but practicable by deep cutting through the summit ridge. From this point I saw the celebrated battle-field of Blenheim.'

During the next few days Vignoles, with his son and the two officers just mentioned, walked through the valley of the Lautersthal (a distance of nine miles), and climbed the summit between Nellingen and Stettingen. He expresses his sense of the difficulties of a practicable line dealing with the ascent and descent of the Alb. He continued his excursions, sometimes on foot, sometimes driving, and very often making use of his theodolite. He notes a vast number of suggestions resulting from his re-examination of the various proposed lines from Geislingen along the valleys of the Fils and the Neckar, of which, and of kindred matters, copious details are given in his closely written diary. The next day he records an interview with Baron Mancler, and adds :—

' The Baron says that I ought to speak to the King very frankly ; that, further, I should set aside everything that had been hitherto done, and make out an entirely new project for

---

[1] The line has been made according to his suggestion.

the railways. I informed him of my intention to visit the lines proposed through the valleys of the Rhems and Brenz.

'*Oct.* 25.—Baron Mancler privately informed me that the King was disposed to give me his full confidence; and that he (the Baron) hoped to get all matters into a satisfactory condition before he set out on a tour with the Prince Royal to Italy.

'*Oct.* 26.—After careful examination of the town, came to the conclusion that the best and most central site for the railway station would be the *trapezium* of buildings immediately opposite the Schloss-Platz, to include Fürstze Street in the station.'

Vignoles gives a sketch plan in a pen-and-ink drawing in his diary, and enters into many suggestions as to arranging the ground, extending and straightening the streets, &c. After working out the plans he showed them to some of his friends connected with the Court, who (he says) 'highly approved of them.' He also received intimation that the Government of the Grand Duchy of Baden wished him to visit their territory, to consult about the junction of the frontier lines with those of Würtemberg.

On the evening of October 28 he dined with Sir George Shee, and met several influential people. M. Köstlin informed him that the Foreign Office had prepared for him a letter of introduction to Count de Bismarck, the Würtemberg Minister at Carlsruhe.[1]

Vignoles mentions the visits of two English gentlemen whom he had met at the Minister's dinner—viz. Mr. Hindley, M.P., and Mr. de Winton, who with his family was wintering in Stuttgart. He also records another excursion with M. Etzel, of which he says:—

'It seems certain that the base of operations for the Würtemberg railways should be the union of Stuttgart with Cannstadt and Ludwigsburg; and from these two places the main lines should run eastward to the Danube and westward to the Rhine, whilst the subsidiary lines may be carried out in any of the directions hitherto proposed.'

---

[1] This nobleman was a member of the Schierstein branch of the Bismarck family. The illustrious prince of that name is descended from the Schönein branch.

On November 1, 1843, Vignoles set out to examine the line of country in the valley of the Neckar to Heilbronn, and thence up the Elsenz Valley, of which he says:—

'This might very well be followed to its confluence with the Neckar, three or four miles east of Heildelberg.' [This has since been done.]

He further says:—

'Examined the country as far as the Baden frontier. Proceeded to Eppingen, and thence to Weilen, where we ascended a fine old tower of the Middle Ages, in a remarkable state of preservation, called the Steinsberg, from which we had a very extensive view. It seems to me that the main line should certainly follow the valley of the Neckar to Heidelberg. A separate line should be made from Stuttgart direct to Pforzheim for the traffic to France and Western Switzerland; or, if that were not agreed to, then a middle course might be taken from Ludwigsburg by Beitingheim to Illengen and Brüchsal.[1] We went at night to this latter place by train from Wiesloch.'

Vignoles records a long and close survey of the country, the next day, from Brüchsal up the Kraich Valley, by Gochsheim and Kurnbach to the summit, and thence into the Zoberthal Valley, and his journal says:—

'*Nov. 3.*—It is evident that the summit gradient must be steep, with heavy works on each side, and a two-mile tunnel. Afterwards examined summit between Siesenbach and Frendenstein, but it was too long and rugged. Explored the summit between Zaiserweiler and Maulbronn. Thence following the valley to Eilfergerhof we crossed to Knittlingen, and thence by the high road got to Bretten, where we passed the night.

'*Nov. 4.*—Left Bretten at daylight and posted down the valley of the Salza as far as Rosith, and crossed again into Würtemberg. I think some of the difficulties of the projected lines may be avoided. Followed M. Seeger's line to the proposed embankment to Pforzheim: found it favourable. Crossed the line at Schonenberg to Erlenbach: easy section to Illingen. No difficulty in crossing valley there to reach the plateau

[1] It is this last suggestion which has been followed out.

between the Enz and the Metter Valleys, by which I can avoid the difficulties in projected line, which would go along the valleys instead of *between* them. MM. Etzel and Räheim seem now more convinced of the fitness of my proposals.'

At Carlsruhe, Vignoles found that the Baden Government attached great importance to the junction of railways at Pforzheim, which was a thriving commercial town. The secretary of the Würtemberg Legation had introduced Vignoles and his companion, M. Etzel, to the director, as well as to the engineer (M. Sauerbeck) of the Baden lines, whose projects he was allowed to criticise on the maps and sections.

The diary says :—

' *Nov.* 9.—The Brüchsal line is a very good one ; the Pforzheim one is bad. Had several tracings made, and discussed the lines with M. Etzel. M. Maréchal [director of the railways] thought that the Würtemberg Government would adopt the wider gauge of the Baden lines,¹ but that his Government would wait to receive my special report, not directly, but from the Würtemberg Government. This concludes my examination of the lines as officially laid before me.

' *Nov.* 10.—To-day I visited *one* out of the *seventy* establishments at Pforzheim for the manufacture of gold and silver ornaments, &c., for which the place is celebrated.

' *Nov.* 12.—Baron Mancler told me that the King wished me to write direct to himself, as to the mode of executing the railways. The first rough draft of this letter occupied me from 8 P.M. till midnight, and I completed the revision of it at 4 A.M., when my son Hutton rose to make a fair copy of it. In the course of the day the document was translated into German, and in evening I sealed and addressed it to his Majesty, to whom Baron Mancler would present it on Tuesday.

' *Nov.* 22.—Our halting-places to-day were at Gmünd, Essingen, Aalen, Wasseralfingen, where we visited the Government iron-works and closely examined the proposed cast-iron

¹ The gauge throughout Germany (and France also) is practically the same as the English narrow gauge, 4 feet 8½ inches. The Russian gauge is 5 feet.

rails, on the so-called American system, which will *not* do for the Würtemberg lines. A tunnel [1] appears inevitable in passing from the Kocher to the Jagst Valley, and the whole of the ground from Lauchheim to Bopfingen is of a very difficult character.

' *Nov.* 24.—To-day we crossed the ridge into the valley of the Brenz, and explored that stream to its source at Königsbronn. Here I inspected the Government establishment for casting of shot and cannon. Turf is used for the puddling of the iron.'

During the next few days Vignoles examined the lines projected through the valleys of the Rems and Brenz, pursuing the latter to the frontier of Würtemberg at Sontheim.[2] He then examined the valley of the Blau, reaching Ulm late at night on the 27th, ' by dint of posting and change of carriages and horses; ' and his diary has this remark on the crossing of the Alb Plateau :—

' *Nov.* 28.—Walked from Darmstadt to the Denker, then across the plateau of the Alb. It appears to me that the proper way of crossing it will be by an inclined plane at each end, to be worked by stationary power; and between the heads of these inclined planes to have a locomotive line chiefly on an embankment. A viaduct and some short tunnels will be required, but open cuttings should be avoided, to prevent the snow-drift in winter.

' *Dec.* 1.—Had a long interview this morning with MM. Köstlin and Bühler, when these gentlemen produced me the drawing of a rail lately proposed, which turned out to be an alteration (for the worse) in the form of rail originally proposed by me in 1830, and which is well known through all Germany as the " *Vignolesche Rail.*"

' *Dec.* 5.—This afternoon I had the honour of dining with his Majesty, who spoke very freely to me on business matters, to which I responded with equal freedom. The King introduced me to the Princesses, with whom I had some agreeable conver-

---

[1] The line as made has no tunnel at this place.

[2] Sontheim-Brenz is on the line from Ulm to Aalen, about 30 kilomètres north-west of Ulm.

sation. In the course of my conference with the King I explained to him fully my views on the general direction of the lines, and that I should be obliged to abandon all the old plans [*scil.* those of the State engineers].

'*Dec.* 9.—This afternoon went with Baron Seckendorff (Maréchal de la Cour) in his carriage along the whole of the proposed line to Cannstadt. Explained the plan of passing the Cavalry Barracks, the exit from Stuttgart, and the mode of crossing the Neckar below Rosenstein. The Count took me over the Rosenstein Palace. Some of the statuary and pictures are very beautiful. He also showed me the King's model farm.

'*Dec.* 13.—This morning, at the request of Baron von Bühler, I rode on horseback with him and my son by Kornthal, &c., to Hemmingen, in the direction by which he supposed the railway might have been taken into the valley of the Enz. The line rose rapidly as far as Kornthal, when the country got to a very high level, then falling into the usual series of deep valleys with numerous lateral ravines, presenting altogether difficulties too great to be thought of. Explained all this as genially as I could to the Baron, who took his engineering disappointment very quietly. We afterwards dined with the Baron and his lady, and in the afternoon he sent me back in his carriage to Stuttgart, my son remaining with him for some shooting.

'*Dec.* 18.—I gave a dinner to a distinguished party. There were fourteen guests, besides myself and my second son, Hutton; and amongst them were H.R.H. Count Wilhelm of Würtemberg, Count de Porbeck (the Baden Minister here), Baron de Berlichingen, Baron Hugel, Baron Cotta, and other high persons of the Court and State.

'*Dec.* 20.—Had a long interview with H.R.H. Count Wilhelm, also with Baron Hugel. Both these noblemen informed me that the King was fast coming round to my ideas, and that probably his Majesty would be induced to create a new department of the Ministry of Public Works.'

Vignoles during the remainder of this year was a good deal occupied in the revision and perfecting of his plans, accompanied by elaborate maps, drawings, and models; and many pages of his

diary for December are filled with references to the plan of operations which he had recommended to the King of Würtemberg.
Of course he then knew nothing of the ' backstairs' intrigues
which were already secretly working to overthrow his designs
and countervail the influence he had acquired over the mind of
the King.

'*Dec.* 23.—Sketched out a design for an iron colonnade in
front and an embankment behind the Cavalry Barracks. Mr.
Müller, the artist, made drawing of the viaduct over the Neckar,
as seen from the Castle of Rosenstein. Began the drawings in
detail of the Rosenstein Viaduct, my son assisting in the same.'

Vignoles and his son spent Christmas Eve at Baron de
Louche's, and he remarks :—

'*Dec.* 24.—On this occasion the German custom of lighting
up a tree and arranging presents for the children of the family
was very prettily exemplified.[1]

'*Dec.* 25.—This Christmas Day (Monday) I completed my
design for the viaduct across the Neckar at Rosenstein. Extended the section of the line from Ludwigsburg to Thann, and
generally pushed on all matters as much as possible. My son
and self took our dinner at the *table d'hôte* at Marquardt's at
half-past four, with a very small company, and drank to family
and friends, &c., in a solitary bottle of champagne. Afterwards
continued my work till 5 A.M.

'*Dec.* 27.—Rose at 5 A.M. and worked at the various plans
and sections, so as to have the fair copies ready to present to
his Majesty to-day. At noon, according to appointment, I
waited on the King and delivered and explained to him the following maps.'

[Vignoles here specifies ten maps, drawings, and sections,
&c., of the works upon the various lines proposed through
Würtemberg.]

' Having given the King a general outline of the results of
my investigations, I made a formal complaint of the delays and
difficulties that had been thrown in my way ; and I also spoke

---

[1] If the writer's memory is to be trusted, this custom had not then been
introduced into England.

strongly of the folly and absurdity of all that had hitherto been done by the Government engineers. I then pressed on the King the necessity for an entire and radical change in the management of the railway concerns. On his Majesty asking for a report in writing to accompany what I had laid out, I demurred, on account of the way in which my first report on the form of rails had been treated; and I positively declined to make any report that was to be subjected to the criticism of his Majesty's Ministers. The King heard me with the utmost attention, and several times addressed me as " Mon cher Vignoles! " He kept the plans, &c., and after one hour and a half's audience his Majesty graciously dismissed me.'

It is evident that this important interview produced at the time considerable impression on the mind of the King, although the sequel was hardly what Vignoles must have hoped for, after so favourable an audience.

The next day President Gärtner, who, as Privy Purse, had considerable influence with the King, called on Vignoles, and begged him to draft a further report specially for the King's perusal, which his Majesty distinctly promised should not be laid before the Railway Commissioners. Such a request Vignoles was prompt to obey; and his diary shows how he (in spite of the indisposition under which he was at the time suffering) bravely set to work, rising early and going late to rest in order to complete the task.

' *Dec.* 30.—Early this morning despatched to M. Gärtner the concluding paragraphs of the report I had prepared at his Majesty's special command. Advising with MM. de Louche and Mährler as to the translation of the same, which they were attempting. My son Hutton engaged in writing the fair copy of the same as fast as I could get it ready, which I carefully revised as I wrote it. M. Gärtner came to see me with a special assurance that the King had given distinct orders to his Ministers, and to Mr. Bühler, the State engineer, that all my requests were to be strictly complied with; and that in a few days I should be supplied with all the materials I had so often asked for.' [This was carried out.]

Vignoles, it seems, had been purposely kept in the dark as to what the exact plans were which had been recommended by some of the State Railway authorities. Indeed, it seems clear that those worthy gentlemen scarcely knew themselves what they intended; or, at any rate, that their proposals were of so indefinite and tentative a character that they evaded all efforts on Vignoles's part to submit them to the test of technical examination. This was all along one of his chief complaints, as it rendered it impossible for him to prepare a clear and distinct system of railway communication which should replace these very visionary projects.

'*Dec.* 31.—This morning the King sent specially to inform me that the Saxon Government had written officially through the Würtemberg Minister at Dresden to make inquiries as to the nature of my arrangements, with a view to invite my services to determine the question of the junction of the Saxon and Bavarian railways, and to ask me to advise generally on lines in that part of Germany.'

We give here Vignoles's concluding reflections for the year 1843 :—

' My occupations here and general state of business make an agreeable contrast in my affairs when compared with the close of the previous year; and I have every reason to be grateful for so happy a change in my circumstances, and that, according to all appearances, the tide of fortune is not unlikely to turn in my favour, after running so long and tumultuously against me. I hope by a little more perseverance to regain my former position as to money matters; and family concerns are also in a more prosperous state, except for the severe illness of my eldest son, whose health is, I fear, seriously affected. The West Indian matter—so long a cause of anxiety—has also drawn to a successful termination. God be praised!'

During the first few days of the new year, Vignoles continued to work at his various plans and designs, and was more particularly engaged on his special report to the King. Some of his friends and advisers still encouraged him to believe in the ultimate success of his proposals; but it is evident that the Railway Commissioners had gained new allies in the military authorities, for, on January 8, Vignoles found it necessary to enter into communication with the Minister of War, General Sontheim. It was probably the proposed mode of passing in front of the Cavalry Barracks that was the cause of this new objection ; but Vignoles with characteristic promptitude immediately gave orders for a full-sized model of four of the pillars and part of the entablature of the proposed colonnade to be erected *in situ*, that the King might be able to judge of the effect of the engineer's design.

His diary says :—

' *Jan.* 11, 1844.—Met the Minister of War on the spot where the wooden full-sized model had been erected. My explanation seemed to give satisfaction. Just after we had left, the King came to inspect the model, and expressed himself thoroughly satisfied with it to the architect. Very much amused at the sensation created in the place. The day being very clear, though bitterly cold, crowds of people flocked to see the model.

' *Jan.* 14.—Engaged all day, and to a late hour of the night, in preparing draft of my report on the Würtemberg railways. I begin with a brief historical account of the whole proceedings, and then examine the system and principles hitherto adopted by the local engineers. The second part will go into a detailed examination of all these lines, so as to support my general remarks. The third part will be a remodelling of my report to the King of December 30 last. The fourth part will relate to other lines through the kingdom, and to a general exposition of railway principles from my point of view.

'*Jan.*18.—This evening attended a ball at Count Beroldingen's. Had an opportunity of speaking to the King about my report, &c. H.M. conversed with me in the kindest and most affable manner, as did also the Princess Marie, his daughter.[1]

' *Jan.* 22. —At noon had an audience of the King of Würtemberg, accompanied by my son Hutton. The Queen and the two

---

[1] This Princess was the oldest of the King's five children, being the elder of the two daughters by his first wife. She was married to Alfred, Count of Weipperg, in 1840.

youngest Princesses were also present. Explained the construction of the timber viaducts, and also showed the models
and plans of that part of the line which crosses the Alb Plateau.

' *Jan.* 25.—Had long interview with Sir George Shee, the
English Ambassador here. Explained to him my designs and
plans for railways in this country. In the evening attended a
great ball given by the Minister of Foreign Affairs. The Queen
conversed with me a long time. I was also introduced to the
Prince of Hohenlohe-Lauenberg, the husband of our own Queen
Victoria's half-sister. The Prince is president of the Würtemberg
House of Peers. Several other influential persons spoke to me,
and all parties united in requesting me not to leave the country
at the present time. Received official notice that M. Bühler
had been removed from the Railway Commission.

' *Jan.* 31.—Attended at the palace of H.R.H. the Princess
Marie, at her express wish, and explained to the Princess and
her husband, the Comte de Weipperg, the various models and
drawings for the railway. Much annoyed to-day at finding that
the Government Railway Commissioners had advertised for timbers for the upper works of the railway, suited to the cross-
sleeping principles.[1]

' *Feb.* 3.—Entertained a large party of scientific and professional men at a *conversazione.* I had placed plans and
drawings round the room, and delivered a short explanatory
lecture in French. Gave them a good supper, with plenty of
wine, and we kept it up to a late hour. Deep snow fell in the
night.

' *Feb.* 5.—This evening I gave a *conversazione* to a party of
sixty ladies and gentlemen of the highest social position in
Stuttgart. The models and drawings were again placed round
the apartments, and were much admired. Explained them to
some of the gentlemen who were best informed in such matters.
The *soirée* was kept up to a late hour.

' *Feb.* 7.—Left Stuttgart on a sledge in middle of the day,

---

[1] This is an incidental proof that at the time he agreed with I. K. Brunel's
opinion, and his preference for longitudinal bearings. Vignoles, however,
eventually adopted the principle of cross-sleepers for all parts of his lines.

with my son and my two assistants, Messrs. Cook and Davies. Got to Geisslingen just at dusk. The snow had gradually increased in depth as we ascended the valleys of the Neckar and Fils, and at the foot of the Alb Plateau it was very heavy.

' *Feb.* 8.—We started at eight o'clock A.M. for Luitzhausen, where we got farmers' sledges, and then, accompanied· by Major Prittwitz, drove upwards of twenty miles by country roads, over the fields, across the ravines, and in all directions, traversing the whole length of the Denkerthal, and also the ground between Scharn-stettin and Halzhausen. The average depth of the snow was about sixteen inches, the maximum (except in a few drifts) being two feet. The country people said that it was deeper than any winter since 1829. They stated that the drifts on the Alb were always in the same places. Examined carefully the various summits and ravines, and I was able to fix pretty nearly in my mind the general course of the lines. Got to Ulm at nightfall.

' *Feb.* 9.—Got a good view of the distant Alps and of the Tyrol from the heights in the course of the morning. I noted the progress of the fortifications now being constructed at Ulm, on which about a thousand men are employed. The work is done very cheaply, but the workmen seem to be unskilful, slow, and idle.'

Vignoles winds up the account of this trip :—

' *Feb.* 11.—Found the snow ceased entirely at Gippingen, where we left our sledges, and posted in a carriage to Stuttgart. In the evening attended a ball given by H.R.H. Prince Frederick.[1] Explained to him, and to the Queen, that the snow was much less than I had supposed, and that we had often a heavier snow-fall in England.

' *Feb.* 13.—Conference in afternoon with M. de Louche, and expressing my vexation and annoyance at the manner in which this railway affair is being carried out. Indeed, I am sick of the whole business. In evening attended the State Ball given by the King at the Palace. His Majesty spoke very graciously

---

[1] He was nephew to the King, being son of H.M.'s brother, the Prince Charles Frederick. This son died in 1870.

with me about my late visit to the Alb. The Queen also was
very affable. M. Gärtner was not cool, but evidently shy of
speaking to me; whilst M. de Schlayer appeared not to see me!

'Feb. 14.—At last succeeded in getting the mode of crossing
the river Enz at the Bissingen saw-mill fixed. The height of
the viaduct will be 790 feet above the sea level, and about 150
feet above the valley; the embankment at each side being
greatly reduced by obtaining a gradient of 1 in 100 at the west
side. On my return I dined with H.R.H. the Princess Marie,
and met a distinguished party.

'Feb. 20.—M. de Malzen, the Bavarian Minister, and M. de
Porbeck, the Baden Minister, both paid me long visits, discussing
the proposed respective junctions on the proposed lines with
those countries. My conference with the former was very
interesting. In evening attended the ball given at the Court
by H.M. the Queen of Würtemberg. Had a very affable conversation with the King.

'Feb. 21.—Continued working at my report from a very early
hour until midnight, chiefly on the comparison of the engineering and statistical points between the two eastern lines. This
was a work of great labour, requiring five or six revisals of each
paragraph, to condense and clearly express all the points. Then
proceeded to the discussion of the military and strategical con-
siderations of the question, and reading all the memoranda and
suggestions I had collected.

'Feb. 22.—Revising my report as far as copied. In consequence of the German writer employed by Professor Mährler
having got drunk repeatedly, I was put to a great deal of trouble
to procure another. Taking up the points of distances and
estimates concerning the lines over the Alb, and those by Rens
and Brenzheim respectively. Did not finish the subject till
three hours after midnight.

'Feb. 24.—Engaged from daylight until two hours after midnight in abstracting and tabulating the estimates. By analysis
I found that the price for earthwork was only 5d. per cubic yard,
and for the masonry 9½d. per cubic foot English. The estimate
for the upper works was a fair one, about 3,275l. per mile for a

single line, with 10 per cent. on the length for sidings, &c. Land averaged about 445*l*. per mile; earthwork about 140,000 cubic yards per mile; masonry, 1,824 cubic yards. But the items for stations, carrying establishment, management, and contingencies, were all much too low—1,200*l*. instead of about 3,000*l*. per mile. The total equals 11,120*l*. per English mile, or about 308,750 florins per Würtemberg league, for which sum I think their railway works could be executed, if properly laid out. Thus 30 millions of florins ought to be the covering sum for all the lines.'

The diary shows that during the last four days of February Vignoles was kept to the house, and only able to rise from his bed late in each afternoon. He had caught cold, and was also suffering greatly from fatigue induced by his recent continuous exertions. Of his now finished report he says on the 29th :—

' Being unable to leave my bed, I spent the time in quietly reading over the fair copy of my report, after it had been bound up. I rose with difficulty toward evening, and added six paragraphs to conclude the second part of it. My final estimate for 98½ leagues of railway brings up the total cost to about two and a half millions sterling.

' *March* 1.—Sir Alexander Malet,[1] the Secretary of the British Legation at Vienna, who had arrived last night, called on me. He has married the daughter of Lord Brougham, and Lady Malet has accompanied her husband to Stuttgart.

' *March* 2. — Interview with Count Beroldingen, who is anxious for me to fix a time with the Saxon Minister of Foreign Affairs for my examination of the railway from Nuremberg to Dresden. Received this morning a large packet of letters from London ; and much annoyed at observing that all the schemes for railways in England which I had proposed in less prosperous times were being taken up now, and falling into the hands of other engineers.

' *March* 4.—Felt still so unwell that I called in the King's private physician, Dr. Ludwig, who prescribed for me. He

---

[1] He was then forty-four years of age, and was Plenipotentiary at the Court of Würtemberg from 1844-1852. His second son, Sir Edward B. Malet, is now the British Ambassador at Berlin.

informed me (to my great disappointment) that his Majesty was rather seriously ill, and that there was no chance of my having an audience with him for some time.

'*March* 5.—Still very poorly, but struggling to keep up, and spent most of day in preparing notes, &c., for the translation of my report. The King appears to be much worse to-day ; and it is understood that a courier has been despatched to H.R.H. the Prince Royal, who is now in Italy. Seriously considering the covert attacks on me by M. Etzel in the Stuttgart papers, to which MM. de Louche and Mährler insist on replying. But I tell them that it is unwise and *infra dig.* to notice them.

March 7 *to* 9.—Vignoles continued to be much indisposed for three or four days. On the state of business he merely expressed his ' disgust thereat ; ' adding : ' All I want now is to wind up affairs and get away.' He records an interview with the ' Privy Purse ' on the 10th, when he stated explicitly to that functionary that his charges would be five hundred guineas for all his expenses, and two thousand guineas for his report and his time.

'*March* 12.—Not able to rise till noon. In the afternoon made a great effort to go out to dine with Sir George Shee, where I met a diplomatic party.[1]

'*March* 13.—In consequence of a message from the King of Würtemberg's daughter, the Princess of Orange,[2] I waited on H.R.H. at the Palace. I expected some communication from the King, whom she had just left, but found that H.R.H. evidently did not like to open the subject, and confined herself to generalities. It was whispered at the Palace that the King had decided about the Stuttgart station, against my plans, and

---

[1] Sir G. Shee was a great lover of classical literature. Vignoles's son Hutton (who was often out with him) says he was never without a copy of Virgil in his hand.

[2] This Princess (Sophie) was the second child of the King by his first wife. She was married to the Prince of Orange in 1839. The King of Würtemberg died in 1864, and was succeeded by his eldest son, whose mother (the King's second wife) was the Princess Pauline of Würtemberg. This King (who was Prince Royal at the time of Vignoles's visit) was married in 1846 to the Grand Duchess Olga, daughter of the Emperor Nicholas of Russia.

in favour of ETZEL'S!!! This was confirmed in the evening, and it is said that it was done at the instigation of the two eldest Princesses, and that the King had not consulted either Schlayer, Gärtner, Mancler, or any of the Ministers or Cabinet.

' *March* 14.—The news of the King's decision is true, and has caused the deepest vexation to my friends. I feel deeply mortified and offended, especially as not the slightest reference was made to me on the subject. The decision of the King, of course, deprives me of all support, and all the weight and influence which ought to attach to my opinion and advice. I consider that I have been subjected to affronts and indignities unworthy of any Government.

' *March* 15.— H.R.H. Prince Jerome called on me, and from him I learned that his Majesty's decision and signature were obtained by Madame Stanberrautz, the actress, who had great influence with the King, and who patronized Etzel! All other parties appear to be indignant, and probably are so, as regards their own disappointed schemes!'

On the 19th he remarks :—

' It is now evident that all my hopes of making these German railways are over! The S. party have beaten me! The foolish old King had not the courage to fight for the engineer he brought out here to tell him the truth! I had a confidential interview with M. de Maelzen, the Bavarian Minister, who urged me to stand my ground; and that very probably I should be called on by the Privy Council to give my opinion as to the railway station, as all the town was crying out against it.

' *March* 21.—Had a long interview with M. Gärtner, as satisfactory as I could expect. It appears that the S. party got hold of the King's friend, with whom Etzel's sister is on terms of great friendship. She seems to have worked on the King's mind while he was ill in bed and in a state of mental and bodily weakness. M. Gärtner thought it possible that his Majesty's decision might yet be rescinded. Called at the Palace to sign the last bulletin of the King, and was favoured with a long audience by H.R.H. the Princess of Orange. I spoke as strongly

as I could about the great mistake made as to the station, and of
the injury that would be done to Rosenstein and to the town;
besides the great expense incurred. The Princess was touched
even to tears! She brought in her little son, who will be the
future King of the Netherlands, should he live. It is probable
that H.R.H. will speak to her father the King, as she is well acquainted with all the circumstances, and is aware that great
discontent exists in the town on this subject.

'*March* 22.—I received this day from the Secretary of State
a letter of thanks from the King of Würtemberg, accompanied
by a magnificent gold snuff-box set in diamonds, as a mark of
his Majesty's esteem.[1] This was accompanied by a formal
letter from the Secretary of State, intimating to me that my
claim of 2,500 guineas had been allowed by the King.

'*March* 23.—Long interview with Count Beroldingen on all
the matters which have recently taken place. Writing letters
to the King acknowledging his Majesty's present, and expressing a wish that my report on the railways may be published.

'*March* 24.—Making all arrangements for leaving Stuttgart.
Writing to the Secretary of University College to say that I
should resume my lectures as Professor of Engineering on April
17. Some gentlemen of the Court dined with me at our hotel.
I also received several calls; and it was a general subject of
regret amongst the Court party that my connection with Stuttgart should be broken off in so abrupt and unsatisfactory a
manner by this wretched " backstairs" intrigue!

'*March* 26.—Attended a grand *soirée* at Count Beroldingen's,
and took leave of a number of ladies and gentlemen of the Court.
The Princess Marie and the Princess of Orange called me over
to speak with them, and both Princesses took a cordial leave
of me.

'*March* 28.—At noon to-day I had a formal audience of the
King to take leave. I pressed hard for the publication of my
report, and pointedly begged his Majesty's attention to the
third part of it, in which I had fully discussed the subject of the

---

[1] This regal gift was bequeathed by Mr. Vignoles to his son Hutton, and it
will be handed down as an heirloom in his family.

stations, the Cannstadt line, the Rosenstein tunnel, &c. His
Majesty was extremely gracious, and intimated his hope of
seeing me again. '

' *March* 29.—At a long interview with M. de Mancler, who
had called on me, that Minister gave me distinctly to understand that the King was more and more pleased with my report;
and that his Majesty hoped I would dine at the Palace before I
left Stuttgart.'

Vignoles does not appear to have visited the Palace again,
and the entry on April 1 records simply :—

' Left Stuttgart per night mail for Heidelberg.'

Vignoles arrived in London on the evening of April 7.

The writer has thought it worth while to transcribe largely
the records of Vignoles's diary for the six months of his professional visit to Würtemberg, as being not only of real interest
in their subject-matter, more especially the insight they give
us into official and Court life in a German state nearly half a
century ago, but also because they contain so graphic an account
of the English engineer's indefatigable labours, and his mature
and careful consideration of the subject of railways in that
country. It has been the aim of the writer of this memoir to
confine himself as much as possible·throughout the narrative
to a plain and straightforward record of the facts and opinions
preserved in Vignoles's journals, and he is content that these
should tell their own story, and that discriminating readers
should be left to draw conclusions for themselves, whether favourable or otherwise, on the unvarnished tale which is laid before
them concerning the subject of this biography.

CHAPTER XX.

The Suspension Bridge at Kieff—Vignoles visits St. Petersburg in winter—
Returns to England—Visits St. Petersburg in summer—Important interview with Emperor Nicholas—Count Kleinmichel, &c.—Meets the Emperor
at Kieff—Chooses site of bridge—Brief account of dimensions of bridge,
&c.

1846–47.

ONE of the most interesting engineering works carried out by
Vignoles was the construction of the great suspension bridge
over the river Dnieper at Kieff, in Russia.

This ancient and renowned city had long been one of
Russia's most important fortified places, and for years the great
desire of the Emperor Nicholas had been for the erection of a
bridge across the river Dnieper, at the foot of the hill on which
the fortress stands, and in such a position that the bridge should
be dominated by the guns of the fortress.

The site was certainly inconvenient, as there was no road
down to the river at that spot, and none along the river banks;
and the difference of level between the fortress and the bridge
was 350 feet.

The Dnieper is here more than half a mile wide, and every
winter it is completely frozen over, with an average thickness of
eighteen inches of ice; whilst the floods in spring caused by the
débâcle and the melting of snow in the upper country are often
dangerously high. The bed of the river consists almost entirely
of sand, except near the right bank, where some clay was found
at the site of the proposed bridge; and the depth of the water
varies from ten to sixty feet, according to the caprice of the floods
each year.

Vignoles first heard of the Emperor's great desire for a

bridge at Kieff from his old friend and brother-officer Colonel du Plat, then Consul-General at Warsaw, who sent him some rough memoranda for his guidance in preparing a design for the bridge, having obtained these from Messrs. Douglas and Alfred Evans,[1] of Warsaw.

This was in the autumn of 1846 ; and Vignoles at once set himself to prepare geometrical drawings on a large scale, to be accompanied by a perspective view of the bridge, as it would appear when completed ; for he perceived that a journey to the Russian capital, and (if possible) an interview with the Emperor himself, would be indispensable to the success of the proposed undertaking. Vignoles never did things by halves, and in this case, when the drawings were finished, he had them mounted on silk, and bound superbly in morocco leather, with an embossed gilt title over the arms of Russia. The portfolios were placed in oak cases, lined with velvet, and they thus formed indeed an imperial set of designs.

On January 4, 1847, Vignoles started for St. Petersburg, accompanied by two of his sons, Hutton and Henry, aged respectively twenty-three and twenty years. Letters of introduction and passports had been duly obtained, furs were procured, and a roomy English travelling carriage was purchased, which largely contributed to the comfort of a land journey of at least 1,400 miles.

Vignoles's diary, containing a detailed account of this journey, is so voluminous that it is not possible to put the narrative in his own words ; the reader, therefore, must be content with occasional quotations from it.

It was thoroughly characteristic of its author that, in addition to his journal, he kept a tabulated itinerary, showing the arrival at and departure from every town or post station, the total distance travelled, and the rate in miles per hour. The travellers proceeded *viâ* Ostend, and thence to Cologne by rail, the speed averaging only fourteen miles an hour. They then posted to

---

[1] This firm (Messrs. Brooke, Alfred and Douglas Evans), in addition to their establishment at Warsaw, were large proprietors of nickel mines in Norway, and owned also extensive works in Birmingham.

Mayence, and we quote the following from the diary of January 6 :—

' The latter part of the journey the snow fell fast, and we could not see much of the banks of the river between Bonn and Coblentz.[1] Notwithstanding the severe weather, the scenery was very striking and interesting; sufficient to prove that the palm of beauty and attraction is borne by the Rhine over the Rhone.'

From Mayence the railway was available *viâ* Frankfort to Heidelberg, from which place Stuttgart was reached by posting at 9 A.M. on January 8, just ninety-six hours from London—very good travelling for those days.

Vignoles had not been in Stuttgart since the spring of 1844, but neither he nor his work were forgotten by the authorities of Würtemberg; and one of his old friends openly lamented that the engineer's advice as to the station for the railway had not been fully carried out. The diary of January 9 says :—

' Having received an official letter from the Secretary of State that the King would receive me at four o'clock in the afternoon, I waited on his Majesty at that hour, accompanied by my two sons, and showed him the drawings of the proposed suspension bridge at Kieff. I had the honour of a long interview, in which the King alluded to my report on the Würtemberg railways in 1843–44. The Minister of Finance, who has charge of the railways, waited to see me in the King's antechamber and invited me to inspect the lines in construction, which I agreed to do.'

The next day Vignoles was graciously received by the Crown Prince (the present King of Würtemberg) and his charming consort, the Grand Duchess Olga of Russia. Finally, on January 12, after the railway inspection, Vignoles left Stuttgart, having previously obtained a letter of introduction from the King to the Emperor Nicholas.

The travellers left for Vienna, *viâ* Ulm, Augsburg, and Munich, posting day and night, and arrived at the Austrian capital on the 16th.

---

[1] Some years later Vignoles was appointed engineer-in-chief of the Frankfort, Wiesbaden, and Cologne Railway, and laid out a large part of the line which now runs on the right bank of the river. Cf. Chap. XXIII.

Several days were passed in Vienna, where interviews were had with the British Plenipotentiary, Lord Ponsonby, also with the Russian Ambassador and others, to obtain information and to provide against the probable difficulties at the Russian frontier, &c.

The party were also fortunate in another respect, as the diary for the same day records:—

'After dinner, owing to the address of our *valet-de-place*, we obtained capital seats in the stage-box of the Joseph's-Stadt Theatre, and heard with delight Jenny Lind, in her character of Marie in the opera of *Li Fille du Régiment*, by Donizetti. Both her singing and acting were perfection.'

From Vienna to Warsaw the journey was accomplished in four days' posting, without a courier or interpreter; and, though the travellers met with nothing but civility *en route*, the difficulties which arose were sometimes very amusing. On one occasion they were for a time completely nonplused by the impossibility of making themselves understood, when fortunately the parish priest appeared on the scene, who, although inaccessible to verbal questioning in any language but Polish, seemed highly gratified to be of service when the queries and answers were written in Latin.

The journal says:—

'*Jan.* 20.—Arrived at Cracow, having travelled the last twenty-four hours at the rate of six miles an hour. The day being dull, we could only get an imperfect view of this ancient city, and of the earthen mound or tumulus of the ancient hero " Krau " on the right, as well as that of the modern hero " Kosciusco " (150 feet high), on the left or north side. I fully concur in the expression that this ill-fated city has all the characteristics of a sepulchre, whitened without by the splendid remains of former greatness, and dark within from the loss of all it once held: a city without a population, and a population without bread.

'*Jan.* 21.—From the frontier the travelling was much more rapid, and only about twelve minutes at each stage were required for changing horses. The names of the towns and post stations were perfectly unwritable, unreadable, and unpronounceable; but with the aid of a map and good pay to the postillions we made fair progress, the supplies for eating and drinking being taken from our own stores provided in Vienna.'

On January 22 Warsaw was reached, and here several days were passed in consultation with Colonel du Plat, the Messrs. Evans, and General Fanshawe, an Englishman who had been many years in the Russian service.

The diary records :—

' *Jan.* 26.—In the evening went with my son Hutton to dine with Prince Paskiewicz. His Highness was extremely polite, and seated me in the place of honour between the Princess and himself.'

Mr. Alfred Evans decided on accompanying the party to St. Petersburg, and a start was made on January 27. The posting was good, but generally six horses were necessary ; and at Kovno, the Russian frontier, there was so much snow that the carriage had to be put on sledges.

Here the travellers had a few hours' respite from the fatigues of incessant travel, and it was all they obtained between Warsaw and St. Petersburg (nearly 800 miles); but as no beds could be procured they had to sleep on straw thrown down on the floor of the post station. Nearing St. Petersburg the cold was intense—20° of frost Réaumur—and fears were entertained that the ' boys,' who occupied the coupé behind, would have their feet frozen; but circulation was restored by snow rubbing.

It is worth while mentioning that Vignoles's sons were wearing the red Hessian boots and green Hungarian stockings which the Viennese deemed indispensable for travellers in Russia. They were, however, compelled to discard these, and replace them by warm slippers and fur bags for the feet and legs, which contrivance formed an effectual defence against the severe cold. *Expertis credite !*

The Russian capital was entered on February 1, a little less than five days' travelling from Warsaw. Vignoles anticipated

Y

only a short visit, but he had to spend several weeks in St. Petersburg.   Lord Bloomfield was the British Ambassador, and Vignoles was indebted to him for much kindness and good advice in the various negotiations which became necessary. The diary of February 2 records his first visit :—

'In the evening, dined with Lord Bloomfield, and met Count Nesselrode, and most of the other principal members of the Russian Ministry, and several of the higher classes of nobility, to whom I was specially introduced.   Count Kleinmichel (Minister of Public Works) not being present as expected, Count Nesselrode undertook, at the special request of Lord Bloomfield, to procure me an interview with him.'

Meanwhile Vignoles made many acquaintances,[1] and procured much important information from every available source. He did not immediately obtain an audience of the Emperor, but through Lord Bloomfield he procured an interview with Count Orloff, private secretary to the Emperor, known also by his Herculean stature.   The diary of February 7 says :—

' Count Orloff received me most affably, and told me that the Emperor was aware of my being in St. Petersburg, and was quite prepared to receive me, but that the matter must come officially through the Minister of Public Works.'

On February 12 Vignoles was favoured with an interview by Count Kleinmichel, to whom he explained the decided superiority of wrought-iron bar chains to iron-wire cables for suspension bridges, and the Count promised to report the engineer's opinion favourably to the Emperor.

First Interview with Emperor of Russia at St. Petersburg.

On February 19 Vignoles and his two sons were admitted to an audience of the imperial potentate of ' All the Russias.' The Emperor was extremely gracious, and Vignoles, who was

---

[1] Amongst other persons Vignoles met Colonel Whistler, whom he had known in the years 1820-21 in South Carolina.   From him he first ascertained that three other Russian bridges would be immediately required at Dunabourg, Janaff, and Kovno.

not a novice in such ceremonials, was perfectly cool and collected. There can be no doubt that the impression made was very favourable ; and Vignoles always afterwards spoke of his Imperial Majesty as being 'the perfect gentleman.'

The Emperor invited Vignoles to give in separate and detailed estimates and drawings for the three bridges mentioned by Colonel Whistler, and his Imperial Majesty expressed himself entirely satisfied with the designs for the Kieff Bridge which Vignoles had submitted to him.[1] The exact total cost was left for future decision ; but the proposals were accepted in principle, Vignoles on his part undertaking on his arrival in England to prepare all the details, with working drawings and estimates, as quickly as possible, and then to return to Russia. He left St. Petersburg on February 23, and after a short stay in Warsaw he reached London on March 10.

SECOND JOURNEY TO RUSSIA.

Vignoles had been dissuaded from attempting a visit to Kieff in the winter, the Dnieper being always frozen over at that season of the year, which would render it impossible to examine the bed of the river for the foundations of the bridge, on which so much depended, and which afterwards proved to be a most serious item in the difficulty and expense of the undertaking.

Having prepared much material in the shape of drawings and preliminary computations, Vignoles left London, with his eldest and his youngest sons, on June 30, accompanied by Mr. Alfred Evans.[2]   After a rough and miserable voyage of fifty-six hours in the steam-ship " Countess of Lonsdale," they reached Hamburg late in the afternoon of July 2.

The railway served the travellers from Hamburg to Berlin and Breslau, and thence to Oppeln, in Upper Silesia. Here

---

[1] Vignoles merely states the nature of this interview as given in the text. A full account (from his diary) of his visit to the Emperor in the summer is given further on.

[2] All the male members of this family have passed away. The only surviving representative is Mrs. Miller, wife of Colonel Miller, J.P., of Shotover, Oxfordshire.

horses were procured, and the heavy English travelling chariot was dragged through sandy bye-roads all night, crossing the Polish frontier about 5 A.M., and reaching the railway at Czenstokau[1] at nine o'clock. The diary has this characteristic remark :—

'*July* 6.—This place is celebrated for its cathedral, which contains the shrine[2] of the "Black Virgin." Evidently the Crusaders had brought an Egyptian mummy of a woman and child in former times here, as well as to other places in Austria and Bavaria, where the Black Virgin is well known.'

Vignoles having proceeded with Mr. Douglas Evans to Kieff, his sons had an opportunity of taking a journey to Cracow, where they visited the grand salt mines of Wieliczka,[3] one of the world's natural wonders.

This was Vignoles's first visit to Kieff, and as the *chaussée* only extended to Lublin, 156 versts (= 104 English miles), the larger part of the journey, which covers a total distance of 807 versts (= 538 English miles), had to be traversed by the rough natural roads of the country.

Vignoles and Mr. D. Evans reached Kieff on July 12. His diary notes :—

'*July* 13.—Examined the site for proposed bridge. Found that no materials had been collected by the Government, nor were any workmen to be had, unless specially brought from the upper country.

'*July* 14.—Called this morning on General Gottmann and General Bibikoff, the Military Governor of Kieff. Again examined the site of the bridge at river side, and from the cliffs above ; also the opposite (east) shore, and the bed of the river, the water being very low. On inquiry I learned that the only foundry in the city declined to make even pile shoes and heads !'

On his return journey to Warsaw with his companion he

---

[1] Pronounced 'Chenstokoff.'

[2] This shrine was not on this occasion *visited* by the travellers. Murray's *Guide* speaks only of a *picture*. No doubt originally there had been an image.

[3] Pronounced 'Vielichka.'

notes that 'Ostrog, a town 350 versts from Kieff, is full of fine
old ruins of monasteries and castles.'

On July 24 Vignoles, with his companion and his two sons,
left Warsaw, and reached St. Petersburg (1,090 versts, or 785
miles) at a quarter to one in the morning of July 28. The
last place of any interest before reaching St. Petersburg is
Gatchina, the present Emperor's favourite resort, 40 versts from
the capital.

The writer has a delightful recollection of the first aspect of
the Russian capital in the silence of the summer night. There
was no real darkness to obscure the vision, but besides there was
the light of a full moon, her silvery beams seeming to give an
ethereal illumination to the white houses, the vast palaces, the
wide streets, and frowning fortresses, as well as making still
clearer the bright stream of the Neva flowing swiftly and silently
along between its granite quays. Vignoles enters in his journal
for July 20 :—

'Found St. Petersburg very dusty and very dull, quite a
different place from the winter. The Emperor either at the
camp or his summer palace at Peterhoff, Count Kleinmichel absent on a tour of inspection, Baird cruising with his yacht in
the Baltic, General D. in France, Lord Bloomfield in the country,
Nicholls in England, the ——'s stopped payment, and scarcely
a nobleman or merchant of eminence in the city.'

On August 1 Vignoles took his sons to visit the Palace of
'Tsarkoe-Selo.' His journal says :—

'*Aug.* 1.—Here we visited the celebrated armoury, the
newly-erected monument of the late Grand Duchess Marie, the
Emperor's youngest daughter; the New Palace, and the interesting old Palace of the Empress Catherine. Most struck with
the " Blue Chapel " and the famous " Amber Drawing-room." [1]
Got back to Benson's Hotel at midnight.' [2]

[1] The writer retains a more vivid recollection of this unique *salon* than of
any other point of interest about St. Petersburg.

[2] The Misses Benson were the kind and much respected proprietors of this
admirable hotel. Vignoles held them both in great esteem. One sister passed
away several years ago; the survivor (Miss Sarah Benson) only died in July
1887.

The strictness of the police administration then existing in the Russian capital was part of a very rigid system of *espionnage* (probably intensified in later days) which exercised a close observation over visitors and strangers, and made it essential for them to avoid any open conversation on political subjects. The alternative was simply that indiscreet persons who could not hold their tongues found themselves politely turned out of the country at twenty-four hours' notice! Vignoles's diary says :—

'*Aug.* 6.—According to arrangement, I gave to-day the formal guarantee required by the police to enable my two sons to leave at once by the Stockholm steamer, on their tour through Finland, Sweden, Denmark, Hanover, &c., and home through Holland. They both went off in high health and spirits.'

We give two or three extracts of interest from the diaries before explaining the issue of this second visit of Vignoles to St. Petersburg :—

'*Aug.* 8.—Visited the Imperial Palace and gardens at Peterhoff to-day in company with friends. It is on the southern shore of the Gulf of Finland, about eighteen miles below St. Petersburg. The day being hot, the shade of the thickly timbered parks and woods was delightful. The original building of Peter the Great is plain and modest, but the modern Palace of the Empress Catherine stands on an eminence, and is very extensive. The waterworks are remarkably good, and the presence of a fine military band added to our enjoyment. There was an illumination after sunset.'

Vignoles also describes his visit to the ' St. Isaac ' Church, then incomplete ; he was much interested in the process of veneering the huge columns with malachite. In their finished state, the effect of these massive lofty *quasi* monoliths of that beautiful mineral is superb indeed.

' *Aug.* 12.—To-day Mr. Evans and myself went on a trip with Mr. Baird in his yacht. There was a fine breeze blowing, and the day was delightful. As we beat out from the anchorage we got a capital view of all the exterior works of Cronstadt—the docks, the old timber and the new granite forts, &c. A number of men-of-war were lying up in ordinary, and there were also several first-rate vessels of the same kind in the anchorage. We got back before dark.

'*Aug.* 15.—Drove out to-day to the encampment at Krasnoe-Selo. The tents were all standing, but, to our disappointment, the troops had all marched away for some manœuvres several miles off. We walked over the common and through the silent camp, and from the adjacent high grounds obtained fine views of St. Petersburg, the Gulf, Cronstadt, &c., the golden dome of St. Isaac's Cathedral shining always like a bright star on the horizon.

'*Aug.* 18.—Visited the "Hermitage" Palace. There are several rooms filled with paintings bearing the names of the old and best masters, but very few of any note. The best are of the Dutch and Flemish schools. In the afternoon went to view the "Winter" Palace, but, the place being in a state of repair, we did not see it to advantage. Many of the rooms are very handsome and the pictures (some at least) are very fine.

'*Aug.* 21.—Went again early this morning with Mr. Evans to the camp at Krasnoe-Selo, and was present at a splendid review of the troops by the Emperor in person.[1] There were about 30,000 Infantry, 20,000 Cavalry, 142 pieces of Artillery, all massed in about fourteen brigades, with one brigade of Pontoons. There was present a most brilliant staff, every officer on the ground being capitally mounted. No firing, but a few manœuvres. I met on the ground Count Kleinmichel, Lord Bloomfield, and for the first time in my life saw Mr. R. Cobden, of Manchester, the celebrated Free Trader. He was making the tour of Europe, and had only just arrived in Russia.

'*Sept.* 3.—This afternoon I had gone out to dine at Lord Bloomfield's with Mr. Evans and Mr. William Miller, when in the middle of dinner an *estafette* arrived with a special message from Count Kleinmichel. I got away as soon as possible and

---

[1] This celebrated camp is about twenty-five miles from the capital. There is a large church for the troops, the architecture and decorations being very handsome and striking. The camp is also noticeable for its great military hospital, which is said to be the finest in the world. Cf. an admirable description of the whole camp and its surroundings in *Morning Post* of November 8, 1848.

reached the Count's residence at nine o'clock. He was frank and friendly, and informed me that the Emperor would see me at Peterhoff on Sunday next at eleven o'clock.'

The following extract, owing to its unusual interest, will not, it is hoped, be deemed too long by the reader :—

Interview with the Emperor and Empress of Russia.

'*Sept.* 5.—This morning at ten o'clock I reached Count Kleinmichel's country seat, five versts from Peterhoff, and drove with him to the Imperial Palace. We waited an hour whilst his Imperial Majesty returned from church. The Count informed me of the general decision of the Emperor to allow me to build the bridge in my own way, but that the portals must be twenty-eight feet wide, and some minor consequent alterations. A little before twelve I accompanied the Count to the reception-room of the Palace. The room was full of high officers and ladies of the Court and members of the imperial family, amongst them being the Grand Duke Constantine, just returned from England; the Princess of Holland; the Emperor's youngest son, the Grand Duke Alexis, and others. At 12.30 a numerous staff of attendants brought in tables, of which there were twelve or fourteen, all laid out for *déjeuner*. A lady suddenly entered the room, and came straight up to me, addressing me in English. I at once perceived that this must be the Empress, as she began to speak of the drawings of *all* the bridges, which I had some weeks ago submitted to the Emperor. The Empress then invited me to partake of breakfast, and her two sons came up and spoke to me, followed by several of the principal courtiers. The Court circle broke up soon after one o'clock, and almost immediately Count Kleinmichel and myself were summoned into the Emperor's private room. Of course I was in military uniform, and on entering the Emperor advanced immediately and shook me by the hand, and expressed himself glad to see me. The various points connected with the Kieff Bridge were then discussed, and the Emperor, after explaining the necessity for the width of the portals to be twenty-eight feet, frankly and nobly decided to leave everything else to my own judgment and experience. The Emperor's words were: "Si vous voulez me répondre sur votre parole d'honneur que le pont sera stablement construit, je vous laisse pleine action, et je vous en donne la main ; " and, shaking my hand heartily, the Emperor added in English, "Is it a bargain?" I answered without a moment's hesitation, and looking him full in the face: " Sur mon honneur, Sire, et sur ma tête."

'After that the Emperor discussed with me several points concerning the "barrage" of the river Dnieper, the floods, the ice, the approach over the plains, and the ascent of the hill on the Kieff side. The Emperor then informed me that he hoped to be at Kieff about the 9th (21st) of this month, "si je ne tombe pas malade en route! " On my taking leave the Emperor again shook hands, and bade me farewell with the utmost kindness and affability. The audience had lasted nearly an hour.'

Vignoles returned to Warsaw at once, reaching that capital on the 13th, and setting out on his second visit to Kieff on September 16. He was only just in time, for on reaching his destination on the 21st he found that the Emperor had already arrived.

We give in his own words the account of his meeting with his Imperial Majesty :—

' *Sept.* 21.—Heard from General Gottmann that there were two things in the agreement which the Emperor objected to : first, allowing Jews to reside in Kieff;[1] second, exemption of the contracts from the stamp duty of ½ per cent. But I felt I could not give way on either of these points.

' *Sept.* 22.—Early this morning I received official notice to join the Emperor in an examination of the proposed site for the suspension bridge. His Imperial Majesty was attended by Generals Gottmann and Falkmann, General Bibikoff, Field-Marshal Prince Paskiewicz, Viceroy of Poland ; also Count Kleinmichel and other officers. The Emperor walked along the face of the sandy cliffs, and examined especially all the difficult

---

[1] This was a point of the utmost importance, for the only possible contractors were Jews, even entirely ignorant as they were with respect to such works as the building of this bridge would necessitate.

places (for the proposed descent to the river), but did not seem to approve of any of the plans, and nothing was decided. On coming to the heights above the site of the bridge, the Emperor called me to his side, and, taking my arm, said to me in English, " There is your work." His Imperial Majesty then spoke of the floods as likely to rise fully fourteen feet, and that I should have much trouble, and added that I must take great care.[1] I replied that I would do my best; and the Emperor said aloud in French, " J'en suis sûr." I then submitted to his Imperial Majesty my idea about changing the site of the bridge. The Emperor said he would leave this matter to me entirely, as I understood it best. Several times in the course of the inspection his Imperial Majesty remarked to me, "I am convinced you will accomplish the work, and overcome all difficulties." After the Emperor had left, Count Kleinmichel informed me that the objections as to the residence of the Jews, and the contract, would both be waived.'

On the 25th a formal contract was signed and sealed, by Vignoles on one part, and on the other by Count Kleinmichel and General Gottmann, as representing the Imperial Government.

Vignoles also entered into an agreement with a wealthy Jew, named Blumberg, for the immediate commencement of the works. This person's principal manager was named Schweitzer, who, after Blumberg's death a year or two afterwards, carried on the works to the end, but at an ultimate cost to Vignoles far exceeding the original estimate.

Vignoles reached Warsaw on September 30, and after a brief stay set out on his return to London, where he arrived on October 7.

After arranging with Messrs. Musgrove, of Bolton, for the

---

[1] This was indeed a prophetic utterance of the Emperor, as the story of the ice-floods in 1849 will presently show. Vignoles in these two visits to Kieff made every inquiry about the bed of the river, and as to a possible foundation for the piers, &c., but he could obtain no reliable information. The only certain fact he ascertained was the dismal one that several previous attemp's had been made in past years to build a bridge over the Dnieper at Kieff, but that the floods had invariably swept away all trace of the works.

machinery, pumping engines, and the general ironwork, he entered into a contract with Messrs. Fox, Henderson, and Co., for the iron chains and links, &c., for the suspension bridge, which work they carried out to his fullest satisfaction.[1] Vignoles then devoted a large portion of his time to an elaborate series of calculations and mathematical investigations connected with the stability of the proposed bridge. In November he took these over to his friend, Mr. Thomas Bergin, of Dublin, the Secretary of the Dublin and Kingstown Railway, and by his advice the papers were submitted to Mr. E. Whiteford, a young mathematician of high repute in Trinity College, Dublin. Vignoles, determined that no possibility of lurking error should remain, then paid a three days' visit (accompanied by Mr. Bergin) to the Rev. Dr. Romney Robinson at the Observatory, Armagh. This accomplished man of science went carefully through the whole series of computations, and fully verified them, thus laying to rest all possible doubts and difficulties as regards the theoretical aspect of the new undertaking.

We conclude this chapter with a very brief technical account of the bridge itself.

PRINCIPAL DIMENSIONS OF THE KIEFF SUSPENSION BRIDGE.

The leading dimensions of the bridge were finally fixed as follows :—

	Feet
Four openings of 440 feet each	1,760
Two openings of 225 feet each	450
One opening of 50 feet for swivel-bridge . . .	50
Swivel bridge abutment, with wing walls on the right bank of river, 100 feet	100
Mooring abutment on right bank of river . . .	80
Mooring abutment on left bank of river, with wing walls	120
Five piers, 20 feet each	100
Total length of bridge	2,660

Or, as nearly as possible, half an English mile.

---

[1] All the ironwork was sent by sea to Odessa, from which port it had to be carted over rough roads of sand or mud, some 300 miles, to Kieff. Great

The total width of the platform of the bridge between the hand railing for the footpaths is 53 feet, and the clear width of roadway is 35 feet.

The footpaths project outside the suspension chains and are carried by cantilevers round the exterior of the piers.

The ways through the piers have a clear breadth of 28 feet, and the height, to the soffit of the semicircular arches of the piers, is 35 feet.

The chains for each pier are four in number, each chain being composed of eight links, each 12 feet long, 11 inches broad, and 1 inch thick, of rolled iron, and the link-pins are 8 inches in diameter.

The total length of the chains, measured along their curves, is four English miles.

The platform is a substantial construction in wood and iron, forming a strong trussed girder, suspended by rods from the chains.

---

difficulties arose from time to time with the authorities at Odessa, and serious delays occurred in the transport. On one occasion a heavy boiler fell off the bullock carts into a large pond, with deep mud at the bottom, and some months passed before it could be even ascertained where it was, as the carters had calmly left it where it fell, and had returned to Odessa. Eventually it was recovered by two English mechanics with a staff of twenty men, at about a hundred miles from Kieff; and then it took some hours' hard work, with the application of screw-jacks and strong tackling, before the boiler was once more got upon the carts ready for final transport.

CHAPTER XXI.

Further visits to Kieff—Floods in Dnieper—Fascine work for coffer-dams—
Inspection of the bridge by Emperor Nicholas, &c.

1848-50.

VIGNOLES'S journal for 1848, besides referring to matters of interest at home, shows that, after visits to various places in England on engineering business, he joined his sons Hutton and Henry in Warsaw early in February, and travelled with them to Kieff, where a very large and commodious house had been engaged, which was speedily fitted with all needful comforts *à l'Anglaise*—a matter involving considerable expense.

Vignoles in his frequent visits to Kieff, and during the lengthened stay he generally made there, was thus enabled to dispense that genial hospitality which to him was a second nature. Many were the courtesies he thus displayed to the leading inhabitants of the venerable city, full of high-born descendants of the ancient Polish nobility; nor were the occasions unfrequent when officers of the imperial army and governors of provinces partook of the festivities so generously provided for them by the English engineer.

His first task was to lay out accurately the direction of the bridge from the west to the east bank of the Dnieper. Constructional work began immediately afterwards, and the first pile was driven on March 25.

This operation was at first conducted in the usual primitive manner, but things improved on the arrival of half a dozen of Gough's six horse-power engines from England. These gave great satisfaction, and were practically more serviceable than

Nasmyth's celebrated 'pile-drivers,' which reached Kieff some months later, for the inventor had not then brought his machines to the perfection which they afterwards reached.[1]

In a special report which he was preparing for Governor Guttmann to forward to St. Petersburg, Vignoles writes :—

'We have now in March on the ground a large quantity of timber for the coffer-dams, about one million bricks, and nearly a thousand piles, with stone of every sort. We have also erected various shops and offices of all kinds, and barracks for the workmen.'

The engineering staff was a large one, Captain Kirchenpauer and Mr. Hutton Vignoles being the principal resident and executive engineers. There was also a gentleman of great promise and high scientific attainments, Mr. Edward Whiteford, to whose memory a few words are certainly due. He had come out as mathematical engineer to the staff, having been strongly recommended to his chief by the Rev. Dr. Romney Robinson, of Armagh. Whiteford had been first 'Madden's Prizeman' in 1847 at the examination for fellowships in Trinity College, Dublin, and if he had competed for this coveted distinction the following year his success was virtually ensured. But he was induced by a very handsome offer of remuneration to join the staff at Kieff, where he died of cholera early in July 1848.[2]

---

[1] The diary has a note, January 17, 1848 : 'Called on Mr. Thomas E. Harrison, the resident engineer on the great bridge at Newcastle-on-Tyne. Saw all the operations, and observed the working of the new pile-driving engines on the coffer-dams. These machines should be made stronger, with larger piston, and better apparatus for draught in furnace; also a simpler arrangement for working and moving. They will probably be useful to me on the great job of pile-driving at Kieff, but the price is at present much too high.' Mr. T. E. Harrison was President of the Institution of Civil Engineers in the years 1874-75. He died at Newcastle on March 19, 1888, aged eighty.

[2] To avoid breaking the continuity of the narrative, a few extracts are given here from Vignoles's diary :—

'June 30, 1848.—The cholera, which was at first slight, appears to have suddenly taken great hold of the men. Several have died, and now I find nearly 400 men have left the works. Soldiers were obtained to work the piles, but they very imperfectly supplied the place of our men; still the coffer-dams were not stopped.

'July 1.—My son Henry and Mr. Whiteford engaged in levelling the new straight line for the working of the self-acting inclined plane.

During the latter half of the year 1848 Vignoles made two journeys to England, each time remaining only a few weeks. His staff, meanwhile, was chiefly engaged in the construction of an inclined plane from the top of the cliff to the river bank; and a new road was also made to connect this approach to the river with the principal fortress, which is, in fact, a huge arsenal, fully stored with arms and ammunition for at least 30,000 soldiers.

For the bridge foundations careful borings had been made on both sides of the river, those on the right (Kieff) bank showing that in one place hard clay existed at a reasonable depth, serviceable for the support of the swivel bridge and the mooring abutment. But the other borings unfortunately demonstrated that nothing but sand to an immense depth would be encountered for all the five piers, and for the mooring abutment on the left or east bank of the river; so that, at the very outset, Vignoles found a stiff practical problem to solve—viz. to build a bridge half a mile long over a river subject to high floods every spring, with no prospect of finding a better foundation than sand for all the piers and one of the abutments.

Young engineers of the present day may be disposed to underrate the formidable difficulties of this state of things forty years ago, knowing there would be little anxiety on such a matter now, when the system of sinking caissons could be carried out with facility. But at the time we are writing of, Vignoles could only decide to drive the piles for the coffer-

' *July 2, Sunday.*—At 3 A.M. this morning Mr. Whiteford (who had only retired to bed at midnight, apparently in good health) was violently attacked by what proved to be true Asiatic cholera. Medical assistance was called in, but by six o'clock he exhibited every symptom of collapse. Later on he rallied a little, but about ten o'clock the attack was renewed, and before eleven in the forenoon *he was dead !*

' Dreadfully shocked and depressed by this heavy stroke of Providence, and my whole family filled with deep feelings of anxiety and sorrow. Before going to rest we had the Church of England Evening Service. (It was Sunday.)

' I was much struck and affected by the excellent conduct and disposition shown by my two sons, and by all the English assistants I had with me, on this melancholy occasion.'

dams as deep as possible, in the bare hope that they would possibly reach harder ground.

The winter of 1848 proved very severe; snow had fallen heavily in the upper country, and, as the spring approached, great apprehension was felt for the safety of the coffer-dams, which had all been completed. The breaking up of the ice in the river towards the end of April was the first enemy to be encountered; and though the strong ice-breakers in front of each coffer-dam completely ensured them against injury, many bays of the temporary bridge were carried away. Such mishaps, however, were looked upon as trifling compared to the danger threatening the coffer-dams from the scour of the flood, which already gave indications of rising to an almost unprecedented height. Day by day, as the river rose, the anxiety was terrible, but we leave the subsequent quotations from Vignoles's diary to speak of this, and likewise to describe the catastrophe which followed. He himself had only returned from England a few days before :—

'*April* 30.—The water in the river continues to rise, and now covers completely the sides of the dams. I begin to feel very uncomfortable about this.

'*May* 1.—This morning the water had completely covered the coffer-dams; the stream also ran very fast as the wind blew down the river. The barges and craft descending the stream are constantly driven against the (temporary) bridge, owing to the gross negligence of the boatmen. I wrote a very strong letter of remonstrance to General Gottmann, calling upon him to enforce better regulations, or else I should be compelled to suspend the works.

'*May* 5.—Weather warm but gloomy, and the water rising at such a rate as to give great cause for apprehension. The barges and craft are coming down fast, and doing great damage, through utter want of any precautions.

'*May* 9.—In the course of last night the strong winds and rapid floods formed so great a current in the river that the deep-water dam to Pier No. II. and the dam of Pier No. I. both blew out, their upper ends rising out of the water, leaving about three-fifths of their body still in the ground. I ordered barges to be loaded with stones and sunk on the Deep-water Dam No. III. and the same on No. VII. as a precaution, though as yet these show no signs of moving.

'During the whole day the wind continued to blow very strong, but towards midnight it grew calmer, although the stream was awful. The barges and craft which had been detained yesterday by the Governor's orders came down again to-day without taking any precautions. Several of the men, however, were arrested and taken before the Governor, when they asserted that they had received no orders from anyone on the subject. This is all owing to the bad faith of the Captain of the Port, who is a desperate rogue!

'*May* 10.—Went with my son Henry and Captain Kirchenpauer, &c., to see the wreck of the coffer-dams. The river continuing to rise, other parts of the deep-water dams floated out, coming up from the bottom with a great jet. Anxiously considering what should be done, and in the evening called on the Governor-General, who expressed a wish to see the wreck of the dams, as he intended to make a special report to Count Kleinmichel.

'*May* 11.—This morning we found that the upper end of Deep-water Dam No. V., on the left side of the channel, had risen several feet, but had not as yet made its appearance above water. It had not upset the barge sunk on it yesterday, but had made it tilt over considerably. No remedy but to sink more barges, and try to keep the dam in its place before it is too late. Towards noon the sun broke out, and, as the water is reported to stand no higher than yesterday, we begin to hope that the worst effects of the snow-melting and the *débâcle* in the upper country are over. At night sat down with a heavy heart to record all these misfortunes, and to write a long letter to Col. du Plat to tell him of all that had occurred.'[1]

[1] The late Col. du Plat often spoke of this letter as being the most vivid piece of descriptive writing he had ever read. Unfortunately it has not been preserved.

FASCINE MATTRESS WORK FOR BRIDGE FOUNDATIONS.

Vignoles left Kieff for Warsaw on May 13, 1849, and returned to London. During this visit he made many inquiries and held consultations with brother-engineers about the foundations for the Kieff Bridge, and amongst others he had written to Herr Hübbe, whose acquaintance and friendship he had made at Hamburg several years before.[1] Herr Hübbe was the engineer-in-chief of the municipality of that city, and was engaged on the works designed for the protection and rectification of the river Elbe, in which operations the fascine system was a very important adjunct. Vignoles at that time (1835) had been greatly interested in the extensive improvements which were being carried out under Hübbe's orders, and had inspected with him many of the large groynes and other contrivances for protecting the river banks from the disastrous scour of the high floods; but his journal does not then make particular mention of the huge fascine mattresses, employed in many places, which were sunk in deep water by being filled with stone, a system also largely utilised by Dutch engineers. It was this kind friend and accomplished engineer who now appeared as the *deus ex machinâ* to relieve Vignoles from the great perplexity he found himself in after the floods in the spring of 1849 already described.

The diary for June 24 says:—

'To-day M. Hübbe arrived from Hamburg, and fully explained to me the method of " fascine-work mattresses " loaded with earth or stones, as protection for bridge foundations, &c., in coffer-dams. Much impressed with the system, which has been followed with great success in Holland, and on the Elbe.'

Soon after this Vignoles set out on his sixth visit to Kieff. But he had already communicated with his staff there, and had instructed them how to proceed until his arrival. At the bridge, when the water had sufficiently fallen, active prepara-

---

[1] Cf. Chapter XIV.

tions had been made to reconstruct the coffer-dams.   Immense
rafts of timber were brought down the river; at least a thousand
workmen and hundreds of skilled carpenters from Central
Russia were engaged, and, some of the Nasmyth pile-driving
engines having arrived from England, the work went on apace;
so that by the time Vignoles reached Kieff in the autumn, all
the coffer-dams had been reconstructed, and ample quantities
of gravel and broken stone provided for concrete—hydraulic
cement, or *pozzolana*, which was manufactured from clay found
near the site of the bridge, and proved equal to the best Portland
cement.   Huge granite blocks were brought from the quarries
forty miles distant, over sandy roads; the self-acting inclined
plane was completed; powerful pumping engines and machinery
were erected; and, in short, all kinds of work were carried on
vigorously, so as to ensure the foundations of the river piers and
abutments being completed before the winter.   Then came a
work of absorbing and novel interest—viz. the construction of the

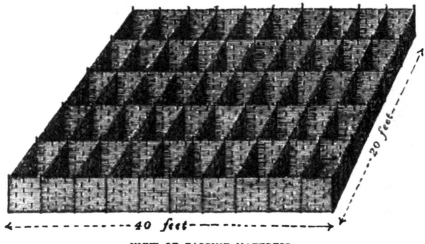

VIEW OF FASCINE MATTRESS.

fascine mattresses for the protection of the foundations.   A staff
of German and Dutch workmen had been sent specially from
Hamburg, and in a very short time these experienced artisans
had completed mattresses forty feet long and twenty feet wide,
which were then floated to the side of the deep river coffer-

dams.[1] Each of these floating mattresses (they had the appearance of large rectangular honeycombs) was carefully anchored, guide ropes were attached to it from the coffer-dams, and several barges laden with stone were moored alongside. All being ready, workmen in each barge, under the direction of a foreman, threw the stone into the cells of the mattress, so regulating the weight that it gradually sank evenly down the side of the coffer-dam, and, when safely settled at the bottom of the river, more stone was thrown into the mattress until every cell was filled. By this method a mass of stone was confined within the cells and deposited close to the coffer-dam, the weight being equal to about 100 tons for each mattress. One after another of these huge contrivances was made, floated to the side of the coffer-dams, and deposited on the bed of the river ; divers being employed to see that each mattress was sunk exactly in its place.

The fascine work was severely criticised by the Russian engineers, who predicted its failure, and naturally some anxiety was felt when the floods came the next spring. But Vignoles had full confidence in Hübbe's positive assertion that these mattresses would serve as an enduring protection to the foundation, and this has proved to be the case, at any rate for forty years.

When the floods of 1850 came, it was ascertained by soundings that the scour in the bed of the river between each pier was very great, and that the mattresses were gradually sinking at their outer edge. This, however, was exactly what Hübbe had predicted—in fact, the scour had failed to make any impression on the mattresses near the coffer-dams ; but as the flood swept under their outer edges, they gradually fell to an angle of 45°, as shown on the sketch opposite. In all other respects they proved immovable, and there they remain to the

---

[1] The bottom of the mattress was constructed of fascine *ropes*, so to say, each about six inches in diameter, closely bound together. The mattress was then divided into squares of about four feet by strong stakes driven perpendicularly into the thick ropes below, after which branches of willow, ash, or birch, were twisted from stake to stake like basket work or wattled fence ; and in this way cells were formed, closed below and open at the top, to allow stones to be thrown in. (See drawing on previous page.)

present day, a bulwark against the tumultuous spring floods. It is really a curious sight, in the middle of summer when the water is very low, to observe how the fascine work has formed, as it were, islands of greenery round each of the shallow-water piers. This is easily understood, as the interstices between the stones in the cells have gradually been filled with sand and mud, which have nourished the branches, and converted the mattresses into living brushwood.

It must be understood that the coffer-dams were not left as represented in the sketch, all the piles being cut off at low-water level.[1]

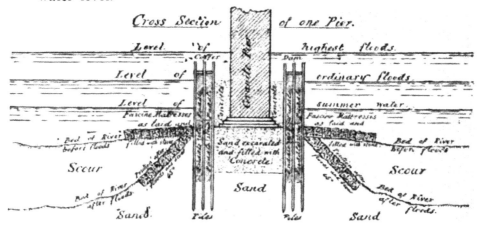

SECTION OF COFFER-DAM OF KIEFF BRIDGE.

An entry in Vignoles's diary, here given, will serve to introduce the notice of a peculiar kind of difficulty, partly diplomatic but still more financial, which was a persistent factor in the varied elements of calculation which had to be understood and carefully provided for in every such undertaking in Russia as Vignoles was at that time engaged on.

'*April* 29, 1850.—Received accounts of the *débâcle* on the river at Kieff fortunately no harm done, a happy contrast to the terrible damage of last spring. Rather pressed to find an immediate advance of 12,000*l.* for the works, besides the avaricious demands of the harpies at St. Petersburg.'

---

[1] The writer is indebted for the substance of these observations, and for the accompanying sketches, to Mr. Henry Vignoles, Memb. Inst. C.E.

It is beyond question that in those days (let us hope the evil is at least ameliorated) financial corruption largely prevailed throughout Russia, in all but the very highest circles. It had become part of a system, from which the most high-minded could hardly escape, and even then not without pecuniary loss to themselves; whilst functionaries of unblemished honour and integrity were obliged, it would seem, to wink at it—certainly they were not able to suppress it. It has been asserted by those most conversant with Russian official life that it was utterly impossible for any bargain or contract to be concluded—at any rate, in affairs under nominal State control—without an ample margin for *largesse*, which formed an indispensable item of cost in all tenders and estimates. Very constant reference is made, and grievous complaints, too, are vented in Vignoles's diaries, regarding this deep-rooted but detestable system. It is impossible for the writer (nor would it be desirable) to quote at large from such entries, but they snow how honest men were both hampered and humiliated in having to deal with such a state of things, from which there was practically no escape, save by the abandonment of their enterprises altogether.

Vignoles's journal notes on May 6:—

'Having heard the sad news of Mr. Craven's death at Kieff, consulted Mr. Robert Stephenson and Mr. Brunel, and on recommendation of latter I agreed with Mr. Gainsford (provisionally) to go out to Kieff as resident engineer at a salary of 800*l.* per annum.'

On May 10 he left London on his seventh journey to Kieff, and the usual details are given in his diaries; but there is nothing of any real interest until his account of an official inspection of the bridge by the authorities of the Imperial Government in the following August.

'*August* 15, 1850.—General Dehar, the chief of the military staff, inspected the bridge and works to-day. To me he made no remark, but I understood afterwards that he observed to a mechanical engineer from St. Petersburg, who was with us, that "everything had been very solidly and conscientiously executed."

'*August* 17.—This afternoon I entertained General Dehar and a large party at dinner. We sat down thirty at table, and everything went off with *éclat*. The old gentleman particularly enjoyed my cigars, and I presented him with a box of them. On taking leave the General remarked : " I can say nothing against you in making my report to his Imperial Majesty; it is impossible that I should, for you have done *more* than your duty."

'*September* 3.—I went down to the bridge to-day, sent for all the staff and the foreman, and took formal command of the works. It is necessary that urgent steps be taken to accelerate progress, especially in view of the approaching visit of the Emperor. The contractor very short of hands, a large number being on the sick list and seven men having died recently.'

The supply of labour was always a difficulty on the Russian works.[1] The men employed on unskilled labour were small and weak, and for the most part extremely ignorant, though generally willing enough, always provided that they were kept away from the *vodka*, a coarse spirit distilled from rye. The better class of workmen were intelligent and rather skilful handicraftsmen from the interior of Russia, some of them from Siberia and other distant provinces. The constantly occurring holidays also of the Greek Church were a source of serious hindrance, as on such days nothing would induce the men employed to do a stroke of work. Besides this there were occasional Jewish holidays, which were observed by the contractors and their co-religionists. The contractor and sub-contractor were Russian Jews, and, judging from the numberless and elaborate references to their incessant demands, it may fairly be concluded that *their* final accounts showed a very favourable credit balance ; whilst the unselfish and industrious man of science, to whose genius, energy, and boundless capacity of labour the success of this great work was entirely due, found himself if anything a poorer instead of a richer man when the Kieff Bridge was completed.

---

[1] Cf. Vignoles's diary for September 20, *infra* (next page

VISIT OF THE GRAND DUKE ALEXANDER.

On September 17 Vignoles notes in his diary :—

' An aide-de-camp of the Governor-General roused me from my bed before 6 A.M. to-day to announce the arrival of the Grand Duke Alexander, heir to the throne of Russia.[1] His Imperial Highness had only arrived one hour before, and would visit the works at noon.

' At 12.30 the Grand Duke reached the inclined plane leading down to the river, and watched the ascent and descent of waggons on the rails by the wire rope. He took a hasty view of the works as seen from this height, and just glanced at the plans, &c., which I had all ready. He asked a few questions and then walked back as quickly as he came, running all the old generals out of breath !

' *September* 20.—Provoked at finding to-day is another great holy day. Not one man at work at the puddling, notwithstanding the great emergency. The water had gained very much on the pumps, and stood now four feet higher than before the last breach.'

VISIT OF THE EMPEROR NICHOLAS.

' *October* 3, 1850.—At 2 P.M. this day the Emperor Nicholas arrived in Kieff, and having first paid his devotions at the "Lavra" Cathedral,[2] he visited the Arsenal, and then received the general officers at the Government House. Soon afterwards General Gottmann sent me up word that the Emperor desired to see me to-morrow morning at ten o'clock at the balcony of St. Andrew's

---

[1] Afterwards Emperor. His deplorable death by the deadly machinations of the Nihilists in December 1880 is fresh in the recollection of Europe.

[2] The most sacred building in the Russian ' Jerusalem,' visited annually by nearly 300,000 pilgrims. It stands in the enclosure of the vast Percheskoi fortress, and is called *Percheskaya Lavra* on that account. It has seven turrets surmounted by gilt cupolas, and its campanile tower rises to a height of 300 feet. The fortress, with all the enclosed buildings, has a grand elevation on the summit of the heights which overlook the west bank of the Dnieper. The writer may perhaps be permitted to refer to a brief account of this cathedral &c., in his series of papers entitled *A Summer Tour in Northern Europe*, originally contributed to the *Leisure Hour* in November 1866.

Church, in order to view from that elevation the sands of the river.[1]

'Great difficulty in getting things straight at the works, owing to the sinking of two barges carrying the floating pier in the heavy gale of last night.

'*October* 4.—I went before ten o'clock this morning to St. Andrew's Church,[2] according to instructions, and waited an hour with Generals Gottmann and Tschetverikoff. Was then summoned to the Emperor's quarters, when I saw his Imperial Majesty for a few moments before he went to a review, having appointed to-morrow at 11 A.M. to see me again. On his Imperial Majesty asking General T. about the bridge, the latter replied that "the work could not be better." This is a satisfactory beginning.

'*October* 5.—We were all early in readiness at the works to receive the Emperor, but he did not arrive till 1.30 P.M., attended by a numerous staff. His manner was exceedingly gracious, and he shook me warmly by the hand.

'I first showed him the working of the inclined plane, on which a waggon with two immense lorries came down beautifully. His Imperial Majesty then examined the engine and boiler house, shafting, &c., and inspected the models of the mooring abutment, of the piers and platform, and of the general elevation of the bridge, and also examined the masonry of one of the abutments. As the Emperor set foot on the temporary bridge, the gale of yesterday, which had increased in severity, seemed to blow a perfect hurricane, and his Imperial Majesty declared it was impossible to cross, as his head was dizzy, and he feared to fall.[3] He then proceeded to the *pozzolana* works, which

---

[1] Vignoles had been engaged for several weeks previously in considering the rectification of the bed of the Dnieper, which he had strenuously pressed upon the Government authorities at Kieff.

[2] This church is built on a site famous in Russian story as being the legendary spot where St. Andrew had planted the Cross, and had predicted that Christianity would in after days be preached in that country.

[3] Mr. Henry Vignoles supplies an interesting addition. When the Emperor hesitated at the bridge, it was proposed that he should cross in a boat built by the staff. The Emperor declined, but added: 'I think, though, that if I went in a boat at all, I should feel myself safer with four Englishmen than with any other persons in the world.'

were in full operation, and at which he expressed great pleasure and surprise. He then discussed with me the rectification of the channel of the Dnieper and the diversion of the Tscheteroi branch. I then showed him the wrought-iron chains; after which I introduced my two sons Hutton and Henry to his Imperial Majesty. He spoke to the former in Russian and to the latter in French; the Emperor afterwards observing to me that Henry was *très joli garçon*! After appointing me to meet him at nine o'clock this evening, the Emperor took his leave, again shaking me warmly by the hand, and expressing himself extremely satisfied with all I had done.'

RECTIFICATION OF BED OF THE DNIEPER.

The same day Vignoles had a long discussion with the Emperor about the rectification, &c., of the Dnieper.[1] Some of the staff were also present. The diary states:—

'I stoutly held out for my views, and pointed out the impossibility of a dam being sufficient, &c. I then exhibited the detailed drawings of my designs for the proposed new bridges, with which his Imperial Majesty several times expressed himself greatly pleased, remarking on what he termed "the extremely careful, minute, and conscientious way" in which they had been executed. The Emperor said the Dunabourg Bridge should be constructed as soon as possible, but, as to the others, the state of the imperial Treasury necessitated their postponement.

'I took the opportunity then of pressing on his Imperial Majesty the loss sustained by the short payments in London; and I also touched largely on the accidents happening by the non-regulation of the river craft. To all these complaints the Emperor paid great attention, and asked me to put them in writing and forward them to St. Petersburg. On one head of complaint, the actual delay in forwarding money when due, the Emperor promised that it should not occur again.

---

[1] This has since been carried out at considerable expense. The effect has been to improve considerably the navigation of the river and increase its depth.

'At the State ball which was given the same night the Emperor's two youngest sons paid me great attention, and they were also particularly civil to my son Henry.'

The Emperor left for Biela on Sunday, October 6, and on November 9 Vignoles returned to London, which he reached on the 28th, staying some time in Warsaw, and consulting, as usual, with the Messrs. Evans and Colonel du Plat.

It is evident these gentlemen had not advised him as judiciously as they were wont to do previous to his late interview with the Emperor. Vignoles had prepared a written memorandum to present to his Imperial Majesty preferring his complaints in the matter of payments, &c. His friends at Warsaw had strongly opposed this, averring that a verbal appeal would answer the purpose equally well; but unquestionably they were wrong on this occasion. The Emperor expressed surprise both to his petitioner and to the imperial staff that a written memoir had not accompanied Vignoles's complaints; and a grievous loss of time was thus occasioned, as he had in the following year to pay another visit to St. Petersburg to remedy the omission.

Vignoles, on more than one occasion, failed to back up his judgment—generally a sound one—by a fixed and resolute will. He was too easily persuaded into adopting the wishes and opinion of others, not in his proper sphere of work, but in matters of diplomacy, especially when the expression of these was couched in strong and determined language!

To conclude this portion of our narrative, one graphic incident of the journey of our engineer from Kieff to Warsaw may be here given. It furnishes a good example of autumn travelling in the muddy cross roads of Russian Poland:—

'*November* 13.—It was long past midnight before we got away from Lutz, and it took the whole night to get over the stones to Rojeest: detained there three hours for want of horses. The morning frosty and roads very bad. At Sernitza we were again detained several hours for horses, and when we did start we only got about 300 yards before we stuck fast in the mud. The postillions coolly unharnessed the horses, and left us in that plight, where we remained the whole night.   It took six oxen the next day to haul us out of the mud ! '

In those days, when no railways existed, and rough by-ways abounded, so soon as travellers left the *chaussée* their troubles began in earnest, and delays and all kinds of hindrance (save to favoured persons with a special *podorojna*) were very frequent. Perhaps the most torturing portion of a journey in summer was through the forests on an uneven track of sand, agreeably diversified by huge outstretching roots of trees ; the jolts which thus resulted seeming to thump one's very heart out, and leaving a lasting impression—on the memory !   The ' corduroy ' roads were as nothing to these, though they were bad enongh.

However, the writer is here, to some extent, glancing more at his own experiences in Russia, where it was his fate to travel some hundreds of miles in a *tarantass*, a sort of trough-shaped wooden cart without springs, than at those of the hero of this story.

Vignoles always traversed the rough country between Lublin, where the *chaussée* terminated, and Kieff in his own strongly-built and very comfortable chariot ; and he was at all times furnished with the most authoritative form of ' permit,' which, of course, commanded prompt obedience at every post station, save when the Emperor or the imperial staff were occupying the route.   Moreover, Vignoles was served as zealously in Russia by postboys as he invariably was in all parts of Europe, as his *pourboires* were always on a very liberal scale.

CHAPTER XXII.

Model of Kieff Bridge—Visit to St. Petersburg—The total eclipse of the sun—
Visit of Emperor Nicholas to Kieff—Completion and opening of the bridge,
&c.—The Crimean War—Death of the Emperor Nicholas—Conclusion of
Vignoles's Russian engagements.

1851–53.

VIGNOLES'S diary at the beginning of the year has this entry :—
' *January* 7.—Received to-day official information that a space
of 120 square feet had been allotted to my model of the Kieff
Bridge in the Exhibition building at Hyde Park.'

This affords a convenient opportunity to speak of this celebrated ' model,' probably one of the most perfect and costly of
its kind in the world. Very soon after the design for the Kieff
Bridge was completed, and all the detailed drawings worked
out, Vignoles determined on having an elaborate model of the
structure made in duplicate by Mr. Jabez James, of Bankside,
Southwark, a well-known and accomplished mechanician.

The first of the two models was ready for transport to Russia
in the autumn of 1849 ; the other was completed in the spring
of 1851, to be shown at the Great Exhibition of that year, in
the memorable ' glass palace ' in Hyde Park.

The first completed model was formally and very graciously
accepted by the Emperor of Russia, Nicholas I., at St. Petersburg, on his name-day, December 6 (18), 1849, and it was
placed in the Winter Palace.

The second model, a duplicate of the other in every minute
particular, was removed to the Sydenham Crystal Palace in 1854,
by the desire of Sir Joseph Paxton, and on the invitation of
Mr. (now Sir George) Grove and the directors, and occupied a
prominent place in the ' model ' gallery of the tropical depart-

ment, where it remained *facile princeps*, admired by the many thousands of visitors, and appreciated as it deserved by the few, until the lamentable fire of December 1866, when this costly and beautiful model, in company with hundreds of other works of art and industry, perished in the conflagration.

The model was upwards of twenty-six feet in length, or nearly 1 to 100 in linear measurement; the area, of course, being 1 in 1,000, and the cubic measure 1 in 1,000,000; and on this minute scale every piece of wood and metal, every plank, link, bolt and screw, and all the handsome granite masonry, were faithfully represented, piece by piece, in the model. A large sheet of plate glass, which reflected the under part of the platform, served well to represent the Dnieper in its tranquil mood; and on the bridge were placed figures which Vignoles had procured at Berlin, perfect models of the various branches of military service, as they would appear in full panoply when crossing the bridge. The cost of the two models was upwards of 7,000*l*.

Resuming the extracts from Vignoles's diaries we read on January 10, 1851 :—

'Received discouraging accounts from Kieff—no frost, no progress, no money! Find to my astonishment that, pending the question of exchange, Count Kleinmichel has given orders to their Consul-General in London to stop all payments here.

'*January* 28 *to* 30.—Left London *en route* to Warsaw and St. Petersburg, accompanied by my wife,[1] and Mr. Brooke Evans. . . . arriving at Hamburg met Mr. Hübbe and other friends. Found that the steamer " John Bull " had made her voyage to this port from the Thames in forty hours, whilst our journey by rail (without intermission) had taken forty-four hours! '

At Warsaw, Vignoles prepared a carefully composed letter to the Emperor of Russia on the subject of the deficient payments, as his Imperial Majesty had invited him to do; this accorded with the promise given him two years previously that the Emperor would always read for himself and favourably consider such a document when properly laid before him.

---

[1] Vignoles had married his second wife in the spring of 1849. She survived him a few years, and died at Hythe, Hants, in March 1880.

Field-Marshal Prince Paskiewicz was then Governor of the Polish capital, and on February 14 Vignoles records :—

' In evening dined with the Prince, whom I found much prejudiced against the proposed direct line [of railway] from Warsaw to St. Petersburg ; but I had learned from General Rookar, the Russian Ambassador at Berlin, that the Emperor decidedly favoured that route. I met General Schilders, of the Engineers, and had some conversation on the subject of the bridges.'

On February 18 Vignoles started once more on the weary six days' journey to the Russian capital, turning aside to view the wire suspension bridge at Moddlina.

The weather he describes as chilly, wet, and raw, but no snow or frost ; and adds that they had six horses to the carriage in the last few stages, which was less trouble than putting it upon a sledge.

The diary of February 25 says :—

' Waited this morning on Count Orloff, who at once consented to deliver my letter to the Emperor. In the evening went to a grand masquerade at the Nobility's Club, which was attended by the Emperor and all the imperial family. In the course of the evening, his Imperial Majesty, as usual, made a promenade of the rooms, and recognised me at once, speaking very kindly to me.

' *February* 26.—Went by appointment to Count Kleinmichel, and had a long conference with him. I exhibited designs, &c., for the various proposed bridges, but firmly declined to mention a price for them. I also broached the project of the construction of the whole series of lines of railway from Warsaw to St. Petersburg by English capitalists. I gave an approximate estimate both of the entire inclusive cost per verst, and also for the time to be occupied.

' *February* 27.—Conferred with my friend Mr. William Miller,[1] British Vice-Consul, and with General Gerstfeldt, as to the various works projected in Russia.

---

[1] Afterwards Sir William Miller, M.P. for Leith, who died in October 1887. He held for many years this important post at St. Petersburg, and is frequently mentioned in the most friendly terms by Vignoles in his journals.

'*February* 28.—Long conferences with Mr. Trewheellan and with Mr. Baird on railway matters. In the evening dined with Lord Bloomfield, the British Ambassador.

'*March* 2.—Heard of the rejection of Mr. William Fairbairn's design for the bridge over the Neva, the Litany Bridge.

'*March* 5.—Heard that the Emperor had given my memoir to Count Kleinmichel, to be laid before the Council of Ministers.

'*March* 6.—Late last night received a complimentary letter from Count Kleinmichel, transmitting a very handsome diamond ring from the Emperor, having on it the imperial coronet and cypher, for which I at once sent my acknowledgments.

'*March* 7.—Examined the state of the model of the Kieff Bridge, which I had presented to the Emperor in December 1849. On the whole it looked very well, and is kept in good order.'

The result of Vignoles's appeal on the question of exchange was favourable, as his diary records on March 15 :—

'Heard to-day that the Council of Ministers had unanimously decided in favour of my claim. Much gratified at the result, as it is founded on right, and not on favour. Received news from my son Henry at Toola,[1] where I have placed him for a year to study the language.

'*March* 30.—Received private information to-day that, notwithstanding the favourable decision of the Council on my claim, the matter would not be finally concluded unless certain *expectations* were settled without delay! The whole amount under this item would be about 24,000 silver roubles.[2]

'*April* 5.—Long talk with Mr. Bell, one of the partners in the firm of Thomson, Bonar, and Co., who informed me of the failure of a negotiation for the Moscow line, ten years ago, similar to mine now for the Warsaw Railway.

'*April* 11.—Long discussion with General D. about the principles on which the new bridges would be constructed. D.

---

[1] Toola (generally spelt *Tula*) is in the centre of Russia, in a district where the language is spoken most purely.

[2] In those days that would be equal to rather less than 4,000*l.* This was considerably more than a fifth of the whole sum awarded.

is a clever scientific man, quick-sighted and capable of taking clear, comprehensive views, but most outrageously venal! Learned from Count Kleinmichel that he would visit Kieff on a tour of inspection about the middle of May.

'*April* 18.—This being Good Friday, I attended the service at the English Church. Lunched with Mr. Miller, who afterwards took me for a drive in his English phaeton. The horses becoming restive, the carriage was upset and we were all thrown out. I was much bruised about the hips and knees, but, thank God, no bones broken.

'*April* 21.—Feeling better to-day, I drove out and paid several formal calls. Learned that the Emperor would be at Warsaw in two or three weeks. Heard from General B., to my great mortification, that the channel through which we had hoped to get at the Grand Duke was stopped by the petticoat influence of Madame F. The ice all gone from the river, but reported to be still in the Gulf.

' *April* 28.—Ice came down so thickly to-day from the Ladoga lake, it was impossible for it all to escape at Cronstadt. Fortunately, being soft ice, and the current very strong, it got free after some time, and no great damage done.

' A horrible affair took place to-day—two women of the town scourged (knouted) nearly to death, for having robbed and murdered a young officer! All the bad women of the town were brought by the police to witness the punishment.

' *May* 15.—Learned that the report of the department on my designs and estimates had been laid before Count Kleinmichel, but that he was in dreadful humour because of the slip on the Moscow Railway, twenty miles from here. As much confusion as if a revolution had occurred! Much annoyed at my detention here, and the general state of uncertainty.'

Vignoles had one or two more interviews with Kleinmichel, but though nothing decisive occurred, the former received every encouragement to be prepared with his designs and estimates for the proposed bridges and other works, which were to be laid before the Count on his official visit to Kieff.

' *May* 21.—Left Benson's Hotel at 2 P.M. and sailed at 7 P.M.

from Cronstadt to Hamburg, in the steamer "Nicholas," with one hundred and fifty passengers.'

Vignoles rejoined his wife at Hamburg on May 25, and arrived in London on his birthday, May 31, after an absence of four months. We give a few extracts from his diary :—

'*June* 3.—Spent most of the day in the Exhibition at Hyde Park. The model very advantageously placed, but the account in the catalogue very meagre.

'*June* 5.—Left London for Windsor with Captain Kirchenpauer,[1] and took the coach to Ascot to see the races. Her Majesty the Queen drove to the course in state, and we had an excellent opportunity of enjoying the scene.

'*June* 7.—Took Kirchenpauer at a very early hour to visit Covent Garden Market. Thence by London Bridge to Woolwich, where we called on young Du Plat at the Artillery Barracks. He was absent on sick leave. Colonel Colquhoun gave us an order to see all the works of the Royal Arsenal.'

For several days in June Vignoles was engaged in an examination of the old North Kent line, which had been once more revived. It would seem that the South-Eastern Company were then planning their Mid-Kent line, over ground which has since been occupied partly by their London and Tunbridge scheme through Chislehurst and Sevenoaks, and partly by the London, Chatham, and Dover Company.

Vignoles's diary records for June 22 :—

'Went from Rochester in an open carriage up the valley of the Medway, accompanied by Mr. F. W. Sheilds. We overlooked the Weald of Kent from the heights on left bank of the river. The whole country rough and difficult.

'Worked our way across country to the town of Farningham. Explored the ground between the valleys of the Darent and the Cray. Got a view of the summit where Bidder had his tunnel, between Bromley and Riverhead. All appears very rough and difficult ground.

---

[1] This gentleman was still acting as principal resident and executive engineer on the works at Kieff, in co-operation with Mr. Hutton Vignoles. The latter was at this time in sole charge.

'*June* 23.—Heard to my great satisfaction that Mr. Page, Engineer to the Woods and Forests, has given a provisional promise to employ Mr. F. W. Sheilds as resident engineer on the Windsor improvements.

'*June* 26.—Corresponded with Mr. G. B. Airy, the Astronomer Royal, as to the observations to be made in the South of Russia at the occurrence of the total eclipse of the sun on July 28.

'*June* 27.—Called to-day on Mr. John Murray, in Albemarle Street, the nephew of Mr. Elliot. Had some conversation with him about Russian church architecture; also on the Kieff Bridge and the model in the Hyde Park Exhibition.'

EIGHTH VISIT TO RUSSIA.

On June 28 Vignoles set out for Kieff on his eighth visit to that city, which he reached on July 9, 1851. His diary says:—

'Found all the establishment well. In evening called on Count Kleinmichel, who received me with open arms, quite overwhelming me with civilities. He engaged himself to dine with us on his first leisure day, and to visit the bridge works as soon as possible.

'*July* 13.—Dined by invitation with Prince Wotchissikoff, the Governor-General, to celebrate the Emperor's birthday. Count Kleinmichel too ill to attend.

'*July* 14.—Corresponded with M. Federoff, Professor of Astronomy, with a view to arrange a meeting at Ooman, 200 miles from this, where the eclipse of the sun will be total for about three minutes, on the 28th inst.'

'*July* 23, 1851.—Left Kieff this evening with my wife in our travelling carriage, accompanied by Mr. Bourne, the resident artist at the Kieff works, and Mr. Shaft. Journeyed on through the night and arrived at 8.30 A.M. at Alexandrevna, the charming residence of the Countess Branitzky, near Bula. Received most kindly and hospitably by the Count Vladiski, the only one of the family at home. When the heat of the day was over, the Count took us through the celebrated gardens, and after dinner part of his stud of horses was paraded before us, and we were then taken for a delightful drive through the park. The walks were lighted up, and the Count's private band played till late.

'*July* 25, 26.—Took leave of the Count at 1 P.M., much gratified at our reception. Stopped at the town of Tarasha, where we dined from our own stores, and, travelling through the night, reached Ooman at 1.30 P.M. Found that a lodging had been provided for us by turning out of his quarters an officer of Engineers. Much annoyed at this, especially on learning that he was a Scotsman by birth, but educated at St. Petersburg. Strangely enough, he had entirely forgotten his English, speaking not a word of anything but Russian! We could not, therefore, hold any communication together. The rooms were small and miserable, so we determined on changing our quarters. Found, however, that, being the Jews' Sabbath, I could get no horses or droshkies till sundown. The heat inside the rooms was intolerable, 27° Réaumur=93° Fahr. In the evening I called on General Fallon, the commandant, a very rough specimen, who only laughed at my scruples in turning out the officers and could give me no information about the scientific persons who had come to see the eclipse. At last I fell in with M. Knorr, Professor of Natural Philosophy at Kieff, who informed me that Professor Federoff had refused to co operate with him! We spent a wretched night in the close rooms, lying on the floor.

'*July* 27.—Procured rooms at an inn, cooler and larger than the quarters which had been assigned to us. The head of the police called in the afternoon to ask why we had changed our abode. We spent good part of the day in the deservedly celebrated public gardens, which quite equalled my expectations. They occupy a valley filled with granite boulders, and are richly wooded as well as most artistically laid out. Shady walks, and artificial cascades, with a goodly collection of flowers, also greenhouses, pineries, vineries, and palm-houses. The head gardener (lately come from Dresden) was very attentive, showed us everything, and gave us a row on the lake. There were several well-dressed promenaders, including some strangers who had come to see the eclipse.

'*July* 28.— A sleepless night, tormented by fleas and disturbed by the howling of dogs.[1] Rose early and went to the lake for a bath, with Bourne and Sharp. After an early dinner, went with Professor Knorr to the cottage where our instruments were placed, and set up the three telescopes in position in the orchard.

' The sky had been cloudy all day, and towards 4 P.M. got more overcast; but we were able to observe distinctly the beginning of the eclipse at 4.34, local time. Just when the sun was three parts eclipsed, a sudden storm of wind brought up a sirocco with whirlwind force, accompanied almost immediately by violent rain, the atmosphere being entirely obscured. Meanwhile the totality drew on, lasting about three minutes : but we were unable to observe any of the phenomena, except the lurid supernatural light along the horizon. Two or three stars were perceived through the intervening clouds, including the planets Jupiter and Saturn.

' Grievously disappointed at this result of our fruitless journey, and at once packed all our things in the carriage, and got away from Ooman at 8.30 P.M.'

There are no entries of much interest in the journal during the few weeks that intervened between this date and that of the Emperor's visit in October.

The works had been hindered by many causes entirely beyond the control of Vignoles or his engineering staff. He himself showed an example of marvellous patience, perseverance, and unflagging industry, and all the Englishmen on the works seconded his efforts with zeal and ability.

In that remote region they were all necessarily hampered by local and official restraints; and at times serious delays occurred owing to the difficulties of transport from Odessa, and the invincible ignorance and obstinacy of the native workmen.

---

[1] These animals prowl about by night in large packs. and are not agreeable to meet with when alone. The writer had a most uncomfortable and somewhat dangerous *quart d'heure* with such a company one dark night at Kieff, and but for the vigorous exercise of a stick he fortunately had with him might not have come out of the fray unharmed.

SECOND VISIT OF THE EMPEROR NICHOLAS TO KIEFF.

On October 1, 1851, the Emperor of Russia arrived at Kieff on a tour of inspection. Vignoles had received intimation of this visit several days before, and his diary gives us the best possible account of what took place :—

' *October* 1.—The Emperor having arrived at Kieff soon after noon to-day, I went down to the river and saw that everything was ready, and we were all in attendance till 6 P.M., but his Imperial Majesty did not come, having been occupied all day with the fortifications and the new designs for additions and alterations of the citadel, to the extent of seven millions of silver roubles. The works generally at the bridge were in a satisfactory state. The portals for the fourth and fifth piers had their centreings erected, and part of the arch was turned on each side, sufficient to show their architectural character. The ropes from the saddle on the fourth pier to the fifth, and from this into the tunnel of the mooring abutment, were suspended, so as to show the central lines of the two chains on the down stream (south) side. Indeed, the aspect of the operations generally was extremely interesting to an engineer, as every part of the works was to be seen in progress from the foundations, with the top of the concrete in Dam No. V. visible, and the swivel bridge completed so as to show the main platform of the bridge itself.

' *October* 2.—At half-past ten this morning the Emperor arrived at the works and gave me a most gracious reception. He first inspected the timber and the granite blocks lying in the field on the right bank, and then diverged to walk across the new *chaussée*, parallel to the Dnieper, and thence to the *capmière*.[1] On returning I had an opportunity of pointing out to the Emperor the accumulation of sand-banks in the river ; and on his questioning me further I explained that the water in the main channel was diminishing, whilst that in the stream of the Tscheteroi was increasing, and that the current of the latter should be *turned*, and not dammed.

'On proceeding to pass over the temporary bridge the

---

[1] The deep trench cut at the side of the *chaussée*.

Emperor experienced the same dizziness as he had felt last year, and he crossed the bridge with difficulty, leaning on the arm of Count Orloff's son. The Emperor looked at and remarked on the various coffer-dams, noticing that there were only a few inches of water in No. V.

'On our arriving at River Pier No. VII., where they were centreing the arch of the portal, the Emperor ascended to the top and was highly delighted with the view, and spoke to the masons engaged at work.

'Finally, the Emperor went on to the mooring abutment (No. II.) on the left bank (east), and discussed the curve of the chains, as indicated by the rope which I had erected. The Emperor expressed himself highly satisfied with the way in which the operations had been carried on, and observed on the immense progress which had been made with the work. After looking at the embankment approach on the left side of the river, the Emperor noticed the iron-works and then re-entered his carriage with Prince Wotchissikoff, taking a gracious leave of me, and expressing his strong confidence that I should continue fully to deserve the trust placed in me, and that he hoped on his next visit he would walk over the finished bridge.'

REMARKS ON VIGNOLES'S POSITION IN THE ENGINEERING WORLD (1853).

There are copious memoranda in Vignoles's journal for 1852 and for the first nine months of 1853. Those referring to matters of real interest and importance are treated of in a subsequent chapter; but there is no necessity to dwell further in this place on points which have already been fully touched upon in the narrative. But a word or two may be said here in justice to the memory of him whose story we are striving truthfully to tell.

It is clear that Vignoles's professional skill and untiring industry were as remarkable as ever; but his periods of long absence from England caused by the anxious and arduous undertaking of the Kieff Bridge, together with the time employed on the gigantic series of projects of new bridges and railways which he had been invited to prepare for the Russian Government, had almost destroyed his connection with the progress of railways in England.

This slow dissolving process had been going on ever since his long sojourn in Würtemberg ten years before; and now, notwithstanding his immense experience and unquestionably high abilities, he had the mortification of seeing many of his original schemes and proposals in connection with English engineering passing into others' hands, whilst, in the new developments of these, their original author and designer was in a great measure pushed aside.

Vignoles undoubtedly felt this keenly in his advancing years; but it was a noble trait in his character that he never made it a subject of complaint, and only occasionally referred to it even amongst his own family.

COMPLETION OF THE KIEFF BRIDGE.

We bring this chapter to a conclusion by the graphic description, supplied from Vignoles's pen, of his final visit to Kieff, and of the formal opening of the suspension bridge, an undertaking which had occupied him almost exclusively for nearly seven years :—

'*September* 7, 1853.—Gratified to find from a slight inspection of the bridge that the whole effect was so grand.

'*September* 15.—To-day H.I.H. Prince Alexander, heir to the throne of Russia, paid a visit to the bridge at 2 P.M. He seemed extremely struck by the appearance of the works, although it was not etiquette for him to say much, until the Emperor had made an inspection. He stopped at every portal along the platform, and as he left could not abstain from a few complimentary remarks.

'*September* 26.—This afternoon General Destreux and General Schriborski paid a visit to the bridge, and expressed their admiration of the excellent mode in which all the works had been executed. Indeed, they were evidently astonished, and I suspect in their hearts a good deal disappointed, at not discovering any-

SUSPENSION BRIDGE AT KIEFF.

thing they could lay their hands upon in the way of fault-finding !

' *September* 29.—The loading of the platform of the bridge with sand, according to the test determined on by the Commission, proceeded all to-day, and was completed towards evening. The load was twenty cubic feet per foot forward of the breadth of the platform.

' *September* 30.—The night having been clear, it was found this morning that much evaporation of the sand had taken place. After some discussion by the Commissioners additional sand was put on, making the total mass equivalent to about twenty-seven cubic feet (or one English cubic yard) for every foot forward of the whole breadth of the platform ; the cubic foot (of dry sand) being taken to weigh about 92 English pounds, or as nearly as possible one and a half tons per foot forward.

' I demurred to this, as there was every probability of rain (which finally came on at sunset), but the Commissioners insisted on it. At 5 P.M. Count Kleinmichel and suite arrived at the end of the bridge, coming along the new *chaussée* which I had constructed. He saw the test load, and was profuse in his thanks and approval, and so forth ; but it was evident he understood nothing at all about it. The bridge stood the test well, and about 5.30 the Commissioners ordered the main load to be thrown off the platform, but that on one whole opening (between Dams VI. and VII.) two-thirds of the weight should be kept on and no counterpoise left on the other side of the piers ! This load got saturated with the rain, and it was nearly two hours after midnight before it was relieved, and the whole platform cleared. Then the great operation was over, without any perceptible damage to the piers, and without permanent deflection of the platform or stretching of the chains. The whole staff were tired out, but we gave a good supper to the men, with plenty of *vodka*, and one shilling each (50 copecks) as a present. The total load on the entire platform was equal to the weight of 40,000 men !

' *October* 1.—Attended Count Kleinmichel's Levée, and was very graciously received. The Test Commission of the bridge finally agreed that a formal statement of the trial yesterday should be drawn up, with all the data and calculations of the strain exerted by the weight of saturated sand, the draft of this (in German) to be sent in for approval, before being finally signed by the staff and myself. Wrote this evening to Sir Charles Fox, who had made the chains, to apprise him of the successful result of the trial of the bridge.

'*October* 2.—Busily engaged this morning in dictating a long letter to Colonel du Plat at Warsaw, giving all details of the testing of the suspension bridge by the Commission, and the very happy result. A copy[1] of this letter was also sent to my son Henry at Biebrich, who was in charge of the works on my Rhenish railway.'

Vignoles gives some startling details of the monetary transactions that were deemed to be (and no doubt were) inevitable on the conclusion of these trials. He always records his protest against this iniquitous system, but was overruled in every case by those most intimately acquainted with the inveterate custom of the country. It is beyond all doubt that to one prominent member of the Imperial Official Staff there was given on that occasion five thousand silver roubles, then equivalent to 830*l.* It is no wonder that Vignoles stamps with execration the venality of these 'harpies of St. Petersburg,' as he frequently calls them ; and it is evident that he must often have bitterly repented that he had ever committed himself to an enterprise which was to him absolutely profitless in a pecuniary sense, a result that was in large measure due to the perpetual drain on his resources, in providing for the demands made by the insatiable greed of those to whom the financial diplomacy of imperial business was entrusted.

FORMAL OPENING OF THE KIEFF BRIDGE.

'*October* 9, 1853.—Received this morning the mortifying news that the Emperor could not find time to visit Kieff in order to open the bridge, but that the Grand Duke Nicholas would arrive to represent his father.

[1] This, unfortunately, is not to be found.

'October 10.—This morning at 9 o'clock had an audience of his Imperial Highness the Grand Duke Nicholas, the third son of the Emperor of Russia, who had been deputed by his father to open the Kieff Bridge. Having given all necessary orders the night before, I went down at 12 o'clock with my wife and a large company of friends, arriving just as the religious ceremony, conducted by the Archbishop of Kieff and Metropolitan of All the Russias, had commenced. The day was most beautiful and auspicious, and while we stood on the bridge the sun was oppressively hot.

'A temporary altar had been erected on the swivel bridge, and some hundreds of priests of every rank and from every church and convent in Kieff were assembled, with their choristers and all the pomp of the Greek ritual. It was a very gorgeous sight, especially the procession of the clergy and the monks, with their banners, crosses and croziers, and pictures of saints, winding down the heights and chanting as they came. The edges and summit of the cliffs were crowded with people, as well as the approaches to the bridge on the Kieff side.[1]

'At 1 o'clock P.M. the Grand Duke arrived, with the Governor-General of Kieff and Count Kleinmichel, and their suite; and after the conclusion of the service the entire ecclesiastical procession wound its way, chanting, over the bridge to the left bank, followed by the whole crowd of people, so that the bridge was tested once more, but by a living load, and not the slightest vibration was observable as the vast assemblage moved along the platform.

'The Grand Duke passed on to the *chaussée* and waited under the shade of the trees till his suite and the carriages had followed over the bridge. The Duke then took leave of me, thanking me in the name of the Emperor, and promising to

---

[1] There were then no habitations at all on the east side of the Dnieper, opposite Kieff; it was the terminus of a far-reaching plain, over which a new *chaussée* had been constructed to give access to the bridge. The western bank of the Dnieper is broken up into picturesque heights, intersected by wooded ravines.

make a good report to his Imperial Majesty. Thus passed off the long-expected opening of my bridge, successful in every respect except in the much-regretted absence of the Emperor.'

Vignoles with characteristic simplicity records his farewell to the city of Kieff, and to the noble suspension bridge, whose erection—in spite of numberless and unforeseen difficulties—was due entirely to his own genius, industry, and patience, of which that great work will always be a standing testimony. The memory of its gifted designer is possibly already waxing dim in the minds of the present scientific generation of his own country ; whilst the only memorial of the bridge (save some faded ' calotypes ') that the writer has been able to procure from abroad is the lithograph represented in the accompanying wood-cut, which he owes to the kindness of a friend.[1] But the bridge still withstands the shock of the ice-floods that sweep down upon its piers every year in tumultuous rage, and the noble structure, though literally ' built on the sands,' has not yielded one inch ! At the date of its construction it was the largest as well as the handsomest work of its kind in the world. Some years later a fine lattice girder bridge was built for the railway from Kursk to Odessa, which approaches Kieff from the east, and crosses the river some little distance below the site of the sus-pension bridge.

Vignoles's last entries in his diary at Kieff for 1853 are here given. He never saw the city or the bridge again :—

' *October* 15.—It was understood that the report of the Com-mission who tested the bridge should be forwarded to me in London.

' Took a last look at the bridge, and arranging with Captain Kirchenpauer for its formal delivery over to the *arrondissement* on November 13.

' *October* 18.—Having got all arrangements completed, I took my final leave of Kieff at 9 A.M. and started on my journey to England.'

We must not part with this famous and picturesque city

---

[1] The Rev. A. S. Thompson, M.A., late Vicar of Arundel, and for many years Senior Chaplain to the British Embassy at St. Petersburg.

without a few further notes on it, and a brief retrospect of its ancient glories. Its situation is delightful, perched on the summits and climbing up the steep acclivities of a series of bluffs and wooded ravines which form part of the border-land of the Ukraine country, beyond which, far away to the east and south, stretch the boundless steppes, the former home of the roving Cossacks. This district—including Volhynia, Kieff, and Podolia —is generally known as 'Little Russia,' but it belonged exclusively to Poland up to 1667, when the Ukraine was halved between that country and its gigantic neighbour, till the final partition in 1793 brought the entire Polish territory under the rule of the Czars.

In the year 885 some warriors from Scandinavia had taken possession of Kieff (or the 'height,' as its name imports) and made it the 'mother city of All the Russias;' and about the middle of the tenth century the famous Grand Duchess Olga, who from the condition of a peasant-girl rose to be the ruler of the country, embraced Christianity, and was baptized at Constantinople, the Emperor Pyrogenitus being her sponsor.

Her grandson was the noted Vladimir whose nature was more than half savage, but who ended by making Christianity the religion of his country in 997, after hearing and rejecting the claims put forward by some Mohammedan envoys, who specially urged total abstinence. To this the Muscovite is said to have replied: 'Drinking is the greatest pleasure of us Russians; we can never give that up.'

Madame de Staël tells us that 'Vladimir had sent to many countries to ascertain which religion would suit him best, and he decided in favour of the Greek Church, partly attracted by its gorgeous ceremonies, but more probably by the consideration that the cult of that ecclesiastical system, being exclusive of Papal influence, would place in the hands of the Russian potentate the supreme headship both of the spiritual and the temporal powers.'

The earliest of the Emperors proper was another Vladimir, who was crowned in the famous church of St. Sophia, at Kieff, founded by Yaroslaf, son of the first Vladimir, and thus in the year 1123 the second of that name became the first Czar of Russia.

At this time Kieff had no less than 600 churches, and was the largest and richest city in Eastern Europe.

It now possesses about sixty, of which four or five have some pretension to antiquity. St. Sophia, called after but very much smaller than its prototype at Constantinople, is a lofty and impressive structure externally, while its interior leaves a very pleasing effect on the visitor by reason of its rich and harmonious colouring. It contains a few original Byzantine frescoes, which (when the church was restored) were left untouched by the special command of the Emperor Nicholas.

Kieff is not only the metropolitan ecclesiastical city of Russia, but also her *Mecca*. Swarms of pilgrims—300,000 it is reckoned—make their annual visit to its various shrines, and Mr. Augustus J. C. Hare tells us that on one night (August 15, 1872) more than 80,000 male devotees slept in the open air on the ground surrounding the principal churches.

Until the middle of the fifteenth century the Metropolitan Archbishop of Kieff was always sent to Constantinople to receive consecration; but from that time the Emperors have dispensed with this usage, and now the Metropolitan is consecrated by a council of Russian bishops.

Russia, which of late years has been making great strides in literature and developing the resources of her copious and beautiful language, only possessed *two* printing presses at the end of the fifteenth century, and she had to wait nearly another hundred years before the first Russian grammar was compiled.

The population of Kieff has risen within forty years from 65,000 to fully 230,000. This is in great measure due to the introduction of railways, by which this fine old city has benefited largely in her educational, social and commercial, as well as in her supreme ecclesiastical capacity.

The Crimean war, which broke out a few months after the completion of the Kieff Bridge, put a stop to all negotiations between Vignoles and the Imperial Government for further work in Russia

The death of the Emperor Nicholas, just before the war was concluded, severed the remaining links of that connection which had so long subsisted between his Imperial Majesty and the English engineer, who had thoroughly won the approval and esteem of the Russian potentate and his chief advisers. Those links were severed, but the friendly feelings that had been created were not allowed to die out altogether, for the remembrance of one who had served the father was cherished by the distinguished son who succeeded to the imperial throne; and on the occasion of Vignoles's visit to St. Petersburg in the winter of 1856–57 he was received with many marks of favour by the Court, and he also obtained every possible facility towards the settlement of his claims on the imperial Treasury.

It may also be stated here, though we are anticipating in point of time, that Vignoles, in conjunction with his friend Mr. Thomas Brassey, obtained in the year 1865 the concession of a line of railway from Warsaw to Terespol. It was almost exclusively a military line presenting no great difficulties; and in this respect it turned out a more profitable affair for the eminent contractor just mentioned than the formidable works he had previously undertaken in Spain on the Bilbao and Tudela Railway, of which we shall speak in the next chapter.

CHAPTER XXIII.

Summary of Vignoles's works in later years—The Cheshire lines—Central Station at Liverpool—Railways on the Rhine, in Switzerland, and in the Brazils— Railway through the Cantabrian Pyrenees—" Himalaya " Eclipse expedition—Astronomers in Spain.

1853–60.

IN this chapter it is necessary in the first place to enumerate a few enterprises which Vignoles carried out successfully after he had completed his sixtieth year, an age when, in a large number of cases, engineers have been able to rest from their labours, and have found an ample recompense for past toil in the evening of life. But Vignoles was destined to work on bravely, cheerfully, and successfully, for twenty years longer; so that if this narrative were extended to cover fully the whole story of the period from 1853 to 1873, it would almost involve the undertaking of another memoir of his life. It must suffice, then, to dwell only on a few interesting and animated pages of his later history, prefacing them with the merest outline sketch of some important professional achievements which, whilst illustrating his unabated energy, will help to fill up the general narrative of his life and work, as well as to mark out his place in engineering records.

Between 1853 and 1857 Vignoles was first occupied in selecting and preparing a line from Liverpool to Garston Docks, and in planning the entrance into that city for the combined Cheshire Junction lines, including the choice of the Central Station in its present position, and other formidable works connected therewith, which he was the first to suggest if he did not

B B

finally carry them out.   They well exemplify that bold grasp of
details and breadth of conception and treatment for which he
was always remarkable.   The words of the first Napoleon, which
Vignoles quotes in his presidential address of 1870, are very
applicable to himself: 'Engineers ought to have magnificent ideas.'

Amongst other engagements of the same period he also conducted fresh surveys for the East Kent and Mid Kent lines, and
laid out a scheme for the Crystal Palace and West End Railways,
all which enterprises, after various delays and modifications,
have taken shape in successful results, and now serve to provide
railway accommodation for the enormously increased travelling
population of the metropolitan suburbs, whose wants are administered to by the London, Chatham, and Dover, and other
railway companies.

On the Continent, Vignoles had been appointed engineer-in-
chief to the ' Frankfort, Wiesbaden, and Cologne Railway,' on
which his two sons, Hutton and Henry, were at different times
the principal executive engineers.

The concession for this railway had been obtained by an
English company, and the capital was almost entirely raised in
London ; but owing to various circumstances only some parts of
the whole project were engineered by Vignoles.   One of these
was the line from Wiesbaden to Rudesheim, which was laid out
by him with peculiar care, as that part of the railway passed
through some of the richest vineyards of the ' Rheingau.'
Vignoles also completed the surveys and sections of the line
from Rudesheim down the right bank of the Rhine opposite to
Coblentz, where the engineer proposed to bridge the river, and
make a junction with the railway which had been constructed
on the left bank.   This project has since been completed, the
Lower Rhine being now crossed at four points by railway bridges
—viz. twice near Coblentz, then a little above Bonn, and again at
Deutz, opposite Cologne.   In Vignoles's days none of these bold
undertakings had been attempted, possibly not even contemplated, save by a few engineers of an enterprising spirit like his
own.   The Government of the Duchy of Nassau, which had
never worked comfortably with the English promoters, eventually

purchased from them the plans and sections of the lines, and on their own account completed the railway to Coblentz.

In the beginning of the year 1854 Vignoles was appointed engineer-in-chief to the 'Western Railway of Switzerland.'[1] His son Henry, as resident engineer, laid out, under his father's direction, the various lines conceded to the Company, which included those from Geneva to Lausanne, from Morges to Yverdon and Neufchatel, from Yverdon to Payerne and Fribourg, and from Fribourg to Berne.

The Company, however, after a time got into financial difficulties, that bane of so many Anglo-Swiss concessions, of which the 'Lake Valley' Railway of Switzerland is at this moment an example, and only the line from Lausanne to Morges and Yverdon was constructed by the English directorate according to Vignoles's designs.

One of the first wrought-iron trellis bridges used in railway construction was erected on this railway near Morges. The natives nicknamed it the 'toothpick' bridge, and predicted its speedy collapse; and when a locomotive was for the first time taken over it by Mr. Henry Vignoles, no one but the driver would go with him on the engine, whilst crowds were collected near to witness the expected fall of the bridge, and the certain death of the two rash individuals who had ventured to conduct the locomotive.

THE BAHIA AND SAN FRANCISCO RAILWAY.

The line from Bahia to the river San Francisco, in the Brazils, was carried out by Vignoles between 1856–63.

It was begun very soon after the commencement of the railway from Pernambuco engineered by Mr. Brunlees; but it has escaped the financial difficulties by which the latter was so long hampered, having been made well within the estimates. The total cost was rather less than 1,800,000*l.* for a single line of 5 feet 3 inch gauge, and in length 77 miles, the contractor

---

[1] This was, we believe, the second railway that was made in that country

being Mr. John Watson, who is still amongst the few survivors of Vignoles's earliest staff of executive engineers.

The railway leaves the shore at Bahia and crosses a head of the bay on an iron viaduct half a mile long, laid upon piles of the same metal. There are two or three tunnels in the course of the line, some of which have at times given a great deal of trouble, owing to the treacherous nature of the ground, occasioning pretty much the same kind of anxiety, vexation, and loss as tunnels are wont to do in every part of the world.

The extreme western terminus of the Bahia Railway was at a small settlement called Alagohines, on the river already mentioned; but within recent years the line has been extended on the *mètre* gauge for about 100 miles into the coffee and sugar producing districts, and this section is being now prolonged some 150 miles farther to the river Johannes.

The first chairman of the Bahia Railway was the late Mr. John Samuels, who was succeeded by the late Mr. Alexander Miller, of Ashford. Amongst the directorate—an unusually strong one—were Mr. Alexander Mitchell, M.P. for Bridport, and Mr. Benjamin Cohen, M.P. Mr. Hutton Vignoles was the chief resident engineer for the execution of the early portion of the railway as laid out by his father.

It is but simple justice and courtesy that the writer should take this opportunity of referring to the good faith and highly honourable conduct of the Brazilian Government in all matters pertaining to the construction of their railways by Europeans, and in the punctual payment of the guaranteed interest on the capital subscribed. Conduct like this reflects honour on the authorities of a country which, though rich in resources, has been necessarily indebted to the wealth of the Old World for the means of its development; and no small part of the credit the Brazils have now attained in the great financial centres of the world belongs to the reigning Emperor.[1]

---

[1] As these lines were penned the writer heard with much satisfaction of the favourable turn taken by the disorder under which his Imperial Majesty had been recently suffering. (June 1888).

It is a point worth noticing that the original Bahia and San Francisco

THE BILBAO AND TUDELA RAILWAY IN SPAIN.

In 1858 Vignoles was appointed engineer-in-chief of the above-named railway, which, next to the Kieff Bridge, was the most interesting engineering work carried out under his directions in foreign countries.

At that time Bilbao had no railway communication with the interior of the country, and fears were entertained by the 'Bilbainos' that the rival port of Santander would obtain precedence of their own, as the province of Santander had already taken the lead·in commencing a railway to the interior. The first section indeed of this line had already been completed and opened for traffic, and it may be remembered that a terrible accident occurred at the opening of a portion of this line, from Santander to Coralles, when a recently made embankment gave way, and the engine turned over down the slope. The engineer-in-chief, Mr. Alfred Gee, and·his brother were on the locomotive, and were both killed, whilst Mr. P. Sewell and two or three others on the engine had an almost miraculous escape.[1]

The projected railway from Bilbao had been previously surveyed by Spanish engineers, but no better ruling gradient than 1 in 40 had been found. The concession was granted, however, on the preliminary surveys, and a subvention from the Spanish Government of 60,000 *pesetas* per kilomètre was allowed.[2] The line followed the course of the river Nervion to the town of Orduña, at the foot of the Cantabrian Pyrenees; thence through the Techas Pass to Miranda, on the Ebro. Here the Northern Railway of Spain (from Irun to Madrid) was joined and crossed; and Vignoles's line—as now made—runs from Miranda to Tudela, down the valley on the right bank of the Ebro, passing through Haro, Logroño, Calahorra, and other towns.

It should be stated that although the town of Bilbao did

Railway is the *only* line on the Stock Exchange list which has never issued either Debentures or Preference Stock.

[1] See the *Times* of that date, October 2, 1858.

[2] The 'peseta' is ⅖₃th of a £.

not at that time contain more than 20,000 inhabitants, the whole
of the capital, which amounted to nearly a million and a half
sterling, exclusive of the Government subvention, was raised by
the Bilbao merchants and their friends in Havanna; the trade between the Biscayan province and Cuba being very considerable.

Vignoles spent several weeks riding over the country [1] in
order to select the best line to traverse the Cantabrian Pyrenees,
and especially to obtain a better ruling gradient than the Spanish
engineers recommended. His trouble was rewarded by the
result of his new surveys, which proved that 1 in 66 was
quite practicable over the route he had selected. It is hardly
necessary so many years later to describe the works of this
difficult and well-known line, but some particulars of general
interest may be here mentioned. Messrs. Brassey and Co. took
the first contract from Bilbao to Miranda at a fixed sum; but
owing to the great difficulties encountered, and the landslips
which occurred, the firm lost about 200,000l. But that noble
and genial man, the prince of contractors—the late Mr. Thos.
Brassey—only remarked afterwards : ' Well, we can't always
gain ; we must lose sometimes and bear our losses patiently.'

The first tunnel near Bilbao proved to be a most formidable
piece of work, as nearly half a mile of it was through a kind
of quicksand or mud studded with enormous boulders, which
had to be supported by columns of masonry built over the arch.
One of these huge boulders slipped from its bearings, and
dropped through the arch into the tunnel, just before the completion of the work, and this accident delayed the opening of
the line for several weeks. Many of the viaducts were so inaccessible that it was found impossible to get the stone to the site,
and in such cases embankments of rock had to be substituted,
some of which were upwards of a hundred feet in height.

The writer cannot refrain here from a few more reminiscences
of Mr. T. Brassey, who was on very intimate terms with all the
Vignoles family. Mr. Hutton Vignoles often speaks of the few
days he spent with Mr. Brassey at Vienna at the time of the

---

[1] In company with Mr. J. O. Mason, of Birmingham, who had brought this
railway to Vignoles's notice.

financial depression in 1866, when the eminent contractor was severely pressed for funds and his work in Austrian Poland was barely saved from a disastrous collapse. 'It is no use crying over spilt milk,' was a favourite proverb with him, but the adage in his case meant that overwhelming difficulties must not only be borne with patience, but met, and if possible lessened, by unflinching courage and a dogged determination to carry on the war somehow. 'We must make the best of it,' he said; 'and if we can pull through, we must be content with less profit, or none!' It was just the same in small things, as the writer well remembers on a railway journey with him in 1868, when the train to the North was delayed by an accident at Crewe. Mr. Brassey's demeanour and imperturbable placidity were really a moral lesson to his fellow-travellers. On the occasion we have already referred to, when news arrived—'not in single spies but in battalions'—of one disaster after another to the works of the Spanish line caused by serious floods, and when urgent messages were sent imploring him to come at once to the scene of destruction, Mr. Brassey remarked to those about him : 'I think I shall wait till the rain has entirely ceased; then we'll go over and find out what is *left* of the works, and I shall thus be saved some useless journeys!'

A beautiful model of about thirty miles of the most difficult part of the line through the Cantabrian Pyrenees was exhibited by Vignoles at the Exhibition of 1862, and well indicated the most remarkable feature of the railway—viz. the horse-shoe or water-bottle shaped valley of Orduña, round which the line was taken in a most ingenious manner, the object being to obtain the required continuous gradient for a distance of about nine miles, and now a traveller, as he emerges from the valley at the neck of the bottle, sees that a stone can almost be thrown on to the railway where it enters the valley, some 500 feet below.

The summit level at Gujuli is 2,163 feet above the sea; and at Lezama, a short distance farther north, the line crosses a stream on a lofty viaduct close to the edge of a precipice, over which there is a waterfall of nearly 700 feet descent, forming a striking and beautiful feature in the landscape.

A short distance from Pobes, a station about nine miles north-west of Miranda, near the river Bayas, may still be seen the little house where the Duke of Wellington and some of his staff slept the night before the battle of Vitoria,[1] June 13, 1813.

The line also passes through a rocky defile in the mountains called the Techas Pass already mentioned, by which, on the same occasion, a portion of the English forces descended into the plain of Vitoria, their timely arrival helping to decide the fortunes of that eventful day. All these points of interest were beautifully shown on Vignoles's model, a work of art in its way only second to his famous model of the Kieff Bridge. This model of the Spanish Railway is now in the Royal Museum at Madrid.

From Miranda to Logroño the works were likewise very heavy ; and not far from the last-mentioned town a great difficulty presented itself, caused by the river Ebro running for about two miles at the base of perpendicular and overhanging cliffs several hundred feet in height. The only alternative route necessitated new and very steep gradients, up and down, to obviate a continuation of the course of the line along the valley of the Ebro.

Vignoles, however, decided to blow down the cliffs and divert the river. He consulted his old friend and brother-officer, Sir John Burgoyne, with respect to the former, and followed his suggestions as to the position of the shafts and galleries, as well as the charges of gunpowder to be used. When all was prepared the mines were fired simultaneously from electric batteries on the opposite bank of the stream, and these formidable cliffs were hurled over into the river. The upheaval caused by the explosion was a magnificent sight; and one very curious circumstance resulted, for when the sulphurous fumes permitted a closer inspection, enormous quantities of honeycomb were found among the *débris*, swarms of bees having built their hives, probably for centuries, within the overhanging ledges of sandstone.

The diversion of the river Ebro was successfully carried out by the aid of fascine mattresses, according to the system Vignoles

[1] This name is from the Basque word ' Beturia '─a height.

had previously adopted for the Kieff Bridge; and these were sunk, one on the top of the other, across the whole channel up to the required height.   As the bed of the river was thus gradually raised, an artificial weir was created in the course of the stream till at last a complete barrier was formed, and the water flowed gently into the new channel which had been cut to receive it.

The Spanish engineers reported against the works as too costly, and indeed they pronounced them impossible; whilst the Spanish local newspapers predicted that the enterprise could never be completed, and that it would remain only as a ' memento of the temerity of English engineers.' [1]

The remaining portion of the line to its terminus at Tudela presents no special features of interest, nor were there any constructive difficulties worthy of record.

The writer has availed himself of a section of the admirable and carefully drawn map, specially prepared by Vignoles for the ' Eclipse ' expedition in 1860, of which we now proceed to speak.

The thin lines which traverse the map obliquely represent a portion of the path of solar obscuration during the actual time of the total eclipse; and all the principal stations occupied by the astronomers on the occasion will be found in this map, on which is also traced the whole course of the Bilbao and Tudela railway.[2]

---

[1] Mr. P. Sewell, M.I.C.E., had come from England at the earnest request of Vignoles to carry out the works which the Spanish contractors had fai'ed to undertake.   A large share of the merit of the success which was ultimately reached is due to his patient and skilful management of men as well as of material in these formidable operations.   Mr. Sewell is to this day (and very properly) proud to remember that it was all accomplished without *Sunday* labour.

[2] Mr. Murray's Handbook for Spain (1858) says:—' The railway from Bilbao to Orduña and Miranda forms a most interesting excursion, from the grandeur of its scenery, its historical associa'ions, and the masterly way in which the line itself has been engineered by our own countryman, Mr. Charles Vignoles.' (Cf. this work, p. 183.)

THE TOTAL ECLIPSE OF THE SUN IN JULY 1860.
THE ASTRONOMICAL EXPEDITION TO SPAIN.

An episode of unusual interest occurred in Spain during the
time of Vignoles's engagement on the Bilbao and Tudela Railway. This was the visit of several astronomers and other
distinguished men of science to the Cantabrian provinces, for
the purpose of witnessing the total eclipse of the sun on July
18, 1860. The opportunities of observation afforded on this
occasion by the presence of a large staff of engineers and contractors in the heart of the shadow-path district were seized
upon with characteristic promptness and energy by Vignoles,
who (as we have seen in the last chapter) had made a long though
fruitless journey in the South of Russia with the object of witnessing a similar phenomenon six years before. But it was
something far above any mere personal feeling which induced
him in 1860 to exert himself to the utmost to secure the success
of the Eclipse expedition. He had discussed with his old friend,
Professor Airy, the then Astronomer-Royal, the importance of
obtaining the help of the English Government in the equipment
of a suitable vessel chartered for this purpose; promising on his
own part to put all the resources of his railway staff, their skill,
instruments, time, and, in some cases, their dwelling-places at
the service of the astronomers.

The response of the Government was all that could be desired.
They with great liberality commissioned their fine transport-
steamer " Himalaya," under the command of Captain Seccombe,
R.N., to make the voyage from Plymouth to the ports of Bilbao
and Santander, with a cargo of astronomers, and all their necessary baggage and scientific apparatus; and a most successful
and delightful trip was the result, on which the writer was permitted to be one of the favoured *voyageurs*. The party on board
numbered about seventy, of whom four were ladies—viz. Mrs.
(afterwards Lady) Airy and her eldest daughter, now the wife
of the celebrated mathematician, Dr. E. J. Routh,[1] Miss Struvé,

---

[1] Dr. Routh has been the 'coach' of no less than twenty-five senior wranglers
within thirty years.

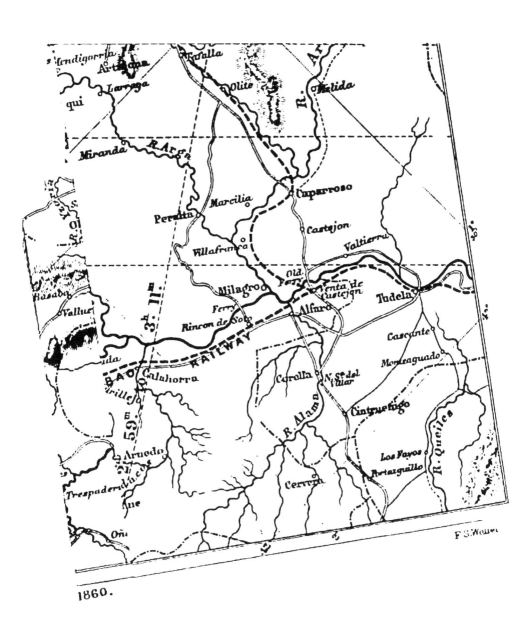

1860.

and one of Vignoles's daughters-in-law. The *savants* on board were too many for distinct enumeration here, but besides the Astronomer-Royal of England there were Professors Struvé (Russian Imperial Astronomer), Pole, Pritchard [1]; Messrs. Wilfrid Airy, Bonomi, Oom, Beckley, Downes, Dr. Winecke, and several other distinguished sons of science, prominent amongst whom must be named the eminent and successful astronomer and physicist, Mr. Warren de la Rue, F.R.S., whose heliographic camera was on this occasion first successfully applied to record automatically the newly-discovered phenomena of the *corona*, and the *red flames* and other striking accompaniments of a total solar eclipse.

Mr. De la Rue's success on this memorable occasion is now a recognised landmark in scientific history; and in his ' Bakerian ' lecture, read before the Royal Society in April 1862, that distinguished astronomer has given a full and most interesting record of the events of the day and the happy results of his own important observations. Only a few passages from this paper can, however, be introduced here, as referring to the subject of this memoir:—

' In the interval of nine years from the total eclipse of 1851, astronomical photography had made great progress, and after inspecting the Königsberg daguerreotype of the eclipse in that year, taken with the heliometer by Dr. Busch, . . . I was led to conclude that it would be very desirable to employ the Kew photo-heliograph on this occasion; but on account of the weight of its pedestal it was thought best to make a new pedestal of cast iron, composed of several pieces, which were eventually left *in situ*, and the iron thus marks the precise locality of my observatory at Rivabellosa. Mr. Vignoles had strongly recommended me to cross to the southern side of the (Cantabrian) Pyrenees, in order to avoid the mists which are caused by the condensation of vapours from the ocean against the northern slopes of the mountains. Subsequently Mr. Vignoles published

[1] Professor Pritchard I ad with him, as guest, the Rev. J. J. Stewart Perowne, now the distinguished Dean of Peterborough.

an " Eclipse map " of Spain on a very large scale,[1] and I selected Miranda de Ebro for my station ; but on that gentleman's recommendation I placed my observatory at Rivabellosa, two miles from the town, and it was fortunate that I did so, as some of the astronomers who selected the former place were prevented by the state of the atmosphere from observing the eclipse.'

Mr. De la Rue further says :—

' On our arrival at Bilbao on July 9, Mr. Vignoles met the "Himalaya" in a small steamer which he had chartered to convey ashore the astronomers who intended to land there with their apparatus and luggage ; but I am under a further obligation to him, not only for his kind and liberal hospitality during my stay at Bilbao, but for despatching my apparatus at once to Rivabellosa, seventy miles away, and which is only accessible through a pass difficult for the transmission of heavy baggage.'

The interesting results obtained by Mr. De la Rue are (as we have said) historical, for he was the first to make it a matter of certainty that the luminous corona and the rose-coloured flames and prominences are *objective phenomena* belonging to the sun, and not merely subsidiary, as if produced by some action of the sun's light upon the moon's edge.

As is well remembered by all who shared in the honour and glory of the expedition, the usual fair weather to be expected in that latitude was replaced by several days of wind and rain, which culminated on the Sunday (July 15) preceding the eclipse in a terrific thunderstorm, that left the atmosphere in a universally moist and disturbed condition, and brought a severe disappointment to the majority of observers on the actual day of the eclipse. Vignoles, with several of his staff and some members of his family, had placed himself on the Gorbea Mountain, at an elevation of 5,000 feet. The sad fate which had befallen him in

---

[1] The map was bound up in a pamphlet of sixty-five pages, full of local information of every kind, making it a complete guide for the scientific visitors. This publication acquired additional value from a series of plain but very precise and lucid directions drawn up by Professor Airy, the scientific captain of the expedition, for the guidance of the army of astronomers under his command.

South Russia was again cruelly meted out. The mountain was wrapped in mist, and the eclipse was unseen.[1]

Two of his sons had a somewhat less unfavourable view of the phenomenon, with an occasional glimpse of the dark body of the moon in its progress over the sun's disc. They were 'positioned' on the ridge of a box-clad hill near Amurrio.

Professor Pole and his party had to beat a hasty retreat from Vitoria to Miranda, and were rewarded by a successful observation on the 18th; whilst Professor Pritchard had even a better view from the summit of the Gujuli ridge. This gentleman hit upon a very simple and ingenious method of enabling the engineers who had been told off as his assistants to observe the phases of the eclipse. This was a string weighted by a stone, forming a vertical line across the body of the sun, which thus became as it were a clock face, and the eye of the observer, using the string as a plumb-line, was in this way guided by it to a rough micrometrical measurement of the course of obscuration. The watchword of this party—constantly reiterated as the totality drew on—and (as the Professor says) one that has proved very useful long afterwards, was 'Mind your plumb-line!'

The two extracts here given from Professor Pritchard's interesting and animated account of the Eclipse expedition will not be deemed irrelevant :—

'In this country great advances had been made in celestial photography by Mr. Warren de la Rue, who by a rare combination of chemical, mechanical, and astronomical skill had obtained automatic *heliographs* and *selenographs* possessing not only unrivalled beauty, but also an amount of accuracy which gave promise (since amply fulfilled) of not merely rivalling but sur-

---

[1] Vignoles was a third time unfortunate, when voyaging to Sicily in H.M.S. "Psyche" in December 1870, with his son Hutton and a scientific party told off to observe the total solar eclipse visible in that island. The vessel struck on a sunken rock off Catania, but no lives were lost. Vignoles was busy over his papers in the cabin, and could only be persuaded to leave when the water was covering the floor. He quietly remarked that nearly half a century had elapsed since his previous shipwreck on the isle of Anticosti ! (See Chapter III.)

passing results hitherto obtained by the most refined instrumental measurements.'

Again, with more immediate reference to Vignoles's share in the success of the visit to Spain, the Professor remarks :—

'It was rightly considered that the existence of railway works in a country where roads are few, and accommodation and the means of transit exceedingly scarce, would prove a circumstance of the utmost importance.[1] Indeed, but for these advantages, and above all for the untiring zeal and unbounded liberality and intelligence of the engineer-in-chief, Mr. C. B. Vignoles, the whole expedition must have been thrown into almost inextricable confusion.'

Amongst the guests of Vignoles at his small but commodious house at Albia, a suburb of Bilbao, were the renowned 'Master of Trinity,' Dr. Whewell, and his amiable and accomplished wife, Lady Affleck. The writer was much amused one evening, when joining a small party who were taking an after-dinner walk by starlight, at an attempt made by an amateur astronomer to call our attention to the planet Mars, then shining with (to our eyes) unwonted brilliancy. The illustrious Cambridge don, who was smoking a splendid ' regalia,' looked up for a moment to the sky, and then with a dignified smile quietly remarked, ' Ah, yes, that is Mars; but you see I know nothing about Mars! But this I do know, that our excellent host, Mr. Vignoles, keeps uncommonly fine cigars.'

Professor Airy and his wife and daughter were also guests

---

[1] Very remarkable progress has been made in Spain in these and many other respects since 1860. Means of communication have increased and a vast improvement has been effected in the accommodation afforded by inns and rural *posadas*. Moreover, the whole tone of Spanish local and ecclesiastical rule has undergone a change for the better. A certain freedom to travel and (more important still) liberty of worship has been conceded to foreigners, which a quarter of a century ago had scarcely a semblance of existence. In 1860 and 1863 the services of the writer were eagerly sought for the administration of baptism to scores of children, born to English navvies and *employés* of all kinds near Bilbao, the rite being solemnized in the house of the Consul, Mr. Horace Young, who happily still presides over the civic rights of his compatriots in that flourishing port. The Holy Communion also could then only be administered in a private house.

at Albia, and the writer cannot refrain from narrating in briefest form a scene unique of its kind, which has left a vivid impression on his memory.

Music used to form an evening relaxation in the little drawing-room of Vignoles's 'château en Espagne,' as it was laughingly called, and a valuable acquisition in the shape of pianoforte playing was occasionally enjoyed when Professor Pole was able to join the party. But a night or two before the " Himalaya " was to re-embark her intellectual cargo, Professor Airy and Vignoles began to quote in turns snatches of old English songs. Sir G. Airy (to give his proper title to one who is still happily spared to England and to science) is gifted with a marvellous memory, and he delighted the little band of listeners with a full and sonorous recitation of Canning's famous poems : 'The Needy Knife-grinder' and 'The U-ni-versity of Gottingen.' This was rather beyond Vignoles's *métier*, so he responded with the ' Lass of Richmond Hill,' and ' Auld Lang Syne,' but he was soon caught up by the Professor with songs still older and rarer, all of which he rapidly went through without a slip of memory. Vignoles retaliated with at least fragments of other ballads, such as 'The Bailiff's Daughter of Islington,' and the like, with a few others unknown to a later generation, although full of quaint humour. But the gage of battle was again promptly accepted by Professor Airy, who at once followed him into the new (or rather *old*) channel of song, and reached a triumphant *finale* in the ballad of ' The Ratcatcher's Daughter,' amidst screams of laughter from the scanty but privileged audience. The writer cannot summarise the contest better than in Virgil's lines, which had thus received a lively illustration :—

> ' Ambo florentes ætatibus, Arcades ambo,
> Et cantare pares, et respondere parati.' [1]

But we must leave these pleasant reminiscences, and revert

---

[1] A very brief memorial obituary notice, contributed by the writer to *The Athenæum* in November 1875, has a few remarks similarly descriptive of the scene here referred to.

to the more important business of this narrative : ' paullo majora canamus ! '

Dr. Whewell did not share the success in viewing the solar eclipse which fell to Professors Airy and Struvé at Pobes, and to the eminent French astronomer, M. Leverrier, near Logroño, by all of whom observations of great interest and value were made and recorded.

Vignoles returned to England in the " Himalaya," and had the pleasure of listening to a vote of thanks proposed by Professor Airy, and passed by acclamation, on the quarter-deck of the steamer. It was to the effect that ' without the great and liberal aid of Mr. C. B. Vignoles, and the disinterested love of science evinced by him on this occasion, the success of the " Himalaya " Eclipse expedition could not have been ensured.'

CHAPTER XXIV.

Vignoles elected President of Institution of Civil Engineers—His position as a man of science—Placed on Ordnance Survey Commission—One of founders of Photographic Society—Estimate of his general work as an engineer—Peculiarities of his character—Concluding remarks—His death in November, 1875.

1865-75.

AFTER the completion of his Spanish railway, Vignoles did not enter upon any very serious or arduous enterprise; but he never laid aside his habits of labour, and even in the sphere of engineering he was engaged from time to time on important works, amongst which may be named the line already spoken of from Warsaw to Terespol, and consultations on the ' Isle of Man ' Railway, both of which undertakings were ably and successfully carried out by his son Henry, who was sole engineer to this first Manx line. Vignoles now devoted much of his leisure to questions connected with the various phases of engineering science, and as these came up for debate at the meetings of the Institution he was constantly in attendance as a member of Council, and contributed from his stores of knowledge and experience to the various discussions that arose. It should here be stated that he had rather lost his proper place in point of seniority as one of the vice-presidents who had not passed the chair. This was in great measure due, though not altogether, to frequent absence from the meetings of the engineers in previous years, owing to his engagements abroad; and, consequently, he had not in regular rotation attained the position which led immediately to the presidency of the Institution. But in 1869 a general feeling arose that Vignoles's age, coupled with his acknowledged ability and character, entitled him without further delay to this highest post of honour in the profession. This desire on the part of the leading engineers of the kingdom was largely promoted by the action of the then President, Sir Charles H. Gregory, and other members of Council; and it was consummated by the high-minded and brotherly conduct of the eminent living engineer, Mr. Thomas Hawksley, F.R.S., who waived his claim to the chair, and thus Vignoles was elected President of the Institution of Civil Engineers in his seventy-sixth year.

His inaugural address as President was marked by great literary ability, and included a comprehensive retrospect of the progress of engineering work on the Continent and in the United Kingdom, in which, with great modesty and self-efface-ment, he recounted many lively reminiscences of the great era of railway engineering, at whose birth he had assisted, and during whose course up to that moment he had assiduously and intel-ligently laboured.

It was something for those who were present on that evening of January 1870 to have listened to 'the old man eloquent,' with his early zeal and enthusiasm unquenched, showing by his voice and gestures, his pleasant smile and his courteous manner, that his heart was still in the profession he loved, and that the most earnest wish he now cherished was for the continued prosperity of the Institution over which he was summoned to preside, of which he had been one of the earliest members, and had so largely contributed to its success and reputation.[1]

Those who knew Vignoles best could not fail to remember how he had been in many a stiffly fought engineering conflict, and had both given and received many a hard blow. Of his professional brethren present there were no doubt some who differed amongst themselves in their estimate of his long and varied labours, and who had even opposed and thwarted him in his career, for this is common to all professions alike, and is of the very essence of the competition by which success can alone be obtained. But none could fail to acknowledge how honourably and fairly their new President had won his present position, and

---

[1] Cf. the opening of Chapter X. (supra, p. 121) for some statistics as to the number of members of the Institution in 1870. At the beginning of the present year (1889), the number of members of all classes is 5,620.

STATUETTE OF C. B. VIGNOLES AT SEVENTY-SIX YEARS OF AGE

with what earnestness and courage he had continued to work during a career of nearly half a century, with energy undiminished by the lapse of years and hope undimmed by many disappointments; his course of life not unmarked indeed by some errors of judgment and some mistaken opinions, but unstained by a single blot on his reputation, his integrity, or his genius.

In the same year in which Vignoles attained the presidency, an admirable bust (life size) was taken by Mr. Miller, the sculptor, of Westminster, which now occupies a niche in the upper corridor of the Institution. From this bust an excellent reproduction was modelled by Vignoles's only daughter, and from this the artist has drawn the life-like figure which is shown in our illustration.

But it is time that this imperfect narrative was brought to a close. Little more need be said in our concluding remarks beyond a word or two as to the general acquirements in the science and practice of his profession which Vignoles possessed, and the position he occupied amongst the distinguished band of railway engineers in the first half of our century.

Vignoles had been elected a Fellow of the Royal Society in 1855, under the presidency of Lord Wrottesley. He was a regular and welcome attendant at its meetings from the date of his election almost to the day of his death, twenty years later, and he numbered many of its leading fellows amongst his friends and admirers. But the range of philosophical discussion in that lofty council of the gods was in some respects beyond the limit of his own attainments in the highest walks of science, and he did not contribute any paper to the 'Transactions' of the Society.[1] We cannot, however, attribute this to his being unequipped for an excursion into the fields of Science, for the records of his achievements, contained in this memoir, entirely refute such a supposition. Rather should we look for the explanation in the lofty, almost ideal, conception he entertained of the merits and

---

[1] Vignoles often contributed to the subjects *verbally* discussed at all scientific societies to which he belonged; and this was markedly so in the debates of the Institution of Civil Engineers.

ability that should characterise any and every paper deemed by
its author worthy of being tendered to the Council of the Royal
Society.   Vignoles, as claiming collateral descent from the great
Newton,[1] had an exalted ideal of 'pure science,' and we may add,
a lowly estimate of himself as but one of her humblest servitors.
Indeed, it was owing to this almost morbid intellectual modesty
that he refrained as a general rule from reading papers before
the meetings of the Institution ; a thing much to be deplored,
as it was certainly within his power to have contributed to its
'Transactions' much that would even now be of value to engineers
in the point both of didactic and of literary skill.   In theoretic
as well as practical mechanical knowledge Vignoles could claim
a high place in his own day ; and some proof of this may be
seen in the fact that from 1836 to 1842 continuously he occupied the post of secretary to the 'Mechanical Section' of the
British Association.   Vignoles's knowledge of bridge-building
(to instance one out of many points), whether in stone, timber, or
metal, was unsurpassed ; and, moreover, he had that artistic
taste which has made a large number of his bridges, both at
home and abroad, recognised models of beauty, as well as of
strength and utility.[2]   What his celebrated Kieff Suspension
Bridge is, the reader can estimate from Chapters XX.–XXII.

But it should also be added, to make our remarks perfectly
consonant with truth, that for the last twenty years of his life
the intellectual activity, as displayed in literary form, which had

---

[1] See Chapter I., page 5.

[2] The principal engineer of the Midland Railway, Mr. A. A. Langley, informs the writer that the handsome cast iron bridge over the Trent, a little
south of Derby (a drawing of which is seen in Chapter XV. of this memoir),
is still as strong and serviceable in all respects as at the time when Vignoles
erected it, fifty-eight years ago.   The stone bridge over the Ribble at Preston
is also an acknowledged masterpiece.

An important passage from Vignoles's diary of April 1, 1850, may be quoted
here, as referring to bridges :—' For the first time passed through the Tubular
Bridge erected by Robert Stephenson across the Menai Straits.   It is a wonderful work of art, and I am much gratified at its complete success, of which I
had never doubted.   Indeed, I was the first engineer who erected a bridge on
this principle, near Blackburn, on my Darwen and Bolton Railway, over the
Liverpool and Leeds Canal and the adjacent turnpike road, about five years
ago.'

distinguished Vignoles up to and beyond his sixtieth year began sensibly to diminish; and his preference was rather for the luxury of reading, and for the quiet social pleasures to whose success he always so largely contributed, especially at his own table, than for the severe strain involved in literary composition. On this last point of distinction in social gatherings, we may say without fear of contradiction that, as host or chairman of any convivial entertainment of his brethren in the world of science, Vignoles was *facile princeps*.[1]

As an engineer, Vignoles was a man of unwearied energy, ardent temperament, and great constitutional power. His work was invariably performed with serious care and conscientiousness, and always with an earnest desire to economise the funds at his disposal; and indeed it was largely for the securing of this end that he advocated the adoption of steeper gradients and sharper curves, earlier than most of his contemporaries.

He was undoubtedly amongst the very first to mark the levels of the ground on railway maps,[2] an improvement so tardily adopted by the directors of the Ordnance Surveys; and on this point of 'contouring' we are justified in making a few remarks, prefacing them with a passage from his diary of March 1853 relating to the contemplated Ordnance Survey of Scotland:—'A long conference with Sir Charles Trevelyan, Secretary to the Treasury, when I explained my views, pointing out the evidence I had given nearly thirty years ago, when the survey of Ireland was first proposed, and referring to my correspondence then with Sir John Burgoyne. I was requested to prepare immediately a report to the Treasury on this subject.'

Other entries show that Vignoles's contention was for a larger scale of maps for the counties; and he was also most desirous for a definite system of contour levels in all the

---

[1] When the writer asked Sir Frederick Bramwell—not long ago—if he possessed any letters from the subject of this memoir, he answered: 'I really do not remember receiving any letters from our late President, except invitations to dinner, and these I invariably made a point of accepting!' Professor Tyndall has recently stated to the writer his opinion that, as a public speaker, whether on the daïs or at the dinner-table, Vignoles had few equals.

[2] Some authorities say he was the first to do this.

Ordnance maps; a plan which he again urged strongly on the Government in 1855, when Vignoles, with Brunel and one or two more civil engineers, together with Sir John Burgoyne and a few other persons of scientific repute, was nominated on a Royal Commission to inquire into and report upon these points. Vignoles showed, from inquiries he had personally made in France, Switzerland, and other countries, that we were far behind our Continental neighbours in such matters; yet he was unable to prevail on his brother-commissioners to recommend the universal adoption of the principle of 'contouring' in the Ordnance Surveys.

We may here remark that the original trigonometrical survey of these isles was begun in 1791, and extended in 1797. During the past ninety years the Treasury has increased the scale in some cases to six inches to the mile, on which the whole of Ireland was mapped out between the years 1824–40. Through this intervening period the survey of Scotland was suspended, and for several years after Vignoles's report the Treasury could not make up its mind as to the scale to be used; but the authorities afterwards laid down general rules under which the *new* survey of the United Kingdom (begun in 1863) was to be on the 1-inch scale, but the county maps on the 6-inch scale. For England and Wales parochial maps are prepared on a much higher scale—viz. 25 inches to the mile—but these even now [1888] only extend over twenty-eight counties in England and Wales, the rest being not completed. Moreover, there are but twenty-nine counties which as yet have their maps finished on the 6-inch scale.

Another illustration of Vignoles's general attitude towards science, and his readiness to appreciate and turn to practical use any improvement in its application, is seen in his earnest and disinterested efforts to foster the infant art of photography. We have already seen that he was amongst the earliest to apply this invention to engineering work in the 'talbotypes' and 'calotypes,' taken under his direction, of the various stages in the progress of the Kieff Bridge, many of which sun-pictures are in the writer's possession; and these were shown as specimens of great interest at photographic exhibitions forty years ago.[1]

A few extracts from his diary of 1853 will serve to record his zeal in helping to found the now flourishing ' Photographic Society,' and its ' Journal ' :—

' *Jan.* 20, 1853.—This afternoon attended a public meeting, held at the rooms of the Society of Arts, when the " Photographic Society " was formed and I was nominated one of the committee.

' *Feb.* 3.—The first general meeting of the Photographic Society was held this evening. [Probably at the Society of Arts' rooms.] Very full attendance, and very good exhibition of photographs from Sir William Newton.

' *Feb.* 17.—Meeting of committee at my house in Duke Street [2] on the question of establishing a " Photographic Journal." I drew up a report, which the Council read and adopted, and general powers were given to the Publication Committee. I wrote letters on the subject to Sir Charles Eastlake, Sir W. J. Newton, Professor Wheatstone, and Mr. Fenton.

' *Feb.* 23.—Engaged all day in preparing matter for the first number of the " Photographic Journal." Conferred with Sir William Newton, Dr. Percy, and others.

' *Feb.* 27.—Occupied several hours, and until late at night, in correcting the proof sheets of the first number of the " Transactions of the Photographic Society." Considering the subject of the leading editorial article.

' *March* 7.—Attended at Judges' Chambers, with Dr. Percy and others. Entered into security against *libels*, &c. Considering the proper means of forwarding circulation of the " Journal."

' *March* 12.—Much engaged with the printer, and with Mr.

---

[1] His diaries prove that at different times between 1847–52 Vignoles had the honour of showing these early protographs to H.M. the Queen and the late lamented Prince Consort, to the Emperor Nicholas of Russia, to Lord Palmerston and the Duke of Wellington, as well as to Lord Westmorland and other persons of high position.

[2] He notes that the Council had accepted his offer to hold the meetings at the house he had newly taken at 21 Duke Street, Westminster, now 17 Delahay Street.

Henfroy, the new editor of the "Journal," to whom Dr. Percy and self transferred the documents, &c., of the forthcoming second number of the " Photographic Journal." [1]

In speaking further of Vignoles's scientific attainments, we cannot claim for him a high place as a mathematician. He had certainly enjoyed rare opportunities in this respect during his sixteen years' continuous residence with his grandfather, Dr. Hutton; but a glance at what we have said in the early chapters of this memoir will show that the old professor did not subject his restless and versatile relative to that strict discipline of industrious and steady work so indispensable to a mathematical student. But his own confessions also prove how little disposed the grandson was ' to bear the yoke in his youth; ' and thus, as he himself laments, time that should have been spent in serious study he ' wiled away in assiduous devotion to the charms of the Muses and the Graces.' Yet, as we have also seen, his aged relative did succeed in pressing him into service as an assistant in his various calculations; and the practical skill thus acquired in preparing tables of logarithms, and other modes of computation, for which young Vignoles displayed singular aptitude, must have materially helped him to attain the expertness and readiness he afterwards displayed in engineering methods, which he often exemplified in bringing out, quickly and accurately, results in a numerical or tabulated form, and on any scale of notation. This acquirement, matured by practical experience, placed him in after life second only to the late Mr. George Bidder as a ' ready reckoner ' amongst his professional brethren. With respect to the other technicalities of engineering, Vignoles was known as an almost unrivalled draughtsman. This distinction he had won very early in his career, as is proved by his letters from Holland in 1814, where he narrates his success in military drawing and measurement at the siege of Bergen-op-

---

[1] Mr. Roger Fenton had previously acted as editor.

The late Chief Baron Pollock was the first chairman of the ' Photographic Society,' and a warm patron of the art. His son, Mr. Henry Pollock, one of the Masters in the Supreme Court of Judicature, has inherited his illustrious father's love of and lively interest in photography. The late Dr. Hugh Diamond was also a zealous worker in the same cause.

Zoom, and there is presumptive evidence that this accomplishment was largely self-acquired.[1] Subsequently to that, his long and arduous practice as a surveyor in Charleston and its neighbourhood gave him increased facilities in this branch of work, to which he often refers in his letters from the Southern States of America, as quoted in our earlier chapters. From the date of the publication of his book and map of Florida, in 1823, which year also marks distinctly his taking up the position of civil engineer in England, up to his eightieth year, Vignoles's keenness of eye, and steadiness of hand, and delicacy of execution had not deserted him.[2]

The importance he attached to accurate mapping, and the skill, precision, and clearness of his topographic work, are well known ; and we have noticed several proofs of this in the applications made to him by the Admiralty from time to time, in such matters as the harbours of Dover and Port Dinlleyn, and in the Irish Railway Commissions, and also in respect of the Ordnance Surveys of Great Britain and Ireland already referred to.

Unfortunately, from circumstances entirely beyond the writer's control, of the vast number of finished drawings, sketches, and maps of all kinds and of various dimensions, which Vignoles brought into existence, very few indeed survive ; save an odd one here and there in the possession of his family and friends, and a certain number of an early date which may still be ferreted out from the shelves of the library of the Institution of Civil Engineers.

The writer of this memoir has a harder task before him in endeavouring to adjudicate on Vignoles's exact position among the leading engineers of the great railway epoch in decade of this century. A decision on this point with much more weight and propriety from an qualified, first, by technical ignorance of the

[1] Cf. Chap. II., p. 24.
[2] Mr. P. Sewell relates that the last time he saw Vig-n him lying at full length on a drawing table, surroun- busily at work on a large map of India.

secondly, by the ties of kindred to him whose place in the Temple of Fame it is sought to determine.

The author thinks that he will pursue a wiser course in endeavouring to review as fairly as possible the exact conditions under which the subject of this biography came to be an engineer at all, he having begun life as a soldier; and also to consider the natural or acquired qualifications he possessed which entitled him to compete with some of the greatest men of the age in practical science, at a time when none but those with exceptional gifts had any chance of success.

In one respect certainly his case resembles that of George Stephenson, whose splendid genius entitles him (in the general judgment of posterity) to the highest place. Like him, Vignoles, though with the advantage of belonging to a higher social sphere, had in no way benefited by the assistance of others. The education he had received (as we have seen) was of the most irregular character, and he had never been disciplined to mental labour; and, as our narrative has shown, no adventitious help of any kind came to him from his grandfather, when he was driven to seek some other employment than a military life, on the disbandment of the army in 1817. He had to carve his own way, as did Stephenson, without counsel or aid from any one, though he was unlike him in having had no training in mechanical or manual labour, and in possessing nothing beyond an elementary acquaintance with any branch of practical science. It must, therefore, be admitted that a young officer, who within seven years of leaving the profession of arms had established for himself, both in the Old and New World, a considerable reputation as a surveyor, a designer, a draughtsman, and a writer, entirely by his own exertions and under very adverse circumstances, may fairly claim a high position amongst the few pioneers who opened out the way that has received so magnificent a development in the triumphs of modern engineering. Let it be well borne in mind that within two years from Vignoles's return to Europe, in 1823, he had worked for, or under the patronage and approval of, the best civil engineers of that day—Telford, Walker, the elder Brunel, the elder Cubitt; that he had been selected by the Rennies to plant this infant branch of science in the South of England; and that immediately afterwards he was despatched by them as their chief surveyor and resident engineer, not (as we have shown) on the line proposed by Stephenson, but on that new and improved line of railway from Liverpool to Manchester which Parliament afterwards sanctioned—the line so celebrated in the history or English science, and the parent of all the great lines of railway throughout the world. Let us remember, further, that within another seven years Vignoles had been elected engineer-in-chief of two important lines in Lancashire; had superseded George Stephenson in being chosen to introduce railways into Ireland; had supplanted Rennie and Jessop in becoming engineer to the Midland Counties line, and Joseph Locke in the election to a similar position on the Sheffield and Manchester line; being in this case the first to pierce the formidable (and as was then thought) insuperable mountain range that barred railway traffic between the southern districts of Lancashire and Yorkshire. All this forms a brilliant record in the history of the earliest stages of modern locomotion, and gives Vignoles a solid claim, which, we fear, has been too much and too long underrated, to a place and a name amongst the great engineers of that day.

But, after all, in the rivalry which existed amongst these gifted men there was nothing that need have been detrimental to Vignoles's future success. True, he had incurred the dislike of George Stephenson; but even that, however unreasonable, ought not to have proved a very serious hindrance to him, as it was known that this remarkable man was not one who could easily overcome a prejudice once conceived against any one. We should also observe that the hostile feeling created towards him in the mind of the elder Brunel by Vignoles's counter-proposals to the directors of the Thames Tunnel in 1829 must have diminished his chances of success in many ways, and certainly they lost him the patronage of one of the greatest men of the century. But, giving full weight to these disadvantages, it is impossible by any such reasons to account for the fact that not till his seventy-sixth year was Vignoles elected to the presidency of the Institution of Civil Engineers. And it is here that a biographer is bound to be faithful to truth, and not merely (as in too many memoirs) feel himself compelled to draw as faultless a picture as possible of the subject of his theme.

It would be foolish to deny that the great hindrance to higher advancement in Vignoles's case, in his middle life, was very largely due to himself—to his impetuosity chiefly, which he was at times quite unable to restrain, and which seemed to drive him on, where any great and pressing object was before him, with irresistible impulse, regardless of opposition, heedless of consequences, and absolutely mindless of his own material interests. There was a certain spirit of heroic self-sacrifice in him, which made him quite indifferent to pecuniary risk or loss, where a cooler man would have held his hand; his temperament impelling to acts of serious imprudence, of hasty determination and impulsive action, that sometimes involved both friend and foe in their far-reaching results. Once let him see that a thing could be done, he determined that it *should* be done, and, if possible, at once. And herein lay another serious source of danger, for his impatience caused him sometimes to be blind to difficulties which could only be overcome by waiting— by allowing for the obstinacy or short-sightedness of others, by yielding at the time that he might prevail in the end. All this he was, as a general rule (especially in his early years of professional success) constitutionally unfitted for, and the most disastrous instance of this is seen in the position he found himself in as to the shares in the Sheffield and Manchester Railway, spoken of in Chapter XVI., by which he was flung in a few months from affluence into poverty, and from professional eminence into (for a time at least) obscurity and neglect. It says very much for his own solid reputation as an engineer, while it speaks volumes as to his marvellous recuperative power, morally, physically, and intellectually, that he was able to withstand such an overwhelming disaster, and enter the lists once more, aye, and win in the end, after having thus given a long start to many who were previously far behind in the race.

But while thus stating the case with some leaning to the side

of severity, it would be most unjust not to bring well into notice
the many admirable qualities belonging to Vignoles's character,
which made amends in a large degree for his confessed failings
of temper and his somewhat arbitrary manner. In fact, these
were faults characteristic of most military men, especially at that
epoch; and those who could bear with the *quondam* officer's
occasional display of hasty temper, and were not too sensitive to
caustic words, were the persons who did not fail to mark and
value the sterling qualities of mind and heart which he possessed.
These it was that so strongly endeared him to the members of
his staff, and have preserved in the minds of his cotemporaries
(there are not many of them left) a very vivid and even affectionate remembrance. His quickness and keenness of perception
were remarkable; but this cut two ways—making him a delightful companion to those who could give and take an abrupt word
and a smart reply; whilst to the somewhat stolid average
Englishman, his quick ways, his ready fence of speech, and his
impatience of dulness and stupidity in any form, were undoubtedly
somewhat provoking. Thus it cannot be denied that he made a
few enemies; and yet probably there hardly ever lived a man
who was so absolutely innocent of malice even to his worst foe,
or so entirely free from professional jealousy towards his most
successful rivals.

His disposition had before this mellowed into the geniality of
age; and no one was more ready with his counsel and his purse
when any benevolent scheme was set on foot, especially if it was
on behalf of those in his own profession who had been overtaken
by sickness or misfortune. He was one of the largest con-
tributors (not of the kind once described by Sydney Smith) [1] to
the eleemosynary fund of the Institution of Civil Engineers,
the benefits of which are gradually being extended as the ranks

[1] The occasion referred to was in the opening sentence of one of the witty
Canon's sermons, and the anecdote was related by a parishioner of Combe-
Florey, who heard the discourse, to Sir George Grove, who told it to the writer
The sermon was for some charitable purpose, and began thus:—'Active bene-
volence is one of the highest of the Christian virtues; but it is remarkable that
no sooner does A set on foot some beneficent scheme, than immediately B sets
himself to discover what C means to give!'

of the profession become more and more thronged and the risks of failure augmented.

In his latter days, Vignoles joined the Volunteer Corps of 'Engineers and Artists,' and was made one of its chief staff officers. He was commonly known as 'the Colonel,' a title he was gratified to own; and he was naturally proud of the long military pedigree he could boast of, which ran back for fourscore years.

Vignoles had enjoyed throughout his long life almost uninterrupted good health, and the illness which terminated fatally was only of three days' duration.

He peacefully breathed his last in his own house at Hythe, in Hampshire, on November 17, 1875, surrounded by his children and grandchildren. His widow survived him for little more than four years.

The subject of our memoir was interred on November 23 in Brompton Cemetery, the officiating clergyman being the Rev. G. A. Crookshank, vicar of Catton, Norfolk, a connection of the family, and one of Mr. Vignoles's trustees. Several distinguished members of the engineering profession stood amongst the family of the deceased around the grave, which lies on the east side of the central avenue of the cemetery. The stone which covers the tomb bears the following inscription :—

IN MEMORY OF

CHARLES BLACKER VIGNOLES,

CIVIL ENGINEER, AND FELLOW OF THE ROYAL SOCIETY,

J. P. FOR HANTS, PAST PRESIDENT OF THE INSTITUTION OF CIVIL

ENGINEERS, AND FORMERLY LIEUTENANT IN

H.M. FIRST ROYAL REGIMENT OF FOOT.

Born, May 31, 1793. *Died, November* 17, 1875.

AGED 83.

With C. B. Vignoles the romantic era of modern engineering science may be said to have passed away.

INDEX.

ADA

ADAMS, Quincy, 78
Airy, G. B. (Astronomer-Royal),
356, 379, 383, 385
Alexander II., Emperor of Russia,
344, 562
Allport, Sir James, 222, 229
America, voyages to, 32, 63
Anticosti, Vignoles wrecked on isle
of, 34
Antwerp, skirmish at, 21
— 500,000l. offered for taking, 21
Aston, Mr. (Secretary to English Em-
bassy, Paris), 167
Athenæum Club, Vignoles a member
of, 155
Athol, Duke of, 122
Atmospheric railways :—
Arundel, 282
Dalkey, 190, 273
S. Devon, 284-5
Kingstown and Bray, 271 *note*
— system, 284-5
Austen, Mrs., 9

BAGSTER (inventor of steam-
whistle), 131 *note*
Bahia and San Francisco Railway,
372-3
Baird, Mr., 325, 326, 353
Baldwin, Mr., 137
Barlow, Professor, 125, 247, 258
— on atmospheric railways, 284,
note

BRA

Barlow, Mr. W. H., and St. Pancras
Station, 227
Beaufort, Admiral, 286
Bell, Captain, 87, 353
Benson, the Misses, 325 *note*
Bergen-op-Zoom, storming of, 22, 23-
28
Bergin, Mr. Thomas, 331
Bergin's spring-buffers, 185
Beroldingen, Count, 295 *et seq.*
Beyser, M., 293
Bianconi, Mr. (introduced jaunting
cars), 272
Bibikoff, General, 324
Bidder, Mr., 203, 393
Birkenshaw, Mr., 154
Birth of Vignoles, 5
Bismarck, Count de, 300
'Black Virgin,' The, 324
Blacker, Mr., 4 and *note*
Bloomfield, Lord, 322, 325, 327
Blumberg (Kieff contractor), 330
Bolivar, General, 69, 70
Bonney, Professor, 214 *note*
Booth, Henry, 109, 130
— multitubular boiler, 130
— and buffers, 186
— lubrication, 186
Boring apparatus, 336
Bradshaw, Mr., 114 *note*
Braithwaite, John, 111, 127, 149, 200,
232
— letter on 'Novelty,' 134
Bramwell, Sir Frederick, 390 *note*

BRA

Brassey, Thomas, 158, 375
Bridge, Southwark, 90
— over the Menai Straits, 389 *note*
— over Severn, 176
— near Morges, 372
Bridges of Vignoles:—
    Grand Canal Docks (Dublin), 187
    Kieff Suspension, 317; ch. xx.–xxii.
    — — model of, 350
    — — opened, 365
    Liverpool and Warrington Road,
    145
    Ribble, 147, 389 *note*
    St. Helens, 141
    of timber, 237 *note*
    over Trent, 240, 389 *note*
Bridgwater, Duke of, 142
Brighton Railway, 202
Brisbane, Gen. Sir Thomas, 9, 48, 52
et seq.
— in Canada, 38
— in New South Wales, 58
— character of, 53
Broglie, Duc de, 172
Brunel, Mark Isambard, 101, 118, 119,
123, 396
— Isambard Kingdom, 118, 125, 180, 196
— I. K. and atmospheric railways,
284–5
— and forms of rail 224 *note*
— and Welsh surveys, 248, 255, 259
Buffers, spring, 185
Bübler, M., 293 *et seq.*
Burgoyne, Sir John Fox, 11, 159, 179,
198, 206, 208, 209, 238, 273
— on railway expenditure, 246
Burton, Decimus, 262
Butler, Colonel, 63
Byron, Lord, and Miss Millbank, 40

' CALORIC ' system, Ericsson's, 131
    Cambridge, Duke of, 191
Capps, T. W. (of Brighton), 204 *note*
Carno Pass, 257
Carriages, luggage, with guard on top
of, 146 *note*
— old first-class, 146

DEH

Carriages, third-class, 146
Charleston, life at, 73, 80
Charlotte, Princess, 53 *note*
Charlton, Dr. Hutton buried at, 67
Chat Moss, 110, 115
Chester and Holyhead, proposed
route, 248
Cholera at Kieff, 334
Christmas tree (German), 305
Clegg, Mr. (inventor of dry gas-
meter), 264, 284
Clive, Lord, 250
Cloncurry, Lord, 181, 183
Coaches at Preston, 143
Cobden, Richard, 327
Collier Dock, 100
Collister, John, 126, 149
Combermere, Viscount, 8
Commission, first Irish Railway, 206
— second Irish Railway, 247 *et seq.*
Commissions in army to infants, 8
and *note*
Committee, Lords', on Liverpool and
Manchester Railway, 110
— — on London and Birmingham
Railway, 157
Conroy, Sir John, 184–5
' Contouring,' Vignoles advocate of,
390
Cook, Mr., 260
Cost of permanent ways, 224
Courtois, M., of Guadaloupe, 6, 49
Cracow, 320, 324
Crawshay of Cyfarthfa, 291
Crimean war, 368
Crosbie-Dawson, Mr., 148 *note*
Croudace, Anna Hester, 77, 211, 293,
388
— Miss Camilla, 77 *note*
Cubitt, William, 159, 186, 249, 284
— and atmospheric railways, 287
Cumberland, Duke of, 15

DARGAN (contractor), 179, 182, 272
    David, M., 166
Davy, Sir H., 264 *note*
Dehar, General, 343

DEO

' Deodand,' 263 *note*
Deserters, shooting, 18
Devonshire, Duke of, 270
Diamond ring from Emperor Nicholas, 353
Dibbin, Mr. H. A., 113
Directors of Sheffield and Manchester Railway and Vignoles, 238
Disasters at Kieff, 337
Dogs in Russia, 358
Dover Harbour scheme, 273
' Dry meter,' gas, Clegg's, 264
Dublin and Kingstown Railway, 177
— — — opened, 187
— terminus, 248
— termini, Vignoles's scheme for connecting, 191

EARLE, Sir Hardman, 143, 147
— General, 143, *note* 1
Ebro, diversion of the, 377
Eclipse of sun in Russia, 356, 358
— — — in Spain, 379
— — — in Sicily, 382 *note*
— — — Vignoles's map of, 381
Edge Hill Tunnel, 112, 113
Edinburgh, 46
' Encyclopædia Metropolitana,' 98
Ericsson, 98, 111, 127 *note*
Erskine, Captain, 14, 15
Esterhazy, Prince, 152
Etzel, M., 295 *et seq.*
Evans, Douglas and Alfred, 218, 321, 347, 351
Express trains first mentioned, 269

FAIRBAIRN, Sir William, 187, 353
Fascine system, 338
Federoff, M. (astronomer), 356
Financial corruption (Russia), 342, 364
Fleetwood, Sir Hesketh, 144
Florida, Vignoles's estate in, 78
— surveys in, 87
— map of, 93
Fort William, 47, 50

HAW

Forth, Mr. Charles, 142 *note*
Fowler, John (Sir), 234 *note*
Fox, Sir Charles, 364
Frost [20 Réaumur], 321
— of 1813–14, 18
F.R.S., Vignoles elected, 388

GAINSFORD, Mr., 343
Gärtner, M., 306 *et seq.*
Gas, former price of, 189
Gauges, various, 180, 189, 302 *note*
German travels, 293 *et seq.*
Giles, Mr., 110
Girard, M., 163
Gold snuff-box from King of Würtemberg, 315
Goldsmid, Sir I. L., 275 *et seq.*
Goold, Colonel, 28
Gordon, General, 63, 79
Goree, island of, 20
Gosport, married at, 65
Gottman, General, 329, 335
Grabam, General, 7
Grand, M. Baptiste le, 160
Graves, Admiral, 85, 91
Greenall, Mr. Peter, 139
— Sir Gilbert, 139, *note* 2
Gregory, Sir Charles H., 96, 101, 104, 124, 196, 386
— Dr. Olinthus, 22, 118, 157, 196
Grey, Sir John, 5
— General Sir C., 7
Grierson, Mr., 183 *note*, 192
Griffiths, Mary, 9, 11
— engaged to Vignoles, 12
— married, 65
— death of, 103
Grove, Sir George, 350, 398 *note*
Guadaloupe, island of, 5
Guest, Sir John James, 291

HACHETTE, M. de la, 163
Hall, Mr., 155
Hanson, Mr., 35, 83
Hawkshaw, Sir John, 279 and *note*
Hawksley, Thos., 387

HEL

Helvoetsluys, 20, 21
" Himalaya " expedition, 379
Hire, La, family name, 1
' History of Midland Railway ' (Wil-
    liams), 215, 217, 225
Holmes, Mr., 152
Hope, Sir Algernon, 81
Hübbe, Herr, 193, 197, 338
— and fascine system, 338 et seq.
Hudson, the ' Railway King,' 222,
    271
Huskisson, Mr., death of, 150, 153
Hutton, Dr. Charles, F.R.S., 4, 5, 91
— death of, 95
— Charles, junior, 37
— Camilla, mother of C. B. Vignoles, 4
— Rev. Henry, 37, note 2
— General, 7, 58
— Isabella, Vignoles's aunt, 5, 9, 12,
    42
— — her kindness, 95, 96
— — character, 97
— — death of, 261
— James, geologist, 5
— Mrs. (wife of Dr. Charles), 29, 30,
    34, 55, 58
— — death of, 62

INSTITUTION of Civil Engineers,
    early days, 121
— Vignoles President of, 387
Ireland, Vignoles's article on, 253_4
Irish surveys, 209
Isle of Man survey, 122
Ivanitzky, Captain, 251

JEFFREY (editor of ' Edinburgh
    Review '), 45
Jenny Lind, 320
Jervis, Admiral, 5
Jessop, Josiah, on Chat Moss, 110 note
— and G. Stephenson, 117
Jews in Kieff, 329 note, 330
Jones, Sir Harry, 206, 209, 274
Journeys to St. Petersburg, 318, 323,
    351

LOC

KEAN, the actor, 41
    Kent, H.R.H. Duke of, 8, 13, 22,
    30, 39, 49, 59, 79
— H.R.H. Duchess of, and Princess
    Victoria, 184, 185
Kieff, 317
— bridge contracts, 329, 330
— — completed, 362
— — dimensions, 331
— — disasters at, 337
— — models of, 350_1
— — official inspection, 359
— — opening of, 365
— — testing the, 363
— — visits of Emperor to, 329, 345,
    350
Kingstown Harbour, 178 note
Kirchenpauer, Captain, 334, 355
Kleinmichel, Count, 322 et seq.
Knouting of women, 354
Köstlin, M., 295, 300
' Kyanized ' timbers, 224 note

LABOUR in Russia, 344
    Langley, Mr. A. A., 389 note
Latin conversation, 320
Lawrence, Charles, 114, 118
Lecky, Mr. W. H., 151 note
Lees, Sir Harcourt, 178, 181, 182
Leigh, Mr., 157
Leipzig, battle of, 16
Leybourne, Professor and Mrs., 12,
    13, 14, 21, 61, 62
— on Vignoles's marriage, 74, 75
— Mrs., death of, 81
Littleton, Mr., 152
Liverpool Central Station, 370
— Lime Street Station, 146
— and Manchester Railway, 113, 114,
    199
— — Vignoles's improved plan, 114
Llanfair, Welsh village with long
    name, 255
Locke, Joseph, on Edge Hill Tunnel,
    113
— engineer of ' Grand Junction
    Railway,' 113, 136

LOC

Locke, Joseph, consulted on North Kent Railway, 277
— on 'Novelty' and 'Rocket,' 129
— on Dublin and Kingstown Railway, 178 9
— and Sheffield Railway, 230 *et seq.*
— and steam blast, 130
— and French railways, 158
Locomotives, Vignoles on, 111
— Ericsson's, 127
— George Stephenson improves, 128
— trial of, 128, 137
London to Dublin, time of passage, 184
Louche, M. de, 295 *et seq.*
Louis-Philippe, King, and railways, 171
Lynn Harbour work, 100

MACGREGOR, Sir G., 69, 70, 72
MacMahon (contractor), strange mistake of, 148
Madeira, Isle of, 68
Mahony, Mr. Peirce, 159, 184
Mührler, Professor, 311, 313
Malet, Sir Alexander, 312
Mancler, Baron de, 291 *et seq.*
Maps, Ordnance, 390
Mawdsley, James, 120
Mersey Tunnel, Vignoles's idea, 119
Miller, Sir William, 352
— Colonel and Mrs., 323 *note*
Models of Kieff Bridge, 350
— of Ribble Bridge, 148 *note*
— of Tudela and Bilbao Railway, 377
Monroe, President, U.S.A., 78
Montalivet, M. de, 161
Montefiore, Sir Moses, 159, 166
Morpeth, Lord, 252
Mother of C. B. Vignoles, 4
Moultrie, Fort, 77
Müller, Colonel, 24, 28, 34, 35, 53
Munich, 299
Murray, Mr. John, 356
Murray, Sir George, 41, 81

POR

NESSELRODE, Count, 322
Newhaven and Shoreham, 203
Newton, Sir Isaac, 5, 388
Nicholas, Emperor of Russia, 317, 322, 325, 329, 330, 345, 350, 359, 368
— Grand Duke, opens Kieff Bridge, 365
Nimmo, Mr. A., and Chat Moss, 110 *note*
— death of, 178
North Kent line *v.* S. E. R., 274
'Novelty' locomotive, 127
— reasons for failure of, 133-4, 149
Nuremberg and Fürth Railway, 197

O'CONNELL and Vignoles, 189 *note*
Ogden, Mr., American Consul, 153 *note*
Olga, Grand Duchess, 319, 367
O'Neill, Miss, 45
Orange, Princess of, 313, 314
Ordnance surveys, Vignoles on, 390
Orloff, Count, 322, 352
Oxford Canal, work on, 123

PADDINGTON Station, origin of, 176
Palmer, Mr. R. S., 241
Parker, Captain, 23
Paskiewicz, Prince, 329, 352
Paxton, Sir Joseph, 269, 350
Peace of 1814, 35
Peel, Sir Robert, and Irish railways, 250
— on railways, 265
Petitvale, M. (surveyor), 84, 85
Photography, Vignoles and, 391-2
Pile-drivers, 334
Pim, James, 179, 184, 258
Plat Du, Colonel, 318, 321, 337
Pointe-à-Pitre stormed, 5
Pole, Professor, 280 *note*, 380
Ponsonby, Lord, 327
Port Dinlleyn, 249, 255-6, 258
Portsmouth, Earl and Lady, 35, 83

POU

Poussin, Major (engineer), 160, 199
President of Institution of Civil
Engineers, 387
Prevost, Sir George, 36, 37, 38, 41
— and Sir James Yeo, 37, 41
Prices at Charleston, 80
— in Scotland (1815), 48
Pritchard, Professor, 380
Prittwitz, Major, 310
Prony, Baron, 163
Purdon, Wellington, 234, 256, 260
— and steam blas‘, 131
Pushing an engine, 144
Pyrogenitus, Emperor, 367

QUEBEC, 33, 35,

RAILS, forms of, 183, 200, 222
    —the ‘Vignoles,’ 201, 224, 303
— cost of laying, 224
— on Würtemberg railways, 303
Railway, Festiniog (smallest gauge),
257
Railways, development of, 107
— cost of working in 1845, 226
— in United States, 137
— travelling in early days, 146
— Blackburn, 275, 389 note
— Cheshire lines, 200
— Cork and Passage, 197, 272
— Dublin and Kingstown, 177
— Holyhead, 256
— Isle of Wight, 286
-- Liverpool and Manchester, 110
— Liverpool and Birmingham, 136
— Lancaster and Skipton, 267
— London and Arundel, 282
— London and Birmingham, 222
— London and Brighton, 202
— London, Chatham, and Dover,
278
— London and Paris, 158
— London and Windsor, 175
— Midland Counties, 196, 221
— North Kent, 274
— North Union, 142

SAV

Railways—continued
— North-Western (Little), 267
— Sheffield, Ashton, and Manchester,
230
— St. Helens, 141, 145
— Spalding and Boston, 270
— Tudela and Bilbao, 374
— Warsaw and Terespol, 369
— Würtemberg, ch. xix.
Rambuteau, Count, 164
Rastrick, J. U., 111, 128, 211
Regent, Prince, 17, 35
Rendel, Mr., 27
Rennie, John and George, 96, 99,
107, 113–16, 125, 177, 203, 249, 262,
277
Report, Vignoles's, on Irish railways,
224
— — on Würtemberg, 308
— of first Irish Railway Commission,
209
Retrospect on attaining fifty years,
244
Richmond, Duke of, 159, 163
Riddle, Edward, 116
Robinson, General, 37 note
‘Rocket,’ the, 128, 129, 130, 150
Romney, Dr. Robinson, 331, 334
Rosse, Earl of, 156
Rothschild and Paris Railway, 159,
162, 166
Royal Society, Vignoles a fellow of,
388
Rue, Warren de la, 380–382
Runcorn and St. Helens Railway, 138,
139
Russell, Mr. E., 148 note
Russian Emperor Nicholas, 317, 328,
&c.
— police administration, 326
— military review, 327

SAMUDA and Clegg, 284
    Sandars, Joseph, 108, 218
Sandhurst, origin of, 12
Sankey Canal, 139
Savannah survey, 81

SEW

Sewell, Mr. P., 109 *note*, 374, 378
Severn Tunnel, 279
Shee, Sir George. 294, 309, 313
Sheilds, Mr. F. W., 262, 355
Shoreham or Newhaven for Dieppe, 203
Sidebottom, Messrs., 289
Sinclair, Mr. Arthur, 140, 145, 267
Smedley, Rev. E., 98
Smiles, Dr., and Vignoles's work, 108, 130
Smith, Sir F., 258
South Carolina survey, 84
— map of, 84
Southern States, travelling in, 80
Southwark Iron Bridge, 262
St. Helens, town of, 141
St. Katharine's Docks opened, 123
St. Petersburg, 321 *et seq.*
St. Thomas, patent slip for island of, 264, 307
Stanberrautz, Madame, 314
Stanhope, Earl, 5 *note*
Stations, old railway, 146
Steam blast whistle, mention of, 131, *note*
Steel sleepers, 225 *note*
Stephenson, George, 109, 112
— and Vignoles, 116
— and his subordinates, 113
— in Ireland, 178
— and locomotives, 129, 132
— and French railways, 162
— and Midland Railway, 221
— compared with Vignoles, 395-6
Stephenson, Robert, 121, 128, 140, 157, 186, 202
— on atmospheric railways, 284
— and Holyhead Railway, 250-5
— 's line to Brighton, 202
Stevenson and Edinburgh and Glasgow Railway, 211
Stewart, Professor Dugald, 45, 46, 47, 50
Stone sleepers, 145, 189, 224 *note*
Stuttgart, ch. xix.
Surrey and Sussex Railway, 107
Sutton Inclined Plane, 154

VIG

TACUMSHIN Lake, proposed drainage of, 272
Talbot, Mr., 270
Talleyrand, M., 168-170
Tedder, Mr. H., 275 *note*
Telford, Mr., 111, 121, 123, 139
— and Oxford Canal, 123
— 's medal, 125 *note*
Terry, J. E. (Vignoles's assistant), 122, 126
— in Isle of Man, 122
— on Preston Railway, 142
Thames Tunnel, Vignoles's plan for the, 118, 124
Thiers, M., 158, 175
— visit to England, 172 *et seq.*
Third-class carriages, 146, 226
'Toothpick' Bridge, 372
Tour of railway inspection, 251
Traffic, Dublin and Kingstown Railway, 188
Travelling in Russia, 321, 324, 348
Tscheffkin, General, 251
Tschetwerikoff, General. 346
Tubular Bridge, Vignoles deviser of, 389 *note*
— — R. Stephenson's, 389 *note*
Tunnels, early, 235

UNIVERSITY College, Vignoles Professor at, 262

VALENCIENNES, siege of, 52
— life and society at, 54 *et seq.*
Vignoles, Very Rev. Charles (Dean of Ossory), 4
— Charles F., 81, 102, 194, 197, 235, 238, 307, 323, 326
— — Henry, Captain, 4, 5
— — — death of self and wife, 6, 7
— John, of Tewkesbury, 41
— Hutton, 98, 235, 256, 267 *note*, 281, 293, 302, 304, 315, 318, 333
— Henry, 102, 235, 318, 333, 342, 346
— Olinthus, 235, 267 *note*, 269, 323, 326

VIG

Vignoles, Charles Blacker, birth of, 5
— characteristics of, 397–8
— commission at a year old, 7
— under his grandfather, 8, 9, 10
— estrangement from grandfather, 10, 11
— at Doctors' Commons, 10
— probable flight to Spain, 11
— at Sandhurst, 12
— engaged to Miss Griffiths, 12
— gazetted to York Chasseurs, 8, 17
— ensign in 1st Royals, 17
— ordered to Holland on active service, 19
— prisoner at Bergen-op-Zoom, 28
— sails for Canada, 32
— shipwrecked, 34, 383
— returns to England, 43
— sails for Scotland, 44
— promoted to lieutenant, 48
— on half-pay, 50
— aide-de-camp to General Brisbane, 54
— at Valenciennes, 52–61
— married at Gosport, 65
— sails for America, 66
— arrives at St. Thomas, 69
— — at Charleston, 72
— loses (temporarily) half-pay, 73
— appointed assistant State surveyor, 75
— daughter, birth of, 77
— surveys Savannah, 81
— voyage to England, 82
— returns to America, 83
— jealousy of Americans, 85
— at St. Augustine, 86
— domestic and other troubles, 89, 90
— visits New York, 91
— returns to England, 96
— engineering work begins, 98
— estimates for Collier Dock, 99
— Witham and Lynn Harbour, 100
— his wife an invalid, 101
— illness of his eldest son, 102
— death of his wife, 103

VIG

Vignoles, Charles Blacker—continued
— Liverpool and Manchester Railway, 107
— connected with G. Stephenson, 109
— House of Lords Committee, 110
— salary under the Rennies, 114
— breaks with G. Stephenson, 117
— and resigns London and Manchester Railway, 118
— elected Member Institution Civil Engineers, 121
— Government survey of Isle of Man, 122
— work on Oxford Canal, 123
— dispute with Brunel senior, 125
— improves navigation of River Slaney, 126
— chief engineer of North Union Railway, 141
— at Rainhill, trial of 'Rocket' and 'Novelty;' 129
— 'St. Helens,' 'Preston and Wigan' Railways, 138
— opening of North Union Railway, 143
— — Liverpool and Manchester Railway, 108
— proposed London and Paris Railway, 159
— in Paris, presented to Louis-Philippe, 171
— Dublin and Kingstown Railway, 177
— — — opened, 187
— Hamburg and Hanover, 193
— Midland Counties Railway, 196
— pressure of work, 197
— surveys in Wales, 304
— — Ireland, 207
— opening of Midland Counties Railway, 226
— Sheffield and Manchester Railway, 199
— difficulties with the same, 232–40
— resigns his connection, 240
— residence at Dinting Vale, 236
— 'begins the world again,' 245
— later Welsh surveys, 248, 254

VIG

Vignoles, Charles Blacker— *continued*
— professor at University College, 262
— various railway work in England
— — — — Ireland ⎫ ch. xviii.
— — — — in or near London
— North Kent scheme collapses, 279
— Leicester and Birmingham Railway, 268
— pressure of work, 281
— proposal to go to India, 287
— Würtemberg Railway, ch. xix.
— first journey to St. Petersburg, 318–321
— second journey to St. Petersburg, 323–325
— arrives at Kieff, 324
— in Kieff, 329
— foundations of Kieff Bridge, 333
— floods and disasters, 337
— saved, 342
— models of Kieff Bridge, 350–1
— second marriage, 351 *note*
— visits of Emperor to Kieff, 329, 345
— third journey to St. Petersburg, 351
— loss of English connection, 362
— completion of Kieff Bridge, 362
— returns to England, 366
— Frankfort, Wiesbaden, and Cologne Railway, 371
— President of Institute of Civil Engineers, 387
— Tudela and Bilbao Railway, 374
— Remarks on life and work, 393–8
Vignolles' (De), ancestors :--
— Etienne (la Hire), 3
— Jacques, Sieur de Prades, 3
Vladimir, first Czar, 367

YOR

WALKER, James, 96, 99, 111, 121, 125, 255
Waterloo, Battle of, 43
Watson, Mr. John, 147 *note*, 271, 373
Webster, Mr. J. Claude, 155
'Wedge' rails, Birkenshaw's, 154 *note*
Wellington, Duke of, 13, 52, 57, 124, 153, 377
Welsh surveys, earlier, 248
— — later, 254 *et seq.*
Wetherall, Captain, 24–27
Wharncliffe, Lord, 199 *et seq.*, 230, 289
Whewell, Dr., and Lady Affleck, 383, 385
Whiteford, E , 331
— dies of cholera, 334
Whitley, Mr. John, 139
— Mr. Edward, M.P., 139 *note*
Wieliczka (salt mines), 324
Wilson, Major, at Charleston, 74, 84, 137
Wilson, Mr. W., 180, *note*
Wilson, Lady, 67
Woodhead Tunnel, 231, 235
Woodhouse, Mr. Thomas, 225
Würtemberg, Crown Prince of, 291, 295, 319
— Count Wilhelm of, 295, 304
— King of, 294, 304, 311, 315
— Queen of, 294, 309
— Princess Marie of, 308, 311
— Prince Jerome of, 314

XANTRAILLES, 3

YORK, H.R.H. Duke of, 15, 63
York Chasseurs, 8, 17

PRINTED BY
SPOTTISWOODE AND CO., NEW-STREET SQUARE
LONDON

INDEX OF AUTHORS.

	Page
Abbott (Evelyn)	3, 14
—— (T. K.)	10
Acland (A. H. D.)	3
Acton (Eliza)	22
Æschylus	14
Allingham (W.)	15
Anstey (F.)	16
Aristophanes	14
Aristotle	10
Armstrong (E.)	3
—— (G. F. Savage-)	15
—— (E. J.)	6, 15, 23
Arnold (Sir Edwin)	7, 15
Arnold (T.)	3
Ashley (W. J.)	13
Atelier du Lys (Author of)	16
Bacon	6, 11
Bagehot (Walter)	6, 13, 23
Bagwell (R.)	3
Bain (Alexander)	11
Baker (James)	16
Baker (Sir S. W.)	7
Ball (J. T.)	3
Baring-Gould (S.)	23
Barrow (Sir J. Croker)	15
Beaconsfield (Earl of)	16, 17
Beaufort (Duke of)	9
Becker (Prof.)	14
Bell (Mrs. Hugh)	15
Bent (J. Theodore)	7
Björnsen (B.)	15
Boase (C. W.)	4
Boedder (B.)	12
Boyd (A. K. H.)	6, 23
Brassey (Lady)	7
Bray (C. and Mrs.)	11
'Brenda'	20
Buckle (H. T.)	3
Bull (T.)	22
Burrows (Montagu)	4
Bury (Viscount)	9
Butler (E. A.)	18
—— (Samuel)	23
Campbell-Walker (A.)	8
Carlyle (Thomas)	23
Caröe (W. D.)	4
Chesney (Sir G.)	3
Chetwynd (Sir G.)	8
Chilton (E.)	17
Cholmondeley-Pennell (H.)	9
Cicero	14
Clarke (R. F.)	12
Clerke (Agnes M.)	14
Clodd (Edward)	14
Clutterbuck (W. J.)	8
Comyn (L. N.)	17
Conington (John)	14
Cox (Harding)	9
Crake (A. D.)	20
Creighton (Bishop)	4
Crozier (J. B.)	11
Crump (A.)	3, 13
Curzon (Hon. G. N.)	8
Cutts (E. L.)	4
Dante	15
Davidson (W. L.)	11, 13
Deland (Mrs.)	17
Dent (C. T.)	9
De Salis (Mrs.)	22, 23
De Tocqueville (A.)	4
Devas (C. S.)	13
Dougall (L.)	17
Dowell (S.)	13
Doyle (A. Conan)	17
Falkener (E.)	10
Farnell (G. S.)	14
Farrar (Archdeacon)	13, 17
Fitzpatrick (W. J.)	3
Ford (H.)	10
Francis (Francis)	10
Freeman (Edward A.)	3
Froude (James A.)	4, 6, 8, 17
Furneaux (W.)	18
Gardiner (Samuel Rawson)	4
Halliwell-Phillipps (J. O.)	7, 23
Harrison (Mary)	23
Harrison (Jane E.)	14
Harte (Bret)	17
Hartwig (G.)	18, 19
Hassall (A.)	6
Hearn (W. E.)	4, 11
Heathcote (J. M. & C. J.)	9
Helmholtz (Prof.)	19
Henry (W.)	9
Hodgson (Shadworth H.)	11, 24
Hooper (G.)	6
Hopkins (E. P.)	10
Horley (E.)	4
Howard (B. D.)	8
Howitt (William)	8
Hullah (John)	24
Hume (David)	11
Hunt (W.)	4
Hutchinson (Horace G.)	9
Huth (A. H.)	14
Hyne (C. J. C.)	17
Ingelow (Jean)	15, 20
Jefferies (Richard)	24
Jewsbury (Geraldine)	24
Johnson (J. & J. H.)	24
Johnstone (L.)	11
Jones (E. E. C.)	11
Jordan (W. L.)	13
Joyce (P. W.)	4
Justinian	11
Kant (I.)	11
Killick (A. H.)	11
Kitchin (G. W.)	4
Knight (E. F.)	8
Ladd (G. T.)	11
Lang (Andrew)	4, 10, 14, 15, 17, 20, 24
Lavisse (E.)	4
Lear (H. L. Sidney)	23
Lecky (W. E. H.)	4, 16
Lees (J. A.)	8
Leslie (T. E. C.)	13
Lewes (G. H.)	11
Leyton (F.)	16
Lodge (H. C.)	4
Loftie (W. J.)	4
Logeman (W. S.)	13
Longman (F. W.)	10
Longmore (Sir T.)	7
Lubbock (Sir John)	14
Lyall (Edna)	17
Lydekker (R.)	19
Lyttelton (R. H.)	9
Lytton (Earl of)	16
Macaulay (Lord)	5, 16
Macfarren (Sir G. A.)	24
Mackail (J. W.)	14
Macleod (H. D.)	13
Maher (M.)	12
Mannering (G. E.)	8
Marbot (Baron de)	6
Marshman (J. C.)	6
Martin (A. P.)	7
Matthews (Brander)	17, 24
Maunder (S.)	20
Max Müller (F.)	11, 13, 24
May (Sir T. Erskine)	5
Meath (Earl of)	13
Meade (L. T.)	20, 21
Melville (G. J. Whyte)	17
Mendelssohn	24
Merivale (Dean)	5
Mill (James)	12
Mill (John Stuart)	12, 13
Milner (G)	24
Molesworth (Mrs.)	21
Monck (H. S.)	12
Moore (E.)	6
Nansen (F.)	8
Nesbit (E.)	16
Norton (C. L.)	8
O'Brien (W.)	6
Oliphant (Mrs.)	16
Osbourne (L)	18
Plato	
Pole (W.)	
Pollock (W. H.)	
Poole (W. H. and Mrs.)	
Praeger (F.)	
Pratt (A. E.)	
Prendergast (J. P.)	
Proctor (Richard A.)	1
Raine (James)	
Ransome (Cyril)	
Reader (E. E.)	
Rhoades (J.)	
Ribot (T.)	
Rich (A.)	
Richardson (Sir B. Ward)	
Rickaby (John)	
—— (Joseph)	
Riley (J. W.)	
—— (A.)	
Robertson (A.)	
Roget (John Lewis)	
—— (Peter M.)	
Romanes (G. J.)	
Ronalds (A.)	
Roosevelt (T.)	
Rossetti (M. F.)	
Round (J. H.)	
Seebohm (F.)	
Sewell (Eliz. M.)	
Shakespeare	
Shearman (M.)	
Shirres (L. P.)	
Sidgwick (Alfred)	
Sinclair (A.)	
Smith (R. Bosworth)	
Sophocles	
Southey (R.)	
Spedding (J.)	
Stanley (Bishop)	
Steel (A. G.)	
Stephen (Sir James)	
Stephens (H. C.)	
—— (H. Morse)	
—— (T.)	
Stevenson (Robert Louis)	1
Stock (St. George)	
Strong (H. A.)	
Stubbs (J. W.)	
Sturgis (Julian)	
Suffolk and Berkshire (Earl o[f])	
Sully (James)	
Suttner (Baron von)	
Swinburne (A. J.)	
Symes (J. E.)	
Thompson (Annie)	
—— (D. G.)	
Thomson (Archbishop)	
Tirebuck (W.)	
Todd (A.)	
Toynbee (A.)	
Trevelyan (Sir G. O.)	
Trollope (Anthony)	
Tupper (C. L.)	
Tyrrell (R. Y.)	
Verney (Francis P.)	
Virgil	
Wade (G. W.)	
Wakeman (H. O.)	
Walford (Mrs.)	
Wallaschek (R.)	
Walpole (Spencer)	
Walsingham (Lord)	
Walter (J.)	
Watson (A. E. T.)	
Webb (T. E.)	
Weir (R.)	
West (C.)	
Weyman (Stanley J.)	
Whately (Archbishop)	
—— (E. J)	
Wheeler (B. I.)	
Whishaw (F. J.)	
Wilcocks (J. C.)	
Wilkin (G.)	

MESSRS. LONGMANS, GREEN, & CO.'S

CLASSIFIED CATALOGUE

OF

WORKS IN GENERAL LITERATURE.

History, Politics, Polity, and Political Memoirs.

Abbott.—A HISTORY OF GREECE. By EVELYN ABBOTT, M.A., LL.D.
Part I.—From the Earliest Times to the Ionian Revolt. Crown 8vo., 10s. 6d.
Part II.—500-445 B.C. Crown 8vo., 10s. 6d.

Acland and Ransome.—A HANDBOOK IN OUTLINE OF THE POLITICAL HISTORY OF ENGLAND TO 1890. Chronologically Arranged. By the Right Hon. A. H. DYKE ACLAND, M.P., and CYRIL RANSOME, M.A. Crown 8vo., 6s.

ANNUAL REGISTER, (THE). A Review of Public Events at Home and Abroad, for the year 1892. 8vo., 18s.

Volumes of the ANNUAL REGISTER for the years 1863-1891 can still be had. 18s. each.

Armstrong.—ELIZABETH FARNESE; The Termagant of Spain. By EDWARD ARMSTRONG, M.A., Fellow of Queen's College, Oxford. 8vo., 16s.

Arnold.—Works by T. ARNOLD, D.D., formerly Head Master of Rugby School.

INTRODUCTORY LECTURES ON MODERN HISTORY. 8vo., 7s. 6d.

MISCELLANEOUS WORKS. 8vo., 7s. 6d.

Bagwell.—IRELAND UNDER THE TUDORS. By RICHARD BAGWELL, LL.D. (3 vols.) Vols. I. and II. From the first invasion of the Northmen to the year 1578. 8vo., 32s. Vol. III. 1578-1603. 8vo. 18s.

Ball.—HISTORICAL REVIEW OF THE LEGISLATIVE SYSTEMS OPERATIVE IN IRELAND, from the Invasion of Henry the Second to the Union (1172-1800). By the Rt. Hon. J. T. BALL. 8vo., 6s.

Buckle.—HISTORY OF CIVILISATION IN ENGLAND AND FRANCE, SPAIN AND SCOTLAND. By HENRY THOMAS BUCKLE. 3 vols. Crown 8vo., 24s.

Chesney.—INDIAN POLITY: a View of the System of Administration in India. By Lieut.-General Sir GEORGE CHESNEY. New Edition, Revised and Enlarged. [In the Press.

Crump.—A SHORT ENQUIRY INTO THE FORMATION OF POLITICAL OPINION, from the reign of the Great Families to the advent of Democracy. By ARTHUR CRUMP. 8vo., 7s. 6d.

De Tocqueville.—DEMOCRACY IN AMERICA. By ALEXIS DE TOCQUEVILLE. 2 vols. Crown 8vo., 16s.

Fitzpatrick.—SECRET SERVICE UNDER PITT. By W. J. FITZPATRICK, F.S.A., Author of 'Correspondence of Daniel O'Connell'. 8vo., 7s. 6d.

Freeman.—THE HISTORICAL GEOGRAPHY OF EUROPE. By EDWARD A. FREEMAN. D.C.L., LL.D. With 65 Maps. 2 vols. 8vo., 31s. 6d.

Froude.—Works by JAMES A. FROUDE, Regius Professor of Modern History in the University of Oxford.

THE HISTORY OF ENGLAND, from the Fall of Wolsey to the Defeat of the Spanish Armada.
Popular Edition. 12 vols. Crown 8vo., 3s. 6d. each.
Silver Library Edition. 12 vols. Crown 8vo. 3s. 6d. each.

THE DIVORCE OF CATHERINE OF ARAGON: the Story as told by the Imperial Ambassadors resident at the Court of Henry VIII. *In usum Laicorum.* Crown 8vo., 6s.

THE SPANISH STORY OF THE ARMADA, and other Essays, Historical and Descriptive. Crown 8vo., 6s.

THE ENGLISH IN IRELAND IN THE EIGHTEENTH CENTURY. 3 vols. Crown 8vo., 18s.

SHORT STUDIES ON GREAT SUBJECTS. Cabinet Edition. 4 vols. Crown 8vo., 24s.
Silver Library Edition. 4 vols. Crown 8vo., 3s. 6d. each.

CÆSAR: a Sketch. Crown 8vo., 3s. 6d.

Gardiner.—Works by SAMUEL RAWSON GARDINER, M.A., Hon. LL.D., Edinburgh, Fellow of Merton College, Oxford.

HISTORY OF ENGLAND, from the Accession of James I. to the Outbreak of the Civil War, 1603-1642. 10 vols. Crown 8vo., 6s. each.

A HISTORY OF THE GREAT CIVIL WAR, 1642-1649. 4 vols. Crown 8vo., 6s. each

THE STUDENT'S HISTORY OF ENGLAND. With 378 Illustrations. Crown 8vo., 12s.

Also in Three Volumes.

Vol. I. B.C. 55—A.D. 1509. With 173 Illustrations. Crown 8vo., 4s.
Vol. II. 1509-1689. With 96 Illustrations. Crown 8vo., 4s.
Vol. III. 1689-1885. With 109 Illustrations. Crown 8vo., 4s.

Greville.—A JOURNAL OF THE REIGNS OF KING GEORGE IV., KING WILLIAM IV., AND QUEEN VICTORIA. By CHARLES C. F. GREVILLE, formerly Clerk of the Council. 8 vols. Crown 8vo., 6s. each.

Hearn.—THE GOVERNMENT OF ENGLAND: its Structure and its Development. By W. EDWARD HEARN. 8vo., 16s.

Historic Towns.—Edited by E. A. MAN, D.C.L., and Rev. WILLIAM M.A. With Maps and Plans. Crow 3s. 6d. each.

BRISTOL. By the Rev. W. HUN

CARLISLE. By MANDELL CREIG D.D., Bishop of Peterborough.

CINQUE PORTS. By MONTAGU ROWS.

COLCHESTER. By Rev. E. L. Cu

EXETER. By E. A. FREEMAN.

LONDON. By Rev. W. J. LOFTIE

OXFORD. By Rev. C. W. BOASE.

WINCHESTER. By Rev. G. W CHIN, D.D.

YORK. By Rev. JAMES RAINE.

NEW YORK. By THEODORE ROOS

BOSTON (U.S.) By HENRY LODGE.

Horley.—SEPTON: A DESCRIPTIV HISTORICAL ACCOUNT. Comprisi Collected Notes and Researches of t Rev. ENGELBERT HORLEY, M.A., 1871-1883. By W. D. CARÖE, M.A tab.), Fellow of the Royal Instit British Architects, and E. J. A. G With 17 Plates and 32 Illustration Text. Royal 8vo., 31s. 6d.

Joyce.—A SHORT HISTORY OF IR from the Earliest Times to 1608. W. JOYCE, LL.D., Author of 'Irish of Places,' 'Old Celtic Romance Crown 8vo., 10s. 6d.

Lang.—A HISTORY OF ST. AN By ANDREW LANG. With Illustrat J. HODGE. [In th

Lavisse.—GENERAL VIEW OF THE F CAL HISTORY OF EUROPE. By LAVISSE, Professor at the Sorbonne. lated by CHARLES GROSS, Ph. D. 8vo., 5s.

Lecky.—Works by WILLIAM E HARTPOLE LECKY.

HISTORY OF ENGLAND IN THE TEENTH CENTURY.
Library Edition. 8 vols. 8vo., £
Cabinet Edition. ENGLAND. Crown 8vo., 6s. each. IRELA vols. Crown 8vo., 6s. each.

HISTORY OF EUROPEAN MORALS AUGUSTUS TO CHARLEMAGNE. Crown 8vo., 16s.

HISTORY OF THE RISE AND INFL OF THE SPIRIT OF RATIONALI EUROPE. 2 vols. Crown 8vo., 16

History, Politics, Polity, and Political Memoirs--*continue*

Macaulay.—Works by LORD MACAULAY.

COMPLETE WORKS OF LORD MACAULAY.
Cabinet Edition. 16 vols. Post 8vo.,
£4 16.
Library Edition. 8 vols. 8vo., £5 5s.

HISTORY OF ENGLAND FROM THE AC-
CESSION OF JAMES THE SECOND.
Popular Edition. 2 vols. Cr. 8vo., 5s.
Student's Edition. 2 vols. Cr. 8vo., 12s.
People's Edition. 4 vols. Cr. 8vo., 16s.
Cabinet Edition. 8 vols. Post 8vo., 48s.
Library Edition. 5 vols. 8vo., £4.

CRITICAL AND HISTORICAL ESSAYS, WITH
LAYS OF ANCIENT ROME, in 1 volume.
Popular Edition. Crown 8vo., 2s. 6d.
Authorised Edition. Crown 8vo., 2s. 6d.,
or 3s. 6d., gilt edges.
Silver Library Edition. Cr. 8vo., 3s. 6d.

CRITICAL AND HISTORICAL ESSAYS.
Student's Edition. 1 volume. Cr. 8vo., 6s.
People's Edition. 2 vols. Cr. 8vo., 8s.
Trevelyan Edition. 2 vols. Cr. 8vo., 9s.
Cabinet Edition. 4 vols. Post 8vo., 24s.
Library Edition. 3 vols. 8vo., 36s.

ESSAYS which may be had separately
price 6d. each sewed, 1s. each cloth.
Addison and Walpole.
Frederick the Great.
Croker's Boswell's Johnson.
Hallam's Constitutional History.
Warren Hastings. (3d. sewed, 6d. cloth).
The Earl of Chatham (Two Essays).
Ranke and Gladstone.
Milton and Machiavelli.
Lord Bacon.
Lord Clive.
Lord Byron, and The Comic Dramatists of
the Restoration.

SPEECHES. Crown 8vo., 3s. 6d.

MISCELLANEOUS WRITINGS
People's Edition. 1 vol. Crown 8vo., 4s. 6d.
Library Edition. 2 vols. 8vo., 21s.

MISCELLANEOUS WRITINGS AND
SPEECHES.
Popular Edition. Crown 8vo., 2s. 6d.
Student's Edition. Crown 8vo., 6s.
Cabinet Edition. Including Indian Penal
Code, Lays of Ancient Rome, and Miscel-
laneous Poems. 4 vols. Post 8vo., 24s.

SELECTIONS FROM THE WRITINGS OF
LORD MACAULAY. Edited, with Occa-
sional Notes, by the Right Hon. Sir G. O.
Trevelyan, Bart. Crown 8vo., 6s.

May.—THE CONSTITUTIONAL HISTORY OF
ENGLAND since the Accession of George II
1760-1870. By Sir THOMAS ERSKINE MAY,
K.C.B. (Lord Farnborough). 3 vols. Crown
8vo., 18s.

Merivale.—Works by the Very Rev
CHARLES MERIVALE, Dean of Ely.

HISTORY OF THE ROMANS UNDER THE
EMPIRE.
Cabinet Edition. 8 vols. Cr. 8vo., 48s.
Silver Library Edition. 8 vols. Crown
8vo., 3s. 6d. each.

THE FALL OF THE ROMAN REPUBLIC:
a Short History of the Last Century of the
Commonwealth. 12mo., 7s. 6d.

Parkes.—FIFTY YEARS IN THE MAKING OF
AUSTRALIAN HISTORY. By Sir HENRY
PARKES, G.C.M.G. With 2 Portraits (1892
and 1892). 2 vols. 8vo., 32s.

Prendergast.—IRELAND FROM THE RE-
STORATION TO THE REVOLUTION, 1660-16
By JOHN P. PRENDERGAST, Author of 'The
Cromwellian Settlement in Ireland'. 8vo.
5s.

Round.—GEOFFREY DE MANDEVILLE: a
Study of the Anarchy. By J. H. ROUND,
M.A. 8vo., 16s.

Seebohm.—THE ENGLISH VILLAGE COM-
MUNITY Examined in its Relations to the
Manorial and Tribal Systems, &c. By
FREDERIC SEEBOHM. With 13 Maps and
Plates. 8vo., 16s.

Smith.—CARTHAGE AND THE CARTHAGIN-
IANS. By R. BOSWORTH SMITH, M.A.,
Assistant Master in Harrow School. With
Maps, Plans, &c. Crown 8vo., 6s.

Stephens.—PAROCHIAL SELF-GOVERN-
MENT IN RURAL DISTRICTS: Argument and
Plan. By HENRY C. STEPHENS, M.P. 4to,
12s. 6d.

Stephens.—A HISTORY OF THE FRENCH
REVOLUTION. By H. MORSE STEPHENS,
Balliol College, Oxford. 3 vols. 8vo. Vols.
I. and II. 18s. each.

Stephens.—MADOC: An Essay on the
Discovery of America, by MADOC AP OWEN
GWYNEDD, in the Twelfth Century. By
THOMAS STEPHENS, Author of "The Litera-
ture of the Kymry'. Edited by LLYWARCH
REYNOLDS, B.A. Oxon. 8vo., 7s. 6d.

Stubbs.—HISTORY OF THE UNIVERSITY OF
DUBLIN, from its Foundation to the End of
the Eighteenth Century. By J. W. STUBBS.
8vo., 12s. 6d.

History, Politics, Polity, and Political Memoirs—*contin*

Todd.—PARLIAMENTARY GOVERNMENT IN THE COLONIES. By ALPHEUS TODD, LL.D. [*In the Press.*

Tupper.—OUR INDIAN PROTECTORATE: an Introduction to the Study of the Relations between the British Government and its Indian Feudatories. By CHARLES LEWIS TUPPER, Indian Civil Service. 8vo., 16s.

Wakeman and Hassall.—ESSAYS INTRODUCTORY TO THE STUDY OF ENGLISH CONSTITUTIONAL HISTORY. By Resident Members of the University of Oxford. Edited by HENRY OFFLEY WAKEMAN, M.A., and ARTHUR HASSALL, M.A. Crown 8vo., 6s.

Walpole.—Works by SPENCER WALF

HISTORY OF ENGLAND FROM THE CLUSION OF THE GREAT WAR IN 18: 1858. 6 vols. Crown 8vo., 6s. eacl

THE LAND OF HOME RULE: bein Account of the History and Institut of the Isle of Man. Crown 8vo., 6s.

Wylie.—HISTORY OF ENGLAND UN HENRY IV. By JAMES HAMILTON WY M.A., one of H. M. Inspectors of Sc 2 vols. Vol. I., 1399-1404. Crown 10s. 6d. Vol. II. [*In the pre*

Biography, Personal Memoirs, &c.

Armstrong.—THE LIFE AND LETTERS OF EDMUND J. ARMSTRONG. Edited by G. F. ARMSTRONG. Fcp. 8vo., 7s. 6d.

Bacon.—LETTERS AND LIFE, INCLUDING ALL HIS OCCASIONAL WORKS. Edited by J. SPEDDING. 7 vols. 8vo., £4 4s.

Bagehot.—BIOGRAPHICAL STUDIES. By WALTER BAGEHOT. 8vo., 12s.

Boyd.—TWENTY-FIVE YEARS OF ST. ANDREWS, 1865-1890. By A. K. H. BOYD, D.D., Author of 'Recreations of a Country Parson,' &c. 2 vols. 8vo. Vol. I., 12s. Vol. II. 15s.

Carlyle.—THOMAS CARLYLE: a History of his Life. By J. A. FROUDE.
1795-1835. 2 vols. Crown 8vo., 7s.
1834-1881. 2 vols. Crown 8vo., 7s.

Fabert.—ABRAHAM FABERT: Governor of Sedan and Marshal of France. His Life and Times, 1599-1662. By GEORGE HOOPER, Author of 'Waterloo,' 'Wellington,' &c. With a Portrait. 8vo., 10s. 6d.

Fox.—THE EARLY HISTORY OF CHARLES JAMES FOX. By the Right Hon. Sir G. O. TREVELYAN, Bart.
Library Edition. 8vo., 18s.
Cabinet Edition. Crown 8vo., 6s.

Hamilton.—LIFE OF SIR WILLIAM HAMILTON. By R. P. GRAVES. 3 vols. 15s. each.
ADDENDUM TO THE LIFE OF SIR WM. ROWAN HAMILTON, LL.D., D.C.L. 8vo., 6d. sewed.

avelock.—MEMOIRS OF SIR HENRY HAVELOCK, K.C.B. By JOHN CLARK MARSHMAN. Crown 8vo., 3s. 6d.

Macaulay.—THE LIFE AND LETTERS LORD MACAULAY. By the Right Hon. G. O. TREVELYAN, Bart.
Popular Edition. 1 volume. Cr. 2s. 6d.
Student's Edition. 1 volume. Cr. 8vo.
Cabinet Edition. 2 vols. Post 8vo.,
Library Edition. 2 vols. 8vo., 36s.

Marbot.—THE MEMOIRS OF THE BA DE MARBOT. Translated from the Fr by ARTHUR JOHN BUTLER, M.A. C 8vo., 7s. 6d.

Montrose.—DEEDS OF MONTROSE: MEMOIRS OF JAMES, MARQUIS OF MONTE 1639-1650. By the Rev. GEORGE WISH D.D., (Bishop of Edinburgh, 1662-1 Translated, with Introduction, Notes, and the original Latin (Part II. now published), by the Rev. ALEXANDER N DOCH, F.S.A., (Scot.) Canon of St. M Cathedral, Edinburgh, Editor and Transl of the Grameid MS. and H. F. MOREL SIMPSON, M.A. (Cantab.) F.S.A. (Sc Fettes College. 4to., 36s. net.

Moore.—DANTE AND HIS EARLY GRAPHERS. By EDWARD MOORE, D Principal of St. Edmund Hall, Oxl Crown 8vo., 4s. 6d.

Russell.—A LIFE OF LORD JOHN RUSS (EARL RUSSELL, K.G.) By SPENCER POLE. With 2 Portraits.
Cabinet Edition. 2 vols. Cr. 8vo., 1
Library Edition. 2 vols. 8vo., 36s.

Seebohm.—THE OXFORD REFORMER JOHN COLET, ERASMUS AND THOMAS MO a History of their Fellow-Work. By FR ERIC SEEBOHM. 8vo., 14s.

Biography, Personal Memoirs, &c.—*continued*.

Shakespeare.—OUTLINES OF THE LIFE OF SHAKESPEARE. By J. O. HALLIWELL-PHILLIPPS. With numerous Illustrations and Fac-similes. 2 vols. Royal 8vo., £1 1s.

Shakespeare's TRUE LIFE. By JAMES WALTER. With 500 Illustrations by GERALD E. MOIRA. Imp. 8vo., 21s.

Sherbrooke.—LIFE AND LETTERS OF THE RIGHT HON. ROBERT LOWE, VISCOUNT SHERBROOKE, G.C.B., together with a Memoir of his Kinsman, Sir JOHN COAPE SHERBROOKE, G.C.B. By A. PATCHETT MARTIN. With 5 Portraits. 2 vols. 8vo., 36s.

Stephen.—ESSAYS IN ECCLESIASTICAL BIOGRAPHY. By Sir JAMES STEPHEN. Crown 8vo., 7s. 6d.

Verney.—MEMOIRS OF THE VERNEY FAMILY DURING THE CIVIL WAR. Compiled from the Letters and Illustrated by the Portraits at Claydon House, Bucks. By FRANCES PARTHENOPE VERNEY. With a Preface by S. R. GARDINER, M.A., LL.D. With 38 Portraits, Woodcuts and Fac-simile. 2 vols. Royal 8vo., 42s.

Wagner.—WAGNER AS I KNEW HIM. FERDINAND PRAEGER. Crown 8vo., 7s.

Walford.—TWELVE ENGLISH AUTH ESSES. By L. B. WALFORD, Author 'Mischief of Monica,' &c. With Portrai Hannah More. Crown 8vo., 4s. 6d.

Wellington.—LIFE OF THE DUKE WELLINGTON. By the Rev. G. R. GL M.A. Crown 8vo., 3s. 6d.

Wiseman.—RICHARD WISEMAN, Surg and Sergeant-Surgeon to Charles II. Biographical Study. By Surgeon-Gen Sir T. LONGMORE, C.B., F.R.C.S., With Portrait and Illustrations. 8 10s. 6d.

Wordsworth.—Works by CHAR WORDSWORTH, D.C.L., late Bishop of Andrews.

ANNALS OF MY EARLY LIFE, 1806-1 8vo., 15s.

ANNALS OF MY LIFE, 1847-1856. 8 10s. 6d.

Travel and Adventure.

Arnold.—SEAS AND LANDS. By Sir EDWIN ARNOLD, K.C.I.E., Author of 'The Light of the World,' &c. Reprinted letters from the 'Daily Telegraph'. With 71 Illustrations. Crown 8vo., 7s. 6d.

Baker.—Works by Sir SAMUEL WHITE BAKER.

EIGHT YEARS IN CEYLON. With 6 Illustrations. Crown 8vo., 3s. 6d.

THE RIFLE AND THE HOUND IN CEYLON. 6 Illustrations. Crown 8vo., 3s. 6d.

Bent.—THE RUINED CITIES OF MASHONALAND: being a Record of Excavation and Exploration in 1891. By J. THEODORE BENT, F.S.A., F.R.G.S. With a Chapter on the Orientation and Mensuration of the Temples. By R. M. W. SWAN. With Map, 13 Plates, and 104 Illustrations in the Text. Crown 8vo., 7s. 6d.

Brassey. Works by LADY BRASSEY.

THE LAST VOYAGE TO INDIA AND AUSTRALIA IN THE 'SUNBEAM.' With Charts and Maps, and 40 Illustrations in Monotone (20 full-page), and nearly 200 Illustrations in the Text from Drawings by R. T. PRITCHETT. 8vo., 21s.

Brassey.—Works by LADY BRASSEY—c

A VOYAGE IN THE 'SUNBEAM'; HOME ON THE OCEAN FOR ELE MONTHS.

Library Edition. With 8 Maps Charts, and 118 Illustrations. 8vo.
Cabinet Edition. With Map and Illustrations. Crown 8vo., 7s. 6d.
Silver Library Edition. With 66 Illustrations. Crown 8vo., 3s. 6d.
Popular Edition. With 60 Illustrati 4to., 6d. sewed, 1s. cloth.
School Edition. With 37 Illustrati Fcp., 2s. cloth, or 3s. white parchm

SUNSHINE AND STORM IN THE E

Library Edition. With 2 Maps and Illustrations. 8vo., 21s.
Cabinet Edition. With 2 Maps and Illustrations. Crown 8vo., 7s. 6d.
Popular Edition. With 103 Illustrati 4to., 6d. sewed, 1s. cloth.

IN THE TRADES, THE TROPICS, AND 'ROARING FORTIES'.

Cabinet Edition. With Map and Illustrations. Crown 8vo., 7s. 6d.
Popular Edition. With 183 Illustrati 4to., 6d. sewed, 1s. cloth.

THREE VOYAGES IN THE 'SUNBEA Popular Edition. With 346 Illustrati 4to., 2s. 6d.

Travel and Adventure—*continued*.

Clutterbuck.—ABOUT CEYLON AND BORNEO: being an Account of Two Visits to Ceylon, one to Borneo, and How We Fell Out on our Homeward Journey. By W. J. CLUTTERBUCK, Joint Author of 'Three in Norway'. With 47 Illustrations. Crown 8vo., 10s. 6d.

Curzon.—PERSIA AND THE PERSIAN QUESTION. With 9 Maps, 96 Illustrations, Appendices, and an Index. By the Hon. GEORGE N. CURZON, M.P., late Fellow of All Soul's College, Oxford. 2 vols. 8vo., 42s.

Froude.—Works by JAMES A. FROUDE.

OCEANA : or England and her Colonies. With 9 Illustrations. Crown 8vo., 2s. boards, 2s. 6d. cloth.

THE ENGLISH IN THE WEST INDIES: or, the Bow of Ulysses. With 9 Illustrations. Crown 8vo., 2s. boards, 2s. 6d. cloth.

Howard.—LIFE WITH TRANS-SIBERIAN SAVAGES. By B. DOUGLAS HOWARD, M.A. Crown 8vo., 6s.

. *This work contains a description of the manners, customs, and daily life of the Sakhalin Ainos, and combines an account of native hunting and other adventures with scientific observation.*

Howitt.—VISITS TO REMARKABLE PLACES. Old Halls, Battle-Fields, Scenes, illustrative of Striking Passages in English History and Poetry. By WILLIAM HOWITT. With 80 Illustrations. Crown 8vo.; 3s. 6d.

Knight.—Works by E. F. KNIGHT, author of the Cruise of the 'Falcon'.

THE CRUISE OF THE 'ALERTE': the narrative of a Search for Treasure on the Desert Island of Trinidad. With 2 Maps and 23 Illustrations. Crown 8vo., 3s. 6d.

WHERE THREE EMPIRES MEET: a Narrative of Recent Travel in Kashmir, Western Tibet, Baltistan, Ladak, Gilgit, and the adjoining Countries. With a Map and 54 Illustrations. 8vo. 18s.

Lees and Clutterbuck.—B. C. RAMBLE IN BRITISH COLUMBIA. Lees and W. J. Clutterbuck, 'Three in Norway'. With Map Illustrations. Crown 8vo., 3s. 6d.

Mannering.—WITH AXE AND ROPE NEW ZEALAND ALPS. By GEORGE MANNERING. With 18 Illustrations Map. 8vo., 12s. 6d.

Nansen.—Works by Dr. FRIDTJOF NAN

THE FIRST CROSSING OF GREENL With numerous Illustrations and a Crown 8vo., 7s. 6d.

ESQUIMAUX LIFE. Translated WILLIAM ARCHER. [*In the*

Norton.—A HANDBOOK OF FLORIDA. CHARLES L. NORTON. With 49 Maps Plans. Fcp. 8vo., 5s.

Pratt.—TO THE SNOWS OF TIBET THRO CHINA. By A. E. PRATT, F.R.G.S. 33 Illustrations and a Map. 8vo., 18s.

Riley.—ATHOS : or, the Mountain of Monks. By ATHELSTAN RILEY, With Map and 29 Illustrations. 8vo., 2

THREE IN NORWAY. By Two of Th With a Map and 59 Illustrations. Cr 8vo., 2s. boards, 2s. 6d. cloth.

Whishaw.—OUT OF DOORS IN TSARLA a Record of the Seeings and Doings Wanderer in Russia. By FRED. J. WHISH Crown 8vo., 7s. 6d.

Wolff.—Works by HENRY W. WOLFF.

RAMBLES IN THE BLACK FOREST. Cr 8vo., 7s. 6d.

THE WATERING PLACES OF THE VOSG Crown 8vo., 4s. 6d.

THE COUNTRY OF THE VOSGES. Wit Map. 8vo., 12s.

Sport and Pastime.

AMERICAN WHIST, Illustrated : containing the Laws and Principles of the Games, the Analysis of the New Play and American Leads, and a series of Hands in Diagram, and combining Whist Universal and American Whist. By G. W. P. Fcp. 8vo. 6s. 6d.

Campbell-Walker.—THE CORRECT CARD : How to Play at Whist ; a Whist Catechism. By Major A. CAMPBELL-WALKER, F.G.S. Fcp. 8vo., 2s. 6d.

Chetwynd.—RACING REMINISCENCES EXPERIENCES OF THE TURF. By GEORGE CHETWYND, Bart. 2 vols. 8vo.,

DEAD SHOT (THE) : or, Sportsma Complete Guide. Being a Treatise on the of the Gun, with Rudimentary and Finish Lessons on the Art of Shooting Game o kinds, also Game Driving, Wild-Fowl Pigeon Shooting, Dog Breaking, etc. MARKSMAN. Crown 8vo., 10s. 6d.

Sport and Pastime—*continued.*
THE BADMINTON LIBRARY.
Edited by the DUKE of BEAUFORT, K.G., assisted by ALFRED E. T. WATSON.

ATHLETICS AND FOOTBALL. By MONTAGUE SHEARMAN. With 51 Illustrations. Crown 8vo., 10s. 6d.

BIG GAME SHOOTING. By C. PHILLIPPS-WOLLEY, W. G. LITTLEDALE, Colonel PERCY, FRED. JACKSON, Major H. PERCY, W. C. OSWELL, Sir HENRY POTTINGER, Bart., and the EARL OF KILMOREY. With Contributions by other Writers. With Illustrations by CHARLES WHYMPER and others. 2 vols. [*In the press.*

BOATING. By W. B. WOODGATE. With an Introduction by the Rev. EDMOND WARRE, D.D., and a Chapter on 'Rowing at Eton,' by R. HARVEY MASON. With 49 Illustrations. Crown 8vo., 10s. 6d.

COURSING AND FALCONRY. By HARDING COX and the Hon. GERALD LASCELLES. With 76 Illustrations. Crown 8vo., 10s. 6d.

CRICKET. By A. G. STEEL and the Hon. R. H. LYTTELTON. With Contributions by ANDREW LANG. R. A. H. MITCHELL, W. G. GRACE, and F. GALE. With 63 Illustrations. Crown 8vo., 10s. 6d.

CYCLING. By VISCOUNT BURY (Earl of Albemarle), K.C.M.G., and G. LACY HILLIER. With 89 Illustrations. Crown 8vo., 10s. 6d.

DRIVING. By the DUKE OF BEAUFORT. With 65 Illustrations. Crown 8vo., 10s. 6d.

FENCING, BOXING, AND WRESTLING. By WALTER H. POLLOCK, F. C. GROVE, C. PREVOST, E. B. MITCHELL, and WALTER ARMSTRONG. With 42 Illustrations. Crown 8vo., 10s. 6d.

FISHING. By H. CHOLMONDELEY-PENNELL. With Contributions by the MARQUIS OF EXETER, HENRY R. FRANCIS, Major JOHN P. TRAHERNE, FREDERIC M. HALFORD, G. CHRISTOPHER DAVIES, R. B. MARSTON, &c.

Vol. I. Salmon, Trout, and Grayling. With 158 Illustrations. Crown 8vo., 10s. 6d.

Vol. II. Pike and other Coarse Fish. With 133 Illustrations. Crown 8vo., 10s. 6d.

GOLF. By HORACE G. HUTCHINSON, the Rt. Hon. A. J. BALFOUR, M.P., Sir W. G. SIMPSON, Bart., Lord WELLWOOD, H.

HUNTING. By the DUKE OF BEAUFORT, K.G., and MOWBRAY MORRIS. With Contributions by the EARL OF SUFFOLK AND BERKSHIRE, Rev. E. W. L. DAVIES, DIGBY COLLINS, and ALFRED E. T. WATSON. With 53 Illustrations. Crown 8vo., 10s. 6d.

MOUNTAINEERING. By C. T. DENT, Sir F. POLLOCK, Bart., W. M. CONWAY, DOUGLAS FRESHFIELD, C. E. MATHEWS, C. PILKINGTON, and other Writers. With 108 Illustrations. Crown 8vo., 10s. 6d.

RACING AND STEEPLE-CHASING. *Racing:* By the EARL OF SUFFOLK AND BERKSHIRE and W. G. CRAVEN. With a Contribution by the Hon. F. LAWLEY. *Steeple-chasing:* By ARTHUR COVENTRY and ALFRED E. T. WATSON. With 58 Illustrations. Crown 8vo., 10s. 6d.

RIDING AND POLO. By Captain ROBERT WEIR, J. MORAY BROWN, the DUKE OF BEAUFORT, K.G., the EARL OF SUFFOLK AND BERKSHIRE, &c. With 59 Illustrations. Crown 8vo., 10s. 6d.

SHOOTING. By LORD WALSINGHAM and Sir RALPH PAYNE-GALLWEY, Bart. With Contributions by LORD LOVAT, LORD CHARLES LENNOX KERR, the Hon. G. LASCELLES, and A. J. STUART-WORTLEY.

Vol. I. Field and Covert. With 105 Illustrations. Crown 8vo., 10s. 6d.

Vol. II. Moor and Marsh. With 65 Illustrations. Crown 8vo., 10s. 6d.

SKATING, CURLING, TOBOGGANING, AND OTHER ICE SPORTS. By J. M. HEATHCOTE, C. G. TEBBUTT, T. MAXWELL WITHAM, the Rev. JOHN KERR, ORMOND HAKE, and Colonel BUCK. With 284 Illustrations. Crown 8vo., 10s. 6d.

SWIMMING. By ARCHIBALD SINCLAIR and WILLIAM HENRY, Hon. Secs. of the Life Saving Society. With 119 Illustrations. Crown 8vo., 10s. 6d.

TENNIS, LAWN TENNIS, RACKETS, AND FIVES. By J. M. and C. G. HEATHCOTE, E. O. PLEYDELL-BOUVERIE and A. C. AINGER. With Contributions by the Hon. A. LYTTELTON, W. C. MARSHALL, Miss L. DOD, H. W. W. WILBERFORCE, H. F. LAWFORD, &c. With 79 Illustrations. Crown 8vo., 10s. 6d.

YACHTING. By the EARL OF PEMBROKE, the MARQUIS OF DUFFERIN AND AVA, the EARL OF ONSLOW, LORD BRASSEY, Lieut.-Col. BUCKNILL, LEWIS HERRESHOFF, G. L. WATSON, E. F. KNIGHT, Rev. G. L.

Falkener.—GAMES, ANCIENT AND ORI-ENTAL, AND HOW TO PLAY THEM. Being the Games of the Ancient Egyptians, the Hiera Gramme of the Greeks, the Ludus Latrunculorum of the Romans, and the Oriental Games of Chess, Draughts, Back-gammon, and Magic Squares. By EDWARD FALKENER. With numerous Photographs, Diagrams, &c. 8vo., 21s.

Ford.—THE THEORY AND PRACTICE OF ARCHERY. By HORACE FORD. New Edition, thoroughly Revised and Re-written by W. BUTT, M.A. With a Preface by C. J. LONGMAN, M.A. 8vo., 14s.

Francis.—A BOOK ON ANGLING: or, Trea-tise on the Art of Fishing in every Branch; including full Illustrated List of Salmon Flies. By FRANCIS FRANCIS. With Por-trait and Coloured Plates. Crown 8vo., 15s.

Hopkins.—FISHING REMINISCENCES. By Major E. P. HOPKINS. With Illustrations. Crown 8vo., 6s. 6d.

Lang.—ANGLING SKETCHES. By ANDREW LANG. With 20 Illustrations by W. G. BURN MURDOCH. Crown 8vo., 7s. 6d.

Longman. — CHESS OPENINGS. By FREDERICK W. LONGMAN. Fcp. 8vo., 2s. 6d.

Payne-Gallwey.—Works by Sir RALPH PAYNE-GALLWEY, Bart.

LETTERS TO YOUNG SHOOTERS (First Series). On the Choice and use of a Gun. With Illustrations. Crown 8vo., 7s. 6d.

Payne-Gallwey.—Works by SIR RAL PAYNE-GALLWEY, Bart.—*continued*.

LETTERS TO YOUNG SHOOTERS. (Seco Series). On the Production, Preservati and Killing of Game. With Directi in Shooting Wood-Pigeons and Breaki in Retrievers. With a Portrait of Author, and 103 Illustrations. Cr 8vo., 12s. 6d.

Pole.—THE THEORY OF THE MODE SCIENTIFIC GAME OF WHIST. By POLE, F.R.S. Fcp. 8vo., 2s. 6d.

Proctor.—Works by RICHARD A. PROCT HOW TO PLAY WHIST: WITH THE LA AND ETIQUETTE OF WHIST. Crown 8v 3s. 6d.

HOME WHIST: an Easy Guide to Co rect Play. 16mo., 1s.

Ronalds.—THE FLY-FISHER'S ENTOMO OGY. By ALFRED RONALDS. With colour Representations of the Natural and Artific Insect. With 20 coloured Plates. 8v 14s.

WHIST IN DIAGRAMS: a Suppl ment to American Whist, Illustrated; bei a Series of Hands played through, illus ing the American leads, the new play, t forms of Finesse, and celebrated coups Masters. With Explanation and Analys By G. W. P. Fcp. 8vo., 6s. 6d.

Wilcocks.—THE SEA FISHERMAN: Co prising the Chief Methods of Hook and Li Fishing in the British and other Seas, a Remarks on Nets, Boats, and Boating. J. C. WILCOCKS. Illustrated. Crown 8 6s.

Mental, Moral and Political Philosophy.

LOGIC, RHETORIC, PSYCHOLOGY, ETC.

Abbott. THE ELEMENTS OF LOGIC. By T. K. ABBOTT, B.D. 12mo., 3s.

Aristotle.—Works by.

THE POLITICS: G. Bekker's Greek Text of Books I., III., IV. (VII.), with an English Translation by W. E. BOLLAND, M.A.; and short Introductory Essays by A. LANG, M.A. Crown 8vo., 7s. 6d.

THE POLITICS: Introductory Essays. By ANDREW LANG (from Bolland and Lang's 'Politics'). Crown 8vo., 2s. 6d.

THE ETHICS: Greek Text, Illustrated with Essay and Notes. By Sir ALEXAN-DER GRANT, Bart. 2 vols. 8vo., 32s.

Aristotle.—Works by.

THE NICOMACHEAN ETHICS: Newl Translated into English. By ROBER WILLIAMS. Crown 8vo., 7s. 6d.

AN INTRODUCTION TO ARISTOTLE' ETHICS. Books I.-IV. (Book X. c. vi.-i in an Appendix). With a continuo Analysis and Notes. Intended for the u of Beginners and Junior Students. By tl Rev. EDWARD MOORE, D.D., Principal St. Edmund Hall, and late Fellow ar Tutor of Queen's College, Oxford. Cro 8vo., 10s. 6d.

SELECTIONS FROM THE ORGANO Edited by JOHN R. MAGRATH, D.D Provost of Queen's College, Oxford. Smal 8vo., 3s. 6d.

Mental, Moral and Political Philosophy—*continued.*

Bacon.—Works by.

COMPLETE WORKS. Edited by R. L. ELLIS, J. SPEDDING and D. D. HEATH. 7 vols. 8vo., £3 13s. 6d.

THE ESSAYS: with Annotations. By RICHARD WHATELY, D.D. 8vo., 10s. 6d.

Bain.—Works by ALEXANDER BAIN, LL.D.

MENTAL SCIENCE. Crown 8vo. 6s. 6d.

MORAL SCIENCE. Crown 8vo., 4s. 6d.

The two works as above can be had in one volume, price 10s. 6d.

SENSES AND THE INTELLECT. 8vo., 15s.

EMOTIONS AND THE WILL. 8vo., 15s.

LOGIC, DEDUCTIVE AND INDUCTIVE. Part I. 4s. Part II. 6s. 6d.

PRACTICAL ESSAYS. Crown 8vo., 2s.

Bray.—Works by CHARLES BRAY.

THE PHILOSOPHY OF NECESSITY: or Law in Mind as in Matter. Cr. 8vo., 5s.

THE EDUCATION OF THE FEELINGS : a Moral System for Schools. Cr 8vo., 2s. 6d.

Bray.—ELEMENTS OF MORALITY, in Easy Lessons for Home and School Teaching. By Mrs. CHARLES BRAY. Cr. 8vo., 1s. 6d.

Crozier.—CIVILISATION AND PROGRESS. By JOHN BEATTIE CROZIER, M.D. With New Preface. More fully explaining the nature of the New Organon used in the solution of its problems. 8vo., 14s.

vidson.—THE LOGIC OF DEFINITION, Explained and Applied. By WILLIAM L. DAVIDSON, M.A. Crown 8vo., 6s.

n.—THE WORKS OF THOMAS HILL GREEN. Edited by R. L. NETTLESHIP. Vols. I. and II. Philosophical Works. 8vo., 16s. each. Vol. III. Miscellanies. With Index to the three Volumes, and Memoir. 8vo., 21s.

earn.—THE ARYAN HOUSEHOLD : its Structure and its Development. An Introduction to Comparative Jurisprudence. By

Hodgson.—Works by SHADWORTH HODGSON.

TIME AND SPACE : a Metaphysical Essa 8vo., 16s.

THE THEORY OF PRACTICE : an Ethic Inquiry. 2 vols. 8vo., 24s.

THE PHILOSOPHY OF REFLECTION. vols. 8vo., 21s.

Hume.—THE PHILOSOPHICAL WORKS DAVID HUME. Edited by T. H. GRE and T. H. GROSE. 4 vols. 8vo., 56s. separately, Essays. 2 vols. 28s. Treati of Human Nature. 2 vols. 28s.

Johnstone.—A SHORT INTRODUCTION THE STUDY OF LOGIC. By LAUREN JOHNSTONE. With Questions. Cr. 8vo., 2s.

Jones.—AN INTRODUCTION TO GENERA LOGIC. By E. E. CONSTANCE JONES, Auth of ' Elements of Logic as a Science of Pr positions '. Crown 8vo., 4s. 6d.

Justinian.—THE INSTITUTES OF JUSTI IAN : Latin Text, chiefly that of Huschk with English Introduction, Translatio Notes, and Summary. By THOMAS SANDARS, M.A. 8vo., 18s.

Kant.—Works by IMMANUEL KANT.

CRITIQUE OF PRACTICAL REASON, AN OTHER WORKS ON THE THEORY C ETHICS. Translated by T. K. ABBOT B.D. With Memoir. 8vo., 12s. 6d.

INTRODUCTION TO LOGIC, AND HIS ESSA ON THE MISTAKEN SUBTILTY OF TH FOUR FIGURES. Translated by T. K ABBOTT, and with Notes by S. T. COLE RIDGE. 8vo., 6s.

Killick.—HANDBOOK TO MILL'S SYSTEM OF LOGIC. By Rev. A. H. KILLICK, M.A Crown 8vo., 3s. 6d.

Ladd.—Works by GEORGE TURNBULL LADD.

ELEMENTS OF PHYSIOLOGICAL PSY CHOLOGY. 8vo., 21s.

OUTLINES OF PHYSIOLOGICAL PSYCHOL OGY. A Text-book of Mental Science fo Academies and Colleges. 8vo., 12s.

Lewes.—THE HISTORY OF PHILOSOPHY from Thales to Comte. By GEORGE HENRY LEWES. 2 vols. 8vo., 32s.

Max Müller.—Works by F. MAX MÜLLER

THE SCIENCE OF THOUGHT. 8vo., 21s.

THREE INTRODUCTORY LECTURES ON

Mill.—ANALYSIS OF THE PHENOMENA OF THE HUMAN MIND. By JAMES MILL. 2 vols. 8vo., 28s.

Mill.—Works by JOHN STUART MILL.

A SYSTEM OF LOGIC. Crown 8vo., 3s. 6d.

ON LIBERTY. Crown 8vo., 1s. 4d.

ON REPRESENTATIVE GOVERNMENT. Crown 8vo., 2s.

UTILITARIANISM. 8vo., 5s.

EXAMINATION OF SIR WILLIAM HAMILTON'S PHILOSOPHY. 8vo., 16s.

NATURE, THE UTILITY OF RELIGION, AND THEISM. Three Essays. 8vo., 5s.

Monck.—INTRODUCTION TO LOGIC. By H. S. MONCK. Crown 8vo., 5s.

Ribot.—THE PSYCHOLOGY OF ATTENTION. By TH. RIBOT. Crown 8vo., 3s.

Sidgwick.—DISTINCTION: and the Criticism of Belief. By ALFRED SIDGWICK. Crown 8vo., 6s.

Stock.—DEDUCTIVE LOGIC. By ST. GEORGE STOCK. Fcp. 8vo., 3s. 6d.

Sully.—Works by JAMES SULLY, Grote Professor of Mind and Logic at University College, London.

THE HUMAN MIND: a Text-book of Psychology. 2 vols. 8vo., 21s.

OUTLINES OF PSYCHOLOGY. 8vo., 9s.

THE TEACHER'S HANDBOOK OF PSYCHOLOGY. Crown 8vo., 5s.

Swinburne.—PICTURE LOGIC: an Attempt to Popularise the Science of Reasoning. By ALFRED JAMES SWINBURNE, M.A. With 23 Woodcuts. Post 8vo., 5s.

Thompson.—Works by DANIEL GREENLEAF THOMPSON.

THE PROBLEM OF EVIL: an Introduction to the Practical Sciences. 8vo., 10s. 6d.

A SYSTEM OF PSYCHOLOGY. 2 vols. 8vo., 36s.

THE RELIGIOUS SENTIMENTS OF THE HUMAN MIND. 8vo., 7s. 6d.

SOCIAL PROGRESS: an Essay. 8vo., 7s. 6d.

THE PHILOSOPHY OF FICTION IN LITERATURE: an Essay. Crown 8vo., 6s.

Thomson.—OUTLINES OF THE NECES LAWS OF THOUGHT: a Treatise on Pu Applied Logic. By WILLIAM THO D.D., formerly Lord Archbishop of Post 8vo., 6s.

Webb.—THE VEIL OF ISIS: a Seri Essays on Idealism. By T. E. WEBB. 10s. 6d.

Whately.—Works by R. WHATELY merly Archbishop of Dublin.

BACON'S ESSAYS. With Annot By R. WHATELY. 8vo. 10s. 6d.

ELEMENTS OF LOGIC. Crown 4s. 6d.

ELEMENTS OF RHETORIC. Crown 4s. 6d.

LESSONS ON REASONING. Fcp. 1s. 6d.

Zeller.—Works by Dr. EDWARD ZEL Professor in the University of Berlin.

HISTORY OF ECLECTICISM IN G PHILOSOPHY. Translated by SARA ALLEYNE. Crown 8vo., 10s. 6d.

THE STOICS, EPICUREANS, AND SCEP Translated by the Rev. O. J. REI M.A. Crown 8vo., 15s.

OUTLINES OF THE HISTORY OF G PHILOSOPHY. Translated by SARA ALLEYNE and EVELYN ABBOTT. C 8vo., 10s. 6d.

PLATO AND THE OLDER ACAI Translated by SARAH F. ALLEYNE ALFRED GOODWIN, B.A. Crown 18s.

SOCRATES AND THE SOCRATIC SCH Translated by the Rev. O. J. REI M.A. Crown 8vo., 10s. 6d.

THE PRE-SOCRATIC SCHOOLS: a Hi of Greek Philosophy from the E Period to the time of Socrates. Tra by SARAH F. ALLEYNE. 2 vols. C 8vo., 30s.

MANUALS OF CATHOLIC PHILOSOPHY.
(Stonyhurst Series).

A MANUAL OF POLITICAL ECONOMY. By C. S. DEVAS, M.A. Crown 8vo., 6s. 6d.

FIRST PRINCIPLES OF KNOWLEDGE. By JOHN RICKABY, S.J. Crown 8vo., 5s.

GENERAL METAPHYSICS. By JOHN RICKABY, S.J. Crown 8vo., 5s.

LOGIC. By RICHARD F. CLARKE, S.J. Crown 8vo., 5s.

MORAL PHILOSOPHY (ETHICS AND NAT LAW. By JOSEPH RICKABY, S.J. 8vo., 5s.

NATURAL THEOLOGY. By BER BOEDDER, S.J. Crown 8vo., 6s. 6d.

PSYCHOLOGY. By MICHAEL MAHER Crown 8vo., 6s. 6d.

History and Science of Language, &c.

Davidson. — LEADING AND IMPORTANT ENGLISH WORDS: Explained and Exemplified. By WILLIAM L. DAVIDSON, M.A. Fcp. 8vo., 3s. 6d.

Farrar. — LANGUAGE AND LANGUAGES: By F. W. FARRAR, D.D., F.R.S. Crown 8vo., 6s.

Graham. — ENGLISH SYNONYMS, Classified and Explained: with Practical Exercises. By G. F. GRAHAM. Fcp. 8vo., 6s.

Max Müller. — Works by F. MAX MÜLLER.

SELECTED ESSAYS ON LANGUAGE, MYTHOLOGY, AND RELIGION. 2 vols. Crown 8vo., 16s.

THE SCIENCE OF LANGUAGE, Founded on Lectures delivered at the Royal Institution in 1861 and 1863. 2 vols. Crown 8vo., 21s.

BIOGRAPHIES OF WORDS, AND THE HOME OF THE ARYAS. Crown 8vo., 7s. 6d.

THREE LECTURES ON THE SCIENCE OF LANGUAGE, AND ITS PLACE IN GENERAL EDUCATION, delivered at Oxford, 1889. Crown 8vo., 3s.

Paul. — PRINCIPLES OF THE HISTORY LANGUAGE. By HERMANN PAUL. Translated by H. A. STRONG. 8vo., 10s. 6d.

Roget. — THESAURUS OF ENGLISH WORDS AND PHRASES. Classified and Arranged as to Facilitate the Expression of Ideas and assist in Literary Composition. By PETER MARK ROGET, M.D., F.R.S. composed throughout, enlarged and improved, partly from the Author's Notes, with a full Index, by the Author's, JOHN LEWIS ROGET. Crown 8vo. 10s.

Strong, Logeman, and Wheeler. — INTRODUCTION TO THE STUDY OF THE HISTORY LANGUAGE. By HERBERT A. STRONG, M.A. LL.D., WILLEM S. LOGEMAN, and BENJAMIN IDE WHEELER. 8vo., 10s. 6d.

Wade. — ELEMENTARY CHAPTERS IN COMPARATIVE PHILOLOGY. By G. WOOSTER WADE, M.A. Crown 8vo., 2s. 6d.

Whately. — ENGLISH SYNONYMS. By JANE WHATELY. Fcp. 8vo., 3s.

Political Economy and Economics.

Ashley. — ENGLISH ECONOMIC HISTORY AND THEORY. By W. J. ASHLEY, M.A. Crown 8vo., Part I., 5s. Part II. 10s. 6d.

Bagehot. — Works by WALTER BAGEHOT. ECONOMIC STUDIES. 8vo., 10s. 6d. THE POSTULATES OF ENGLISH POLITICAL ECONOMY. Crown 8vo., 2s. 6d.

Crump. — AN INVESTIGATION INTO THE CAUSES OF THE GREAT FALL IN PRICES which took place coincidently with the Demonetisation of Silver by Germany. By ARTHUR CRUMP. 8vo., 6s.

Devas. A MANUAL OF POLITICAL ECONOMY. By C. S. DEVAS, M.A. Crown 8vo., 6s. 6d. (*Manuals of Catholic Philosophy.*)

Dowell. — A HISTORY OF TAXATION AND TAXES IN ENGLAND, from the Earliest Times to the Year 1885. By STEPHEN DOWELL. (4 vols. 8vo.) Vols. I. and II. The History of Taxation. 21s. Vols. III. and IV. The History of Taxes. 21s.

Jordan. — THE STANDARD OF VALUE. By WILLIAM LEIGHTON JORDAN. 8vo., 6s.

Leslie. ESSAYS IN POLITICAL ECONOMY. By T. E. CLIFFE LESLIE. 8vo., 10s. 6d.

Macleod. — Works by HENRY DUNNING MACLEOD, M.A.

THE ELEMENTS OF BANKING. Crown 8vo., 3s. 6d.

THE THEORY AND PRACTICE OF BANKING. Vol. I. 8vo., 12s. Vol. II. 14s.

THE THEORY OF CREDIT. 8vo. Vol. I. 7s. 6d. Vol. II., Part I., 4s. 6d. Vol. II. Part II., 10s. 6d.

Meath. — Works by The EARL OF MEATH.

SOCIAL ARROWS: Reprinted Articles various Social Subjects. Crown 8vo.,

PROSPERITY OR PAUPERISM? Physical Industrial, and Technical Training. 8vo. 5s.

Mill. — POLITICAL ECONOMY. By JOHN STUART MILL.

Silver Library Edition. Crown 8vo., 3s. Library Edition. 2 vols. 8vo., 30s.

Shirres. — AN ANALYSIS OF THE IDEAS ECONOMICS. By L. P. SHIRRES, B sometime Finance Under-Secretary of Government of Bengal. Crown 8vo., 6s

Symes. POLITICAL ECONOMY: a S Text-book of Political Economy. With Problems for Solution, and Hints for plementary Reading. By Professor J. SYMES, M.A., of University College, Nottingham. Crown 8vo., 2s. 6d.

Toynbee. — LECTURES ON THE INDUSTRIAL REVOLUTION OF THE 18th CENTURY ENGLAND. By ARNOLD TOYNBEE. 8vo. 10s. 6d.

Wilson. — Works by A. J. WILSON. Chiefly reprinted from *The Investors' Review.*

PRACTICAL HINTS TO SMALL INVESTORS Crown 8vo., 1s.

PLAIN ADVICE ABOUT LIFE INSURANCE. Crown 8vo., 1s.

Wolff. PEOPLE'S BANKS: a Record Social and Economic Success. By HENRY W. WOLFF. 8vo., 7s. 6d.

Evolution, Anthropology, &c.

Clodd.—THE STORY OF CREATION: a Plain Account of Evolution. By EDWARD CLODD. With 77 Illustrations. Crown 8vo., 3s. 6d.

Huth.—THE MARRIAGE OF NEAR KIN, considered with Respect to the Law of Nations, the Result of Experience, and the Teachings of Biology. By ALFRED HENRY HUTH. Royal 8vo., 21s.

Lang.—CUSTOM AND MYTH: Studies of Early Usage and Belief. By ANDREW LANG, M.A. With 15 Illustrations. Crown 8vo., 3s. 6d.

Lubbock.—THE ORIGIN OF CIVILISATION and the Primitive Condition of Man. By Sir J. LUBBOCK, Bart., M.P. With 5 Plates and 20 Illustrations in the Text. 8vo., 18s.

Romanes. — Works by GEORGE JOHN ROMANES, M.A., LL.D., F.R.S.

DARWIN, AND AFTER DARWIN: an Exposition of the Darwinian Theory, and a Discussion on Post-Darwinian Questions. Part I. The Darwinian Theory. With Portrait of Darwin and 125 Illustrations. Crown 8vo., 10s. 6d.

AN EXAMINATION OF WEISMANNISM. Crown 8vo.

Classical Literature.

Abbott.—HELLENICA. A Collection of Essays on Greek Poetry, Philosophy, History, and Religion. Edited by EVELYN ABBOTT, M.A., LL.D. 8vo., 16s.

Æschylus.—EUMENIDES OF ÆSCHYLUS. With Metrical English Translation. By J. F. DAVIES. 8vo., 7s.

Aristophanes. — THE ACHARNIANS OF ARISTOPHANES, translated into English Verse. By R. Y. TYRRELL. Crown 8vo., 1s.

Becker.—Works by Professor BECKER.

GALLUS: or, Roman Scenes in the Time of Augustus. Illustrated. Post 8vo., 7s. 6d.

CHARICLES: or, Illustrations of the Private Life of the Ancient Greeks. Illustrated. Post 8vo., 7s. 6d.

Cicero.—CICERO'S CORRESPONDENCE. By R. Y. TYRRELL. Vols. I., II., III., 8vo., each 12s.

Clerke.—FAMILIAR STUDIES IN HOMER. By AGNES M. CLERKE. Crown 8vo., 7s. 6d.

Farnell.—GREEK LYRIC POETRY: a Complete Collection of the Surviving Passages from the Greek Song-Writting. Arranged with Prefatory Articles, Introductory Matter and Commentary. By GEORGE S. FARNELL, M.A. With 5 Plates. 8vo., 16s.

Harrison.—MYTHS OF THE ODYSSEY IN ART AND LITERATURE. By JANE E. HARRISON. Illustrated with Outline Drawings. 18s.

-HOMER AND THE EPIC. By EW LANG. Crown 8vo., 9s. net.

Mackail.—SELECT EPIGRAMS FROM THE GREEK ANTHOLOGY. By J. W. MACKAIL, Fellow of Balliol College, Oxford. Edited with a Revised Text, Introduction, Translation, and Notes. 8vo., 16s.

Plato.—PARMENIDES OF PLATO, Text, with Introduction, Analysis, &c. By T. MAGUIRE. 8vo., 7s. 6d.

Rich.—A DICTIONARY OF ROMAN AND GREEK ANTIQUITIES. By A. RICH, B.A. With 2000 Woodcuts. Crown 8vo., 7s. 6d.

Sophocles.—Translated into English Verse. By ROBERT WHITELAW, M.A., Assistant Master in Rugby School; late Fellow of Trinity College, Cambridge. Crown 8vo., 8s. 6d.

Tyrrell.—TRANSLATIONS INTO GREEK AND LATIN VERSE. Edited by R. Y. TYRRELL. 8vo., 6s.

Virgil.—THE ÆNEID OF VIRGIL. Translated into English Verse by JOHN CONINGTON. Crown 8vo., 6s.

THE POEMS OF VIRGIL. Translated into English Prose by JOHN CONINGTON. Crown 8vo., 6s.

THE ÆNEID OF VIRGIL, freely translated into English Blank Verse. By W. J. THORNHILL. Crown 8vo., 7s. 6d.

THE ÆNEID OF VIRGIL. Books I. to VI. Translated into English Verse by JAMES RHOADES. Crown 8vo., 5s.

THE ECLOGUES AND GEORGICS OF VIRGIL. Translated from the Latin by J. W. MACKAIL, M.A., Fellow of Balliol College, Oxford. Printed on Dutch Handmade Paper. Royal 16mo., 5s.

Wilkin.—THE GROWTH OF THE HOMERIC POEMS. By G. WILKIN. 8vo., 6s.

Poetry and the Drama.

Allingham.—Works by WILLIAM ALLINGHAM.

IRISH SONGS AND POEMS. With Frontis-
of the Waterfall of Asaroe. Fcp. 8vo.,
6s.

LAURENCE BLOOMFIELD. With Portrait
of the Author. Fcp. 8vo., 3s. 6d.

FLOWER PIECES; DAY AND NIGHT
SONGS; BALLADS. With 2 Designs by
D. G. ROSETTI. Fcp. 8vo., 6s.; large
paper edition, 12s.

LIFE AND PHANTASY: with Frontispiece
by Sir J. E. MILLAIS, Bart., and Design
by ARTHUR HUGHES. Fcp. 8vo., 6s.;
large paper edition, 12s.

THOUGHT AND WORD, AND ASHBY
MANOR: a Play. With Portrait of the
Author (1865), and four Theatrical Scenes
drawn by Mr. Allingham. Fcp. 8vo., 6s.;
large paper edition, 12s.

BLACKBERRIES. Imperial 16mo., 6s.

*Sets of the above 6 vols. may be had in uni-
form Half-parchment binding, price 30s.*

Armstrong.—Works by G. F. SAVAGE-
ARMSTRONG.

POEMS: Lyrical and Dramatic. Fcp.
8vo., 6s.

KING SAUL. (The Tragedy of Israel,
Part I.) Fcp. 8vo., 5s.

KING DAVID. (The Tragedy of Israel,
Part II.) Fcp. 8vo., 6s.

KING SOLOMON. (The Tragedy of Israel,
Part III.) Fcp. 8vo., 6s.

UGONE: a Tragedy. Fcp. 8vo., 6s.

A GARLAND FROM GREECE: Poems.
Fcp. 8vo., 7s. 6d.

STORIES OF WICKLOW: Poems. Fcp.
8vo., 7s. 6d.

MEPHISTOPHELES IN BROADCLOTH:
a Satire. Fcp. 8vo., 4s.

ONE IN THE INFINITE: a Poem. Crown
8vo., 7s. 6d.

Armstrong.—THE POETICAL WORKS OF
EDMUND J. ARMSTRONG. Fcp. 8vo., 5s.

Arnold.—Works by Sir EDWIN ARNOLD,
K.C.I.E., Author of 'The Light of Asia,' &c.

THE LIGHT OF THE WORLD: or the
Great Consummation. A Poem. Crown
8vo., 7s. 6d. net.
Presentation Edition. With Illustrations
by W. HOLMAN HUNT, &c. 4to., 20s. net.

POTIPHAR'S WIFE, and other Poems.
Crown 8vo., 5s. net.

ADZUMA: or the Japanese Wife. A Play.
Crown 8vo., 6s. 6d. net.

Barrow.—THE SEVEN CITIES OF THE DEA
and other Poems. By Sir JOHN CROKE
BARROW, Bart. Fcp. 8vo., 5s.

Bell.—Works by Mrs. HUGH BELL.

CHAMBER COMEDIES: a Collection
Plays and Monologues for the Drawi
Room. Crown 8vo., 6s.

NURSERY COMEDIES: Twelve Tiny Pla
for Children. Fcp. 8vo., 1s. 6d.

Björnsen.—PASTOR LANG: A PLAY. I
BJÖRNSTJERNE BJÖRNSEN. Translated
WILLIAM WILSON.

Dante.—LA COMMEDIA DI DANTE.
New Text, carefully Revised with the aid
the most recent Editions and Collation
Small 8vo., 6s.

Goethe.

FAUST, Part I., the German Text, wit
Introduction and Notes. By ALBERT
SELSS, Ph.D., M.A. Crown 8vo., 5s.

FAUST. Translated, with Notes. By T.
WEBB. 8vo., 12s. 6d.

FAUST. The First Part. A New Tran
lation, chiefly in Blank Verse; with I
troduction and Notes. By JAMES ADI
BIRDS. Crown 8vo., 6s.

FAUST. The Second Part. A Ne
Translation in Verse. By JAMES AD
BIRDS. Crown 8vo., 6s.

Haggard.—LIFE AND ITS AUTHOR: I
Essay in Verse. By ELLA HAGGARD. Wi
a Memoir by H. RIDER HAGGARD, and P
trait. Fcp. 8vo., 3s. 6d.

Ingelow.—Works by JEAN INGELOW.

POETICAL WORKS. 2 vols. Fcp. 8vo
12s.

LYRICAL AND OTHER POEMS. Selecte
from the Writings of JEAN INGELO
Fcp. 8vo., 2s. 6d. cloth plain, 3s. clo
gilt.

Lang.—Works by ANDREW LANG.

GRASS OF PARNASSUS. Fcp. 8vo., 2s.
net.

BALLADS OF BOOKS. Edited by ANDRE
LANG. Fcp. 8vo., 6s.

THE BLUE POETRY BOOK. Edited b
ANDREW LANG. Special Edition, prin
on Indian paper. With Notes, but wi
out Illustrations. Crown 8vo., 7s. 6d.

Lecky.—POEMS. By W. E. H. LECKY. Fcp. 8vo., 5s.

Leyton.—Works by FRANK LEYTON.

THE SHADOWS OF THE LAKE, and other Poems. Crown 8vo., 7s. 6d. Cheap Edition. Crown 8vo., 3s. 6d.

SKELETON LEAVES: Poems. Crown 8vo. 6s.

Lytton.—Works by THE EARL OF LYTTON (OWEN MEREDITH).

MARAH. Fcp. 8vo., 6s. 6d.

KING POPPY: a Fantasia. With 1 Plate and Design on Title-Page by ED. BURNE-JONES, A.R.A. Crown 8vo., 10s. 6d.

THE WANDERER. Crown 8vo., 10s. 6d.

Macaulay.—LAYS OF ANCIENT ROME, &c. By Lord MACAULAY.

Illustrated by G. SCHARF. Fcp. 4to., 10s. 6d. ————————————— Bijou Edition. 18mo., 2s. 6d. gilt top.

————————————— Popular Edition. Fcp. 4to., 6d. sewed, 1s. cloth.

Illustrated by J. R. WEGUELIN. Crown 8vo., 3s. 6d.

Annotated Edition. Fcp. 8vo., 1s. sewed, 1s. 6d. cloth.

Nesbit.—Works by E. NESBIT (HUBERT BLAND).

LEAVES OF LIFE: Verses. Cr. 8vo

LAYS AND LEGENDS. First S Crown 8vo., 3s. 6d. Second Series. Portrait. Crown 8vo., 5s.

Piatt.—AN ENCHANTED CASTLE, OTHER POEMS: Pictures, Portraits, People in Ireland. By SARAH F Crown 8vo. 3s. 6d.

Piatt.—Works by JOHN JAMES PIAT IDYLS AND LYRICS OF THE VALLEY. Crown 8vo., 5s.

LITTLE NEW WORLD IDYLS. Cr.

Rhoades.—TERESA AND OTHER By JAMES RHOADES. Crown 8vo.,

Riley.—OLD FASHIONED ROSES: P By JAMES WHITCOMB RILEY. 12mo

Shakespeare. — BOWDLER'S FA SHAKESPEARE. With 36 Woodcuts. 8vo., 14s. Or in 6 vols. Fcp. 8vo., 2

THE SHAKESPEARE BIRTHDAY BOO MARY F. DUNBAR. 32mo., 1s. 6d. ing Room Edition, with Photog Fcp. 8vo., 10s. 6d.

Stevenson. — A CHILD'S GARDE Verses. By ROBERT LOUIS STEVE Small Fcp. 8vo., 5s.

Works of Fiction, Humour, &c.

ATELIER (THE) DU LYS: or, an Art Student in the Reign of Terror. Crown 8vo., 2s. 6d.

BY THE SAME AUTHOR.

MADEMOISELLE MORI: a Tale of Modern Rome. Crown 8vo., 2s. 6d.

THAT CHILD. Illustrated by GORDON BROWNE. Crown 8vo., 2s. 6d.

UNDER A CLOUD. Crown 8vo., 2s. 6d.

THE FIDDLER OF LUGAU. With Illustrations by W. RALSTON, Crown 8vo., 2s. 6d.

A CHILD OF THE REVOLUTION. With Illustrations by C. J. STANILAND. Crown 8vo., 2s. 6d.

HESTER'S VENTURE: a Novel. Crown 8vo., 2s. 6d.

IN THE OLDEN TIME: a Tale of the Peasant War in Germany. Crown 8vo., 2s. 6d.

THE YOUNGER SISTER: a Tale. Cr. 8vo., 6s.

Anstey.—Works by F. ANSTEY, Autl 'Vice Versa'.

THE BLACK POODLE, and other St Crown 8vo., 2s. boards, 2s. 6d. clotl

VOCES POPULI. Reprinted from 'Pt With Illustrations by J. BERNARD RIDGE. First Series. Fcp. 4to Second Series. Fcp. 4to., 6s,

THE TRAVELLING COMPANIONS. printed from 'Punch'. With Illustr by J. BERNARD PARTRIDGE. Post 4

THE MAN FROM BLANKLEY'S: a in Scenes, and other Sketches. Illustrations by J. BERNARD PART Fcp. 4to., 6s.

Baker.—BY THE WESTERN SEA. JAMES BAKER, Author of 'John West Crown 8vo., 3s. 6d.

Beaconsfield.—Works by the Ea BEACONSFIELD.

NOVELS AND TALES. Cheap Ed Complete in 11 vols. Cr. 8vo., 1s. 6d.

Vivian Grey.	Henrietta Temp
The Young Duke, &c.	Venetia. Tan
Alroy, Ixion, &c.	Coningsby. S
Contarini Fleming, &c.	Lothair. Endy

Beaconsfield.—Works by the Earl of BEACONSFIELD.

NOVELS AND TALES. The Hughenden Edition. With 2 Portraits and 11 Vignettes. 11 vols. Crown 8vo., 42s.

Chilton.—THE HISTORY OF A FAILURE, and other Tales. By E. CHILTON. Fcp. 8vo., 3s. 6d.

Comyn.—ATHERSTONE PRIORY : a Tale. By L. N. COMYN. Crown 8vo., 2s. 6d.

Deland.—Works by MARGARET DELAND, Author of 'John Ward'.

THE STORY OF A CHILD. Cr. 8vo., 5s.

MR. TOMMY DOVE, and other Stories. Crown 8vo. 6s.

DOROTHY WALLIS: an Autobiography. With Preface by WALTER BESANT. Crown 8vo., 6s.

Dougall.—Works by L. DOUGALL.

BEGGARS ALL. Crown 8vo., 3s. 6d.

WHAT NECESSITY KNOWS. 3 vols. Crown 8vo.

Doyle.—Works by A. CONAN DOYLE.

MICAH CLARKE : A Tale of Monmouth's Rebellion. With Frontispiece and Vignette. Cr. 8vo., 3s. 6d.

THE CAPTAIN OF THE POLESTAR, and other Tales. Cr. 8vo., 3s. 6d.

THE REFUGEES: A Tale of Two Continents. Cr. 8vo., 6s.

Farrar.—DARKNESS AND DAWN: or, Scenes in the Days of Nero. An Historic Tale. By Archdeacon FARRAR. Cr. 8vo., 7s. 6d.

Froude.—THE TWO CHIEFS OF DUNBOY: an Irish Romance of the Last Century. by J. A. FROUDE. Cr. 8vo., 3s. 6d.

Haggard.—Works by H. RIDER HAGGARD.

SHE. With 32 Illustrations by M. GREIFFENHAGEN and C. H. M. KERR. Cr. 8vo., 3s. 6d.

ALLAN QUATERMAIN. With 31 Illustrations by C. H. M. KERR. Cr. 8vo., 3s. 6d.

MAIWA'S REVENGE : or, The War of the Little Hand. Cr. 8vo., 1s. boards, 1s. 6d. cloth.

COLONEL QUARITCH, V.C. Cr. 8vo. 3s. 6d.

Haggard.—Works by H. RIDER HAGGARD —*continued.*

CLEOPATRA. With 29 Full-page Illustrations by M. GREIFFENHAGEN and CATON WOODVILLE. Cr. 8vo., 3s. 6d.

BEATRICE. Cr. 8vo., 3s. 6d.

ERIC BRIGHTEYES. With 17 Plates and 34 Illustrations in the Text LANCELOT SPEED. Cr. 8vo., 3s. 6d.

NADA THE LILY. With 23 Illustrations by C. H. M. KERR. Cr. 8vo., 6s.

MONTEZUMA'S DAUGHTER. Cr. 8vo.,

Haggard and Lang.—THE WORLD'S DESIRE. By H. RIDER HAGGARD ANDREW LANG. Cr. 8vo. 6s.

Harte.—Works by BRET HARTE.

IN THE CARQUINEZ WOODS. Fcp. 8vo. 1s. 6d.

ON THE FRONTIER, &c. 16mo., 1s.

BY SHORE AND SEDGE. 16mo., 1s.

•.• Three Works complete in one Volume. Cr. 8vo., 3s. 6d.

Hyne.—THE NEW EDEN : a Story. C. J. Cutcliffe Hyne. With Frontispiece and Vignette. Cr. 8vo., 2s. 6d.

KEITH DERAMORE : a Novel. By the Author of ' Miss Molly'. Cr. 8vo., 6s.

Lyall.—THE AUTOBIOGRAPHY OF A SLANDER. By EDNA LYALL, Author of ' Donovan,' &c. Fcp. 8vo., 1s. sewed.

Presentation Edition. With 20 Illustrations by LANCELOT SPEED. Cr. 8vo.,

Matthews.—Works by BRANDER MATTHEWS.

A FAMILY TREE, and other Stories. Cr. 8vo., 6s.

WITH MY FRIENDS : Tales told in Partnership. With an Introductory Essay the Art and Mystery of Collaboration. Cr. 8vo., 6s.

Melville.—Works by G. J. WHYTE MELVILLE.

The Gladiators.	Holmby House.
The Interpreter.	Kate Coventry.
Good for Nothing.	Digby Grand.
The Queen's Maries.	General Bounce.

Cr. 8vo., 1s. 6d. each.

O'Brien.—WHEN WE WERE BOYS: Novel. By WILLIAM O'BRIEN. Cr. 8vo. 2s. 6d.

Works of Fiction, Humour, &c.—*continued.*

Oliphant.—Works by Mrs. OLIPHANT.

MADAM. Cr. 8vo., 1s. 6d.

IN TRUST. Cr. 8vo., 1s. 6d.

Parr.—CAN THIS BE LOVE? By Mrs. PARR, Author of ' Dorothy Fox '. Crown 8vo. 6s.

Payn.—Works by JAMES PAYN.

THE LUCK OF THE DARRELLS. Cr. 8vo., 1s. 6d.

THICKER THAN WATER. Cr. 8vo., 1s. 6d.

Phillipps-Wolley.—SNAP: a Legend of the Lone Mountain. By C. PHILLIPPS-WOLLEY. With 13 Illustrations by H. G. WILLINK. Cr. 8vo., 3s. 6d.

Robertson.—THE KIDNAPPED SQUATTER, and other Australian Tales. By A. ROBERTSON. Cr. 8vo., 6s.

Sewell.—Works by ELIZABETH M. SEWELL.

A Glimpse of the World.	Amy Herbert.
Laneton Parsonage.	Cleve Hall.
Margaret Percival.	Gertrude.
Katharine Ashton.	Home Life.
The Earl's Daughter.	After Life.
The Experience of Life.	Ursula. Ivors.

Cr. 8vo., 1s. 6d. each cloth plain. 2s. 6d. each cloth extra, gilt edges.

Stevenson.—Works by ROBERT LOUIS STEVENSON.

STRANGE CASE OF DR. JEKYLL AND MR. HYDE. Fcp. 8vo., 1s. sewed. 1s. 6d. cloth.

THE DYNAMITER. Fcp. 8vo., 1s. sewed, 1s. 6d. cloth.

Stevenson and Osbourne.—THE WRONG BOX. By ROBERT LOUIS STEVENSON and LLOYD OSBOURNE. Cr. 8vo., 3s. 6d.

Sturgis.—AFTER TWENTY YEARS, and other Stories. By JULIAN STURGIS. Cr. 8vo., 6s.

Suttner.—LAY DOWN YOUR ARMS (*Die Waffen Nieder*): The Autobiography of Martha Tilling. By BERTHA VON SUTTNER. Translated by T. HOLMES. Cr. 8vo., 7s. 6d.

Thompson.—A MORAL DILEMMA: a Novel. By ANNIE THOMPSON. Crown 8vo., 6s.

Tirebuck.—Works by WILLIAM TIREBUCK.

DORRIE. Crown 8vo. 6s.

SWEETHEART GWEN. Crown 8vo., 6s.

Trollope.—Works by ANTHONY TROLLOPE.

THE WARDEN. Cr. 8vo., 1s. 6d.

BARCHESTER TOWERS. Cr. 8vo., 1s. 6d.

Walford.—Works by L. B. WALFORD, Author of ' Mr. Smith '.

THE MISCHIEF OF MONICA: a Novel. Cr. 8vo., 2s. 6d.

THE ONE GOOD GUEST: a Story. Cr. 8vo., 6s.

West.—HALF-HOURS WITH THE MILLIONAIRES: Showing how much harder it is to spend a million than to make it. Edited by B. B. WEST. Cr. 8vo., 6s.

Weyman.—Works by STANLEY J. WEYMAN.

THE HOUSE OF THE WOLF: a Romance. Cr. 8vo., 3s. 6d.

A GENTLEMAN OF FRANCE. 3 vols. Cr. 8vo. [*In the Press.*

Popular Science (Natural History, &c.).

Butler.—OUR HOUSEHOLD INSECTS. By E. A. BUTLER. With numerous Illustrations. [*In the Press.*

Furneaux.—THE OUTDOOR WORLD; or The Young Collector's Handbook. By W. FURNEAUX, F.R.G.S. With numerous Illustrations including 6 Plates in Colours. Crown 8vo., 7s. 6d.

Hartwig.—Works by Dr. GEORGE HARTWIG.

THE SEA AND ITS LIVING WONDERS. With 12 Plates and 303 Woodcuts. 8vo., 7s. net.

THE TROPICAL WORLD. With 8 Plates and 172 Woodcuts. 8vo., 7s. net.

THE POLAR WORLD. With 3 Maps, 8 Plates and 85 Woodcuts. 8vo., 7s. net.

Popular Science (Natural History, &c.)—*continued.*

Hartwig.—Works by Dr. George Hartwig—*continued.*

The Subterranean World. With 3 Maps and 80 Woodcuts. 8vo., 7s. net.

The Aerial World. With Map, 8 Plates and 60 Woodcuts. 8vo., 7s. net.

Heroes of the Polar World. 19 Illustrations. Cr. 8vo., 2s.

Wonders of the Tropical Forests. 40 Illustrations. Cr. 8vo., 2s.

Workers under the Ground. 29 Illustrations. Cr. 8vo., 2s.

Marvels Over our Heads. 29 Illustrations. Cr. 8vo., 2s.

Sea Monsters and Sea Birds. 75 Illustrations. Cr. 8vo., 2s. 6d.

Denizens of the Deep. 117 Illustrations. Cr. 8vo., 2s. 6d.

Volcanoes and Earthquakes. 30 Illustrations. Cr. 8vo., 2s. 6d.

Wild Animals of the Tropics. 66 Illustrations. Cr. 8vo., 3s. 6d.

Helmholtz. — Popular Lectures on Scientific Subjects. By Professor Helmholtz. With 68 Woodcuts. 2 vols. Cr. 8vo., 3s. 6d. each.

Lydekker.—Phases of Animal Life, Past and Present. By. R. Lydekker, B.A. With 82 Illustrations. Cr. 8vo., 6s.

Proctor.—Works by Richard A. Proctor. *And see Messrs. Longmans & Co.'s Catalogue of Scientific Works.*

Light Science for Leisure Hours. Familiar Essays on Scientific Subjects. 3 vols. Cr. 8vo., 5s. each.

Chance and Luck: a Discussion of the Laws of Luck, Coincidence, Wagers, Lotteries and the Fallacies of Gambling, &c. Cr. 8vo., 2s. boards. 2s. 6d. cloth.

Rough Ways made Smooth. Familiar Essays on Scientific Subjects. Cr. 8vo., 5s. Silver Library Edition. Cr. 8vo., 3s. 6d.

Pleasant Ways in Science. Cr. 8vo., 5s. Silver Library Edition. Cr. 8vo., 3s. 6d.

The Great Pyramid, Observatory, Tomb and Temple. With Illustrations. Cr. 8vo., 5s.

Nature Studies. By R. A. Proctor, Grant Allen, A. Wilson, T. Foster and E. Clodd. Cr. 8vo., 5s. Silver Library Edition. Crown 8vo., 3s. 6d.

Proctor.—Works by Richard A. Proc—*continued.*

Leisure Readings. By R. A. Proctor, E. Clodd, A. Wilson, T. Foster and A. C. Ranyard. Cr. 8vo., 5s.

Stanley.—A Familiar History of Birds. By E. Stanley, D.D., formerly Bishop of Norwich. With Illustrations. Cr. 8vo., 3s. 6d.

Wood.—Works by the Rev. J. G. Wood.

Homes without Hands: a Description of the Habitation of Animals, classed according to the Principle of Construction. With 140 Illustrations. 8vo., 7s. net.

Insects at Home: a Popular Account of British Insects, their Structure, Habits and Transformations. With 700 Illustrations. 8vo., 7s. net.

Insects Abroad: a Popular Account of Foreign Insects, their Structure, Habits and Transformations. With 600 Illustrations. 8vo., 7s. net.

Bible Animals: a Description of every Living Creatures mentioned in the Scriptures. With 112 Illustrations. 8vo., net.

Petland Revisited. With 33 Illustrations. Cr. 8vo., 3s. 6d.

Out of Doors; a Selection of Original Articles on Practical Natural History. With 11 Illustrations. Cr. 8vo., 3s. 6d.

Strange Dwellings: a Description of the Habitations of Animals, abridged from 'Homes without Hands'. With 60 Illustrations. Cr. 8vo., 3s. 6d.

Bird Life of the Bible. 32 Illustrations. Cr. 8vo., 3s. 6d.

Wonderful Nests. 30 Illustrations. Cr. 8vo., 3s. 6d.

Homes under the Ground. 28 Illustrations. Cr. 8vo., 3s. 6d.

Wild Animals of the Bible. Illustrations. Cr. 8vo., 3s. 6d.

Domestic Animals of the Bible. Illustrations. Cr. 8vo., 3s. 6d.

The Branch Builders. 28 Illustrations. Cr. 8vo., 2s. 6d.

Social Habitations and Parasitic Nests. 18 Illustrations. Cr. 8vo., 2s.

Children's Books.

"Brenda."—Works by "BRENDA".

OLD ENGLAND'S STORY IN LITTLE WORDS FOR LITTLE CHILDREN. With 29 Illustrations. Imp. 16mo., 3s. 6d.

WITHOUT A REFERENCE. A Story. Cr. 8vo., 3s. 6d.

Crake.—Works by Rev. A. D. CRAKE.

EDWY THE FAIR; or, The First Chronicle of Æscendune. Crown 8vo., 2s. 6d.

ALFGAR THE DANE: or, the Second Chronicle of Æscendune. Cr. 8vo. 2s. 6d.

THE RIVAL HEIRS: being the Third and Last Chronicle of Æscendune. Cr. 8vo., 2s. 6d.

THE HOUSE OF WALDERNE. A Tale of the Cloister and the Forest in the Days of the Barons' Wars. Crown 8vo., 2s. 6d.

BRIAN FITZ-COUNT. A Story of Wallingford Castle and Dorchester Abbey. Cr. 8vo., 2s. 6d.

Ingelow.—VERY YOUNG, and QUITE ANOTHER STORY. Two Stories. By JEAN INGELOW. Crown 8vo., 6s.

Lang.—Works edited by ANDREW LANG.

THE BLUE FAIRY BOOK. With 8 Plates and 130 Illustrations in the Text by H. J. Ford and G. P. Jacomb Hood. Crown 8vo., 6s.

Lang.—Works edited by ANDREW LANG—continued.

THE RED FAIRY BOOK. With 4 Plates and 96 Illustrations in the Text by H. Ford. and LANCELOT SPEED. Crown 8vo., 6s.

THE GREEN FAIRY BOOK. With Plates and 88 Illustrations in the Text by H. J. FORD and L. BOGLE. Cr. 8vo.

THE BLUE POETRY BOOK. With Plates and 88 Illustrations in the Text by H. J. FORD and LANCELOT SPEED. 8vo., 6s.

THE BLUE POETRY BOOK. School Edition, without Illustrations. Fcp. 8vo. 2s. 6d.

THE TRUE STORY BOOK. With Plates and Illustrations in the Text, by H. Ford, LUCIEN DAVIS, LANCELOT SPEED and L. BOGLE. Crown 8vo., 6s.

Meade.—Works by L. T. MEADE.

DADDY'S BOY. With Illustrations Crown 8vo., 3s. 6d.

DEB AND THE DUCHESS. With Illustrations by M. E. EDWARDS. Crown 8vo. 3s. 6d.

Children's Books—*continued.*

Meade.—Works by L. T. MEADE—*continued.*

THE BERESFORD PRIZE. With Illustrations by M. E. EDWARDS. Cr. 8vo., 5s.

Molesworth.—Works by Mrs. MOLESWORTH.

SILVERTHORNS. Illustrated. Crown 8vo., 5s.

THE PALACE IN THE GARDEN. Illustrated. Crown 8vo., 5s.

THE THIRD MISS ST. QUENTIN. Crown 8vo., 6s.

NEIGHBOURS. Illustrated. Crown 8vo., 6s.

THE STORY OF A SPRING MORNING, &c. Illustrated. Crown 8vo., 5s.

Reader.—VOICES FROM FLOWER-LAN a Birthday Book and Language of Fl By EMILY E. READER. Illustrated by BROOKE. Royal 16mo., cloth, 2s. vegetable vellum, 3s. 6d.

Stevenson.—Works by ROBERT LOU STEVENSON.

A CHILD'S GARDEN OF VERSES. Sm Fcp. 8vo., 5s.

A CHILD'S GARLAND OF SONG Gathered from 'A Child's Garden Verses'. Set to Music by C. VILLIE STANFORD, Mus. Doc. 4to., 2s. 3s. 6d., cloth gilt.

The Silver Library.

CROWN 8vo. 3s. 6d. EACH VOLUME.

Baker's (Sir S. W.) Eight Years in Ceylon. With 6 Illustrations. 3s. 6d.

Baker's (Sir S. W.) Rifle and Hound in Ceylon. With 6 Illustrations. 3s. 6d.

Baring-Gould's (Rev. S.) Curious Myths of the Middle Ages. 3s. 6d.

Baring-Gould's (Rev. S.) Origin and Development of Religious Belief. 2 vols. 3s. 6d. each.

Brassey's (Lady) A Voyage in the 'Sunbeam'. With 66 Illustrations. 3s. 6d.

Clodd's (E.) Story of Creation: a Plain Account of Evolution. With 77 Illustrations. 3s. 6d.

Conybeare (Rev. W. J.) and Howson's (Very Rev. J. S.) Life and Epistles of St. Paul. 46 Illustrations. 3s. 6d.

Dougall's (L.) Beggars All: a Novel. 3s. 6d.

Doyle's (A. Conan) Micah Clarke. A Tale of Monmouth's Rebellion. 3s. 6d.

Doyle's (A. Conan) The Captain of the Polestar, and other Tales. 3s. 6d.

Froude's (J. A.) Short Studies on Great Subjects. 4 vols. 3s. 6d. each.

Froude's (J. A.) Cæsar: a Sketch. 3s. 6d.

Froude's (J. A.) Thomas Carlyle: a History of his Life.
1795-1835. 2 vols. 7s.
1834-1881. 2 vols. 7s.

Froude's (J. A.) The Two Chiefs of Dunboy: an Irish Romance of the Last Century. 3s. 6d.

Froude's (J. A.) The History of England, from the Fall of Wolsey to the Defeat of the Spanish Armada. 12 vols. 3s. 6d. each.

Gleig's (Rev. G. R.) Life of the Duke of Wellington. With Portrait. 3s. 6d.

Haggard's (H. R.) She: A History of Adventure. 32 Illustrations. 3s. 6d.

Haggard's (H. R.) Allan Quatermain. With 20 Illustrations. 3s. 6d.

Haggard's (H. R.) Colonel Quaritch, V.C.: Tale of Country Life. 3s. 6d.

Haggard's (H. R.) Cleopatra. With 29 Fu page Illustrations. 3s. 6d.

Haggard's (H. R.) Eric Brighteyes. With Illustrations. 3s. 6d.

Haggard's (H. R.) Beatrice. 3s. 6d.

Harte's (Bret) In the Carquinez Woods other Stories. 3s. 6d.

Helmholtz's (Professor) Popular Lectures Scientific Subjects. With 68 Woodcuts. vols. 3s. 6d. each.

Howitt's (W.) Visits to Remarkable P 80 Illustrations. 3s. 6d.

Jefferies' (R.) The Story of My Heart: Autobiography. With Portrait. 3s. 6d.

Jefferies' (R.) Field and Hedgerow. I Essays of. With Portrait. 3s. 6d.

Jefferies' (R.) Red Deer. With 17 Illustratio by J. CHARLTON and H. TUNALY. 3s. 6d

Jefferies' (R.) Wood Magic: a Fable. W Frontispiece and Vignette by E. V. B. 3s.

Knight's (E. F.) The Cruise of the 'Alerte the Narrative of a Search for Treasure the Desert Island of Trinidad. With Maps and 23 Illustrations. 3s. 6d.

Lang's (A.) Custom and Myth: Studies of Usage and Belief. 3s. 6d.

Lees (J. A.) and Clutterbuck's (W. J.) B. 1887, A Ramble in British Columbia. Wi Maps and 75 Illustrations. 3s. 6d.

Macaulay's (Lord) Essays and Lays of Ancl Rome. With Portrait and Illustrati 3s. 6d.

Macleod's (H. D.) The Elements of Ban 3s. 6d.

Marshman's (J. C.) Memoirs of Sir Hen Havelock. 3s. 6d.

The Silver Library—*continued.*

Max Müller's (F.) India, what can it teach us? 3s. 6d.

Max Müller's (F.) Introduction to the Science of Religion. 3s. 6d.

Merivale's (Dean) History of the Romans under the Empire. 8 vols. 3s. 6d. each.

Mill's (J. S.) Principles of Political Economy. 3s. 6d.

Mill's (J. S.) System of Logic. 3s. 6d.

Milner's (Geo.) Country Pleasures: the Chronicle of a Year chiefly in a Garden. 3s. 6d.

Newman's (Cardinal) Apologia Pro Vitâ Sua. 3s. 6d.

Newman's (Cardinal) Historical Sketches. 3 vols. 3s. 6d. each.

Newman's (Cardinal) Callista: a Tale of the Third Century. 3s. 6d.

Newman's (Cardinal) Loss and Gain: a Tale. 3s. 6d.

Newman's (Cardinal) Essays, Critical and Historical. 2 vols. 7s.

Newman's (Cardinal) An Essay on the Development of Christian Doctrine. 3s. 6d.

Newman's (Cardinal) The Arians of the Fourth Century. 3s. 6d.

Newman's (Cardinal) Verses on Various Occasions. 3s. 6d.

Newman's (Cardinal) The Present Position of Catholics in England. 3s. 6d.

Newman's (Cardinal) Parochial and Plain Sermons. 8 vols. 3s. 6d. each.

Newman's (Cardinal) Selection, adapted to the Seasons of the Ecclesiastical Year, from the 'Parochial and Plain Sermons'. 3s. 6d.

Newman's (Cardinal) Sermons bearing upon Subjects of the Day. 3s. 6d.

Newman's (Cardinal) Difficulties felt by Anglicans in Catholic Teaching Considered. 2 vols. 3s. 6d. each.

Newman's (Cardinal) The Idea of a University Defined and Illustrated. 3s. 6d.

Newman's (Cardinal) Biblical and Ecclesiastical Miracles. 3s. 6d.

Newman's (Cardinal) Discussions and Arguments on Various Subjects. 3s. 6d.

Newman's (Cardinal) Grammar of Assent. 3s. 6d.

Newman's (Cardinal) Fifteen Sermons Preached before the University of Oxford. 3s. 6d.

Newman's (Cardinal) Lectures on the Doctrine of Justification. 3s. 6d.

Newman's (Cardinal) Sermons on Various Occasions. 3s. 6d.

Newman's (Cardinal) The Via Media of the Anglican Church, illustrated in Lectures, &c. 2 vols. 3s. 6d. each.

Newman's (Cardinal) Discourses to Mixed Congregations. 3s. 6d.

Phillipps-Wolley's (C.) Snap: a Legend of the Lone Mountain. With 13 Illustrations. 3s. 6d.

Proctor's (R. A.) Other Worlds than Ours. 3s. 6d.

Proctor's (R. A.) Rough Ways made Smooth. 3s. 6d.

Proctor's (R. A.) Pleasant Ways in Science. 3s. 6d.

Proctor's (R. A.) Myths and Marvels of Astronomy. 3s. 6d.

Proctor's (R. A.) Nature Studies. 3s. 6d.

Stanley's (Bishop) Familiar History of Birds. 160 Illustrations. 3s. 6d.

Stevenson (R. L.) and Osbourne's (Ll.) The Wrong Box. 3s. 6d.

Weyman's (Stanley J.) The House of the Wolf: a Romance. 3s. 6d.

Wood's (Rev. J. G.) Petland Revisited. With 33 Illustrations. 3s. 6d.

Wood's (Rev. J. G.) Strange Dwellings. With 60 Illustrations. 3s. 6d.

Wood's (Rev. J. G.) Out of Doors. 11 Illustrations. 3s. 6d.

Cookery and Domestic Management.

Acton.—MODERN COOKERY. By ELIZA ACTON. With 150 Woodcuts. Fcp. 8vo., 4s. 6d.

Bull.—Works by THOMAS BULL, M.D.

HINTS TO MOTHERS ON THE MANAGEMENT OF THEIR HEALTH DURING THE PERIOD OF PREGNANCY. Fcp. 8vo., 1s. 6d.

THE MATERNAL MANAGEMENT OF CHILDREN IN HEALTH AND DISEASE. Fcp. 8vo., 1s. 6d.

De Salis.—Works by Mrs. DE SALIS.

CAKES AND CONFECTIONS À LA MODE. Fcp. 8vo., 1s. 6d.

DRESSED GAME AND POULTRY À LA MODE. Fcp. 8vo., 1s. 6d.

DRESSED VEGETABLES À LA MODE. Fcp. 8vo., 1s. 6d.

DRINKS À LA MODE. Fcp. 8vo., 1s. 6d.

ENTRÉES À LA MODE. Fcp. 8vo., 1s. 6d.

OYSTERS À LA MODE. Fcp. 8vo., 1s. 6d.

Cookery and Domestic Management—*continued*.

De Salis.—Works by Mrs. DE SALIS—*cont.*

PUDDINGS AND PASTRY À LA MODE. Fcp. 8vo., 1s. 6d.

SAVOURIES À LA MODE. Fcp. 8vo., 1s. 6d.

SOUPS AND DRESSED FISH À LA MODE. Fcp. 8vo., 1s. 6d.

SWEETS AND SUPPER DISHES À LA MODE. Fcp. 8vo., 1s. 6d.

TEMPTING DISHES FOR SMALL INCOMES. Fcp. 8vo., 1s. 6d.

FLORAL DECORATIONS. Suggestions and Descriptions. Fcp. 8vo., 1s. 6d.

NEW-LAID EGGS: Hints for Amateur Poultry Rearers. Fcp. 8vo., 1s. 6d.

WRINKLES AND NOTIONS FOR EVERY HOUSEHOLD. Crown 8vo., 1s. 6d.

Harrison.—COOKERY FOR BUSY LIVE AND SMALL INCOMES. By MARY HARR SON. Crown 8vo., 1s.

Lear.—MAIGRE COOKERY. By H. SIDNEY LEAR. 16mo., 2s.

Poole.—COOKERY FOR THE DIABETIC. B W. H. and Mrs. POOLE. With Preface Dr. PAVY. Fcp. 8vo., 2s. 6d.

West.—THE MOTHER'S MANUAL OF CHI DREN'S DISEASES. By CHARLES WES M.D., &c., Founder of and formerly Phy cian to the Hospital for Sick Childre Fcp. 8vo., 2s. 6d.

Miscellaneous and Critical Works.

Armstrong.—ESSAYS AND SKETCHES. By EDMUND J. ARMSTRONG. Fcp. 8vo., 5s.

Bagehot.—LITERARY STUDIES. By WALTER BAGEHOT. 2 vols. 8vo., 28s.

Baring-Gould.—CURIOUS MYTHS OF THE MIDDLE AGES. By Rev. S. BARING-GOULD. Crown 8vo., 3s. 6d.

Boyd ('A. K. H. B.').—Works by A. K. H. BOYD, D.D., First Minister of St. Andrews.

AUTUMN HOLIDAYS OF A COUNTRY PARSON. Crown 8vo., 3s. 6d.

COMMONPLACE PHILOSOPHER. Crown 8vo., 3s. 6d.

CRITICAL ESSAYS OF A COUNTRY PARSON. Crown 8vo., 3s. 6d.

EAST COAST DAYS AND MEMORIES. Crown 8vo., 3s. 6d.

LANDSCAPES, CHURCHES AND MORALITIES. Crown 8vo., 3s. 6d.

LEISURE HOURS IN TOWN. Crown 8vo., 3s. 6d.

LESSONS OF MIDDLE AGE. Crown 8vo., 3s. 6d.

OUR LITTLE LIFE. Two Series. Cr. 8vo., 3s. 6d. each.

OUR HOMELY COMEDY: AND TRAGEDY Crown 8vo., 3s. 6d.

RECREATIONS OF A COUNTRY PARSON. Three Series. Crown 8vo., 3s. 6d. each. Also First Series. Popular Edition. 8vo., 6d.

Butler.—Works by SAMUEL BUTLER.

Op. 1. EREWHON. Cr. 8vo., 5s.

Op. 2. THE FAIR HAVEN. A Work Defence of the Miraculous Element in o Lord's Ministry. Cr. 8vo., 7s. 6d.

Op. 3. LIFE AND HABIT. An Essa after a Completer View of Evolutio Cr. 8vo., 7s. 6d.

Op. 4. EVOLUTION, OLD AND NEW. C 8vo., 10s. 6d.

Op. 5. UNCONSCIOUS MEMORY. Cr. 8vo 7s. 6d.

Op. 6. ALPS AND SANCTUARIES OF PIE MONT AND CANTON TICINO. Illustrate Pott 4to., 10s. 6d.

Op. 7. SELECTIONS FROM OPS. 1. With Remarks on Mr. ROMANES' 'Men Evolution in Animals'. Cr. 8vo., 7s. 6

Op. 8. LUCK, OR CUNNING, AS T MAIN MEANS OF ORGANIC MODIFICATIO Cr. 8vo., 7s. 6d.

Op. 9. EX VOTO. An Account of t Sacro Monte or New Jerusalem at Varal Sesia. 10s. 6d.

HOLBEIN'S 'LA DANSE'. A Note a Drawing called 'La Danse'. 3s.

Carlyle.—LAST WORDS OF THOMAS CA LYLE—Wotton Reinfred—Excursion (Fut Enough) to Paris—Letters to Varnhag von Ense, &c. Crown 8vo., 6s. 6d. net.

Halliwell-Phillipps.—A CALENDAR OF T HALLIWELL-PHILLIPPS' COLLECTION SHAKESPEAREAN RARITIES. Enlarged ERNEST E. BAKER, F.S.A. 8vo., 10s.

Miscellaneous and Critical Works — *continued.*

Hodgson.—OUTCAST ESSAYS AND VERSE TRANSLATIONS. By W. SHADWORTH HODGSON. Crown 8vo., 8s. 6d.

Hullah.—Works by JOHN HULLAH, LL.D.

COURSE OF LECTURES ON THE HISTORY OF MODERN MUSIC. 8vo., 8s. 6d.

COURSE OF LECTURES ON THE TRANSITION PERIOD OF MUSICAL HISTORY. 8vo., 10s. 6d.

Jefferies.—Works by RICHARD JEFFERIES.

FIELD AND HEDGEROW: last Essays. With Portrait. Crown 8vo., 3s. 6d.

THE STORY OF MY HEART: my Autobiography. With Portrait and New Preface by C. J. LONGMAN. Crown 8vo., 3s. 6d.

RED DEER. With 17 Illustrations by J. CHARLTON and H. TUNALY. Crown 8vo., 3s. 6d.

THE TOILERS OF THE FIELD. With Portrait from the Bust in Salisbury Cathedral. Crown 8vo., 6s.

WOOD MAGIC: a Fable. With Vignette by E. V. B. Crown 8vo., 3s. 6d.

Jewsbury.—SELECTIONS FROM THE LETTERS OF GERALDINE ENDSOR JEWSBURY TO JANE WELSH CARLYLE. Edited by Mrs. ALEXANDER IRELAND. 8vo., 16s.

Johnson.—THE PATENTEE'S MANUAL: a Treatise on the Law and Practice of Letters Patent. By J. & J. H. JOHNSON, Patent Agents, &c. 8vo., 10s. 6d.

Lang.—Works by ANDREW LANG.

LETTERS TO DEAD AUTHORS. Fcp. 8vo., 2s. 6d. net.

BOOKS AND BOOKMEN. With 2 Coloured Plates and 17 Illustrations. Fcp. 8vo., 2s. 6d. net.

OLD FRIENDS. Fcp. 8vo., 2s. 6d. net.

LETTERS ON LITERATURE. Fcp. 8vo., 2s. 6d. net.

Macfarren.—LECTURES ON HARMONY. By Sir GEORGE A. MACFARREN. 8vo., 12s.

Matthews.—PEN AND INK: Papers on Subjects of more or less importance. By BRANDER MATTHEWS. Crown 8vo., 5s.

Max Müller.—Works by F. MAX MÜLLER.

HIBBERT LECTURES ON THE ORIGIN AND GROWTH OF RELIGION, as illustrated by the Religions of India. Crown 8vo., 7s. 6d.

Max Müller.—Works by F. MAX MÜLLE —*continued.*

INTRODUCTION TO THE SCIENCE OF R LIGION: Four Lectures delivered at Royal Institution. Crown 8vo., 3s. 6d.

NATURAL RELIGION. The Gifford Le tures, 1888. Crown 8vo., 10s. 6d.

PHYSICAL RELIGION. The Gifford Le tures, 1890. Crown 8vo., 10s. 6d.

ANTHROPOLOGICAL RELIGION. Th Gifford Lectures, 1891. Crown 8vo 10s. 6d.

THEOSOPHY OR PSYCHOLOGICAL R LIGION. The Gifford Lectures, 189 Crown 8vo., 10s. 6d.

INDIA: WHAT CAN IT TEACH US Cr. 8vo., 3s. 6d.

Mendelssohn.—THE LETTERS OF FELI MENDELSSOHN. Translated by Lady W LACE. 2 vols. Cr. 8vo., 10s.

Milner.—COUNTRY PLEASURES: the Chro nicle of a Year chiefly in a Garden. B GEORGE MILNER. Cr. 8vo., 3s. 6d.

Perring.—HARD KNOTS IN SHAKESPEARE By Sir PHILIP PERRING, Bart. 8vo., 7s.

Proctor.—Works by RICHARD A. PROCTO

STRENGTH AND HAPPINESS. With Illustrations. Crown 8vo., 5s.

STRENGTH: How to get Strong an keep Strong, with Chapters on Rowin and Swimming, Fat, Age, and the Wais With 9 Illustrations. Crown 8vo., 2s.

Richardson.—NATIONAL HEALTH. Review of the Works of Sir Edwin Cha wick, K.C.B. By Sir B. W. RICHARDSO M.D. Cr., 4s. 6d.

Roget.—A HISTORY OF THE 'OLD WATE COLOUR' SOCIETY (now the Royal Societ of Painters in Water-Colours). By JOH LEWIS ROGET. 2 vols. Royal 8vo., 42s.

Rossetti.—A SHADOW OF DANTE: bein an Essay towards studying Himself, h World and his Pilgrimage. By MARI FRANCESCA ROSSETTI. With Illustratio and with design on cover by DANT GABRIEL ROSSETTI. Cr. 8vo., 10s. 6d.

Southey.—CORRESPONDENCE WITH CAR LINE BOWLES. By ROBERT SOUTHE Edited by E. DOWDEN. 8vo., 14s.

Wallaschek.—PRIMITIVE MUSIC: an I quiry into the Origin and Development Music, Songs, Instruments, Dances, an Pantomimes of Savage Races. By RICHAR WALLASCHEK. With Musical Example 8vo., 12s. 6d.

Lightning Source UK Ltd.
Milton Keynes UK
UKHW02f1811201217
314809UK00008B/499/P